SOCIAL ONTOLOGY

Social Ontology

COLLECTIVE INTENTIONALITY AND GROUP AGENTS

Raimo Tuomela

OXFORD
UNIVERSITY PRESS

OXFORD
UNIVERSITY PRESS

Oxford University Press is a department of the University of Oxford.
It furthers the University's objective of excellence in research, scholarship, and education by publishing worldwide.

Oxford New York
Auckland Cape Town Dar es Salaam Hong Kong Karachi
Kuala Lumpur Madrid Melbourne Mexico City Nairobi
New Delhi Shanghai Taipei Toronto

With offices in
Argentina Austria Brazil Chile Czech Republic France Greece
Guatemala Hungary Italy Japan Poland Portugal Singapore
South Korea Switzerland Thailand Turkey Ukraine Vietnam

Oxford is a registered trademark of Oxford University Press
in the UK and certain other countries.

Published in the United States of America by
Oxford University Press
198 Madison Avenue, New York, NY 10016

Library of Congress Cataloging-in-Publication Data
Tuomela, Raimo.
Social ontology : collective intentionality and group agents / Raimo Tuomela.
pages cm
Includes bibliographical references and index.
ISBN 978–0–19–997826–7 (alk. paper) — ISBN 978–0–19–997827–4 (updf)
1. Social groups. 2. Group identity. I. Title.
HM716.T86 2013
305—dc23
2013000898

9 8 7 6 5 4 3 2 1
Printed in the United States of America
on acid-free paper

To my wife Maj

Contents

Preface

THE MAIN TITLE of this book is *Social Ontology*, with a focus on the two topics of *collective intentionality* and *group agency*. These two topics do not cover all that there is to social ontology, which can be broadly understood to cover all kinds of entities and properties that rational study of the social world is taken to need. Understood in this wide sense, social ontology is not only a study of the basic nature of social reality but at least in part a study of what the best-explaining social scientific theories need to appeal to in their postulated ontologies. This book largely focuses on conceptually group-based notions. The theory presented in this book is based on the full we-perspective (the "we-mode") and on collective construction of the social world by means of the collective acceptance by group members.

To say a few words about *collective intentionality* ("aboutness"): a good example of situations involving collective intentionality is given by cooperation. As we know, human beings have the capacity to cooperate in a variety of contexts, including those involving an element of conflict between the participants. Cooperation in its core sense requires collectively intentional attitudes such as joint intentions and shared beliefs, which have the same content and can be taken to be satisfied by the same token state. For instance, watching a flying eagle together, conversing, painting a house together, making an agreement, and forming an organization are examples of phenomena involving collective intentionality. Collectively intentional mental states and actions based on them involve reference to a "we", a social group capable of collective reasoning and action. When the group members jointly intend, believe, have emotions jointly, and so on, and act on the contents of these mental states, it is from their group's point of view, typically from a "we-perspective", that is, it is "our" group that intends, believes, has emotions, and acts on the contents of these states. (Of course, a group can function only through its members' activities.)

Collective intentionality can be regarded as "the cement of society". This view can be substantiated by reference to three central or "criterial" features of the we-mode framework, namely, *group reason* (a unifying reason for group members to participate in group-based activities), a *collectivity condition* for all members ("necessarily being in the same boat"), and *collective commitment* (basically a product of joint intention and the members' group reason involved). These three elements unite the group members and "cement" them together in all contexts where they function as group members, for example, in the contexts of cooperation and institutional action. They also have a central role in the case of hierarchical groups where authoritative use of power sets limits to people's and groups' activities. Chapter 1 discusses these notions and surveys the contents of the book.

The theory presented in this book assumes that some social groups, including large organized groups, can be viewed as functional *group agents*. This means that we can on functional grounds attribute as-if mental states such as wants, intentions, and beliefs, as well as actions and responsibility to these groups. Such group agents are not intrinsically intentional agents ("persons") comparable to human beings, but they can on functional and epistemic as well as practical grounds be viewed and accepted as extrinsically intentional agents with attributed quasi-mental properties. The group members may engage in group-based reasoning of the following kind: "When functioning as group members, we want X and take this to require that we jointly do Y and hence do it as a group". This kind of reasoning and acting helps to make them a we-mode group that can act as a group—a functional group agent. The group agent view helps to explain group members' behavior and is often useful for theorizing about intergroup phenomena (e.g., cooperation and conflict between large groups like corporations and states).

The group agent approach, I argue, is especially useful with respect to large, typically hierarchical groups (e.g., corporations and states), cases in which theorizing about individuals and their interrelations is impractical. In the specific analyses of various group notions in the book the starting point often is a hierarchical group with "internally" or "externally" authorized leaders.

Comparing the weakly collectivistic we-mode group view with the individualistic (or "I-mode") idea, according to which people act as private persons and as autonomous and primary actors, I show not only that they are conceptually different but also that there are empirically testable functional differences between we-mode and I-mode groups concerning, for example, acting in collective dilemma situations where individual and collective rationality are in conflict. Indeed, the present book provides precise new results based on a "team game-theoretic" approach. Some experimental testing concerning the we-mode and I-mode approaches has been performed, and the results indicate that there indeed are collective action dilemmas in which people engage in we-mode reasoning and acting.

The present book widens the framework of my previous book, *The Philosophy of Sociality* (2007a), to encompass cases allowing the use of power by external authorities. This significantly extends the scope of the theory, as it now can deal with groups governed by external authorities and with we-mode concepts that are analogously based on external power.

This book discusses a variety of related topics, including situations where the people in effect constitute a group and share collectively intentional states that depend on the group's main goals, interests, values, beliefs, norms, and so on, as well as act together as group members. In addition, some topics new to the social ontology and collective intentionality literature are analyzed. These include group solidarity, group reasons, and we-reasoning, as well as institutionality based either on routine, typically nonintentional activities or on intentional collective construction. As said, the book also provides conceptual tools for the study of various intergroup phenomena. The book presents a systematic, analytically argued theory that is broadly naturalistic and "science-friendly". The upshot is that the group-based collective intentionality framework (the we-mode framework) is needed to complement the individualistic, I-mode framework that is commonly endorsed in the social sciences and philosophy.

Acknowledgments

I WISH TO thank the Academy of Finland for a grant (for the years 2010–2013) for hiring researchers. A great part of the work for this book was done during the mentioned period. Thanks are due to the members of the research group (Raul Hakli, Arto Laitinen, Kaarlo Miller, Mikko Salmela, Pekka Mäkelä, and Maj Tuomela) for stimulating discussions and for reading versions of the chapters. This research group belongs to the Academy of Finland Centre of Excellence in the Philosophy of the Social Sciences.

My very special thanks go to Kaarlo Miller and Matti Heinonen. Both read through the penultimate version of the book and presented good criticisms and comments. Kaarlo Miller has been the overall best and sharpest critic of my work throughout the years, and the present book is no exception. Our respective views of the matters discussed in this book differ somewhat, and this has provided for stimulating comments and interchange. In many cases I have changed my text to accommodate his points, going to the roots of the topic in question. This book owes much to his excellent comments. Matti Heinonen read all of the chapters and helped to make stylistic improvements to them as well as to improve the arguments.

As always, my wife Maj has been highly supportive of this project and has also provided me with good criticisms and ideas during the writing of this book, which I dedicate to her.

Of my friends in Munich I wish to thank especially Wolfgang Balzer and Martin Rechenauer for discussions and comments on the matters discussed herein.

Finally, I wish to thank the philosophy editor Peter Ohlin for support. In addition editorial assistant Emily Sacharin deserves my thanks for quick and highly efficient help in practical problems related to the completion of the manuscript. The referees for Oxford University Press are to be thanked for their critical comments on my manuscript. I have presented some of the materials in the book in international workshops and conferences, and I wish to express my gratitude to commentators.

Some paragraphs and sections in the book are based on my recently published papers. I thank the publishers for the appropriate copyright permissions to use some passages from the following papers published elsewhere:

"Two Kinds of We-Reasoning" (jointly with Raul Hakli and Kaarlo Miller). *Economics and Philosophy* 26 (2010): 291–320.
"Cooperation as Joint Action". *Analyse und Kritik* 33 (2010): 65–86.
"Searle's New Construction of Social Reality". *Analysis* 71 (2011): 706–19.

Helsinki, April 2013

Raimo Tuomela
Professor Emeritus, University of Helsinki
Permanent Visiting Professor, University of Munich

SOCIAL ONTOLOGY

1

Introduction

1. SOCIALITY AND GROUPS

1.1.

Humans are social beings and adapted to living in groups, indeed, to functioning in several different groups during their lives. Anthropologists have provided evidence that for at least two million years the Homo family has lived in groups and has become genetically adapted to group living, plainly to survive and be able to reproduce and raise offspring. Both common-sense evidence and psychological experiments indicate that humans have the need and the consequent desire to belong to groups and enjoy the order and well-being afforded by group living, and the underlying motive for this need and desire might simply be the conscious or unconscious need to survive.[1] This need, involving as an obvious consequence also the need to be recognized and respected by others, motivates people to seek institutional and other collectively satisfactory solutions to collective action dilemmas, viz., dilemmas where individual and collective interests are in conflict. Indeed, it seems warranted to say on evolutionary and psychological grounds that group sociality is an inherent aspect of humanness and hence that it is intrinsically valuable for humans to belong to groups.

While all humans can be taken to have this social need and desire, not all of them adjust themselves to the created social order, obeying social rules and norms (especially fairness norms). This uncooperative behavior may be due to their selfish desires to gain something for themselves while exploiting others or perhaps due to their desires to distinguish themselves and be different from others. Yet orderly group life on a local, as well as on a global, level is a must in the current world of increasing dependence between people and peoples. Indeed—despite some free-riding, noncooperation, conflicts, and aggressive action—human groups tend to succeed in maintaining social order. This seems to be due not so much to acting out of prosocial motivation (and sometimes selfish underlying motives) as to acting on group-based motivation and commitments, i.e., to the authoritative reasons that membership in social groups gives for action that promotes the group's interests. Human individuals are thus often disposed to think in terms of "we", of their group, and to act in a solidary way for the benefit of the group or to further the group's interests, where the group's views and attitudes give them a reason to do so.[2]

The mainly psychological and evolutionary facts and assumptions outlined above give rise to the question of what would be the most adequate conceptual and explanatory framework for characterizing human sociality. The right social scientific framework must obviously accord an important role to social groups, but the central problem here is whether its descriptions of group behavior can on some level be reduced to descriptions of individual intentional behavior. The direction in which this book points is that the latter kind of description is not instrumentally feasible, and probably cannot be carried out either for more general theoretical reasons. The ultimate social scientific framework must allow individuals to make reference to social groups—conjectured to be individualistically irreducible—in the contents of their mental states. This view has by now been accepted by most contemporary philosophers writing on collective intentionality. Nevertheless, we may go even further and accord to social groups a functional and intentional existence as social systems in a sense to be elucidated below. Hence it can be claimed that the social world cannot be adequately explained and rationally understood without postulating groups as intentional agents.[3]

This is why the key theory of this book takes thinking and acting as a group member in terms of "we-thinking" (in my terminology, the *we-mode*) as its starting point and contrasts this with thinking and acting individualistically, as a private person (the *I-mode*). With respect to the resulting "I-mode/we-mode" alternatives, this book focuses on the role of the conceptually group-based we-mode way of thinking and acting, and hence I often use the shorter term "we-mode approach" for the theory of this book. The we-mode approach is based on the intuitive idea that, conceptually, the primary acting agent in central group contexts is the group viewed as an intentional agent, while the individual members of the group are the primary ontological agents acting as representatives for the group. The members' social identity is centrally constituted by his group (or groups).

Accordingly, a group organized for action is regarded as an agent from a conceptual and justificatory point of view, although in the causal realm it exists only as a functional social system capable of producing uniform action through its members' intentional action.[4] A group agent in the sense of this book is not an *intrinsically* intentional agent with raw feels and qualia, as contrasted with ordinary embodied human agents. The functional and intentional existence of the group is *extrinsic* and basically derives from the joint attitudes, dispositions, and actions of its members, and from the irreducible reference to the group that these attitudes and actions involve and that is here assumed to make groups conceptually irreducible to the members' individual properties and relationships not based on the group (see chapter 3). Thus agents functioning as proper group members may be assumed conceptually to entify the group by their group-invoking actions and attitudes. This weakly collectivistic conception of groups as intentional agents contrasts with the intentionality of intrinsically intentional group agents on the one hand and with group agents merely instrumentally and/or epistemically conceived on the other hand.

I.2.

The theory developed in this book may be contrasted with earlier, historical views of group agency and collective minds. As old myths and tales indicate, these ideas have been spoken about in various senses for several thousands of years.[5]

There is some ancient Greek and Roman discussion in the history and philosophy of law and, more generally, in political philosophy and theory. This discussion has continued through medieval times up to now—or in any case till the early decades of the past century. Groups as corporate agents in a judicial sense were acknowledged by ancient Roman law, where the terms *universitas*, *corporatio*, and *collegium* referred to "group persons" (intentional group agents) who were capable of entering into agreements involving the making of promises and their fulfillment, and included the idea of corporate responsibility.[6] A corporate group in this sense was contrasted with *societas*, a collective based on interaction between individuals who were less tightly connected and did not form an intentional group agent called a "group person" (where the term "person" or *persona* refers to theatrical mask).[7] A *corporatio* thus was understood as a *persona* and as a group agent capable of action and of making promises and fulfilling them. Groups as persons have been discussed (e.g., by Catholic theologians) from the Middle Ages until the present day. In addition, Locke and Hobbes are theoreticians who entertained some idea of the group person in the English-speaking world, while in the German community idealism was an influential doctrine in philosophy from the eighteenth century on. Thus, Hegel has become well known for his idea of the collective spirit, the Absolute. Another similar example is provided by Otto von Gierke. According to him, the state is a person, "a human organism with a unified collective life distinct from the life of its members".[8] My own functional view of group agents is quite different and does not accept the idealistic ontological view.

The idea of a collective (or group) mind has been employed to account for the kind of mental unity that has been seen in a nation, an army, or in a culture. The term *esprit de corps* (group spirit) has been used in this context. Typically it is not only the mental unity of certain kinds of collectives or groups that is involved here but also the reflective self-consciousness of a group. For instance, "We, the French people, are the bravest in the world" could express this kind of self-consciousness in a group, involving its "group spirit" and "we-feeling". In addition, sociologists, social psychologists, and philosophers of sociality have discussed group minds and group agents at least since the mid-nineteenth century.[9]

In the contemporary landscape, our defense of the relative autonomy of group agents contrasts with the strict individualism that is characteristic of much current social scientific theorizing influenced by rational choice theory. The weak conceptual and epistemic collectivism of this book may accordingly be seen as defending a common-sense alternative that lies somewhere between the extreme group-centeredness of German idealism and the conceptually impoverished framework of rational choice theory as we now have it.

I.3.

The theory of this book is based on a science-friendly philosophical naturalism, and is accordingly committed to the idea that major claims of the theory are at least indirectly and partially empirically testable. I accordingly prefer to treat individualism and collectivism not as ideologies but as competing approaches to the explanation of social phenomena, reformulated for my purposes under the guise of the I-mode/we-mode distinction. The primary way in which the I-mode and the we-mode may be compared is in terms of their consequences. The we-mode will be shown to have objectively real dispositional features, which generate action predictions different from those the I-mode account entails. Neither the I-mode nor the we-mode is conceptually or explanatorily reducible to the other, nor constructible from concepts pertaining to the other. However, I will argue that neither individualism nor collectivism is capable of expressing the whole truth, so to speak: both individualistic (I-mode) and collectivistic (especially, we-mode) concepts and mental states are needed to explain, for example, social action and social institutions. Hence individualism needs to be supplemented by irreducible we-mode states and attitudes in order to fulfill the social scientific task of describing and explaining the social world as accurately and defensibly as possible. Ontologically the theory of this book takes individuals ultimately to be the only action-initiating "motors" in the social world, even if social groups objectively exist as (often irreducible) social systems.

As for specific ontological claims about the nature of we-mode mental states, the claims that I will make are mostly tentative, because one cannot a priori give adequate answers to ontological questions (such as whether people do indeed have we-mode mental states with specific neural bases). While such questions are to be answered a posteriori by scientific means, performing correct experiments and correctly gathering and interpreting the data obviously depend on an adequate conceptual framework for formulating the right questions and making the conclusions understandable and testable. The goal of this book is in part to make relevant conceptual clarifications and explications to this effect, compatibly with the best current scientific research.

2. THE I-MODE AND THE WE-MODE

This book presents an analytic and conceptual theory of how the social world is constructed. The theory presents the basic building blocks of society with an emphasis on group-based notions. My account is accordingly based on a group-level description of the social world, which in many cases can be conceptualized in terms of the we-mode approach on the member level. The we-mode framework forms an indispensable conceptual framework for the study of social life. It consists of interconnected concepts that, according to the arguments of this book, are not in general reducible to I-mode concepts. Much of our social life consists in living in a group context where people often are guided "from above" by authorities (despite people's attempts to reform society by locally democratizing it). An adequate description and explanation of social life accordingly requires that we-mode thinking and acting covering large and hierarchical groups be included in one's theorizing about the social world. The intuitive idea here is that the central agent often is a group, a "we" (expressing the speaker's or thinker's self-identification with a group). On the member level we have its members' we-thinking and we-acting, that is, thinking and acting together as a "we" to promote the interests of "us". The primary conceptual and justificatory direction in the we-mode is "top-down", from group level to member level, whereas in the I-mode the primary conceptual and justificatory as well as ontological direction is "bottom-up", from member level to group level. Thus an individual may act in a group context either in the we-mode or in the I-mode (including acting for the group in the "pro-group" I-mode), although some we-mode thinking and action is functionally needed for the stability and robustness of group life (see below for arguments). Note that a person can have a we-mode attitude with a certain content but fail to have the same attitude in the I-mode.[10]

We-thinking expresses collective intentionality ("aboutness"). There are many different kinds of collectively intentional states and activities. For instance, collective intentions involve shared commitments to action, while mutual beliefs are shared doxastic states (often involving iterated, higher-order beliefs), and collective emotions are or involve shared affective phenomena. There are also various different senses of collective intentionality. The weakest sense of collective intentionality is based on the I-mode, and it simply requires that the agents have an attitude with the same content and mutually believe that they have it. A somewhat stronger sense of collective intentionality (either I-mode or we-mode, in my terms) has it that agents intend to do or believe something together. An even stronger kind of collective intentionality (we-mode, in my terms) requires that agents intend to act together *as a group* and thus, according to my approach, for the same *authoritative group reason*, and also satisfy the criteria or markers of *collective commitment* and the *collectivity condition* (a kind of "necessarily being in the same boat" condition). This kind of acting as a group is collectively (or, if you prefer, jointly) intentional action, where not only the component actions are intentionally performed but the very joint action is intentional in the sense of being based on a full-blown joint intention. The we-mode approach of this book emphasizes full-blown, we-mode forms of collective intentionality in social matters that are up to the group to make true judgments about and does it at the expense of their weaker, I-mode counterparts. The phrases "full-blown" and "as a group" in general are taken in this context to refer to the we-mode in this book, the latter phrase referring to unitary jointness.[11]

There are cases of we-mode thinking and acting where some people are acting together without having organized themselves into a group, a we-mode group that is capable of action. When there is not yet such a we-mode group but the participants still psychologically act in the we-mode, we can speak of a we-mode *group-to-be* (or of a *prospective* we-mode group). This idea will be put to use in some chapters of this book (especially in chapter 5).

We-mode collective intentionality is concerned with functioning fully as a group member when in a group context.[12] In contrast, there is pro-group I-mode collective intentionality that is concerned with functioning as a "private" person but still at least in part for the group when in a group context.[13] For example, two persons may privately or personally share a goal, for example, to go to the movies with the other one and act in virtue of their private reasons, being only personally committed to the shared activity. This is conceptually and psychologically weaker than acting in the we-mode and requires less togetherness and weaker functioning for their group than the we-mode involves. Both kinds of collective intentionality express a "we-perspective", a set of basic assumptions concerning, especially, what a group's functioning from its members' point of view involves.[14] In addition, I will be concerned with the plain I-mode that does not require functioning for one's group, even when one is functioning in a group context.[15] Comparing pro-group I-mode thinking with we-mode thinking, the crucial differences are, respectively, the change of agency from individual to collective (or group agency) and the change of I-reasoning to we-reasoning. These differences also account for the claimed irreducibility of the we-mode to the I-mode (or at least indicate how and where an irreducibility argument can be grounded).

The need for the hypothesis of *irreducible* we-mode collective intentionality stems from the important conceptual and functional differences between I-mode and we-mode collective intentionality (see below). The we-mode is not only conceptually irreducible to the I-mode but is often preferable to the I-mode both for general theoretical reasons and for reasons that have to do with the functionality of collective behavior. Especially in the case of large groups the we-mode is computationally more economic because it helps agents make up their minds by restricting the range of feasible (or group-conducive) action alternatives, and because it limits the extent to which the individuals need to be aware of others' mental states to plan their individual actions as group members. One of my main arguments for the we-mode is that in many game-theoretical contexts we-thinking and we-reasoning (in the we-mode) are capable of handling collective action dilemmas better than standard game theory, as will be shown in chapter 7. I-reasoning in a decision situation asks, "What should I do?" whereas we-reasoning basically asks, "What should we do as a group?" (or, more informatively, the three-part question, What do we want? What should we do to satisfy the want? What should I do as my part of our satisfying it?). It can be shown that in choice-theoretic contexts we-mode reasoning can (1) decrease the number of equilibria (but cannot increase them) and (2) rationally be more rewarding in the sense of maximizing expected utility than (pro-group) I-mode reasoning. For example, in the Hi-Lo game we-mode reasoning gives only Hi-Hi as an equilibrium (in the two-person case), whereas the (pro-group) I-mode gives both Hi-Hi and Lo-Lo as equilibria (see chapters 4 and 7 for discussion and qualifications that this claim needs).[16] The we-mode accordingly tends to create more social order and thus provides a better explanation of social institutions and other macrosocial phenomena. Hence it is arguable that the social world can be adequately understood and rationally explained only with the help of we-mode concepts in addition to I-mode concepts.

The we-mode is based on the aforementioned three criterial notions of group reason, collective commitment, and the collectivity condition, which will be elucidated in more detail in chapter 2. The members of a we-mode group give part of their natural authority to act to the group and take the group as giving them authoritative reasons to think and act. This is expressed by the three musketeers' principle, "All for one and one for all"—the members are supposed to act as a unit, and they are committed, to the group as well as to each other, to perform their parts of the collective deed. Each member is in principle replaceable by any of the others, who are always ready to step in and perform whatever actions are required for the satisfaction of the common goal. According to the collectivity condition, the group's goal is satisfied simultaneously and interdependently for all of the members of the group, rather than for its individual members separately. The reasons for action that the group confers on its members may differ from their private reasons, and are generally not even supervenient on them. In the ideal we-mode case, the group acts tightly as a unit, and so countervailing private reasons are completely set aside and there accordingly is no incentive to free-ride, and each of the members acts in a solidary way towards the others.

The members of a we-mode group construct their collection as a social group. In addition, the group's goals and other attitudes are explicated in terms of the members' collective construction by way of their performative, reflexive collective acceptance (see chapter 5). My view of groups as agents thus depends on collective construction, and construction in the sense meant involves the capacity to imagine and pretend things, to entertain counterfactual contents, and to hold them true in one's mind. Collective construction is conventional in the sense that one can imagine alternative constructions that could be taken to be true. However, collective construction is not unconstrained as to its content, because, e.g., causality and the physical laws of the universe and also human culture underlie what can be feasibly rationally constructed, and also determine much of what social constructions such as institutions will ontologically lead to in the social world. Furthermore, humans have natural dispositions to act in orderly and routine ways, which block chaotic arbitrariness in collectively constructed social practices. For instance, children can be taught to behave in uniformity with social norms and to take them as their reasons for acting, and all of this can become their "second nature" (*natura altera*). Why specifically these social practices (and not some others) are taught to them is answered partly circularly in terms of collective construction and the collective social acceptance on which such construction is ultimately founded. To be feasible, what is accepted must of course normally accord with basic human needs and other—e.g., physical—constraints, and this gives us a dual condition on what can be accepted. Although the "second nature" dimension of social institutions and institutional action helps to create order and stability in the social world, some arbitrariness or openness as to the content of what is constructed remains, and this shows in the differences between the cultures that exist in the social world.[17]

The theory of this book differs from earlier work that I have carried out on the I-mode/we-mode framework by emphasizing the *hierarchical* and *authoritative* nature of central kinds of we-mode groups. An indispensable part of social theorizing should, according to my present account, be done in terms of theories postulating not only groups based on we-thinking but organized groups with structures of positions (offices, roles, etc.) to be filled by individuals. The "positional" account is meant to apply to all we-mode groups, but is especially illustrative with respect to organizations like business and civil corporations when they function as we-mode groups, indeed group agents. Even such large agential social structures as states may qualify as we-mode groups. The point for our present discussion is that the positions in such organizations are, so to speak, conceptually independent of the particular psychological setups of the individuals filling them. Note that when functioning in the "positional mode," they can think and act either in individualistic or in collectivistic ways as long as the organization's main interests, views, etc., tend not to be violated. This book nevertheless largely concentrates on individuals functioning in the we-mode and thus on groups that function in the we-mode. Yet it is critical to see that from the point of view of social theorizing it is basically a contingent issue whether in particular contexts we-mode thinking and acting will be better or worse than I-mode thinking and acting (or some mixture of these).

Furthermore, the we-mode is in this book understood in a liberal sense that allows, e.g., external leaders and, more generally, even some amount of external coercion, as long as the group members go along with it (see chapters 2, 4, and 6).

3. INDIVIDUALISM AND COLLECTIVISM IN SOCIAL SCIENCE

The I-mode/we-mode distinction may be contextualized from the point of view of the by now classical social-scientific debate between individualism and collectivism. Individualism is a doctrine that privileges the individual over the group and emphasizes individual autonomy and self-determination. [18] It is in part based on the general and correct view that in normal circumstances individual human agents are in charge of what they do: an individual's behavior is normally to be seen as her action (normality here excludes, e.g., reflexes and behavior fully controlled by an external agent). This view is still compatible with the existence of irreducible groups and group properties and with the theory developed in this book. But methodological individualism (MI, for short), which is the scientific version of individualism to be focused on below, makes stronger individualistic claims related to matters of conceptual understanding (meaning), explanation, and ontology. [19] We can say that the core of MI consists of property-expressing predicates that refer to individuals' psychological or (broadly) physical properties of the kind that do not involve, or presuppose, irreducible social groups, or group properties. [20]

MI has both factual and normative aspects. Below I will focus on the former and consider individualism and collectivism as competing conceptual frameworks for theorizing in the social sciences, i.e., for building true and informative descriptions and explanations of social phenomena. This book argues that for various reasons individualism in the sense of MI does not suffice for giving an adequate description and explanation of social facts and structures, which is the main task of social science.

A central underlying reason for the insufficiency of MI is the mentioned fact that human beings are inherently disposed to live in groups and to think and act as group members, which is also an experimentally supported fact. They tend to share goals, values, beliefs, and standards with others in their social groups and collectively act on the just mentioned factors, often with the motive of getting approval from others by the right kind of behavior. Indeed, seeking approval and imitation are often mentioned as motivational factors leading to sharing and to conforming behavior.

Focusing on intentional action, thus action performed for a reason, the following rather liberal principles (that accept reducible group notions) can now be proposed for methodological individualism (MI): [21]

(a) Conceptual understanding of an individual's action (viz., what she does) is ultimately based on the individual's own attitudes and motivating reasons, which may concern or be about other agents' attitudes and reasons. This basis may include reducible group attitudes and reasons and may, in addition, include physical and other nonsocial features. (*Meaning and understanding*).
(b) Explanation of an individual's action (viz., why she does what she does) ultimately has as its explanatory basis the individual's own attitudes and motivating reasons, which may concern some other agents' attitudes and reasons and include reducible group attitudes and reasons as well as physical and other nonsocial features. (*Explanation*)
(c) The basic social ontology consists solely of the activities and properties (including mental activities and properties) and interactions (including mental interactions and relations) between individuals and it may contain groups and group properties that are reducible to the individualistic (and possibly other nonsocial) basis referred to in (a) and (b). (*Ontology*)

The distinguishing mark of methodological individualism accordingly is that it limits the applicability of the conceptual framework of agency and intentional interpretation basically to individual agents. Thus MI cannot deal with irreducible groups and group attitudes without (inconsistently) invoking genuinely collective elements.[22] Our above principles (a)–(c) of MI concern both entity and property individualism and do not accept that irreducible groups and features are referred to in social scientific theorizing. Indeed, such leading methodological individualists as Max Weber, (the early) Friedrich von Hayek, Floyd Allport, Karl Popper, John Watkins, and Jon Elster eschew the employment of group concepts supposedly expressing (at least explanatorily) irreducible groups or group properties.[23]

However, according to the theory presented in this book, a person functioning as a group member, e.g., acting jointly with others or performing his institutional duties, should at least in general base his reasons for participatory acting on the group (see chapter 4). Accordingly, the agent's action-favoring attitude will be grounded in and generated by the (in many cases irreducible) group reason, rather than by his private, possibly conflicting reasons. The group reason may exclude or override the members' private reasons (concerning matters not related to their group) and will do so in standard situations in the case of "we-moders", who normally identify with the group and recognize the group reason as authoritative.

A full-blown group reason in general is not reducible to the private reasons of its members from a rational functional point of view (concerning rational action toward equilibrium states). My argument below complements the much-discussed multiple realizability and supervenience arguments. According to my new argument concerning the irreducibility of we-mode reasons, reducibility fails because we-mode reasoning leads to a set of action equilibria different from what individualistic, I-mode theorizing leads to. (In the simple example below only one possible we-mode action equilibrium exists.) Here each equilibrium state can when collectively chosen both objectively and subjectively serve as a group reason for the participant to act rationally. (In the we-mode case the group reason consists of the existence of an equilibrium qua collectively accepted by the participants as their group reason—chapter 7.)

Let me illustrate the argument in terms of the following simple Hi-Lo game

	Hi	Lo
Hi	3, 3	0, 0
Lo	0, 0	1, 1

This Hi-Lo (a coordination game without communication) has two equilibria (individualistically described), HiHi and LoLo, of which HiHi payoff dominates over LoLo. Classical game theory (an individualistic theory) for situations without agreement making cannot recommend HiHi over LoLo (or indeed anything at all), but group game theory can (see chapter 7).

From the possible four choice combinations HiHi, HiLo, LoHi, LoLo a rational group chooses HiHi. The group reason it gives for the members' participation is the fact that HiHi maximizes expected group utility and thus is best for the group. Hence, acting as a group for that group reason entails the members' choice of Hi. This is the we-mode solution to Hi-Lo for a rational group.

The equilibrium states can (in both an objective and a subjective sense) serve as group reasons for rational participatory action. Yet we-mode and I-mode group reasons can be, and in some cases are, different: In our example, we-mode gives HI (= HiHi) as the unique group reason, while I-mode also offers LO (= LoLo) as an alternative group reason (see the arguments in chapter 7 against the payoff dominance principle as blocking LO).

Thus a rational we-mode reason need not be reducible to rational I-mode reasons—the disjunction of HI and LO in the I-mode case fails to be functionally equivalent to HI in the we-mode case mainly because the we-mode case leads to action while the I-mode case does not. This result, if indeed empirically tenable, refutes MI, because a we-mode reason here is not, and thus we-mode reasons need not at least in all cases be, reducible to I-mode reasons or other nonsocial sources. (See chapter 7 for discussion.)

The present irreducibility argument can be applied to show that we-mode reasons not only conceptually but also explanatorily and ontologically differ from I-mode reasons in a way making them irreducible to them also in these two other senses. (I leave a detailed discussion of this for another occasion.)

Note that one may yet conceive of a form of individualism (which hardly can qualify as MI) that accepts *irreducible* groups as long as such groups are created through individuals' action, interaction, and interdependencies.[24] What in such a case distinguishes the we-mode approach from the I-mode is basically the fact that individuals functioning in the I-mode reason and act individualistically—even when performing joint actions.[25]

To remark on the collectivism-versus-individualism debate from the point of view of the much-used notion of social identity within our present approach, we may speak of the full-blown collective social identity of persons consisting of their we-mode states and activities (that are conceptually group-dependent). On the other hand we may speak of interpersonal social identity that is individualistic and analyzable in terms of I-mode (including pro-group I-mode states and activities).

To provide a short-term historical perspective on the debate about individualism and collectivism, especially in the modern era, individualism and collectivism (broadly understood) have been the main competing frameworks in social theorizing. After the Second World War, in part due to the impact of positivism and the emergence and great influence of rational choice theory (i.e., mathematical decision theory and game theory), individualism got the upper hand against collectivist thinking that had earlier been influential (think of, e.g., the tradition in sociology inspired by Spencer and Durkheim). This kind of individualistic theorizing has had successes, but due to its impoverished conceptual framework, it has also received abundant criticism. Indeed, it does not seem to be capable of explaining satisfactorily such central phenomena as cooperation in collective action dilemmas (for example, in a situation with the objective payoffs of a Prisoner's Dilemma) or even simple coordination cases such as the Hi-Lo situation.[26] The conceptual framework of rational choice theory is based on the notions of action, preference, and (degree of) belief. It does not contain among its primitive concepts even the important and central notions of goal, reason, commitment, or any other normative notions (although some attempts to mimic these notions in terms of choice-theoretic notions have been made). Textbook rational choice theory also refuses to ascribe intentional attitudes and actions to social groups (and this applies also to coalitions in cooperative game theory). However, both common sense and linguistic conventions commonly treat groups as agents. Accordingly, nonaggregative notions of joint attitude and social group seem to be plausible prima facie candidates for inclusion in a social theory. However, the social sciences contain other, less individualistic theories than those based on rational choice theory or its basic notions and ideas. Yet the kind of individualism incorporated in letter or in spirit in this influential theory is common in current social science, not least because the major theories of economics are based on this kind of individualism.[27]

The approach of this book is based essentially on group acceptance and construction, and hence conflicts with individualism in the sense of MI. The account regards organized groups that are capable of action as functional group agents through their members actions (see section 7 of chapter 2). This view of group agents may be defended in terms of its capacity to fare better than even the most "group-friendly" kind of individualism in accounting for social institutions, cooperation (especially in social dilemma situations), intergroup phenomena, and collective responsibility (see chapter 7). My weakly collectivistic approach is nevertheless far from full-blown anti-individualism, because it does not regard groups as intrinsically intentional agents, but rather characterizes individual human beings as the only agentive causal motors in the social world. In a nutshell, groups accordingly can act only through their members' activities.

This book does not advocate a political ideology or program, but is compatible with liberal communitarian views.[28] As will be emphasized later in this chapter, this is a view that arguably is needed for "saving the world" from various global threats (such as serious overpopulation, energy and food crisis, climate change, and so on).

4. THE MAIN IDEAS SUMMARIZED

4.1.

The present book improves and develops further the systematic philosophical theory of sociality (or conceptual and theoretical framework) presented in my earlier book entitled *The Philosophy of Sociality: The Shared Point of View* (2007a). While this theory emphasizes the role of we-mode thinking and acting, the full theory also accounts for I-mode (especially pro-group I-mode) phenomena.

Since the publication of the 2007 book central improvements to the theory have been made, and it has been applied to some new areas. In this book I will present the main features of the (revised) theory in a self-contained manner. The present book is about *social ontology* with the focus on *collective intentionality* and *group agency* phenomena. The theory is concerned especially with shared and joint aspects of the social world such as joint intentions, mutual beliefs, common knowledge, joint action, joint authority, collective commitment, and collective action dilemmas—as well as social groups and institutions. It will complement the individualistic conceptual framework of concepts and principles that commonly underlie current social theories. Economics is a prime example of a field dominated by rational choice theory, but individualism is prevalent in many disciplines where precise mathematical tools are applied to theorizing.

Which features are new in the present theory as compared with the 2007 theory? The new insights and improvements have to do with a stronger emphasis on *group agency* and *group reasoning* than before. Importantly, the present book extends the notion of *we-mode group* to cover *non-autonomous cases*, e.g., cases in which the group members do not themselves democratically create their ethos (viz., the group's constitutive goals, beliefs, norms, standards, practices, etc.) and cases where a group is led by a leader who possesses externally given power and is not strictly authorized by the group. The present feature makes it possible to account for various kinds of interrelationships between groups, ranging from cooperation to coercion. By implication, the notion of *we-mode* activity (e.g., cooperation and collective acting for a group reason) is given a much more liberal and broader scope and is called a *non-autonomous we-mode* activity. In addition to this, the book also improves my previous accounts of some central elements in the theory, such as collective intention (joint intention, we-intention, group agent's intention) and collective acceptance. Totally new topics are the history of group agency and collective intentionality, indicating interesting connections between current theorizing (especially my own account) and some historical accounts from the beginning of last century. Furthermore, an original account and discussion of group-based solidarity is given in terms of the we-mode approach. The central notion of group reason is discussed at length, and a distinction between a group agent's reason and the members' participation reason (member-level group reason) is made and analyzed. The book also gives a game-theoretic account of group reasoning and applies it to argue that there are important functional differences (concerning action equilibria) between we-mode and pro-group I-mode theorizing. (Indeed, in an ideal we-mode group, in contrast to an I-mode group, there cannot even be conflict-involving collective action dilemmas.) The theory presented in the book applies not only to small groups but also to large groups organized for action and organizations such as business corporations (partly in view of the "positional" account referred to earlier in this chapter). [29]

4.2.

Some of the central theses defended in the book are the following:

(1) The social world can be adequately understood and rationally explained only with the help of we-mode concepts expressing full-blown collective intentionality and sociality in addition to I-mode concepts.[30] We-mode thinking and reasoning is not conceptually reducible to I-mode reasoning; i.e., it is not definable by, or functionally constructible from, I-mode notions, nor does it seem fully explainable in terms of the I-mode framework. The central reason for this is that it employs a different reasoning mechanism that relies on groups (collective agents) as the basic agents of reasoning. These differences lead to functional differences.

(2) The we-mode approach is based on the intuitive idea that the acting agent in central group contexts is the group viewed as an intentional agent, whose members are engaged in *we-reasoning from the group's point of view* (e.g., "We will do X" and "What does our doing X require me to do?"). Conceptually, the individual agent is not the primary agent (as in the I-mode approach) but rather a representative acting for the group—although ontologically, in the causal realm, individuals are the only initiating "causal motors". In general, the conceptual and justificatory direction for theorizing and conceptual construction in the we-mode account is "top down" rather than "bottom up," as in the I-mode account.

(3) The intuitive picture expressed in (2) can be explicated for the group-member level and be seen to involve the central ideas of an *authoritative, uniformly motivating group reason*, the *collectivity condition*, and *collective commitment* as a priori framework features of the we-mode approach (to be discussed in detail in chapter 2). These features all serve to *unify* the group around its *ethos*, i.e., the constitutive goals, values, and purposes to which group life is dedicated.[31]

(4) The we-mode account explicates the group's attitudes in terms of the members' reflexive performative collective construction of contents for the group. Collective construction conceptually involves explicit or implicit agreement (although not

always the activity of agreement making) between the participants. In the we-mode case it also involves collective commitment to satisfying the content of the agreement. While collective acceptance sometimes is an attitude, it also involves acceptance action, viz., acting in the right way concerning the accepted content in order to "validate" this content.

(5) The we-mode tends to create more *collective order*, *stability*, and *persistence* than the I-mode in some contexts. These features give a reason for preferring the we-mode to the I-mode in some institutional and organizational contexts. The we-mode is also *"computationally" economic*, because it, in contrast to I-mode cases, does not necessarily require finding out the other group members' specific thoughts and attitudes about relevant cooperation. In general, cooperation is a presupposition in the we-mode (rather than a contingent and conditional matter).The members are presumed to go along with the group's activities, and they may also be more *flexible collectively* in new situations than I-moders because of their guidance by the group ethos the satisfaction of which they are collectively committed to (in partial contrast to aggregated private commitments in the case of an I-mode group). We-mode groups can be more *creative qua groups* than I-mode groups in cases where the group provides good infrastructure and the right kind of interpersonal and other stimulation for creative work. The we-moders function together uniformly for *shared group reasons*, "being necessarily in the same boat", and tend to find new ways of dealing with emerging problems. The we-mode can *prevent collective action dilemmas* (e.g., those with the structure of the Prisoner's Dilemma or Chicken) from appearing, as will be seen in chapter 7. In that chapter, a game-theoretic account of group reasoning is employed to show that there are important *functional differences* between the we-mode and the (pro-group) I-mode.

(6) The members' we-mode (thus group-based) goals, beliefs, etc., may differ from their private goals, beliefs, etc., and generally may not even be relevantly supervenient on them (see chapter 3). In the pure (or ideal) we-mode case, private desires are completely set aside—because the group is the agent—so that in principle there is no incentive for properly functioning group members to free-ride, in contrast to the (pro-group) I-mode case.

(7) A we-mode group is necessarily *solidary* in the intragroup sense of its members' being pro tanto required to cooperate with each other in group affairs when acting to promote the group ethos. It is also solidary in a structural group-level sense, which serves to explain intermember solidary activities. The better the group satisfies the requirements of the we-mode, the better this integrated and solidary group manages (1) to enable the individual member to satisfy her group-based goals, and (2) to help the individual member when she is in trouble in a group context. (See chapter 9 for group solidarity.)

(8) A *paradigmatic* we-mode group is democratic and autonomous (free from external domination), able to decide about its internal affairs (e.g., its ethos and other goals and views). This is compatible with such a group still being internally unfree concerning its member freedom (e.g., some members may try to use power to coerce others and in other ways to prevent their freedom of action). There are weaker we-mode groups that may involve external use of power and the members going along with that. (See chapter 2 for a classification of we-mode groups and chapters 6 and 8 for examples of weak we-mode groups.)

4.3.

The research conducted in this book has a bearing on several contemporary social, moral, and political issues and problems that require urgent solution. We are living in a world of crises, one after the other. The biggest crisis that we have to face in the near future is sustaining appropriate living conditions for the nations of the world in view of excessive population growth (perhaps the main single factor) and diminishing resources (such as fossil energy, minerals, clean water and air, fertile soil, etc.), not to speak of climate change and international terrorism. The peoples of the world today are highly interdependent and are thus in the same boat and share the same fate concerning these problems. One thing that can contribute to solutions is obviously innovative scientific research and new technologies built on it. It can be suggested that more unifying we-thinking both within nations and between nations will promote sustainable development. Thus, more relevant global economic, political, and cultural policies seem to be called for. Accordingly, collective intentionality research and policies based on it may help in this survival problem, possibly the biggest that mankind has ever faced. Of course, empirical studies are central for giving relevant factual information, but the present kind of philosophical and conceptual work is important in providing a guide to what kinds of questions and answers ultimately can give tenable solutions to these problems.

What collective intentionality in actual practice can amount to in relation to the aforementioned problems is the creation of relevant cooperative collective action based on joint goals and intentions, as well as common beliefs. The related moral and political aspects of this matter are obviously important. Mankind should take responsibility for its future and the future of all living creatures and nature on the whole. This means that not only the public sphere (especially states and coalitions of states) but also private enterprises like big business corporations should be required to take on relevant social responsibility. A liberal communitarianism (which the present theory is compatible with) enriched by the conceptual tools and theses of this book might result in a normative political doctrine contributing to "saving the world".

How relevant collective intentionality and moral responsibility could arise is of course a problematic matter. This requires not only further scientific research but also education, starting by teaching children to understand the aforementioned problems and to become cooperative. I do not here provide concrete solutions—that would go beyond the scope of this work and indeed would require much empirical research as well.

As to the importance of philosophical and theoretical work in solving the big global problems mentioned above, I will just say the following here. The basic research on collective intentionality and social ontology problems is presently expanding at a fast pace and is spreading not only into such fields as moral and political philosophy, philosophy of social science, epistemology, semantics, and aesthetics but also into other fields in the humanities and social studies. Predictably, applications to concrete problems like those concerning sustainable development will be presented in the near future.

5. SURVEY OF THE CHAPTERS OF THE BOOK

Chapters 1–3 give the central building blocks for the theory, at least in passing and in an introductory way. Yet all chapters are important and contribute to the theory created in the book. The detailed index should be useful for those who wish to get a quick idea of how the present theory approaches a certain specific problem.

Below the reader will find a brief survey of the contents of the various chapters following the present introductory chapter.

Chapter 2 discusses functional group agents—groups organized for action typically in terms the members' we-mode activities—and explains the main features of the we-mode approach. The central notions involve the three criteria of the we-mode (authoritative group reason, collectivity, collective commitment), all of which depend on collective acceptance-as-true (of a proposition). All these central notions are conceptually group-dependent. This thus holds true of joint intentions and wants and common (or mutual) beliefs and knowledge, as well as joint action. The most remarkable new result in this chapter is that it liberalizes the notions of we-mode group and we-mode attitude by accepting that group-external power use can be decisively involved in the functioning of we-mode groups. This results in what can be termed "non-autonomous" we-mode groups and attitudes, the term *non-autonomous* referring to the presence of external power—instead of an internal power-based consensus of the members.

Chapter 3 gives an account of collective intentions including especially joint intentions, we-intentions, and intentions attributed to groups. It emphasizes the conceptual group dependence of collective intentions and makes we-intentions strongly dependent on relevant joint intentions. The difference between collective intentions when had in the I-mode versus when had in the we-mode, is clarified. There is also a new irreducibility argument for we-mode mental states (e.g., we-mode intentions) in general. There are also comments on some previous, mainly historical, accounts of collective intention. I show that interesting similarities exist between some historical accounts (such as those by Jean-Jacques Rousseau, William McDougall, Ferdinant Tönnies, and Alfred Vierkandt) and my own (e.g., we-mode and pro-group I-mode collective intentions were discussed in a rudimentary way by some of these early theoreticians). In addition, John Searle's views are critically commented on.

Chapter 4 is about social reasons, especially group reasons, for action. While there has been much discussion of reasons for action in the case of single agents, no systematic theory of social reasons for collective action and group action has so far been developed. This chapter presents an account based on groups organized for action, i.e., functional group agents. Especially central for the present book are authoritative group reasons for members' activities qua group members and a group's (group agent's) reasons for its action. I also consider group reasons based on external authorities' orders and directives, and present a summary of my earlier account of social power as social control.

Chapter 5 discusses the formation of a group's attitudes (attitudes attributable to a group) and presents an account that differs both conceptually and in emphasis from the standard choice theory approach. It also gives a new description of collective acceptance, claiming that explicit or implicit agreement is conceptually involved in collective acceptance. Otherwise the participants' collective commitment to what has been accepted would be left without adequate justification. Some applications to concrete situations are given (in terms of the "bulletin board" view and the "going-along-with" approach).

The topic of chapter 6 is cooperation and authority. As elsewhere in the book, power considerations are involved here, and the central problem is under what conditions cooperation and the existence of powerful authorities are compatible. Authority-based power is considered especially in the context of organizations, illustrated by the example of a business company. I also argue that organizations are more functional when their members perform in the we-mode, although perhaps most organizations involve significant amounts of I-mode activity.

Chapter 7 concerns we-reasoning in game-theoretic contexts and is to a large extent based on a recent article I coauthored with Raul Hakli and Kaarlo Miller. (For this chapter I have written a long new section on the empirical validity of the results.)

Chapter 7 describes a difference between we-mode and pro-group I-mode reasoning in terms of the equilibria they lead to, especially in collective action dilemmas.

The we-mode we-reasoning approach in many cases excludes individualistic equilibria (and, e.g., Prisoner's Dilemmas), whereas the pro-group I-mode accepts them. Thus the we-mode approach may result in more collective order and can even be recommended for institutional design.

Chapter 8 presents new observations on institutional facts, especially their nature as collective human constructions. An account of social institutions as systems of positions and normatively governed, routine-like social practices (collective "pattern-governed behaviors") is given and applied to social organizations such as business corporations. Searle's new theory of "making the social world" is also discussed in this chapter.

Finally, chapter 9 presents my theory of group solidarity. This chapter argues that the we-mode is *the* mode of solidarity, resulting in a significant increase in intragroup cooperation in comparison to the I-mode. A distinction is made between solidarity of the members toward other members and the group's structural, ethos-based solidarity (which explains member-level solidarity). A group can be solidary toward its members (internal solidarity) or solidary toward other parties.

2

Groups and We-Thinking

1. THE WE-MODE APPROACH

1.1.

According to our common-sense view, a person can be regarded as an intentional agent, and an intentional agent is conceptually to be understood in terms of our ordinary framework of agency. It contains the following central elements: Intentional agents can have representational mental states such as beliefs, wants, and intentions, and they can also have emotions and feelings with their bodily accompaniments (e.g., shame may involve blushing). On the ground of these kinds of states, agents in the full sense are capable of intentional action, which typically is action for a reason. Intentional human agents are also taken to understand normativity and to be capable of obeying (and for that matter, breaking) norms, for example, the norms involved in promises and agreements and those involved in communal laws and informal social norms. Accordingly, human agents are both causally and morally responsible for their intentional actions.

An organized social group (broadly understood to cover, e.g., corporations and even states) exists as an interactive social system (a kind of social whole) that consists of interrelated individuals such that this system is, through them, capable of producing uniform actions and outcomes. This unity arises through the members' bringing about these actions and outcomes jointly, as a group. This kind of group organized as a social system is generally not conceptually reducible (e.g., in terms of explicit definitions or bijective functions in a mathematical sense) to the properties and relationships between the members, at least insofar as only their intentional individual (viz., I-mode) properties are considered (see chapter 3). This irreducibility is in part due to the emergent features that an organized social system (group) has because of its members' interdependencies and interaction, as well as changing membership in the group. Furthermore, if the group is regarded as an intentional group agent, it is based on its members' regarding and constructing it as a group agent with which they come to identify in the sense of adopting its goals, views, and norms as their own and, so to speak, giving up to the group, when functioning as group members, part of their natural de facto authority to act.[1] They then function as if they were limbs of a collective body, to adopt an apt metaphor. However, the only causally initiating agentive motors are the individual agents, and hence the agency of group agents must ontologically bottom out in the behavior of its members. The group may nevertheless enjoy an autonomy that makes reduction to the private intentional psychologies of its members unfeasible, if not impossible, for the aforementioned reasons.

To give a preliminary account of the notion of group agent, we start with the fact that the behavior of a group agent, at least on instrumental grounds, can be described in intentional agency terms—just like the behavior of individual agents (see section 7 for a fuller account). Thus intentional states such as beliefs and desires are attributed to the group (understood as a social system) to make sense of its behavior. These states roughly account for the functional *world-to-mind*, *mind-to-world*, and *mind-to-mind* relationships and interactions between its intentional states and the external world as well as the interrelations between its intentional states.[2] The present conception of group agents ontologically depends in a central way on its members' psychological states and activities. Simplistically put, the members act jointly with the purpose of achieving some shared goals according to some common beliefs, thereby functioning as a coherent, uniform unit. This kind of action can be given a group-level description on epistemic and practical grounds. The match between the *group-level account* and the *member-level account* is not always tight—yet in many cases the former relevantly supervenes on the latter (see section 7). The postulation of a group agent as a group-level notion corresponds or resembles the use of theoretical notions in science, especially at the initial stages of scientific research. The value of the group-level description of groups as group agents lies largely in its economizing and systematizing, but also its explanatory value (concerning, e.g., groups' actions and members' collective action), in general its epistemic and practical advantages. A group-level description makes it much easier to discuss interaction and interdependence between various macrosocial groups and social structures (cf., e.g., France or Microsoft). Such a group agent basically has the capacity to act as a unit; while a citizen-level description of its particular activities would be an overwhelming task, a group-level description is viable.[3]

The functionalistic account of intentional groups as social systems nevertheless leaves out important conceptual and factual features of agency, such as phenomenal features (e.g., qualitative sensations) and emotions, which belong to full-blown human agency. Bodiless group agents do not blush when ashamed, although their members may take part in collective guilt or pride and in similar shared emotions in the we-mode. Groups can never be full-blown agents (or persons) in the flesh-and-blood sense, but at best entities that share some similar functional features with intentional human agents.

Although even the attribution of intentionality to individual agents is sometimes justified instrumentally by its capacity to make sense of behavior and to predict it, I tend to accept at least partial realism concerning individuals' intentional states. Thus we will assume that individual mental states are generally *intrinsically* intentional in virtue of their biological nature, whereas group agents are intentional only in a *derived, extrinsic sense* in virtue of their members' collective construction of the group as an intentional entity that they identify with. As group agents do not have bodies, their intentionality cannot depend on biological states and processes as an ontological and epistemic source of intentionality, but they are real as social systems capable of action. Of course, construction (or, more generally, acceptance) is involved in the individual case as well, and mental states need not strictly supervene on brain states in a direct fashion (think, e.g., of the mental state of knowing something).[4] The intentional properties of group agents, then, are not intrinsic but *extrinsic* in the sense that they are based on the members' (and possibly other people's) collective attribution of attitudes to the group (cf. chapter 5 for such attribution and below, section 7, for the extrinsic intentionality of group agents and their quasi-mental states).[5]

I.2.

To recall some of the central distinctions from chapter 1: my theoretical approach to describing and explaining the social world relies centrally on the broad distinction between "we-thinking" and "I-thinking" (be these in the we-mode or in the I-mode). We-thinking involves the notion of group viewed from the "inside", viz., from its members' point of view, as a "we" for them. I distinguish between two kinds of we-thinking and, accordingly, two kinds of collective intentionality: we-mode and I-mode collective intentionality. Both express a "we-perspective" (the group's "intentional horizon", its goals, views, emotions, etc.). The we-mode as strong, conceptually group-based collective intentionality, concerns functioning fully as a group member. In full-blown joint activities the agents intentionally function together *as a group* and thus, according to my approach, for the same *authoritative group reason* and satisfying the criteria of *collective commitment* and the *collectivity condition* (the "necessarily being in the same boat" condition); these group-based criterial features (necessary conditions) of the we-mode will be discussed in detail below. Note that we may also speak of we-thinking related to group matters from a we-perspective without the people involved yet forming a we-mode group, instead only forming a "prospective we-mode group". They aspire to become a we-mode group and reason in terms of hypothesized membership.

As I have said, strong collective intentionality is to be distinguished from weak collective intentionality, called the *pro-group I-mode*, concerned with functioning as a private person, though in a group context and for the satisfaction of the interests of the group. In a nutshell, the most significant difference between the we-mode and the pro-group I-mode is that the former employs we-thinking and we-reasoning in what clearly seems to be an irreducible group-based sense, while the latter employs individualistic reasoning that may occasionally involve a thin we-notion, but not the full "togetherness-we" satisfying the collectivity condition and expressing the members' social identification with the group it refers to (see chapters 3 and 7 for a precise account). There is also the private I-mode that does not require functioning for the interests of one's group. A notion of "we" may accordingly figure in both I-mode and we-mode contexts, but it is to be interpreted in different ways in these cases, and similarly one may think linguistically in terms of "I" either in the I-mode or in the we-mode (e.g., "I will do my part of our joint action X").

As we have seen, the *we-mode approach* is based on the intuitive idea that the acting agent in central group contexts conceptually is the group, and the members are to be conceptually understood as representatives acting for the group rather than as acting from their own, private points of view. The group constitutes the social identity of each individual "we-moder". (A we-moder is a person predominantly functioning as a group member in the we-mode.)

The adoption of the we-mode framework is justified by the fact that individuals' behavior may in some contexts be better conceptualized and explained in terms of group membership than in terms of their private (viz., merely personal) mental states (also when the latter are pro-group private states). When the instrumental attribution of mental states and actions to the group works, i.e., the group members' (collective and singular) behavior matches the behavioral predictions that the we-mode framework yields, we have a partial vindication of the we-mode framework.[6] In addition, the we-mode framework (re)solves some collective action and coordination dilemmas, such as the Prisoner's Dilemma (PD) or the Hi-Lo, better than the I-mode framework (especially when the latter is based on standard rational choice theory). I also argue that operating in the we-mode may in some instances produce collectively more rational and stable behavior than operating in the I-mode. This feature provides the we-mode framework with a central role in the design of social institutions and other collective institutional phenomena.

Furthermore, group agents may be able to operate "in the logical space of reasons and justification" because they, e.g., through their leaders, can make intergroup agreements and promises and can at least on some occasions be regarded as normatively responsible for their intentional actions (and in some cases also for their nonintentional actions). This gives groups a central role in the normative domain—a feature especially important in the case of such large groups as corporations and (political) states. Sometimes collective activity may lead to a kind of normative emergence also on the member level with the appearance of novel normative commitments, which are not readily deducible from the private level (see chapter 4 for more discussion).

This chapter discusses the main conceptual features of the we-mode framework starting with a distinction between we-mode and I-mode social groups (section 2), then moving on to thinking and acting in the we-mode on the member level (sections 3–4). Section 7 contains a deeper discussion of the nature of group agents. It includes comments on a recent account of group agents by List and Pettit. The chapter ends with a brief conclusion (section 8) and two appendices. Thinking and acting in the we-mode is elucidated in terms of the three criterial features of the we-mode framework (briefly, group reasons, collectivity, and collective commitment). The second section presents an argument for these three we-mode criteria in groups organized for action, while the consequent sections elucidate these criteria in more detail. The first appendix is concerned with a liberalized interpretation of the we-mode allowing for restrictions on group-internal autonomy and allowing the use of external power, while the second appendix presents a functional argument for the introduction of the notion of group agent into social scientific theorizing. As a result, we have extended our conceptually group-based we-mode approach to cover non-autonomous groups and can speak of non-autonomous we-mode groups and non-autonomous we-mode states and activities. The present expository strategy of proceeding from we-mode groups to the member-level we-mode criteria reflects a deeper theoretical commitment based on the conceptual group-dependence of we-mode states and attitudes. The we-mode, strictly speaking, has content only in the context of a social group. Nevertheless, we will also consider we-thinking from a shared we-perspective without a preexisting group but conceptually dependent on a prospective group.[7]

The elucidation of the I-mode, in contrast, does not conceptually require starting from the notion of a social group. Yet since our main interest in this book is with social activity in a group context, we will in the I-mode case concentrate on the pro-group I-mode, which does require a group context due to our conceptual stipulation (this category is formed from the plain I-mode category by restriction to pro-group individuals). Hence the present manner of proceeding from an elucidation of I-mode and we-mode social groups to the main member-level counterparts of these kinds of groups is justified on both methodological and theoretical grounds.

2. WE-MODE VERSUS I-MODE SOCIAL GROUPS

2.1.

The conceptual and explanatory framework presented in this book draws on the idea that groups organized for action, such as we-mode groups, qua group agents can be viewed as not only conceptually and epistemically existing entities but also as existing in the causal realm—even if they have some fictitious features.[8] Bluntly put, groups seem to be needed for social theorizing as irreducible posits of the best-explaining social scientific theories because of their causal roles, which are based on their members' joint causal powers qua members (see section 7). A social group qua group agent may be understood as a task-right system with fillable positions.[9] The members may perform their positional tasks either in the I-mode or in the we-mode, but best-functioning groups that are capable of unified action are taken to require at least a substantial number of we-moders in their member base. The we-mode approach accordingly claims that groups viewed from the inside in terms of their members' we-thinking are indispensable for social theorizing. Ideally these are paradigmatic we-mode groups, groups that can act autonomously on the basis of their internally controlled decision structures, but, importantly, the present chapter extends the we-mode approach to comprise non-autonomous groups and we-mode activities.[10]

A central element in a we-mode group is its *ethos*, viz., the group's central, typically action-related constitutive properties, and other group-related properties that are collectively accepted as true or right for the group by some persons who become the group's founding members.[11] The members can be regarded as position-holders not only in formally structured groups like corporations but also in informal we-mode groups, partly because the individuality of members in a we-mode groups is not conceptually central (but may yet contingently be important) and because the members qua position-holders represent the group and act for the group no matter if the group is an egalitarian, same-status group or has a power hierarchy with a division of tasks and duties.

Through acceptance of group membership (most centrally the ethos) the members become "group-normatively" obligated to promote the ethos and in any case to act compatibly with it in group contexts. This criterion of membership is group-internal, and we may speak of a *paradigmatic* we-mode group when the group has authority to decide about its ethos and its internal affairs without external intervention. The members may also, perhaps upon satisfying some special conditions, in principle enter and exit such a group freely without internal or external coercion that compromises their free agency. If it is to be able to function well, the members ought to (intrinsically or extrinsically) value the group—and this is necessary also for the welfare of the members. Accordingly, proper group members have to function in a group-centered way when in a group context.

The general capacity for we-thinking—an assumed capacity for the members of we-mode groups—may partly be a product of culture-gene evolution, although many cultural and social specifics related to we-thinking are learned in early childhood.[12] Given that the members have the readiness for we-thinking and joint acting, when forming a group they are assumed to share a *realm of concern*, a set of topics that are of importance to the group, about which they collectively share some attitude contents that form their *we-perspective* (their intentional horizon). Most centrally, they are assumed to collectively commit themselves to a group ethos (certain constitutive goals, beliefs, standards, norms, etc.—a subset of the intentional horizon contents) and to acting accordingly.[13]

Here is my specific technical account of we-mode groups, which is to be understood in the light of the comments made above. If collective acceptance is understood in liberal terms, this account covers both paradigmatic we-mode groups and other we-mode groups, as will soon be seen:[14]

(WMG) A collective g consisting of some persons (or in the normatively structured case, position-holders) is a *we-mode social group* (if and) only if

(1) g has accepted a certain ethos, E, as a group for itself and is committed to it;
(2) every member of g group-normatively ought to accept E as a group member (and accordingly to be committed to it as a group member), at least in part because the group has accepted E as its ethos;
(3) it is a mutual belief in the group that (1) and (2).

As to (1), it makes at least functional sense to attribute mental states (e.g., acceptances, goals, intentions) to a we-mode group. A we-mode group is taken to be able to reason and act as a unit (via its members) on the basis of those mental states and to be committed to what it has accepted.[15] It is accordingly taken to be capable of making judgments, molding its physical surroundings, and constructing institutions in virtue of its commitment to the group ethos. On the member level, this entails that the members are collectively committed to what they have collectively accepted (or constructed) for the group with the understanding that the ethos is to function as providing them with authoritative reasons to think and act as group members.[16] In short, a we-mode group is a quasi person without literally being a person—rather it is the individual members of the group who collectively enact or realize the person-aspect of the group agent. In simple cases, a we-mode group acts if and only if relevant group members act.

Clause (1) presupposes that the group members have some mastery of the concepts involved; for example, they must know at least roughly what it is for a group to have an ethos (identity-determining constitutive goals, beliefs, norms, etc.) and what it is for them to be collectively committed (to have bound themselves) to the ethos. Note that, because of (2), a we-mode group is internally normative (or group-normative). A group cannot rationally have a goal (like an ethos, E) without being committed to it, and thus its members—especially its new members—ought to accept E and be (collectively) committed to it.

On the level of its members, (1) entails that at least a substantial number of the members of g have as group members (thus in a broad sense as position-holders in g) collectively accepted E as g's (namely, their group's) ethos and hence are collectively committed to it, with the understanding that the ethos provides authoritative reasons for thinking and acting qua group members. This means that those members function as full-blown group members and thus in the we-mode so that the central we-mode criteria (group reason, collectivity, and collective commitment) are satisfied. This will be discussed in detail later in this chapter and the next one.

Clause (2) presupposes that one cannot act as a member of g unless one believes that one is a member of g, and (3) adds a social awareness assumption in part to make collective acting as a group member successful (leaving it possible that the normative expectation in (2) is not fulfilled). Going beyond the present requirements, even more can be required in the case of groups with members capable of group-level reflection: The members of a we-mode group must in principle be able to represent themselves as a group (e.g., "We are the best ice hockey team in town"). Specifically, the ethos of the group and the (conceptual and psychological) entity nature of the group are collectively constructed. For instance, the members' collectively construct (accept) something E (a set of propositions) as the group's ethos.[17] Through their collective acceptance the members "entify" the group in their thoughts around its ethos and in effect think that they necessarily "are in the same boat" (the collectivity condition, to be discussed below, thus will be satisfied). The members have thereby constructed g as a we-mode group. Rational collective acceptance entails mutual true belief that there is such collective acceptance, and derivatively also such belief in what has been accepted (in virtue of the principle CAT of chapter 8).[18]

An important feature of we-mode grouphood is that in its core sense it is internal: A we-mode group's central basis is the collective acceptance of E with collective commitment and entailed mutual belief about collective acceptance (see clause (3)). The group in the paradigmatic sense exists for the members. (An example of a purely internal group might be a secret association meant to promote the members' understanding and practice of some political doctrine.) Not all we-mode groups need to be based on purely internal criteria, though. Thus, the addition of new conditions, such as symbolic markers, is possible, as long as (1)–(3) remain satisfied. But in the typical case of a partly externally defined group, (1) will have to be modified, and that is why we have the parentheses around the phrase "if and" in the above account (WMG). Conditions (1)–(3) are in any case necessary in the case of any constructed group, partly because it is basically the members who by their collective acceptance construct the group. No external conditions can by themselves be fully sufficient for the existence of such a group (cf. the "only if" in (WMG)).[19]

A we-mode group is typically described in intensional rather than extensional terms, and the group members' descriptions may differ somewhat from each other. Still, they cannot differ very much extensionally, on pain of the group failing to have an identity and to act uniformly. This point concerns the criteria of grouphood and group membership. Note that this is different from the practical epistemic matter of how correct their actual classification of individual people into group members and nongroup members is. If there indeed objectively are persons who accept the same E and mutually correctly believe that E has been accepted but are completely mistaken about who the other members are, one may still say that they have created a group. In principle, the individual identities of the position-holders are not conceptually central in the case of a we-mode group, although whether the members know each other personally can of course psychologically matter considerably concerning their functioning together.

Note finally that transient, "on the spot" we-mode groups fit (WMG), for an ethos may only include a goal that is shared. These groups are probably the most common in everyday life and the conditions of (WMG) are often satisfied: for example, cases where you and I carry a table upstairs together, or where I am conversing or answering a question, or buying a ticket, or depositing or withdrawing money. In the last example the teller and I together may well form and be a we-mode group and satisfy the three criteria of the we-mode. (1) By our verbal and other behavior we express that we collectively accept the goal of performing the transaction—that we share the goal as a group is our group reason. (2) My goal is satisfied if and only if the teller's is (the collectivity condition is satisfied). (3) We are collectively committed to performing the transaction successfully. We are even willing to offer help to the other if needed, etc.[20]

2.2.

A paradigmatic we-mode group was above taken to be a group that is able autonomously to decide about its own affairs, such as creating and maintaining its ethos, and to be one that the members can freely enter and leave. I will next interpret the account (WMG) of we-mode groups to give it a wider scope, allowing the use of external power to control the group.

In real life collective acceptance is often based on something less than the participants' first preferences for we-mode attitudes and actions. What is more, the participants' proposals for the group's preferences and collective acceptance may be affected externally by the use of *power*, when the group is not internally autonomous. A we-mode group can be externally governed as long as it can act and function (almost) like a paradigmatic one in normal circumstances. I will speak of a non-autonomous we-mode group in this case. A non-autonomous we-mode group can be subject to intentional coercion by an external authority. The ethos of the group may be externally determined yet be collectively accepted as true or right or "good enough for going along with it" by the members. Collective acceptance in the above account of a we-mode group accordingly does not require creation of the ethos by the group but only acceptance in the relatively weak "going along with" sense, and the same applies to the acceptance of directives and orders by an external authority that are imposed on the group. Acceptance here need be only implicit and unreflected acceptance-in-action (collective pattern-governed behaviors discussed in chapter 8 provide examples of this).

A paradigmatic we-mode group is not only democratic in that it itself can determine its ethos and try to promote it, but is also autonomous in the sense that the members may freely enter or exit the group conditionally on their participating (or ceasing to participate) in the collective acceptance and promotion of the ethos. Thus a paradigmatic we-mode group is *open* relative to its actual and potential members, although special conditions may concern individuals who have made explicit agreements or contracts in their capacity as group members. Yet the members typically need the permission of the other members to rescind their commitment once more specific goals and intentions have been accepted for the group, since the feature of group-normativity (to be discussed below) binds the members strongly together around a shared ethos. Appendix 1 shows how these ideas can be schematically investigated and how they can be used to broaden the scope of we-mode groups to take into account externally authorized leaders and the external use of power concerning the group. This is done by assuming that liberalized we-mode groups nevertheless satisfy the conditions in (WMG) under the broad interpretation of collective acceptance specified above.

To summarize the results of appendix 1, we get the following classification of we-mode groups. *First*, we have a *paradigmatic we-mode group* that is democratic in that the group itself is in charge of its own activities. If there is a leader, he is internally authorized. The conditions of voluntary entrance and exit as well as the formation of the ethos by the group apply. *Second*, we have other we-mode groups that also are *democratic* in the sense that they otherwise control their activities except that their ethos may be externally determined (yet collectively accepted by the members as viable or as one to go along with). *Third*, we have even more liberally conceived we-mode groups with internally authorized leaders, where the members may to some extent be constrained regarding their freedom to enter or exit the group at their discretion, and the group may be constrained regarding ethos determination. *Fourth*, there are *non-autonomous we-mode groups* with externally authorized leaders who have not been collectively accepted as leaders by the members, although the members still comply with the leaders' directives—perhaps because of the threat of coercion or of sanctions.

Note finally the important consequence that as all we-mode states and actions are on conceptual grounds group-dependent, we now, most importantly, have available *a more liberal, broader notion of the we-mode* (viz., we-mode states and actions) than before, corresponding to the more liberal notion of the we-mode group. The members of a non-paradigmatic we-mode group (viz., groups in classes 2–4 in the preceding paragraph) behave in the we-mode in the liberalized sense even when they grudgingly go along with the group's directives because of external exertion of power.[21] The three criteria of the we-mode, viz., group reasons, the collectivity condition, and collective commitment, apply to all we-mode groups treated above, as long as collective acceptance is allowed to be weak enough and to represent just *going along with* an external leader's orders and directives. The present important extension of the theory makes it much more realistic than the earlier account focusing on the paradigm case. Group life typically involves some dependencies due to the people's and the group's past history or current situation. Full de facto autonomy seldom exists in real life.

Another point to make is that the ethos of a we-mode group can be purely *procedural* and consist of norms and procedures to be followed. The procedural we-mode case generalizes garden-variety cases like playing a game of tennis together. The participants share ground rules or presuppositional rules, but their roles or parts are antagonistic. Two important cases involving a procedural ethos are economic and political "markets" in a liberal democracy, the first obviously concerned with matters of economic welfare and the latter with people's general welfare and with leadership. People here have their own partly opposing private interests (respectively economic and political). But they share a "joint action bottom" such as the rules of fair trade that the group (e.g., the government in a state) or its host society upholds. In this sense markets resemble procedural we-mode groups, even if there is also some competitive I-mode acting involved. We could here also speak of mixed we-mode/I-mode groups (viz., groups with a mixture of we-mode and I-mode acting) with open membership. (The European Union provides an example of a second-order group the structure of which fits well a we-mode group but which today seems more like an I-mode group.)

2.3.

Compatibly with the above, I regard my *positional* view of groups and social institutions (including organizations)—and also what one might call the *positional mode* of functioning as group members—as useful for social theorizing, whether the positional activities are based on I-mode or we-mode thinking and reasoning. According to the positional view, organized groups (including we-mode ones) can fruitfully be seen as structures of positions (offices, roles, etc.) that are to be filled by individuals. When a position-holder authorized to act for the group performs an action X in this capacity, action X can be attributed to the group, and, loosely speaking, the group can be said to perform X.

Positional groups in general are capable of change of members without this essentially affecting its activities. When one position-holder leaves the group the position is filled and group life continues much as before: Positional structure guarantees smooth maintenance of group functions.[22] This gives permanence to the group but also flexibility, as the particular members can be changed (think of state governments or governing boards of business corporations). This holds both for we-mode cases and pro-group I-mode cases, viz., partly independently of whether the agents filling the positions function in the we-mode or in the I-mode, although we-mode groups seems to have advantages both in the moral realm (e.g. fairness, strongly prohibited free-riding) and the factual effectiveness realm (see chapter 7 for this point). Especially, we-mode groups are informally or formally organized groups with positional structure, operating by we-thinking.[23] Even in groups that a priori do not have differentiated member tasks and interlocking positions, the very notion of acting as a group member, when contextually specified for each member, results in a division of tasks and positions.

To each specific position belong normative tasks (duties, etc.) and rights. There can also be power relations and communication relations between the positions (see chapters 6 and 8). The positionality feature is especially important in the case of business organizations and the like where people are hired and where the position-holders may often change. Positional tasks can in principle be performed and positional roles be filled either with I-moders (persons predominantly acting individualistically, in the I-mode) or with we-moders (persons predominantly acting in the we-mode) or perhaps in some way consisting of a combination of these modes. Organized groups typically involve shared activities, and either (pro-group) I-mode or we-mode shared mental states may come into play, depending on whether the members are I-moders or we-moders. (Recall that account (WMG) of we-mode groups allows the presence of some I-moders in the group.) However, the stability and robustness of group life typically require at least a significant amount of we-moders in a well-functioning group. Accordingly, I argue that self-controlling we-mode groups are highly central for social institutions; indeed they are needed as host groups for fully functioning social institutions.[24]

2.4.

An I-mode group need not be based on the members' collective construction of the collectivity as their group but is rather based on the members' sharing their privately (i.e., personally) held goals, beliefs, etc.[25] An I-mode group centrally consists of the members' interdependencies and interactions and requires pro-group thinking and acting.[26] In contrast to a we-mode group, in an I-mode group the members are only privately committed to an ethos. The I-mode group is not constructed by the members as a group in the way that a we-mode group is, and thus (i.e., without additional agreements or other normative constraints concerning the members) it is not capable of acting *fully* as a group: The members do not act as full-blown group members, which allows that not even the cognitive content of the collectivity condition is satisfied and that they are not collectively committed (in an action-generating way) to participation in the members' promotion of the group ethos (shared private goals, beliefs, standards, etc.).[27] However, the members may act toward the same goal so that the group can be said to "intend" the goal in virtue of generating a collective state by their interdependent behaviors (by their joint action toward the individualistically shared goal).

Here is my stylized account of I-mode social groups:[28]

(IMG) A collective g consisting of individual agents is an *I-mode social group* (if and) only if

(1) The members of g privately accept some goals, beliefs, standards, and so on as constitutive for the collective, forming the privately shared ethos, E, and accordingly are committed to E at least in part because the others in g privately accept E, and that they are so committed is mutually believed in g.
(2) The members of g believe that they themselves are group members—they need not believe of all of the other members that they also are members.

In an I-mode group a kind of pro-groupness exists in the members' private mental states and attitudes. The "because" in clause (1) accordingly expresses a private, I-mode reason that in this context need only be a means-end reason, in contrast to the self-standing motivational reason that we must have in the we-mode case (see chapter 3 for more commentary). The commitment in the I-mode case is weaker than in the we-mode case because it is private and can therefore more easily be given up.

3. WE-MODE THINKING AND ACTING

3.1.

The idea of a group agent can be based on an intuitive analogy:[29] Analogously to intentional action (or at least a central kind of singular intentional action) by an individual agent, intentional action by a group agent (and its parts, the members) is normally based on reasons for action.[30] Analogously to an individual having to coordinate the movements of her body parts when performing singular action (e.g., a bodily one), the members of a (we-mode) group coordinate their action (indeed all activities including mental ones) both synchronically and diachronically in order to achieve group goals. Analogously to an individual agent who is committed to her intended actions, the group members are committed as a group, that is, collectively committed, to the group's actions. Let us also assume along with common sense that at least some groups, viz., group agents such as we-mode groups and corporate agents more generally, indeed can intentionally perform actions (e.g., a business company buys another one). This intuitive analogy together with the common-sense premise tells us that if a we-mode group acts as a group, its members in general (perhaps not all of them) must act in the we-mode, for a group only acts through its members; and if the group acts in the we-mode, this means that a substantial amount of we-mode acting by the members occurs.

To elaborate, in a we-mode group the members are supposed to function as group members almost as if they were intentionally functioning as parts of an organism. Because of this, the group's ethos, as a central goal-like "jointness" element, is assumed to be (extensively) accepted by the group members and gives them their central reason for acting as group members. The reason is an authoritative one for the members—and de facto authoritative, at least if they themselves have appropriately participated in the creation of the ethos by their collective acceptance.[31] Similarly, because they are members of a group (qua agent), the group members will necessarily "be in the same boat" when acting as a group. This is explicated by the collectivity condition, the satisfaction of which comes about through the members' collective commitment to the ethos and through action on the basis of this commitment. Obviously, a group agent must be committed to what it purports to achieve in order to act effectively, and on the member level this becomes the requirement of collective commitment.

While the group reason, collectivity, and collective commitment criteria depend on collective acceptance, such acceptance need not in all cases be full we-mode acceptance that conceptually depends on the criteria in question and tends to create circularity. This matter will be considered in chapter 5, and the charge will be rebutted by showing that in fact an individualistic acceptance process from a we-mode perspective does suffice, although in collective decision making it must lead to group attitudes and assumes a prospective we-mode attitude of the participants toward the formation of a group property (e.g., group attitude). Yet we-mode collective acceptance in a fuller sense covering the very decision making process is not required, and thus vicious circularity can be avoided.

The upshot so far is that a we-mode group can act only if its members (or their majority or the group's delegates, etc., as the case may be) can function as full-blown group members. This can happen only if their thoughts and actions respect the three criterial we-mode conditions. Of course, they need not explicitly formulate these criteria and reflect on them, but they need to function in the right ways so that it can be said that the members collectively satisfy the criteria to an extent that enables successful group action.

Let me present the above group action argument more pedantically in terms of a stylized piece of deductively valid reasoning that gives a ten-step argument for the need of we-mode cooperative acting by the members when a group acts as a group agent:

(1) Intentional action requires intention toward a relevant action—presently the action is regarded as a goal, for simplicity's sake. (Generally accepted principle.)
(2) A group agent g intends to achieve a goal if and only if its members (at least the operative ones) intend jointly, as a group, to achieve it. (Bridge principle connecting a group's intended goal with its members' joint intention.)
(3) Intention involves at least instrumental commitment. (Generally accepted property of intention.)
(4) If group agent g is committed to an action-goal X, its members $A_1, \ldots, A_m$ must be collectively committed to it as a group as well as to their part performances. (Bridge principle, making use also of (2) and (3).)
(5) Group action X here requires the members' $A_1, \ldots, A_m$ participation in X in terms of their respective part actions $X_1 \ldots, X_m$, and it is here (simplifyingly) assumed that the latter either factually bring about or conceptually constitute X. (Analysis of group action in terms of members' actions; recall (2).)

(6) If the members of g have intentionally satisfied their joint intention by performing X as a group, they have acted for a group reason (viz., a group reason for the members' part performance), the reason here being group agent g's having the intention to bring about X or a further goal to which the members' bringing about X contributes.

(7) If the members collectively act for a group reason as a group, they necessarily satisfy the collectivity condition with respect to X and its parts: Necessarily due to acting as a group, if the group reason is satisfied (fulfilled) for any one of them, it is satisfied (fulfilled) for all of them and the group. (The collective action in consideration represents intragroup cooperation and in general will satisfy the account (CWM), to be given in chapter 6.)

(8) Group g acts intentionally as a group to bring about X. (Categorical premise instantiating the antecedent of (6) and (7).)

(9) The members of A act intentionally as a group for that group reason, being collectively committed to doing so, and satisfying the collectivity condition (From (2)–(8).)

Therefore:

(10) The members of A acted cooperatively in the we-mode. (From (9) and the three central criteria of the we-mode (viz., the group reason, collectivity, and collective commitment criteria.)

The upshot is that the group fully acts as a group agent if and only if its members (or at least the operative members) act jointly as a group, viz., in the we-mode, hence cooperatively. When a group acts, it causally (or conventionally) generates the action that it brings about. Even if the causation goes through the members qua members causing or at least generating the intended result, we can still use collectivistic language and say that the group caused that result, the group being in these circumstances necessary for the result in question.[32]

3.2.

To comment further on the notion of a *mode* as used in the context of the we-mode and the I-mode, we might also speak of a positional or institutional mode that psychologically can involve either we-mode or I-mode thinking and action. Let us here concentrate on the we-mode approach—the most central mode for the purposes of this book—and say as earlier that to think (e.g., have an attitude) and act in the *we-mode* is to *think and act fully as a group member*. This represents a mode of thinking and acting, to act *we-mode-ly*, to express it adverbially. Thus, e.g., attitudes can be in the we-mode or in the I-mode, and this concerns the respective mode of having them or, in the important collective case, of sharing them. As such the mode can be conceptually separated from the attitude content. This is the first, "narrow" mode-aspect. Second, functioning in the we-mode also involves the teleological aspect of benefaction (in a broad sense), that the action is for the satisfaction of the group's goals and interests—which might be even fully altruistic concerning some external party. The group's goals and intentions are for the group in the sense that the group "owns" the work that is involved in its satisfying or trying to satisfy them and that the means-actions that this involves are attributable to the group (see chapter 3). But depending on the group's attitude (e.g., goal) contents, the intended particular beneficiary or beneficiaries of its actions can be the group itself or some other parties. Thus, the group and its members may have the goal of affecting another group or individual agent; e.g., the goal may be the altruistic one of helping the victims of an earthquake in Haiti ("We—our group—will help the victims"). The intended beneficiaries here are those victims. Of course, typically the group itself is at least one of the beneficiaries of the outcome of its attitude satisfaction. Third, while a *group* may act altruistically or selfishly toward outsiders, depending on its attitudes and emotions, independently of this, ideally, its *members* must act out of *group-centered* motives to be *genuine* we-moders.

In all, we-mode activity or functioning involves three aspects: (1) the narrow *adverbial aspect*, (2) the *teleological* aspect related to benefaction through the obtaining of the *contents of the group's attitudes*, and (3) the *underlying psychological member-level motive* aspect (e.g., altruism or group-centeredness; in the case of fully socialized, group-centered persons, only loyalty seems to be appropriate).

In contrast, to think and act in the I-mode is to think and act as a private person. The I-mode further divides into the *private I-mode* and the *pro-group I-mode*. The private I-mode concerns any activity by an individual for herself, be the activity selfish or altruistic. The pro-group I-mode concerns a member's action (or activity in the sense of holding an attitude) as a private person performed in part for the satisfaction of the goals of the group. The pro-group I-mode may be based on various underlying motives such as selfishness or altruism or group-centrism. For instance, the group's goal may be altruistic, and thus the action that the members' attitudes are about is altruistic. (Still, the members' hidden, underlying motives can be something else.)

I have argued elsewhere that we-thinking, especially in the full we-mode sense, is (*a*) in some cases conceptually necessary, for example, in contexts where the we-mode members hold (and thus construct) full-blown group notions—collective artifacts—such as group beliefs and social institutions, (*b*) functionally required in many contexts, especially in cases of joint action requiring synergy effects for collectively (and individually) beneficial results, (*c*) theoretically sufficient for rationally solving (or rather dissolving) central collective action dilemmas (e.g., the PD) and thus for collectively rationally creating collective order, and (*d*) needed for group-based cultural evolution in developed cases, and capable of handling large groups better than the I-mode (in part because it functions on the basis of a uniform group reason, often issued though a directive of a leader, rather than using as the motivational and reason-basis only intermember dependencies and interaction).[33] It may be argued that the we-mode approach can properly account for the generality, member changeability, and alienation (from the group) that the group level may involve, especially in large groups, while still accounting for group solidarity.[34]

4. GROUP REASON

In this section and in sections 5 and 6 I will respectively discuss—still in a somewhat preliminary way—the criterial features of the we-mode, viz., those concerned with group reasons, collective commitment, and the collectivity condition.

We-mode action is based on a group reason and is thus performed for the reason of promoting the group's interests. The underlying psychological motives (possibly subconscious ones) may be of several kinds, but *group-centeredness* must be involved on constitutive normative grounds so that the right kind of thinking and acting is psychologically consistent with those attitudes. This requirement excludes extreme self-centeredness. Indeed, it can be said that paradigmatic or genuine we-mode functioning excludes conflicting individualistic motives: *An ideal we-moder can think and act only for group-centered motives*, regardless of whether they conflict with individualistic motives. This indicates an important difference and contrast between we-mode and I-mode functioning. Thus, in a we-mode group, properly functioning members ought to act as group members, and thus to "identify with the group" and show solidarity toward the group and its members (in contrast to an I-mode group—see below). Wholehearted identification and acting for the group is not required, but when such identification is present we are dealing with "genuine" we-mode thinking and acting that, in addition, is typically but not necessarily accompanied by shared group emotions, such as those expressible by statements like "I am proud of our group".

Let me offer a description of group-related reasons in some detail. A group agent can be taken to be able to act intentionally for a reason according to our common-sense view (cf. premise (1) above in the argument for the three we-mode criteria). However, on conceptual and ontological grounds it may act only through its members' appropriate behaviors. Since the members of a group agent are themselves intentional agents, we must distinguish reasons for action on the level of the group agent and on the level of its members. The reasons that a group agent has for its action are in this book called the *group agent's reasons*, whereas the reasons of its members for their participatory actions are called *group reasons* simpliciter. Since the behavior of a group agent bottoms out in the behavior of its members, we need a link to tie these two notions together. The tie is provided by the we-mode *we-reasoning* (we-mode "team reasoning") that the members engage in when they act as group members (see chapter 7 for a precise account), thereby reasoning from the group's point of view and taking the group's directives as authoritative by deriving member-level group reasons from them. Such strong we-mode we-thinking requires the members think and reason in terms of a thick, "togetherness" notion of "we" with respect to attitudes, actions, and emotions attributable to the group and its members. There may be cases where one deals with a "switch" from the I-mode to the we-mode, e.g., a switch from the members' private thoughts expressible by "I take satisfying the group ethos to be good for me as a private person" to their participation in the we-mode thought "We take satisfying the group ethos to be good for us, for our group". It entails both the *change of agency from individual agents to group agents* and the *change from I-mode thinking and acting to we-mode "we-thinking" and "we-acting"* (see chapter 7).

If a group plans to paint its clubhouse, its motivating reason may simply be that the old paint has worn out. So the group qua group agent through its members, e.g., its leaders, forms the intention to see to it that the clubhouse is painted, say, by the members. This intention by the group agent can serve as the members' reason for participating in the painting activity. Here the members are to function appropriately as group members, but they need not in all instances be motivated and act for the same reason that the group agent acts. The group reasons of the members are in the present case simply based on the members' internal authorization of the group by virtue of their collective acceptance, rather than on the substantive contents that are accepted for the group. Thus the members may act for the reason that the group has accepted a certain goal for itself (e.g., to build a moat around a castle), rather than for the substantive external reason that the goal is based on (e.g., the presence of external threat, viz., the group agent's reason). The members are accordingly disposed to derive member-level group reasons for their participation, which correspond or are closely related to the directives that the group confers upon its members. The relevant reasoning may sometimes be unequally distributed, as when a subset of internally authorized operatives decides about the specific positional tasks of each of the group members.[35] The central conceptual difference between the group agent's reasons and the group reasons of its members is that member-level group reasons often involve properly normative elements, since the members are bound together in virtue of their constituting the same group agent and hence normatively cannot abandon the group in virtue of their membership. Group reasons in the present sense of participation reasons accordingly are desire-independent reasons, which also involve some strong normative bonds between the members, which minimally include mutual expectations with significant normative entailments. (See chapter 4 for a detailed discussion of the present topic.)

To comment on a group's obligations versus its members' obligations, we may think that a group agent, g, has promised to another agent to do something X. This involves that g has the obligation to perform X. All members in simple egalitarian groups can be taken to have the obligating reason to contribute to the group's performance of X. The case with all-things-considered obligation (in contrast to pro tanto obligation) is strict and does not fit well with our ideas of human agents as persons who are in multiple ways socially connected to their surroundings. Thus in many cases it is realistic to allow, e.g., their central moral obligations and commitments to count against their group-based obligating reasons. Given this, it seems conceptually possible that even when all of the members simultaneously are excused, the group still has the obligation to perform X. It can at a later point of time be capable of performing X. Indeed, we may here accept that "ought implies can", which entails that the group at least eventually must be capable of performing X.

5. COLLECTIVITY CONDITION

The members of a we-mode group are assumed to participate in a collective intention (or collective intentions) toward the group ethos in virtue of their belonging to that group (e.g., if they agreed to be members of a club, they ought to participate in the activities that the satisfaction of their group intention requires). In the case of collectively intending members, their intention cannot generally be satisfied for the members separately—it must on conceptual grounds be satisfied for all of the members collectively and, as it were, simultaneously. (This contrasts with the I-mode case.) The present idea I call the *collectivity condition*. It may be elucidated informally in terms of the idea that the members are "in the same boat" relative to the satisfaction of the group ethos in virtue of satisfying the underlying group-solidarity ideal of "All for one and one for all", which is also intimately connected to the notion of group-normativity. The collectivity condition may be formulated as follows for the special case of goal or intention satisfaction (or more generally, for world-to-mind satisfaction cases):[36]

(CC_i) It is necessarily true (based on the group's acceptance of P as group g's goal) that P is satisfied for a member A_i of g (qua member of g) if and only if it is satisfied for every (other) member of g (qua member of g).

(CC_i) concerns the members of unstructured groups where the having and the satisfaction of the goal distributes to the members.[37] There is also a corresponding group version that connects satisfaction for the group to satisfaction for individual group members:[38]

> (CC_g) Necessarily, based on group acceptance, a group g's goal P is satisfied for g if and only if P is satisfied for any group member qua group member.

This condition ties together a group's goals (thus the group's intentions) and member goals as to their satisfaction and does it with quasi-conceptual necessity: P's satisfaction for an individual member entails, and is entailed by, its satisfaction for the group. The notion of truth on conceptual grounds in the collectivity condition can be regarded as an analytic a posteriori truth: Because of the fact that the participants have collectively accepted the goal as their collective goal, the goal has conceptually necessary satisfaction for all members as its feature. Collective acceptance can vary in strength, so to speak, and range from joint, plan-based acceptance to shared acceptance-belief (cf. below).[39] Figuratively speaking, the firmer the collective acceptance, the stronger is the necessity. It can be noted that the agents need not even have beliefs about the strong collectivity condition—the connection can come about in a roundabout way through their *de re* beliefs that they are engaged in the same project. If the collectivity condition were satisfied on contingent grounds only, g would not be a collective goal in our group-based sense but only a shared private goal.

To illustrate the differences between the collectivity condition and weaker, I-mode shared goals, consider the following example of going to the movies together. In the I-mode, I may intend to go to the movies tonight and you may intend to go to the movies tonight. If one of us goes to the movies, the goal is satisfied for that person irrespective of what the other does. There may also be interpersonal action-dependence such that each of us intends to go to the movies only on the condition that the other intends to go to the movies too. Hence the satisfaction conditions of our intentions are linked on situation-dependent, contingent grounds relative to the contents of our intentions. The we-mode case may be contrasted with these weaker cases by considering a corporate agent such as the Movie Club, which forms the intention to go the movies tonight—perhaps as part of a larger plan to go to the movies every second Sunday. In the we-mode case, the goal of going to the movies is satisfied for each of us simultaneously and interdependently qua members of the Movie Club. In general, I-mode cases can be made more complex by taking representatives and delegates into account, but the point is that this does not as such involve giving away to the group a part of one's authority to act. Thus there is no quasi-conceptual connection to the group as in the we-mode case. (Note, however, that I-moders can make additional agreements to achieve stronger ties resembling those in the we-mode case.)

Note that for a goal to be satisfied for the participants in a full subjective sense, we must require more than the objective occurrence of the goal-state due to the participants' action. Analogously with the case of intentional action, we must require that the participants believe that the goal has been satisfied and, given (CC_i), also believe that it has similarly been satisfied for the others.

A fully intersubjective version of (CC_i) is obtained if it is required, in addition, that the above condition is *mutually believed* in g:

> ($CC_{i,mb}$) Based on the participants' collective acceptance of P for the group, it is necessarily true that P is satisfied for a member A_i of g (qua member of g) if and only if it is satisfied for every (other) member of g (qua member of g); and this is mutually believed in g.

We can distinguish between the objective and intersubjective components involved in ($CC_{i,mb}$) as follows. The objective aspect is this: given that the members have collectively accepted P as their goal, it is true that P either is satisfied for no member or it is satisfied for every member. The intersubjective aspect in turn is that the members mutually believe this fact about satisfaction. Together these two aspects cover the central content of ($CC_{i,mb}$). Completely analogously with this condition, we also have a group version ($CC_{g,mb}$) corresponding to (CC_g), but I will not here write it out explicitly.

The I-mode case satisfies neither (CC_i) nor (CC_g) because it is not based on the meant kind of collective acceptance for the group, but only on shared private (merely personal) acceptance and private commitments. Briefly, the collectivity condition shows that we-mode and I-mode groups differ in the way that their goals are satisfied. Importantly, the connections between the satisfaction conditions of member intentions are quasi-conceptually necessary in the former because they are based on collective acceptance, but are contingent in the latter kinds of groups.

It can be noted that, because of individualistic rationality, in the I-mode case the goals and intentions in typical cases are not unconditional—because private rationality may prevent it (think of collective action dilemmas such as the Prisoner's Dilemma). Thus from a rational point of view, the promises and agreements in the (pro-group) I-mode case will typically be conditional on others' actions or perhaps promises and agreements (or the like). In contrast, the we-mode is based on the presupposition that sufficiently many will participate. Such a presupposition is a kind of default condition on which the members act as group members. This presupposition is entailed by a version of the collectivity condition that covers acting as a group member—roughly, the idea is that a member cannot act as a group member unless others also do.[40]

Related to the comment just made, we can generalize the collectivity condition for goal satisfaction (and more generally for world-to-mind direction-of-fit cases) to cover mind-to-world direction-of-fit cases, thus, e.g., actions performed as group members and attitudes had as group members when these actions and attitudes are joint ones, viz., when it is required by the group that all members participate in performing them or having them respectively. Thus, in the case of such a group action required to be performed by all members qua group members and to be joint in this sense, we have, e.g., for the generic case of acting fully as a group member (a requirement applying, of course, to all members) the following: necessarily, a member cannot alone act as a group member, i.e., he cannot perform an action X as a group member unless also other members perform X (or try to perform it) as group members. (Here a member can perform X alone, but then he would not be performing it properly as a group member, even if he believes that others are also performing X.) In general, on conceptual grounds, one cannot alone participate in a joint attitude or in a joint attitude as a group member.

6. COLLECTIVE COMMITMENT

The intentional satisfaction of a group agent's attitude (especially one related to its ethos) requires the group be committed (bound, typically voluntarily) to its activity. On the level of its members, this involves that the members in a group-normative sense should be *collectively committed* to the satisfaction of the group's goals (especially its ethos) and to performing their parts qua group members. This requirement can be justified partly in terms of its being an entailment of group membership (in a we-mode group) and the assumption that the group is relevantly committed.[41] The group's intention and hence commitment to a goal, for instance, involves the members' collective intention and the entailed collective commitment to satisfying it.[42] Such collective commitment is in general closely related to joint intention: joint intention entails collective commitment, and collective commitment to a constitutive group item involves joint intention (see chapter 3 for a more precise statement). Collective commitment also involves that the members have group-based normative rights and obligations towards one another, which glue them together more strongly around the shared ethos than in the I-mode, where such group-normative commitment is missing. A member cannot unilaterally rescind her commitment to the ethos without the others' permission. This is because, so to speak, she has given up part of her authority to act to the group and needs the others' permission to get it back. More concretely put, a member participating in collective commitment does not have the right to leave the joint project under way, because that might *harm* the other participants, as it might not be possible to complete the project as well, if at all, without the member in question, and because, in any case, the member has bound herself more strongly to the group than in the I-mode case, where a participant does not similarly give up part of her authority to the group.[43] If the harm ensuing from a member's abandoning the commitment is small, merely *informing* the group (or something weaker) may suffice. (Depending on the case, what has been said above may need liberalizations in the case of large groups, but I will not here discuss the matter.)

Collective commitment is the central ingredient that accounts for the stability and robustness of group life. It is largely in virtue of collective commitment that the group is *organized for action* and that it is able to act effectively to achieve its goals. If the group were not committed, it could more easily rescind its goals (even central ones contained in the ethos). If the members were not collectively committed, they could lapse more easily from the we-mode to the I-mode or fail to perform their parts. (When the lapse is intentional and causes much harm, such a lapse may in the we-mode group entail the free-rider's having to leave the group.) Note that if the members were not group-normatively committed to one another, they might fail to coordinate their actions or cease to correct one another's performances, thereby weakening group-normativity and cohesiveness. Hence it can be argued that there is a central kind of collective commitment in well-functioning groups, and that any group that does not satisfy this condition is not a group agent that is able to act purposively to achieve its goals. This argument for the presence of collective commitment in we-mode groups and for the superiority of we-mode groups over their I-mode counterparts will be discussed in more detail in chapters 6 and 7.

Three basic features that distinguish collective commitment from collective private commitments in the I-mode case are the following in the case of social items (contents) that in principle are fully up to the group to decide about, carry out, or make true (e.g., the joint activities of the group, what the group's institutions are; see chapter 8):

(1) We-mode collective commitment is based on a group agent's commitment (be it due to an internal or external leader or the members' collective acceptance).

(2) Qua being collectively committed, the members of a we-mode group are group-normatively committed to one another to perform their parts of the required collective activity, since the group agent's intention cannot typically be satisfied by a single member.

(3) Qua being based on the group's commitment, a member is accordingly committed to the group and to its members to further the group's interests

> and to perform her part. In contrast, in the plain I-mode case a person is committed to herself to further her own interests, and in the pro-group I-mode case she is committed to herself to at least partly further the (I-mode) group's interests.

The main route to collective commitment goes via joint intention. Briefly, group members' joint intention to see to it that something p (e.g. the group's ethos) is or will be the case even on conceptual grounds generates collective commitment for the members to see to it that p.[44]

Collective commitment in the group-based, we-mode sense has two basic, intertwined roles. First, it binds the members together around an ethos, serving to ground the unity and identity of the group.[45] Second, collective commitment provides the group with the authority to decide about its members' activities in a practically efficient way. The members must in their own thinking and acting take into account the group's commitment to its ethos and their group-normative commitment to one another to perform their parts of the collective activity required to satisfy the ethos. Every group member is accountable for his participatory actions, not only to himself but also to the other members.

To summarize the conceptual considerations presented in this section, a we-mode group's commitment to its ethos basically amounts to the members' collective commitment to it on the member level. Here the conceptual starting point is the group's accepting an ethos with commitment to its satisfaction and maintenance.[46] On the group-member level, this amounts to the group members' collective acceptance (indeed, collective construction) of an ethos (e.g., a goal) as the group agent's ethos (goal) to which they collectively commit themselves (see chapter 5 for collective acceptance). More generally, the members' collective commitment to a content p involves their having jointly or collectively bound themselves to seeing to it that p, where collective commitment is grounded by the group's commitment (when substantively different from it) and where collective commitment also involves that the members are group-normatively committed to each other to function as group members and thus typically to further and maintain the ethos when trying to see to it that p.[47] Collective commitment is required for the group to function as an agent, because without it the members could not coordinate their activities or perform together effectively to achieve group goals. As will be shown in later chapters, the stability and robustness yielded by collective commitment to group agency can also be used to argue for the central role of we-mode groups in the design of social institutions and in general for increasing the likelihood of cooperation in group contexts. In all, the members are assumed to view and construct their (we-mode) group as an entity partially guiding their lives when their group membership is salient, and also requiring them to function as collectively committed ethos-obeying and ethos-furthering group members.

A precise characterization of collective commitment in the intention-induced sense is given in subsection 3.4 of chapter 3, to which the reader is referred.

7. GROUP AGENTS

7.1.

Group agents in the sense of this book are social groups collectively accepted (and constructed) as functional entitative group agents. (For collective acceptance see chapter 5.) The group agent's attitudes as well as its actions can be viewed as collectively constructed and constituted mind-dependent features of the social world—the other part being the causal-functional states and activities of the group. The main argument for employing the notion of group agent (or that of a group capable of action) is that it has indispensable *explanatory*, *predictive*, and *descriptive* usefulness for theorizing about the social world, especially in the case of large groups (e.g., corporations as group agents for the purposes of macroeconomics and political states for the purposes of the study of international relations). The group-level description of the social world, making use of notions like that of a group agent, instead of trying to get along with micro-level notions (involving directly individual human beings) helps a researcher to get knowledge about, e.g. a large group's properties (attitudes and actions) and intergroup relationships—even if having both detailed micro-level and macro-level information might be even more desirable. The individualistic approach cannot do all that the group-based account can, and when saying this I also refer to the arguments in chapters 2, 3, 6, and 7 for the irreducibility and functional importance of the we-mode. I will below argue for the usefulness of the postulation of group agents for scientific and general communicative use.

To illustrate, we have descriptions like "The United States and Israel are strongly opposed to Iran's alleged attempt to build nuclear weapons and believe that that should be prevented". These kinds of *group-level* attributions are grounded in relevant participating group members' (e.g., politicians') joint and other attitudes and resulting activities. (It is both the members and out-groupers who may ascribe group attitudes and a group mind to group agents.)[48] These descriptions may work functionally (e.g., predictively and explanatorily) concerning concrete happenings in the social world, despite their being features (think of "opposing" and "believing") attributed to partly fictitious agents, and this makes instances of such features partly fictitious and individualistically irreducible. The fictitious elements are concerned with matters going beyond the *individual-level* basis, consisting basically of joint attitudes (joint intentions and actions) and actions.[49] These fictitious features include the quasi-mental attitudes and intentional actions attributed to group agents and in some cases also, e.g., normative elements based on legal constraints in the case of corporations, but not the nonintentional properties of group agents (groups organized for action).

What does it mean to say that a group agent is fictitious and has fictitious features? My view is that group agents are mind-dependent entities and fictitious in the mind-dependence sense that involves collective imagination, idealization, and construction. They do not exist as fully intentional agents except perhaps in the minds of people (especially group members). This also makes the intentional states attributed to them fictitious because the bearers (viz., group agents) of these states are fictitious (not real except in the minds of the group members). That a group's intention or belief, etc., is fictitious entails that it is not literally true that it intends or believes, etc. Its intentions and beliefs are extrinsically attributed to it by group member and others. Yet the group functions as if it really, viz., intrinsically intended or believed, etc. Note that group agents consist of real, non-fictitious members (people) and have other real properties—e.g., the members' joint and other beliefs are real. Only the intentional properties attributed to group agents are fictitious in the mere mind-dependence sense. Group agents qua nonintentional systems have causal powers and are capable of causing outcomes in the real world.

The fictitious features—qua imagined properties—are nevertheless related to and at least partly based on the group members' intentional states and actions. In many cases the relation is that of supervenience or approximate supervenience. But it seems that neither (what I in chapter 3 call content-preserving) supervenience nor, of course, explicit definability applies to all cases, and this speaks for the indispensability of the postulation of functional group agents. Even if strict theoretical indispensability would fail, the aforementioned fictitious features simplify our descriptions of the social world (when compared with member-level descriptions) and help to make group-level matters epistemically tractable (see the discussion of organizations in chapters 6 and 8 for illustration).

A collectively constructed group agent exists for the purposes of the group as a *mind-dependent* (and at least for external observers as fictitious) but *epistemically objective* and *extrinsically intentional agent*.[50] As I have said, it also exists *causally objectively as a social system capable of causal production of outcomes in the world in virtue of its we-thinking and "we-acting" members*.[51] Similarly, the collective acceptance of a property or other item for the group amounts to its existence *for* the group and thus its epistemic objective existence in the first place. Collective acceptance has this kind of "performative" character on conceptual grounds, although only *for the group* in the first place. However, for external observers, there need be no real group agent, although there will be people interacting in a systemic way, producing outcomes jointly. In any case, a social group is objectively (and not only group-relatively) real when not conceptualized as an intentional group agent but as a social system that is composed of interrelated and interdependent intentional individual agents.

When the members of an actual we-mode group (or a group that is intended by the individuals to become a we-mode group) individually make their *we-mode proposals* for what the group should do and what attitudes it should have, the result of group discussion may be that *emergent* combinations of proposals get accepted as group's attitudes. A simple kind of example is group compromises that differ from single group members' we-mode proposals (see chapter 5 for we-mode proposals). Emergence e.g., in this simple sense can thus exist—as of course can emergence in other contexts with respect to I-mode features. The upshot is that emergent combinations of we-mode features can be attributed to the group agent.

Note that in the present context the members' we-mode proposals are based on we-thinking but might not properly satisfy all the central we-mode criteria—not, e.g., the group reason criterion as long as a we-mode group is only being formed and only in the prospective we-mode group are all the relevant criteria expected to be fulfilled.

A stronger argument for the lack of tight correspondence between group-level attitudes and corresponding member-level joint attitudes (and an argument for the sought-for indispensability of group agents) can be found in the case of organizations, e.g., in business corporations that are basically *created by laws* or *decrees* in a top-down fashion (see section 4 of chapter 8). The indispensability point here is that such organizations cannot perform their obligated law-based actions unless they are conceptualized as group agents (and as "legal persons"). The partly fictitious, top-down-created group-level states in these organizations might not always be relevantly supervenient on the member-level features in a content-preserving sense (see chapter 3).[52]

As we have seen, a functional group agent has fictitious, collectively imagined and constructed features in addition to its other features. The fictitious features in many cases depend on taking group agents to be analogous with individual agents (which we at least in the present discussion generally treat as non-fictitious). In my view group agents such as corporations conceptualized as intentional agents are fictitious (objectively nonreal) and have fictitious intentional features (e.g., reasoning and other features that require a biological brain and are impossible for group agents to have). On the other hand, when viewed from a pragmatic and epistemic point of view, group agents, it seems right to say, can have such attributes as selling goods, waging wars, and even overt emotions (e.g., be aggressive). While their intentional features may be (partly) fictitious, the pragmatic understanding of these kinds of fictitious features on a practical level is usually relatively easy on the basis of their analogy with individuals' features. People do meaningfully speak of such features and do see how they connect to concrete events in the world. (To see this, read the main news in your daily newspaper.)

To illustrate, we consider this example. John and Jane jointly intend to paint their house together. For our present purposes this interrelational joint intention can be assumed to be constituted by real states in them (perhaps states in their brains). Now consider the dyad, a group agent, consisting of John and Jane. This group agent is collectively constructed. Simplistically put, John and Jane form a group because they (and others) take them to form a group. This view it is ontologically grounded by John's and Jane's relational state of joint intention (i.e., the individual we-intentions and the mutual awareness that it is ontologically composed of) and by their joint action dispositions. What the dyad involves in addition to the joint states and activities and their relevant dispositions is the members' (and/or perhaps some others') collective construction (under their own conceptualization) of them together constituting a functional group agent, viz., the dyad in question. In this case the ontological gap between the non-fictitious joint states and actions and the fictitious intentional attitudes and actions attributed to the group agent figuratively speaking is rather "small" in relation to, e.g. a corporation.

In the discussion of the ontology of group agents and their properties, collective construction is taken to be collective acceptance that is based on people's capacity to imagine and pretend things, compose wholes of them, and entertain counterfactual contents in one's mind. Construction in this present sense thus involves an imagined, fictitious element. Yet such collective acceptance (construction) and the central we-mode requirements (the group reason, collectivity, and collective commitment requirements) may be naturalistically grounded (cf. the above example), although perhaps they cannot naturalistically analyzed—mainly because of the group agent's fictitious features.

We have seen that groups are "multiply realizable" concerning their members: a group (a corporate agent, for instance) need not lose its identity with the change of its members. On the other hand, it is a familiar feature that groups in general are intensional entities: two or more groups with the very same members can be different. In our above example, John and Jane might constitute not only a house painting group but also, say, a stamp-collecting group. These groups of course would differ not only concerning different conceptualization but in terms of these groups' ethoses and group activities. So there is a real member-action difference in the causal realm based on difference in conceptualization and construction. The collective construction of the fact that some individuals constitute a group agent is a unifying, partly fictitious intensional and identity-giving element. That unifying element is causally effective (concerning predictions and explanations of outcomes) only when there is a relevant similarity or correspondence concerning member-level versus group-level counterpart features (such as mutual beliefs on the member level and the group agent's belief or rather quasi belief attributed to it). E.g., if "we" or our leaders make an agreement for the group as group members, this fact of course will affect the members' activities. This is central, as in my view individuals are ultimately the only causal "motors" in the social realm—groups can only act through their members.[53]

It would seem that, in contrast to we-mode groups, I-mode groups in general cannot be functional group agents in our sense. I will leave this matter open here, mainly because I take it to be ultimately a contingent empirical question whether a group agent has the capacity to function as it should—e.g., a business company should be able to sell its product, to make deals with other companies, and be responsible for its intentional activities. Suppose that we only had members jointly intending, believing, acting, etc., in the I-mode. While the individuals' joint action can be viewed as a conceptually and psychologically weak kind of group action, it is far from the we-mode sense of group action. As seen above, full group action requires a unification that only collectively accepted group reason, collective commitment, and collectivity (viz., the criterial elements of the we-mode) seem able to provide. This suggests that we-mode groups in some central ways function better than I-mode ones (see chapter 7).

7.2.

As claimed, the notion of group agent can and often will make theorizing about large groups—with, say, millions of members—more economical and practical than individualistic theorizing and explaining by means of interindividual relationships and interaction and by classification of the members into subgroups. An example of group-level explanation by means of the notion of state might concern, e.g., why the EU states cooperate to help other states in economic trouble, why some states refuse to join international agreements that go against national interests, or why one country invades another country so as to be able to get hold of its oilfields. Such explanations may in part have to do with differences in their powers and resources to act adequately, which in turn may be dependent on their size, wealth, the health of their economy, and so on. This kind of group-level information may give a proximate and indispensable explanation of state-level cooperation, at least in large groups with a huge number of factors to deal with (if, for example, pairwise combinations of individuals' properties are needed for mutual beliefs or joint goals for arriving at the group level). In many cases it requires that the individual level is partly defined in terms of the group level—e.g., in case it requires that the explanatory power is conceptually based on acting as the member of the group in question (see below). Here are a couple of additional points related to explanation in terms of group agents. First, the explanandum (of individual or collective action) should be describable in noncircular terms vis-à-vis the explanans. Second, the indispensability of the group agency explanans should be demonstrated. Consider this example. Some people are found spying against a state. Perhaps there is a network spies involved. A simple explanation might be that they belong to a certain spy organization of a foreign state. Thus that state is at least partly responsible for the spying activity, and it also serves as a partial explanans of the spying activity. The important thing in this kind of case is that a valid explanation of the explanandum requires describing it as action taken qua member of certain group (here state) The behavior and its outcomes are to be constituted as group action (acting as a group member) and explained at least in part by reference to a group agent in the explanans.

7.3.

Let me now summarize the central features of the above discussion of group agency:

(1) *Group agent as a collectively constructed functional social action system*: A group agent as an (extrinsically) intentional agent is a collectively conceptually constructed and "fictitious" functional entity with real features (when viewed as a nonintentional system): (a) The mental states and actions of the group agent are generally extrinsically constructed and attributed to the group by the members (or their leaders). In many (but not all) cases the group agent's quasi-mental properties (viz., properties that are mental but not literally applicable to groups) supervene on the members' joint mental states and actions. The functional construction involves world-mind, mind-mind, and mind-world connections (both causal and normative ones) somewhat in analogy with how individual-level functionalists typically view mental states in the single agent case, and (b) the group agent is functional in that it functions in many contexts as if it were a person. (c) Features (a) and (b) involve postulating group attitudes that, e.g., in some organizations such as business corporations may serve to explain the individual group members' activities. (d) From the naturalistic causal point of view, a group agent is constituted by a (sometimes emergent) collection of interdependent and interacting individuals, and it acts as a group in virtue of its members' actions.

(2) *Group agent as an action system with the power to act*: Despite being a fictitious agent with fictitious intentional features, a group agent can have causally objective existence as a social action system based on intentional member actions and also epistemically objective existence as an extrinsically intentional group agent satisfying the (CAT) formula of chapter 8, section 2. In simple cases a group agent as a social action system amounts to a group of (individual) agents capable of joint

action and control over the group's performance (e.g., concerning satisfying its ethos). A group can exercise causal and other control over its members, but such exercise must of course bottom out in relevant members' joint action in the sense in which all group action is joint and which, importantly, must be action as group members. Such a joint action is a causally objective event that is brought about by an epistemically objective group agent that has been collectively constructed by the group members. Speaking in group-level terms, a group agent's power to act typically involves not only the capacity to act qua group but also the capacity to interact with other groups. An intentional group agent's action is mainly guided by its ethos as well as its contextual goals and beliefs (and other possibly partly fictitious, constructed attitudes).

(3) *Group agent with derived intentionality and without phenomenal* properties: A functional group agent has only derived, extrinsic intentionality and, as bodiless, lacks the phenomenal features of normal individual agents (e.g., shared feelings and qualia are not possible group agent states). Group agents accordingly do not have phenomenally unitary conscious minds.

(4) *Emergence with respect to individual members' we-mode proposals and their I-mode properties*: A functional group agent in the we-mode sense may be emergent (in a sense that might not satisfy the supervenience condition) not only with respect to the group members' private, I-mode properties but also with respect to the members' we-mode proposals for what the group should do and which attitudes to accept. The group agent may indeed have attitudes that none of its members has in the I-mode (as her purely personal attitudes), and there may also be other kinds of discrepancies between the group level and the member level (e.g., failure of *content-preserving* supervenience with respect to the members' we-mode proposals); see chapter 3, section 2.

(5) *Group agent as an economical explanatory system especially in the case of the large groups*: At least in the case of large groups (e.g., states and countries) a theorist's notion of functional group agent may sometimes, e.g., in the case of some organizations, be employed to *indispensably causal-intentionally explain* (a) its members' actions and outcomes that they produce as group members and (b) intergroup cooperation and conflict and other intergroup relationships and activities and, especially in the case of large groups, may do all this in a more *economical* and *epistemically* more tractable way than does an individualistic theory that does not employ the notion of group agent but rather operates in terms of members' interaction and interdependence (think, e.g., of the number of pairwise comparisons if that is what the theory operates with).[54]

(6) *Attribution of mental states from outside the* group: In addition to group members, group-external agents (e.g., from the surrounding society) may also

explanatorily and predictively successfully attribute mental states to group agents—typically on the basis of the actions of the group agents (cf. the behavioristic attribution of mental states to individuals).

(7) *Autonomous versus non-autonomous group agents*: As we-mode groups can generally be viewed as present kinds of functional agents, the classificatory distinctions made in section 2 of this chapter (and in appendix 1) concerning we-mode groups of course apply to group agents, as all we-mode groups can be viewed as functional group agents. In particular, the broad distinction between *autonomous* and *non-autonomous* we-mode groups applies and yields respectively autonomous and non-autonomous group agents.

7.4.

In their recent book Christian List and Philip Pettit (2011) discuss the nature of group agents from different points of view, but with a strong emphasis on the formation of group attitudes as based on aggregation of the individual members' attitudes. I will below briefly consider these authors' ideas about group agents and compare them with mine.[55]

An agent is assumed to satisfy the following three rather uncontroversial criteria for agency, proposed in the first chapter of these authors' book: An agent has representational states that depict how things are in the environment, has motivational states that specify how it requires things to be in the environment, and has the capacity to process its representational and motivational states, leading it to intervene in the environment whenever that environment fails to match a motivating specification. Assuming that these criteria are both necessary and sufficient for agency, List and Pettit go on to argue that group agents may satisfy these criteria and hence count as real agents, rejecting what they call eliminativism about group agency. They nevertheless claim to hold on to a version of *methodological individualism*, since they go against the rather obsolete view that group agency must contain some mysterious kind of spirit, or *vis vitalis*, that adheres to group agents in addition to individuals.

The version of methodological individualism that List and Pettit are committed to permits even the existence of irreducible group agents as long as no mysterious spirit is postulated. List and Pettit say that group agents "holistically supervene" on their members but without saying precisely what the ground of a supervenience relation is (see chapter 5 of this book). In any case supervenience in their work is important in that it shows with some precision how aggregates of individual attitudes produce group attitudes. Supervenience also gives a group agent some autonomy and irreducibility. The authors' notion of supervenience roughly expresses that individual facts necessarily fix (or determine) group facts. Supervenient group facts are not strictly definitionally reducible to individual facts. (See chapters 3 and 5 below for supervenience.)

Group agents are claimed to be "relatively autonomous entities—agents in their own right with minds of their own".[56] These phases may suggest intrinsic intentionality and a holistic view, yet this is not the official view in the book. Rather, the phrase "minds of their own" above does not mean intrinsic intentionality but extrinsic intentionality in the light of the individualistic epistemic, and functionalistic perspective of the authors.

In which specific sense, then, are group agents real? List and Pettit reject the idea that group agency requires something above and beyond the possibly emergent, coordinated, psychologically intelligible dispositions in individual members. When their view is described in group-level language and when the satisfaction of the supervenience requirement is assumed, we have this: a group agent is an agent that consists of individual persons with suitable coordinated dispositions to think and act such that the group properties holistically supervene on those dispositions (and their manifestations). Note, first, that my account accepts this, when understood in the normal naturalistic sense, as a necessary but not strictly as a sufficient condition for group agency because of the argued irreducible fictitious features of group agents. Second, my account mostly relies on we-mode groups and we-mode thinking and acting, while List and Pettit do not operate with the we-mode/I-mode distinction. Third, my account of group agents is not based on methodological individualism, in contrast to List's and Pettit's account.

As to the formation of group agents, List and Pettit say that the joint intention to form a group around a shared goal is the basic way of forming a group. Here joint intention is individualistic joint intention. Given such a group agent, a story is told about how its attitudes are aggregatively rationally formed. The group's attitudes are formed from the individual attitudes and activities, and the relation between the individual and the group level is that of (holistic) supervenience. (See chapter 5.)

Group agents in the List-Pettit sense are too weak to capture what they call "group persons", and what I have called "group agents". They take a performative and Hobbesian view of group persons: functioning as a person consists of giving one's word to others, claiming the ability to represent to others what one thinks and wants, and living up to the expectations this representation supports under local conventions of honesty and fidelity. Personhood accordingly is a special normative status in addition to rational agency. A person is an agent who can perform effectively in the space of obligations. (Note that in the present book the terminology is different: group agents are taken to satisfy the criteria that List and Pettit impose on group persons—cf. the discussions of we-mode groups making promises and entering agreements.)

8. CONCLUSION

Human beings seem to be evolutionarily adapted to living in groups, and the we-mode forms the central core of this form of living. The present chapter has clarified the notion of the we-mode and argued for its central role in the study of the social world. Some central features of the we-mode approach are as follows. Individuals' we-mode attitudes and actions are conceptually dependent on their salient (we-mode) group that can conceptually be regarded as the primary actor. However, the group is capable of action in the causal realm only through the members' action. For instance, if the group members form a we-mode joint intention to act as a group, this basically suffices for making their group a we-mode group, a group agent capable of action, e.g., through the members' realizing the joint intention by their action.

Note that a mode of having an attitude or performing an action is an adverbial notion: having or doing something "we-mode-ly". In many cases attitudes can be had either in the (weakly) collectivistic we-mode or in the individualistic I-mode. The we-mode depends on certain criterial features that are not part and parcel of the individualistic I-mode approach, and this makes the we-mode a conceptually and ontologically strong notion. These criteria require that the group members, first, have attitudes and actions that depend on a *group reason*, a reason grounded by the group; second, satisfy a special *collectivity condition*; and, third, be *collectively committed* to their attitudes and actions qua group members. The present chapter has argued for these requirements and discussed the contents of these requirements in some detail. In all, the chapter presented the central conceptual and philosophical notions that the theory of this book, the we-mode approach, depends on.

Most important, this chapter has presented a new view of we-mode groups (hence group agents) and we-mode mental states and action that allow an *external authority's control* over a we-mode group. This gives a new division of we-mode groups into *autonomous* or *non-autonomous* types, and the analogous distinction applies to the very notion of the we-mode. A detailed but somewhat simplified account of we-mode groups in a relevant sense is presented in appendix 1.

Further discussion related to these central conceptual building blocks of the we-mode approach will take place in later chapters.

APPENDIX 1: A SCHEMATIC STUDY OF WE-MODE GROUPS IN AN EXTENDED SENSE

We have seen that we-mode groups are based on we-thinking and we-acting. In addition, de facto autonomy to a substantive degree is required. A *paradigmatic* we-mode group (but not every kind of we-mode group to be considered below) determines its own ethos and appoints its own leaders (more generally, operative members) and is generally capable of promoting the ethos in virtue of its collective commitment to it. Furthermore, this kind of group is conditionally *open* if according to its rules a member may voluntarily give up her membership conditionally on the group's permission and may analogously conditionally enter the group. As to entrance, the group may have decided that the conditions require that some special, group-specific qualifications be met by a candidate for entrance. Such qualifications will often have to do with the special skills and capacities that are required of the group members, such as adeptness in using tools in the house-painting case (considered in the text), but they may also be intrinsic: e.g., a racist group might not accept people of a different color as members. (Of course, in a categorically open group there are no restrictions for entrance or exit.) What is meant by autonomy here is that groups may decide about such special conditions, and that the members may freely enter or leave the group upon satisfying any relevant conditions without the intervention of any group-external parties. From a group-internal perspective, once specific goals have been adopted by the group, voluntary exit can become restricted because of the members' group-normative commitment to those special goals, since in general one cannot leave a joint project that is under way without the group's permission.

The notion of a paradigmatic we-mode group may be liberalized by weakening the autonomy requirement and thus by considering groups that are not able fully to determine their ethos or to govern the fluctuations in their member base. I will below present a simple schematic classification of groups according to the amount of external control that they may tolerate qua we-mode groups without failing to satisfy account (WMG) of section 2. This liberalization requires that the members' collective acceptance be allowed to be only the weak "going along with" kind that was discussed briefly in section 2 of this chapter and will be discussed in detail in chapter 5. The point of this simple exercise is to propose some central ways for liberalizing the notion of a we-mode group.

The main dichotomy of this appendix is the one that was discussed in this chapter as the distinction between autonomous and non-autonomous we-mode groups, i.e., we-mode groups that are internally governed versus we-mode groups that are under the governance (possibly under threat of coercion) of an external authoritative power. Hence we start with the following classification of social groups into two main categories:

(A) Autonomous group (governed by internal authority)
(B) Non-autonomous group (governed by external authority with power over the group).

As will be seen, we-mode groups satisfying account (WMG) can exist in both main categories. Groups are below initially understood in a very general sense as groups of people sharing an ethos, viz., common goals, beliefs, standards, norms, practices, constraints, history, etc., such that the groups still are capable of action (i.e., are organized for action).

We will focus on the three central variables mentioned in the text. They are

(1) VEN = voluntary group entrance
(2) VEX = voluntary group exit
(3) AET = formation of group ethos based on internally autonomous collective acceptance and (possibly) appointment of position-holders.

A *paradigmatic* (or "genuine") we-mode group presupposes voluntary entrance, voluntary exit, and voluntary, internally free formation of ethos; however, the more liberal account of we-mode groups accepts many more cases, as will be illustrated below. Groups are here initially understood in a very general sense as collections of people sharing an ethos, viz., common goals, beliefs, standards, norms, practices, constraints, history, etc. Hence explicit organizational norms or rules are not presupposed as long as the members are disposed to function as a group in the sense of (WMG). Minimally a shared goal or belief is required for an ethos in (WMG).

The classification of the A-cases below will be understood in general terms to be about an autonomous group's decision or acceptance of a value for each of the three variables VEN, VEX, and AET. Thus, for instance, the value +VEN means that group had decided that voluntary entrance to the group is in general possible, or possible under such and such special conditions; −VEN means that the group has decided that such entrance is not possible (in general or perhaps ever); similarly for VEX and AET. In B-cases it is always an external authority that decides about the values of the three variables.

As we have three dichotomous variables there are $2^3 = 8$ cases both in A and in B. We get these kinds of cases:

A1. +VEN and +VEX and +AET (e.g., paradigmatic we-mode group)
A2. −VEN and +VEX and +AET (e.g., an exclusive club, say Mensa, capable of democratic ethos formation)
A3. +VEN and −VEX and +AET (e.g., group with exit prohibited by a norm)
A4. +VEN and +VEX and −AET (not possible)
A5. −VEN and −VEX and +AET (e.g., ethnic group organized for decision making)
A6. −VEN and +VEX and −AET (not possible)

A7. VEN and –VEX and –AET (not possible)
A8. –VEN and –VEX and –AET (not possible)

I claim now that the cases with the value +AET can include we-mode groups in the sense of the account (WMG) (viz., all of its clauses (1)–(3)), even with the standard interpretation of collective acceptance, which is compatible with acceptance of the most preferred alternative in the situation (see chapter 5 for this). (A1) represents the most *democratic group* relative to our variables, but (A2), (A3), and (A5) can also be regarded as democratic in virtue of the internal determination of the ethos, but to a different degree because of the lack of the possibilities of voluntary entrance or exit. Cases (A4), (A6), (A7), and (A8) are strictly speaking impossible combinations as A-cases. In saying this I here ignore the possibility of a group temporarily being in too poor shape to take care of its affairs yet retaining its identity or perhaps even identity qua we-mode group. Note that there is a difference between the group's delegating its authority to decide about its ethos and an external authority taking that power from the group (or something analogous being the case). The former is still a case of +AET, while the latter is a case of –AET.

I will not here consider I-mode groups at all except to say that in principle the variables under discussion can of course also be considered in their case. I will not discuss the A-cases in more detail, but will leave it to the reader to verify for herself that the examples mentioned above indeed can instantiate the account (WMG) of we-mode groups.

The above classification in terms of three variables can also be made in the B-cases, which involve external coercion or threat of it. Here an external institutional authority will have the ultimate say, but it may appoint an internal decision-making body such as a territorial government, giving it the power to determine some internal affairs under the general monitoring of the external authority. Those group members who are under the governance of this decision-making organ may then collectively authorize the internal government to speak for them without collectively accepting the ultimate say-so of the external authority, which inhibits that government from achieving full autonomy (e.g., a regional government with separatist ambitions in a federalist country would fit the bill). Here is the relevant taxonomy of the *externally governed* case including relevant examples:

B1. +VEN and +VEX and +AET (e.g., a typical non-autonomous we-mode group with internal leadership)
B2. –VEN and +VEX and +AET (e.g., state in a union state with, say, ethnic criteria for entrance)
B3. +VEN and –VEX and +AET (e.g., Catholic marriage)

B4. +VEN and +VEX and −AET (e.g., business company qua part of a consortium)
B5. −VEN and −VEX and +AET (e.g., intrastate ethnic group with self-government)
B6. −VEN and +VEX and −AET (e.g., commercially ruled sports team)
B7. +VEN and −VEX and −AET (e.g., Catholic marriage without internal autonomy)
B8. −VEN and −VEX and −AET (e.g., national army unit based on national conscription)

Analogously with the A-cases, all the B-cases can in principle be instantiated by a group satisfying account (WMG) of a we-mode group. They can simply be called "non-autonomous" we-mode groups because of external control; that is, the term *non-autonomous* here refers to the fact of potential power use. The authority always has the option of changing the situation by its use of power, and, for example, putting conditions on the three variables discussed above.[57] But if it does not, the group may function more or less like an autonomous we-mode group. The main point here is that in such a group the members often function as typical we-moders accepting the ethos (although perhaps grudgingly), and acting for a group reason with collective commitment and as if "in the same boat".

I will not here prove that all the above cases with external power can be satisfied by a we-mode group but do it for one case, namely, the extreme case B8 and the example mentioned. Every man is obligated by law or by a dictator to do his military service and fight for the group, and so it is obvious we have −VEN and −VEX and also −AET. Still, both in exercise and in real combat a team of soldiers can obviously function in the we-mode; they can perhaps set their subgoals or at least accept (at least in the sense of comply with) what their superordinates tell them to do. This can well be the normal way in the daily life of the unit, and what we have here is a non-autonomous we-mode group.

The above stylized and strongly simplified classifications are based on dichotomous variables, and only three of them. Despite this limitation, the above classification system shows that there are many possibilities of variation and kinds of we-mode groups.

APPENDIX 2: A FUNCTIONAL ARGUMENT FOR GROUP AGENTS

The following argument really fits medium-size and large groups best, but it also works in the case of small groups. Consider a group G consisting of three members

A, B, and C. These members could be teams or suborganizations of a larger organization, a group of groups, G. G functions on the basis of its members' interaction. Say we are dealing with a business corporation G where members A, B, and C are producing different kinds of goods and selling them. They need each other in their production. They are partly autonomous economic agents, and they have to function efficiently concerning each other. Let us just schematically assume that A produces something for B and B something else for the use of A. Both A and B optimally should do well with respect to each other. They should produce quantitatively and qualitatively enough to keep their balance sheets in the black. Suppose, we are dealing with k relationships between A and B; e.g., k = 2 and the relationships are quantity and quality, measured in appropriate ways (that we need not care about here). Basically the same holds for the pairwise relationships between A and C and between B and C. C might be a sales firm that puts together and sells suits, viz., what A and B have produced (A produced trousers and B jackets). C still has to be able to make a profit relative to what it paid for the trousers and the jackets and the work needed to put them together when selling suits in the market.

Let me reconsider the above in structural terms. We have a second-order group, consortium G that I now interpret as a group agent, not ontologically but conceptually and epistemically. G is a social system producing an output, say overall profit from what A, B, and C achieve when considered together. G sees to it that A, B, and C considered together act adequately as a system.

In general, we assume there are n members in G. When n = 3, as here, and when there are n(n − 1), i.e.,, six pairwise relationships to handle, we get, with k = 2, twelve cases altogether. But when G is in charge and gives A, B, and C a group reason to do (produce, etc.) what they do as members of G, we only have one relationship of ordering by G that simultaneously concerns A, B, and C. In contrast, all of A, B, and C report back to G what they have achieved. So there are altogether only n + 1, i.e., four relationships (and eight cases). This is more economical than in the case without a group agent, where there were six pairwise relationships to keep track of. In the general case, there will be n(n − 1) pairwise relationships to handle but only n + 1 relationships to take care of in the group agent case.

Put more carefully, the above argument says that the introduction of a group agent will economize the functioning of the system G, the price being that the elements or subgroups of G agree to take and obey orders from the group agent—which they may (but need not) themselves have instituted (the central case of a collectively and democratically created group agent). The group agent is a kind of we-agent at least in the sense that the members must think in terms of a "we" (e.g., "we" consisting of A, B, and C). This means that the members of G function in the we-mode *or* the pro-group I-mode (or perhaps some mixture of these). The present structural considerations do not as such let us argue that G must be a we-mode group agent, let alone a fully intentional agent with consciousness (which latter feature I have excluded in any case). However, we assumed that G can act as a group, and if it does act so, as just assumed above, we get the result, in view of our earlier discussions in this chapter, that when G acts *fully* as a group, it must act in the we-mode. Thus group agent G here is a functional and economizing we-mode group agent.

3

Collective Intentions

1. INTRODUCTION

Humean psychology gives a causal account of actions in terms of desires (wants) and beliefs. In recent decades approaches based on intentions and beliefs have been gaining ground, and the so-called BDI (belief-desire-intention) conceptual architecture of mental antecedent conditions for action has become regarded as viable and is needed especially in the case of ordinary human beings qua boundedly rational agents with limited cognitive resources.[1] In contrast to desire, intention entails commitment and is needed especially in cases like the Buridan's ass dilemma with equally strong wants pushing in separate directions. Intentions serve to initiate, control, and guide action. Furthermore, the full intentionality of an action requires that the agent intends the action (or a closely related action or state).[2] Analogously to individual intentional action, full-blown collective action requires the participants' relevant collective intention directed to a collective goal. The notion of collective intention is used in various different ways in the literature, as will be seen. There are also practical and functional difficulties related to the controlling and guiding nature of individualistically conceived collective intentions. In chapter 7 it will be shown that we-mode reasoning and intending will in many cases lead to rationally and functionally better action equilibria than individualistic, I-mode reasoning and intending.

I will below improve upon the existing accounts of collective intention by presenting my own updated account of we-mode collective intentions and by comparing them with shared intentions in the I-mode. The beginning of this chapter introduces and discusses some general properties of intentions.

The notion *collective intention* is sometimes used to refer to an intention ascribed to a group or to a collective and sometimes to the group members collectively, as a group. In this chapter, my main purpose is to disambiguate several different notions of collective intention. In particular, I will focus on a *group agent's intention*, on a *joint intention* ascribed to several individuals collectively, and on a *we-intention* understood below as a kind of individual "slice" of those individuals' joint intention and involving a participant's intention to take part in the jointly intended collective action.[3] These collective-intention notions are interrelated because they are all intrinsically dependent on the group. In addition, I-mode interpretations of these notions are possible and will be commented on in relevant parts of the chapter. However, in general I prefer to talk of *shared intention* rather than joint intention in the I-mode case, because the collective commitment and the other unity-creating criterial elements of the we-mode are not present; the members are not "glued" together in a strong sense of jointness.

Collective intentions in the we-mode are conceptually based on the notion of a group. Full-blown joint intentions exist as relational properties between two or more individuals collectively viewed as forming a group, and individual agents are the only initiators of causal chains in this context. To discuss we-mode collective intentions in some more detail, we may speak of joint intentions as functioning as a kind of conceptual and metaphysical bridge between the group's intention and the personal we-mode we-intentions of its members. Accordingly, it is primarily on the "jointness" level that the three criteria of collective commitment, group reasons, and the collectivity condition interact to bind together interdependent individual actions into normatively coherent and cohesive group action. From the group's point of view, the members must function together "as parts of an organism"—*as a group* in the terminology of the present book. This in many cases requires them to adopt the we-perspective and to function appropriately. Yet, e.g., corporations and political states viewed as group agents may operate without we-mode and we-perspective notions (see chapter 6).

In the we-mode case, which I will mostly focus on, we thus have three kinds of collective intention that we need to tie together in order to achieve a complete construal of intentional group agency. From the conceptual point of view, the group level is nonetheless primary in the sense that the member level here involves irreducible reference to a group, be it a small or a large one (cf. a football team, a corporation such as Apple, or a state such as France). A we-mode group's intention in turn entails the existence of joint intention with the same content or a member-level counterpart content, and it also entails that the members have appropriate we-intentions.

The structure of this chapter is the following. In the next section, I distinguish between I-mode and we-mode intentions in group contexts. In the third section, concentrating largely on egalitarian we-mode groups, I elucidate joint intentions and show how they function as a conceptual and metaphysical bridge between a group's intention and the personal we-mode we-intentions of the members. In the fourth section, I analyze the group's intention in the autonomous and non-autonomous we-mode cases and also in cases where particular kinds of psychological states (such as we-mode states) and actions on the member level are not required. Finally, in the fifth section an argument for the irreducibility of we-mode states and attitudes to their I-mode counterparts is presented. There is also an appendix on joint equilibria and a conclusion with reference to some historical authors, viz., Jean-Jacques Rousseau, William McDougall, Ferdinand Tönnies, and Alfred Vierkandt, whose views on collective volition ("will") interestingly resemble my account of collective intention.

2. WE-MODE INTENTION VERSUS I-MODE INTENTION

2.1.

In this chapter, intentions are analyzed as pro-attitudes the content of which describes what the agent(s) intend(s). For simplicity's sake, I will concentrate on cases where an agent A intends to bring about a state P, e.g., that the window will become open because of his action (or, more generally, that A intends to see to it that P, which covers also maintenance intentions).[4]

I first propose a list of simple, idealized principles that the full-blown notion of intention and intender must satisfy on conceptual grounds and on pain of criticizable irrationality or "conceptual immaturity". Below "if—then" means conceptual or, at least, noncontingent entailment:

(1) If a singular or group agent A intends to perform (or see to it that) X and believes that normal conditions obtain, then he tries to bring about X (or some suitable means to X).
(2) If A decides to perform X, then he also intends to perform X.
(3) If A intends to perform X, then he is committed to performing X.
(4) If A believes that he cannot perform X, he cannot intend to perform X.
(5) It is not rationally possible for A to intend to perform both X and –X on the same occasion.
(6) If A intends to perform X and believes that he cannot do it without performing some action Y, he will intend to perform Y.

(7) A intends to perform X if and only if he intends to perform X in accordance with and because of his intention to perform X.
(8) If A intends to perform X and believes that Z is an effect of the performance of X, then it possible that he does not intend Z.
(9) If A intends to perform X, then he has no momentarily stronger incompatible wants or, in the case of risky situations, stronger want-belief combinations, concerning the performance of X (or at least has set aside such other factors and considerations).

As the above principles are rather well known and accepted in the literature, I will not here use space to discuss them.[5] The above features of single-agent intentions, mutatis mutandis, apply to we-intentions and group intentions—viz., intentions of a group—and also to agents' joint intentions. These concepts will be discussed below.

There is a well-known ambiguity in common parlance about intentions and other representational mental states such as belief. One can speak of a psychological state having a specific content. As an example, consider the sentence "John intends to paint the house". This is in part a description of the *state of intending* that John is in, which we may write out as "Int(John, that the house is painted by him)". Here "that the house is painted by John" gives the *content of the intention.* Often one refers to the content simply by calling it John's intention. Briefly, the two aspects of intending can be called the *attitude sense* and the *content sense*, where the former conceptually presupposes the latter.[6] In most normal contexts the distinction need not be explicitly made but is revealed by the context. However, when I make the distinction between we-mode and I-mode intention, this distinction will prove to be crucially important, since one may collectively hold either an intention state (be in a certain psychological state) or an intention content. This provides a new way to carve apart we-mode collective intentions from their I-mode counterparts—in which only an intention content (rather than the intention state) can be shared.[7]

Intentions qua commitments to action affect our lives in many respects in which mere wants do not. Intentions pose problems that can be solved by means of practical reasoning and—because of their special cognitive aspects involving believed consistency and possibility of satisfaction—may serve to screen off other intentions and, indeed, action scenarios. What we have so far discussed less is the following feature of an intention: Through its transformation to "willing" or "intention-in-action" it serves to initiate, energize, direct, and monitor behavior believed by the intending agent to contribute to its satisfaction and in the case of joint intention-in-action to guarantee the required kind of interpersonal coordination.[8] Joint we-willings are joined by their shared content to bring about what the agents in that situation jointly aim at, this normally being the content of the prior joint intention (if there was one) that generated the joint we-willings.[9] Obviously, intending and acting jointly require that the participants have some underlying capacities that, e.g., children between one and two years of age do not seem to have in full but three- to four-year-olds may have. These include the capacities to jointly attend a phenomenon and share common knowledge about it and other relevant matters, to think of the others as different persons with their own mental states, to be disposed to help others, and to understand joint commitment and to be jointly committed to a task.[10]

2.2.

In general, the content of any *pro*-attitude, including intention, can be characterized in terms of its conditions of *satisfaction*. These conditions describe, roughly, "what it would be like if the pro-attitude were satisfied". Accordingly, these conditions characterize the content of the intention. As usual, the satisfaction conditions of an intention and the conditions of having the intention are to be distinguished. When the latter conditions obtain, the agent *has* the intention. When the former conditions obtain, the intention is *satisfied*, and it is these conditions that fix the *content* of the intention (in the sense of the truth-condition account of content).

Next we consider some central structural attributes that we-mode social intentions may have. Suppose that you and I have constituted us as a group and collectively accept that our house will be painted by us and thus form the (we-mode) joint intention to perform this action. In that case we *share* the intention and believe so. In this example, because of collective acceptance the sharing is strong, we-mode sharing and the intention can be said to be *joint* (in the sense of jointly held) intention but also a *joint* (or, here equivalently, *collective*) intention because of its content, viz., because we will do the painting together).[11] This is a dividable intention; e.g., your task may be to paint the front of the house and mine to do the back. Our we-mode joint intention is collectively constructed (accepted) by us to have *collective* content: it is necessarily the case as a conceptual or quasi-conceptual framework feature (based on the participants having constructed themselves as being intrinsic parts of the group) that none of us can satisfy it for herself only. Collectivity here requires collective acceptance and conceptual necessity based on it.[12] These features connect the satisfaction of the participants' intentions in the we-mode case. In the I-mode case there is no such necessity but the participants' intentions may be connected by their contingent mutual promises or something weaker. The aforementioned collectively constructed features of having intentions jointly (the state aspect) with collective contents (intention content aspect) hold in the we-mode case in virtue of the collective acceptance (at least acceptance-in-action) of the group, whereas in the I-mode these conditions need not hold true.

2.3.

We-mode intentions are intentions that one has in virtue of functioning as a group member. For instance, suppose the members of an organization work together to promote its ethos (under some description or by entailment, e.g., by intending something that a member believes is ethos-promoting). Think of a professor correcting term papers as nonjoint action while also teaching a joint seminar as part of his required duties.[13] He is doing his correction work alone in one sense. but in another sense he is also by his correction of term papers performing his duties and working jointly with the staff to satisfy and promote the ethos of the university. His work (correction work or joint teaching) is in the we-mode (assuming that some further conditions such as the three criterial features of the we-mode are satisfied).

There are also (more) *general* we-mode intentions such as the intention to satisfy and promote the ethos of the group in question or, put in other words, the general intention to function as a group member in the we-mode. Such a general intention can generate specific we-mode intentions like the intention to correct term papers or to teach a joint seminar.

In the case of a we-mode intention the important thing is not the specific content of the intention but the *mode of having* the intention. One and the same intention (content) can thus be had in different modes, e.g. in the collectivistic we-mode or in the individualistic I-mode. (Note that mode in the present sense is to be distinguished from the "attitudinal" mode, e.g. intending, hoping, or believing, applied to a certain content.) In the we-mode case the intending subject is "we," and in the I-mode case it is "I". It prefixes the content, P, of an intention. Below the content can be, e.g., "that we perform X together" or the infinitival "to do X together". It can also represent a state to be brought about or maintained, etc., and in this case the phrase "we intend to see to it that P" expresses both the state of intending of the intending subject and the content P. It can also represent a state to be brought about or maintained, etc., and in this case the phrase "we intend to see to it that P" expresses both the state (fact) of intending and the intention content P. The content P can also refer to a single agent, e.g., "that John participate in our joint action X", or something similar. Note that an agent's intention that we do X together of course rationally requires that he intend to do something furthering the satisfaction conditions of the intention with collective content that we do X together.

Here is a partial account of the notion of we-mode intention in an egalitarian group (i.e., one with members with equal status):[14]

(WMI) Agent A has the intention with the collective content P in the *we-mode* in a group, g, of agents if

(1) A is functioning qua member of g,
(2) A's intention presupposes that the agents in g collectively accept P as their intention (content) for satisfying the interests of g,
(3) A intends to participate in the satisfaction of the intention for g, and
(4) A presupposes that the central we-mode criteria are satisfied for the participants.[15]

A we-mode intention in the above sense is jointly (here equivalently, collectively) held by the participants, but it need not have joint (here equivalently, collective) content.[16] A we-mode intention is jointly held in the we-mode by the participants, but there are weaker ways of sharing intentions, viz., sharing them in the I-mode.[17]

In (WMI) the satisfaction of the intention is *for* g. This "for-groupness" involves that a paradigmatic we-mode group is taken to "own" the products of its activities and thus to be able to make either itself or some other party the beneficiary. The aspect of owning and that of being a beneficiary are to be kept apart. To own the satisfaction activity entails it being allowed in principle for a paradigmatic, thus autonomous, we-mode group to choose the party that will be the intended beneficiary, be it the group itself, some group member(s), or another group or person (recall the discussion in chapter 2).

Note that our discussion here primarily concerns the paradigmatic we-mode case. To account for the notion of the non-autonomous we-mode that was discussed in chapter 2, the wording of (WMI) in fact can be kept intact, but the notion of (collective) acceptance in clause (2) must be understood in a broad sense, primarily as "going along with" (see chapter 5). In that case what was just said about owning needs qualifications, which are going to be of different kinds depending on the kind of we-mode group in question (viz., the autonomous versus non-autonomous we-mode cases distinguished in chapter 2).

The intention P is an intention to participate in a *joint* intention and not merely a *shared* one when (WMI) is satisfied. In general, a joint intention in this sense is below taken to be in the we-mode, while a merely shared intention is shared only privately in the I-mode.[18] We could say that if a person truly acts *on* his we-mode intention, he acts qua group member. Assuming that there is a part for each agent to perform, the we-mode entails that they intend to participate in satisfying the intention together with the others. The participation can be direct or indirect (in the latter case the member still participates in some way in the group's seeing to it that the intention will be satisfied, e.g., by taking part in the group's discussion of who should be the operative agent carrying out the task). And if a participant then acts qua member, he does not independently perform a part, but he performs his part as his part of the members' satisfaction of the joint intention.

As the members' functioning in the we-mode also entails that the participants are collectively committed to what they have accepted, (WMI) has a guiding and controlling function. If they then form an intention for the group, the existence of that group intention will be their authoritative group reason for action as group members. There is group authority in the present case primarily because the participants are functioning as a group, and this is out in the open. They must, so to speak, give up part of their authority to act to the group. So even in the most simple we-mode cases there is collective commitment and also a group reason involved.

In virtue of being collectively accepted by the group members *qua* group members, the we-mode intention (WMI) satisfies three central criteria involved in the we-mode, namely *group reason*, the *collectivity condition*, and *collective commitment*. Suppose that our group, consisting of you and me, collectively accepts as its goal (intention) to get the house painted (see chapter 5 for this kind of collective acceptance). When I have a we-mode intention to participate in our seeing to it that P in the we-mode, my group reason is not the mere content P of our acceptance, but the reason also involves the fact of our acceptance of it as our intended goal. The reason here can be taken to involve the fact that P has been collectively accepted by us to be our intention or goal.[19] In our example, the proximate reason is that we have collectively accepted getting our house painted (e.g., by the group members). This intention content, spelled out as "the house gets painted by us", intrinsically requires our collective acceptance of this content as our (joint) intention content. Our collectively accepted intention to get the house painted provides me with a reason, indeed a group reason, which I would not have otherwise; and I intend to perform my share of the painting at least in part *because* of this group reason. Accordingly, in the first-person case, my group reason is not merely *what* we accept as our intention, but in the first place the very social fact *that* we accept that content as our intention.

In addition to the presence of this group reason, there is also collective commitment to act for this reason; viz., we have voluntarily committed ourselves to seeing to it that the house gets painted as agreed. This collective commitment also entails for both parties the intention to see to it that mutual awareness of the satisfaction of the intention will eventually be achieved, or, if it turns out that it cannot be satisfied, to see to it that this fact will become mutually known. According to the collectivity condition, if the intention is satisfied, then it is necessarily satisfied for both of us.

2.4.

It is useful to contrast we-mode intentions with I-mode intentions, as they have different functional roles in thinking and acting in virtue of their different satisfaction conditions, which also entail different commitments and action recommendations. The following kinds of I-mode intentions or rather ways of having an intention in the I-mode can now be distinguished:

(IMI) Agent A has the intention that P in the *I-mode* if and only if A is privately committed to satisfying P (or participating in the satisfaction of P) and he intends to satisfy P (or participate in its satisfaction) at least in part for himself qua private person (rather than qua group member).

(PIMI) Agent A has the intention that P in the purely *private I-mode* if and only if A is privately committed to satisfying P (or participating in the satisfaction of P) and he intends to satisfy it only for himself qua private person.

(PROGIMI) Agent A has the intention that P in the *pro-group I-mode* in group g if and only if A is functioning qua member of g (in a weak sense), is privately committed to participating in the satisfaction of P and intends to do it in part for (the members of) group g but in part for himself qua private person. [20]

The general notion (see (IMI)) of an I-mode intention is independent of whether A functions purely privately or (in part) for the group. The beneficiary (in the sense of chapter 2) of the satisfaction of P can in the present case be agent A himself, his group, or some other party. In terms of our house-painting example, the difference is that in the case of (PIMI) the result of the action in question (e.g., painting a house) is solely for advancing the interests of A (whatever they are), whereas in the case of (IMI) it may be in part also for A's group or for another party. Here "for" does not always entail "for the benefit of", but the satisfaction of the intention is in any case understood to be for satisfying A's goals and interests, which may be egoistic or altruistic or something else.[21] In the I-mode case an agent in principle always can act normatively autonomously unless he has restricted his autonomy by a special commitment entailing promise or agreement. He is not intrinsically acting as a group member and thus has not delegated part of his individual authority to the group, in contrast to what happens in the we-mode case. In a we-mode group a member is functioning as a group member and taking part in group action whenever the group acts. His action is intrinsically connected to the group's action. We can say somewhat metaphorically that when a member acts as a member in a we-mode group, the group also acts through his action. The member represents the group and through his commitment to the group he intrinsically (rather than contingently and *in casu*) gives part of his authority to act to the group in the group action case.[22]

In the pro-group I-mode case the group members share their private (viz., personal) intention P with the other group members in the sense of sharing the satisfaction conditions of P. Sharing in the I-mode case need be only shallow sharing: e.g., I have the intention to participate and you have the same intention, and we mutually believe this.

In contrast to the we-mode case, we may not infer that the intention always is (or is at least by redescription or entailment) for the promotion of the ethos of the group, since the members may function as a loose I-mode group (rather than as a group agent in the sense of this book), and their intentions may be only interpersonally related rather than dependent on the group as an irreducible social entity (cf. the functional argument for the we-mode in appendix 2 of chapter 2). In the house-painting case, for example, the house getting painted must thus be at least in part for the interests of g and thus the members of g. Yet in (PIMI) and (PROGIMI) the beneficiary or beneficiaries of the satisfaction of P in principle are open as in (IMI).[23]

Comparing the we-mode (WMI) and the pro-group I-mode (PROGIMI), in the latter case an intention strictly speaking cannot satisfy any of the three constitutive criteria of the we-mode: group reason, the collectivity condition, and collective commitment or, rather, their counterparts that concur with individualistic reasoning instead of reasoning fully as a group.[24] This is because these we-mode criteria are all based on preanalytic collective acceptance that must be for the group qua group agent and based on a process of group reasoning (see chapter 5 for details). Let me elaborate on this.

First, although the agent who has the intention that P in the pro-group I-mode intends to contribute to the satisfaction of P for the group, she need not (and strictly speaking cannot) intend to act *because* of the right kind of group reason, viz., because of the participants' strong, we-mode collective acceptance of the intention that P for the group. Second, in the absence of such strong collective acceptance, the pro-group I-mode intention cannot satisfy the collectivity condition that requires necessity based on collective acceptance. Third, a member acting in the pro-group I-mode (e.g., as a group "benefactor") is not a participant in a *collective* commitment to achieve P.[25]

In the present context we have to deal not only with the we-mode and the I-mode, viz., the *mode* or way of having an intention or of acting, but also of the *content* of the attitude or action from the point of view of whether it involves single agency or multiple agency. Single agency is expressed by the pronoun "I" and I-thinking, whereas shared or collective agency is expressed by "we". *"We-thinking" and "I-thinking" do not have an unambiguous mode-specific linguistic form: there can be we-thinking both in the we-mode and in the pro-group I-mode.* I-mode joint action is based on individualistic reasoning (while possibly employing "we" in an aggregative "linguistic" sense) instead of proper we-reasoning as in the we-mode case.

Here is an example that typically is instantiated as I-mode rather than we-mode joint action. Suppose two drivers, you and I, are coming from opposite directions, and we get out of our cars to remove a fallen tree from the road, our shared goal of course to get the tree removed from the road. We share that goal in the I-mode—based on our private reasoning that we will do the job together (as both are physically needed for it). We—you and I—here share an I-mode we-intention expressible by "We will remove the tree together". I intend to participate in our joint action and so do you (and we share the information needed). On the other hand, two persons obviously can remove a log acting jointly in the we-mode when functioning as a group. The same we-intention expression as above can be used. What is added to the I-mode case is that the we-mode criteria (the group reason, collectivity, and collective commitment criteria based on collective acceptance correctly apply). Our participation intentions, e.g., that I will do my part of the joint action, now are in the we-mode. Thus, more generally, on the one hand I-thinking (e.g., intending) can be in the we-mode or in the I-mode and, on the other hand, we-thinking can also be in the I-mode or in the we-mode.[26]

Note that if a group agent is a we-mode group, its members' activities (intendings and actions, etc.) ought to be in the we-mode. So one might say that such a group agent acts in the we-mode (using the term in an extended sense).

2.5.

To end this section, I will make some further remarks on the relationship between the we-mode and the I-mode. First note that a person, A, can at least on conceptual grounds have the intention that P simultaneously both in the I-mode and in the we-mode (although these two intentions have different satisfaction conditions). However, A's we-mode intention entails neither that he has nor that he does not have the corresponding I-mode intention, and vice versa. Second, we may ask how a group's intention or goal is related to the collective intentions of its members. These notions obviously are dependent. This dependence can be explicated in terms of a *supervenience relation*: Every change in the group's intention (in the full, we-mode sense) is necessarily accompanied by some change in the we-mode intentions of at least some of the members. However, the members' we-mode intentions do not depend on their private, I-mode intentions with the same content. For instance, a group (e.g., a group of extremists) could have the intention P (e.g., to destroy capitalism) and the members could have P as their derived we-mode collective intention but not have P as their private intention. The group's intention P could change without any change in the members' privately held P-related intentions taking place (while some relevant change in the members' P-related intentions held in the we-mode would have to take place). In any case, supervenience with respect to I-mode intentions with the same content thus fails.

Supervenience of we-mode attitudes with respect to other I-mode attitudes that are not about the content P is another matter. I claim that giving up the *same-content* condition would lead to highly uninformative connections, for obviously when people think that P, for example, something is happening in their central nervous system. Perhaps such an unspecified holistic basis could be connected to the we-mode attitude P in the way that supervenience requires, but making this basis and this connection epistemically informative and respectable is certainly a hard task. Note that the we-mode approach has the ontologically individualistic feature that it asserts that we-mode states and activities ultimately ontologically pertain to individuals, despite the fact that they may be group-dependent, dependent on a (partly) fictitious group agent, and one with both naturalistically understood causally relevant properties and imagined properties (recall chapter 2, section 7).[27]

It has recently been argued by List and Pettit that a broader notion of "holistic supervenience" relation (that does not always satisfy the above same-content requirement) is needed for the general case.[28] This relation also might be at stake within the we-mode approach where a *contingent holistic supervenience relation* (between the we-mode and the I-mode) might obtain concerning neural happenings in a holistic sense.

3. JOINT INTENTIONS AND WE-INTENTIONS

3.1.

Suppose that some agents intend jointly to perform an action, or to achieve a goal, together—e.g., they intend jointly to build a bridge or sing a song together or to write a joint paper. From a linguistic point of view, the participants might collectively accept the joint intention expression "We will do X jointly", which will be seen to entail that each participant has the we-intention to perform the joint action X together with the others. Such a we-intention (which here is assumed to be a we-mode one) entails a participant's intention to participate in their performing X together—either in an "actional" sense or in the sense of taking part in the group's, "our", collective responsibility for X. This is the core of we-intention, and it refers to an action that the participant normally can be assumed to be able to perform on her own, while the joint intention may involve a content that the participants may only achieve together. Accordingly, while the agent typically cannot perform X alone, what he can do is to participate in the joint action X either in the actional sense or only in the mentioned collective responsibility sense. This relates to the group's "owning" the activity and as a result of it to the collectivity condition concerning participation and satisfaction of the part performances.[29]

My account views X as a joint action type, which is, roughly, a jointly tokenable action structure based on we-thinking and which involves part actions for at least two participants.[30] In a simple choice situation, joint tokening of an action type minimally involves that the participants choose as a unit, their choices thus being bound together by collective commitment. These considerations indicate that one cannot satisfy a we-intention alone (at least in the present we-mode sense), because the we-intending agent presumes that there is a joint intention that is *conceptually prior* to we-intention. Thus we can say that there is an intending group (as an underlying responsible agent) consisting of or at least including the jointly intending members for there to be a we-intention by any individual member of the group. (For more on this veridicality assumption, see below.) In this chapter I will avail myself of certain "canonical" linguistic expressions of we-intentions (without assuming that my account strictly requires language users).

From a group's perspective, there will have to be unified group action for a group's intention to become properly satisfied. This requires that the group members' actions be suitably bound together and coordinated with each other to yield jointly intentional action, namely, joint action based on the participants' joint intention. The relevant intermember bond here is the group's intention and commitment to action—recall chapter 2.

The participants of joint intention are here assumed to act as group members and thus to comply with the group's ethos (and other goals and standards, etc.). This applies also to fleeting temporary task groups—think, for instance, of some people carrying a table jointly upstairs. When the members act as group members in such simple egalitarian, same-status groups, they represent their group, and their joint intention can be attributed to their group. In more complex cases there may be a special power structure and delegation of authority within the group, or asymmetries in the possession of relevant information such that not all members need to (or even are allowed to) participate in the formation of group attitudes.

A group agent's intention being formed by the members' collective acceptance, such acceptance activity is an ontological prerequisite for the existence of the group's intention. In forming the group's intention the members are answering in that situation the question "What should our group do?" or "What should we do as a group?" The resulting group agent's intention is both conceptually and causally prior to the members' participatory action aiming at the satisfaction of the group intention. To illustrate, suppose that the group members or the operatives have formed the intention for the group to paint the house. The fact that the group so intends is conceptually prior to what the group members do, and this fact, through the members' joint intention and their we-intentions, contributes to and explains the resulting painting actions of the members. (See the practical inference schema in section 5 below.)

A we-mode joint intention presupposes that the participants understand—at least in a rudimentary sense—that a joint action is involved. This goes even for instances where their actions apart from the group context would as such be separate and non-joint. Acting as members of a we-mode group necessarily brings in jointness (viz., acting jointly to satisfy or promote the ethos). The joint action must be taken to include a "slot" for each participant's intention, where in principle the identity of a participant does not matter much.[31]

In general, all the relevant generic action concepts need to be possessed at least to a degree by the participants—a kind of "hermeneutic circle" is at play. Thus the agents have to believe, in general, that they can perform the action together—or at least that such performance is not impossible. Next, certain situation-specific information must be presupposed. If the performance of joint action X in a situation, S, is at stake, the concept of X must be possessed by the potential participants at least in an actional if not in a reflective and cognitive sense, and they must also understand what S involves concerning the performance of X. It is also required, at least ideally, that each participant believe that the participants mutually believe that the "joint action opportunities" for X hold in S, e.g., that a sufficient number of willing participants for the performance of X will exist. To put the point concisely, the participants must know what they are up to, where, and when.

Some direct or indirect public communication (or signaling) between the participants is in general needed for joint intention formation because the participants are autonomous agents who, nevertheless, must make up their minds depending on what the others are thinking and doing. The indirect communication may be previously "codified" and may relate to certain kinds of situations (e.g., "In situation S we always have a joint plan of a certain kind and act together appropriately"). Another reason for group-internal publicity is that such central social notions as the speech acts of agreement making, promising, commanding, and informing—all relevant to joint-intention formation—are public in their core sense.

As to we-intentions, a person's acceptance as a group member of the joint intention expression "We will do X together" normally involves that he is prepared to participate and perform his part of X—or at least that he is prepared to take responsibility for X together with the others—and that a we-intention expression such as "I we-intend to do X together with the others" is true of him. The participants' joint intention justifies his participatory intention (the main component of a we-intention; see (WI) below). The above locutions express that the participants all collectively accept doing X together, and hence the intention expression "We will do X together" is true of and for them ("us"). If one in this context uses the locution

"I we-intend to do X", where X refers to a joint action (viz., an action performed jointly), it can be taken to refer just to the fact that the person accepts that he participates in the joint action X (e.g., to have lunch together) and thus also accepts that they will do X together, where acceptance has the world-to-mind direction of fit. Acceptance in this case is conative acceptance that involves the agent's ("my") true intention to contribute to or take responsibility for the group's ("our") performance of X jointly, as a group.

As indicated, some participants' joint intention consists of interdependent member intentions (we-intentions) all of which are also expressible by "We will do X together". I regard the notion of *we-mode joint intention* as a conceptually primitive notion, one that is not at least a priori explicitly analyzable in terms of individuals' mental states without invoking the notion of group in a we-mode sense (see section 5 for irreducibility). Consider a group g consisting of you and me. The core idea is that if we, viz., you and I qua members of g, jointly intend to perform X together, this requires that you and I, qua members of g, both intend to participate in our joint performance of X for us (qua members of g) while being collectively committed to performing X jointly. You and I mutually know (or correctly believe) all this. That the joint performance of X is intentional action for g involves that there is a group reason consisting of the fact that our group has, through our collective acceptance (or, in the non-autonomous case, because of an external leader's directive) formed the intention to perform X.

Note that in simple egalitarian cases where on the member level there is a joint intention toward X as a group on the group level we have the fact that the group intends X. Our group's intention may here give us a group reason for us to participate (in the sense to be analyzed in chapter 4). Because we are functioning as group members for this group reason, we are necessarily "in the same boat" concerning our joint performance of X. The joint intention is necessarily satisfied for you, for me, and for our dyad if and only if it is satisfied for you and for me. We are also collectively committed to satisfying our joint intention (see section 4 below). That we really must be collectively committed can be seen by looking at what a group's successful action amounts to from the members' point of view: we must be collectively committed in a coordinated way for being able to see to it that X really comes about as planned; and this requires that we not only do our parts properly but also that we may help or even pressure others, if needed for X's successful coming about.[32] Thus the three we-mode criteria of group reason, collectivity, and collective commitment are appropriate also for the case of joint intention.

If the participants in joint intention are full-blown we-moders who act as proper group members and if this is mutual knowledge among them, this already entails the kind of unity that amounts to an agreement between the members to act as the group requires. Thus among participants functioning fully in the we-mode, there will be no "deconditionalization problem", viz., the problem of inferring from "I will participate if you will participate" to "I will participate", requiring my premise "you will participate" (and similarly for you)—all this leading to a standstill. That premise is indeed basically provided by the we-mode approach, as each of us knows or at least initially presumes nonconditionally that sufficiently many others will participate, other things being equal. The presumption is in principle testable and may prove to be wrong. You may after all fail to have the participation intention and thus not be a we-moder, or the failure may be due to some kind of situational error. Anyhow, a we-moder will cooperate at least initially in normal circumstances. (For comments on free-riderism and its exclusion, see especially chapter 7, section 3.)

3.2.

I will next say in more precise terms what collectively accepted we-mode joint intentions and we-intentions amount to, and here the we-mode attitudes and actions can also be non-autonomous in the sense of chapter 2. I will assume, as before, that these non-autonomous we-mode intentions also are conceptually group-dependent, for the group has accepted them, however grudgingly. As in effect said, the core idea in my view of joint intention (i.e., a jointly held intention) for egalitarian cases is that for you and I qua members of g to intend jointly to perform X together it is necessary and sufficient that you and I, qua members of g, both intend to participate in our performing X jointly for us and do it qua members of g being collectively committed to performing X jointly; and you and I mutually know (or correctly believe) all this. (This account is partly circular, for intentional joint action must here make reference to joint intentions.)[33]

In view of the above, it can be said that if the members of a group collectively accept the truth (correctness) of "We will do X together as a group", understood as an expression with the world-to-mind fit, and if the central we-mode criteria of group reason, collectivity, and collective commitment are satisfied, then and only then do they jointly intend qua group members to perform X together as a group.[34] Given this view, what will be said of we-intentions below will, in view of the idea that we-intentions are "slices" of joint intentions, also give more information about the notion of joint intention.[35]

It is worth noticing here and in other similar contexts in this book that the participants in joint intention can be group agents. For instance, in the present case the member states of the second-order group European Union can form joint intentions that in the we-mode case are conceptually dependent on its ethos (the constitutive features of the EU).

The locution "We will do X as a group" in the present context applies to the members both collectively and individually, i.e., with regard to both their joint intention and their personal we-intentions. The notion of we-intention will next be analyzed in a way that makes we-intentions strictly dependent on joint intention and group intention, in contrast to the earlier versions of the account that I have presented in my books and articles—or at least in partial contrast to what has been explicitly spelled out in those accounts.[36]

In my account a we-intention is not merely a subjective state of an individual, not something only in the "individual's head". Rather it is a relational state, in a sense a token part or "slice" of the participants' joint intention, as, we recall, joint intention requires the participants' interrelated conative acceptances of "We will do X" (or its equivalent) and as those acceptances, when spelled out, turn out to yield we-intentions. The relational nature of we-intentions may be further elucidated by the following stylized account of we-intentions in the we-mode—although notice that the account does not explicitly assume the we-mode understanding and is therefore open to a pro-group I-mode interpretation. I assume that the participants accept a linguistic expression for their we-intention, but this is not an essential feature. Accordingly I propose the following account for a member A_i of a social group (in the first place, a we-mode group or a non-autonomous we-mode group) g consisting of the members $A_1, \ldots A_i, \ldots, A_m$ who have formed a joint intention to act together as a group:

> (WI) Member A_i of group g *we-intends* to perform X together as a group with the other members if and only if, given that the account (WMI) of we-mode intention is satisfied,

(1) A_i intends to participate in the members' ("our") doing X together and to do his part of X as his part of X;

(2) A_i truly believes that the group members (including himself) collectively accept "We will do X together as a group" in that context and thus that a joint intention to perform X jointly exists between the participants, and this fact is his main justificatory reason for (1);[37]

(3) A_i has a true belief to the effect that the joint action opportunities for an intentional performance of X will obtain (or at least probably will obtain), especially that a right number of the full-fledged and adequately informed members of g, as required for the performance of X, will (or at least will with a nonnegligible probability) perform their parts of X, which under normal conditions will result in an intentional joint performance of X by the participants;

(4) A_i truly believes that there is (or will be) a mutual true belief among the participating members of g (or at least among those participants who

[handwritten margin notes:]
very Brodmannesque.
But A_i has to assume the group. His theory here includes no indiv.-to-grp creation. This is a problem: how else are grps formed?

perform their parts of X intentionally as their parts of X) to the effect that the joint action opportunities for an intentional performance of X will obtain (or at least will obtain with a nonnegligible probability);

(5) (1) and (2) are in part true because of (3) and (4).

(WI) applies not only to the case of autonomous we-mode groups but in principle also to non-autonomous ones, mutatis mutandis (recall especially what was said in chapter 2 concerning the interpretation of collective acceptance in the non-autonomous case). Joint intentions and we-intentions in the case of non-autonomous we-mode groups will not be specifically analyzed below, but my account of a group-agent's intentions in section 4 will be seen to contain the main elements for such analysis through the fact that typically in non-autonomous groups, at least in "we-mode-driven" cases, leaders' joint intentions will be central.

Clause (1) of (WI) formulates the basic intention content of a we-intention: it refers to the agent's *participation intention*. So a we-intention entails the intention to perform one's part of (or contribution to) the joint action in question. While this participation intention is an "I-intention" (e.g., "I intend to perform my part of X as my part of X"), it is *not* an I-mode (purely personally had) intention but rather a we-mode intention trivially derived from a we-intention and dependent on a joint intention.[38] The proximate reason for the participation intention in this egalitarian case is the fact that the agents have the joint intention. That the others will participate is not conceptually a primary reason for an agent's participation but rather a presupposed (but testable) rationality requirement and a secondary reason (but de facto proximate reason) for his participation (cf. clause (3)).

Clause (2) is a presupposition that shows that a joint intention is conceptually and sometimes temporally prior to a we-intention, that is, "We will do X together as a group" as accepted by us, the participants in the situation. Note that as the notion of joint intention appears only in a belief context in (2), this allows that the participants need not know very precisely what a joint intention is. It suffices that they believe that the joint intention involves the participants' connected acceptances of "We will do X jointly", where the connectedness must involve at least mutual belief about the others' similar acceptances. The existence of a joint intention that A_i take part in X gives him a "coordinative" social reason to participate. Clause (2) involves the veridicality (truth of belief) assumption that the joint intention in question must really exist, as we are dealing here with central cases where the agents do really function as group members and—based on the existence of the joint intention—rely on the others' participation for their own participation (it may require empirical checking that the others really are participating in the we-mode sense).

Clause (3) veridically makes an agent's intention to perform his part of X dependent on the correctly believed fact that the others are similarly involved in the joint intention and ensuing joint action. More specifically, (3) states that the right doxastic presuppositions are in place, briefly, that the participants truly believe that the "joint action opportunities" (conditions concerning, e.g., the required number of participants, the presence of some and the absence of some other agent-external conditions, etc.) relating to X are or will be in place.

Clause (4) requires that these true beliefs be socially shared in terms of a mutual belief that they are in place. In general, social belief loops of the kind expressed in the two-person case by "I truly believe that you truly believe that I will do my part" are needed for my being assured in my own part performance. Clauses (3) and (4) are rationality presuppositions whose holding can and should be checked by A_i.

Clause (5) expresses a motivating justificatory reason for reflective participants and thus requires the doxastic conditions to be non-idle.

As to the veridicality feature, to be sure, one may hold mistaken beliefs about the existence of a joint intention (hence about the other agents' we-intentions). One may also mistakenly believe that the intention one has is a we-intention and thus be mistaken about one's intention to this extent (although perhaps not about its phenomenal features). The mistake in beliefs can be or include that no actual "we" exists in the situation, there being no other we-intenders. In the absence of a real "we" I might still mistakenly start doing my part of the joint action that I thought we jointly intended. One can thus radically fail to interpret correctly even one's own social intentions.

Note that the present stylized account ties the jointly intending members together in a rather strong sense. The participants must all we-intend on the basis of the joint intention held by the same participants. If one of them gives up his we-intention, the original joint intention—dependent on those particular members—vanishes and none of the participants retains his we-intention qua we-intention based precisely on that joint intention. Of course, the participants may form a new joint intention by checking first that the joint action opportunities will still obtain for the changed group and will as a consequence have a partly new we-intention in relation to X.

The embedded veridicality requirement is based on the view that we-intentions at bottom are based on a real "we" (i.e., a group) that intends to perform a group action. But as groups can only function through their members functioning in unison, we-intentions must for the sake of coherence be regarded as conceptually dependent on joint intentions, the latter being a member-level counterpart of a group's intention. The ontological veridicality assumption is an addition to this, one partly due to the requirement of the (intragroup) *public* nature of group affairs that I have accepted in this book.

Let me still explicitly verify that we-intentions as discussed above are we-mode intentions. Considering the three criterial features of we-mode mental states, in our simple case with an egalitarian group we can say the following. Clause (2) in conjunction with (3) and (4) gives a group(-based) reason for the members to participate in the joint intention and thus to form their part-performance intention and normally to perform their part action. The members thus perform X *for* the group and are "in the same boat" with respect to X here, the collectivity condition thus being satisfied. As intention entails commitment and, specifically, joint intention entails joint commitment, the three criterial conditions of the we-mode are satisfied in the present case, and we are thus dealing with a we-mode case.[39]

When a group agent intends to perform an action, the group agent is viewed as intending and consequently acting as a unit. It is constructed as possessing a single intention state token and producing a single action token at a time. Corresponding to this we have the requirement in the causal ontological realm for the we-mode case that there be only a single joint intention token and only a single joint action token. To consider this matter, suppose you and I have the joint intention to carry a table together (X). You and I represent this linguistically by endorsing the same statement expressing joint intention:

I: We will perform X jointly.
You: We will perform X jointly.

We have here two token mental states of intending with the same content. It can be stipulated that a single joint token of the joint intention to do X jointly—i.e., a single token of the intention of the group agent formed by the two of us—requires that the contents of our intentions indeed are the same and mutually truly believed to be the same. In addition, some further connecting conditions will also be required, e.g., that our being collectively committed to satisfying the intention content by participating in our joint performance of X. A joint action token realizing X can be taken to be what results when a token of joint intending is successfully carried out. The existence of such a joint action token is a partly fictitious feature although also a group-internal fact, and this fact also often gives some evidence for the inference to our group-relative joint intention token claim, because intentions tend be manifested by the intended action (although not perhaps uniquely). The existence of joint action and intention tokens in a group may still be regarded as an objective fact within the group. No group mind in the sense of idealism is needed. (Note, however, that your and my acceptance of the joint intention to do X together involves different dispositions for the two of us when it comes to satisfying the intention: you intend to do your part of X and I intend to do my part. So we have different participation intention tokens.)

3.3.

There are some relevant reasoning patterns that necessarily apply to proper we-intenders, elucidating the motivational dimension of (WI).[40] The following two practical reasoning schemas that we-intenders ought to infer with may be taken to elucidate the manner in which the participation aspect of we-intentions is motivationally based on joint intention:

(W1):
(1) We will do X jointly.
(2) I am one of "us" (the present group).
Therefore,
(3) I will do my part of our joint performance of X.

(W2):
(1) We will do X jointly.
(2) X cannot be performed by us jointly unless we perform action Z, for instance, teach, help, or pressure a group member to perform his part action.
Therefore,
(3) We will do Z.
(4) Unless I perform Y, we cannot perform Z.
Therefore (because of (3) and (4)),
(5) I will do Y (as my contribution to Z).

Schemas (W1) and (W2) somewhat indirectly express part of what group membership and collective commitment and what their satisfaction conditions involve. The notion of joint intention in my theory is a strong one in the sense that it entails not only the applicability of these practical reasoning schemas, but also that the participants in a joint intention are collectively committed (i.e., have bound themselves, not necessarily in a proper normative sense) to the content, X, of the intention and also to some extent to jointly intending—as long as it is collectively rational to continue intending jointly. (One can of course be concerned with joint intentions and we-intentions in weaker senses as well, as I have done in my previous work.)[41]

3.4.

The notion of *collective commitment* is the glue that binds the members of a we-mode group together in relation to the group's ethos, and hence we must consider the notion of collective commitment in more detail before moving on. The main way to arrive at collective commitment is through the group's intention. As already seen, if a group agent intends to perform an action or, more broadly, to see to it that something is or will be the case, it is even on conceptual grounds committed to realizing what it intends. On the member level this amounts to the members' being collectively committed to seeing to it that what the group is committed to will come about. Here is my (partial) account of collective commitment:

> ($CoCom_{Int}$) Members $A_1, \ldots A_i, \ldots, A_m$ of group g are collectively committed to performing X jointly as a group if they jointly intend to perform X together as a group, that is, "Jointly-intend-qua-members(we, we perform X jointly as a group)" is true of them qua members of g, and this whole sentence, which is about the fact that they so intend, has the mind-to-world direction of fit, while the intention content, viz., "We perform X jointly as a group", has the world-to-mind direction of fit. In addition, because they have the aforementioned intention, the members "group-normatively" ought to participate in the performance of X together as a group (and thus to we-intend so to participate).

Thus, joint intention entails collective commitment to the intention content, which in turn entails an instrumental imperative to perform one's part of X in addition to a group-normative "ought" to perform X for the members, because one is accountable ("group-normatively committed") to the others for performing one's part. Note that the reasoning schemas (W1) and (W2) rely on the group members' group-normative collective commitment to the group's ethos. Especially in the case of (W2), which is referred to in many contexts in this book, this is important to keep in mind.[42]

3.5.

John Searle's theorizing in his 1995 and 2010 books on institutional facts and related matters is an important contribution to recent literature in the field. In the commentary below I will not discuss institutionality but rather his account of we-intentions in the latter book (see chapter 8 for my discussion of "making the social world"). Searle presented an account of we-intention in his paper of 1990. In his 2010 book he gives a revised account of we-intention that I will briefly comment on below.

Searle starts his discussion by offering what he takes to be a general counterexample that works against all of the attempts to reduce "we-intentionality" (which he also seems to call "collective intentionality") to "I-intentionality" ("individual intentionality"). His counterexample concerns an imagined case of Harvard Business School graduates who were taught to believe in Adam Smith's theory of the invisible hand. Each of them tries to benefit humanity by being as selfish as he possibly can and by trying to become as individually rich as he can, in conditions of common knowledge. Searle now emphasizes that there is no cooperation between the agents and hence no collective intentionality, although there is a shared goal and common knowledge that it is shared.[43]

The above case is then contrasted with the imagined case in which the graduates make a pact that they will each go out and try to help humanity by becoming as rich as they can and by acting as selfishly as they can. All this will be done in order to help humanity. Searle says that in this case there is cooperation and collective intentionality—even if it is a higher level of cooperation to the effect that there should be no lower-level cooperation. Nevertheless this second case is a case of collective intentionality, Searle argues, although the cases according to him are the same concerning the agents' external behavior. He says that there is a tremendous difference in the two cases because in the second case there is an obligation assumed by each individual member. In the first case, the individuals have no pact or promise to act in this way. If a person changes her mind, she is free to drop out at any point, but in the second case there is a promise made by each to all of the others.

So here we have two cases that overtly (behaviorally) are the same but different from the point of view of the participants' intention. My first comment is that as mental states are in general dispositions to act, there must be at least a potential (and probably an actual) difference in behavior as well. For instance the assumed obligations will eventually lead to different behaviors in the second case as compared with the first case. My second point is more important and says that Searle's account does not really offer a clear theoretical argument against the reducibility of collective intentionality (we-intentionality) to individual intentionality (both notions understood in his sense).

By irreducibility Searle seems to mean, in the first place, conceptual irreducibility. He does not say very clearly what we-intentionality amounts to or what the individualistic basis precisely consists in. However, here is a central clue to his intuitive view: "There is a ground-floor form of collective intentionality, one that exists prior to the exercise of language and which makes the use of language possible at all".[44] This seems to me a good idea to work on partly because it does not make the explicit use of intentionality-expressing language conceptually and ontologically primary.[45]

In chapter 5 I will give an account of weak collective acceptance in terms of joint intentions in the case of persons *implicitly agreeing* on a joint activity. This account relies on a kind of prelinguistic idea that in some cases can be illustrated by speaking of "mental handshaking" as joint activity and depending on the we-mode we-perspective. (See especially the appendix to chapter 5.) It seems that this line of thought is not as such available to Searle. Why not? The reason seems to be that what he calls "we-intentionality" (and seemingly equivalently "collective intentionality") can be exemplified both by *we-mode we-intentionality* and *pro-group I-mode we-intentionality*, in my terminology. At least to my knowledge he never makes the latter distinction, and thus he ends up lumping together these both conceptually and functionally different notions.[46] Furthermore, for him individual intentionality or I-intentionality amounts to I-mode intentionality. This entails that Searle's and my accounts carve up the social world in different ways. Accordingly, in my account (methodological) individualism can contain a weak kind of collective intentionality and we-intentionality, namely pro-group I-mode collective intentionality (although with reducible groups—recall chapter 1, section 3).

Searle has not given us a precise argument against individualistic reducibility of we-thinking (or even we-thinking of the we-mode kind), although he has sketched the intuitive basis for such an argument. While I basically agree with his intuitions, it should be recalled that my own account of collective intentionality goes in terms of we-mode thinking that is conceptually connected to a group through the irreducible features of group reason, collectivity (viz., satisfaction of the collectivity condition), and collective commitment. This gives a conceptually and ontologically stronger account than his theory does.

Let us still briefly consider Searle's analysis of we-intentions in his 2010 book and try to see if a more precise irreducibility argument can be obtained from it.[47] Consider you and me playing Beethoven's Spring Sonata together, as a duet. Assume that we share the we-intention to play the sonata together (call this joint action X). It can be said that this intention content is our collective goal here. Our means are that I play the piano and you play the violin. Searle's account of this case from my, the piano player's, point of view would entail this: I have the we-intention to achieve collective X. Indeed, in his similar example, we-playing is already taking place and there is a we-intention that is a we-intention-in-action, in his terminology. To quote (here A refers to a single-agent action and B to a collective action): "The content of that intention [viz., the we-intention to perform B, viz., to play the duet, with you playing the violin] is: this intention-in-action causes it to be the case, as A, that the piano plays, which, in that context, constitutes its being the case, as B, that the duet is performed".[48] This is the "constitutive" case; the causal case is parallel (cf. our making mayonnaise by me pouring and you stirring the ingredients).

From Searle's present account of we-intention no precise argument is obtained for the irreducibility of we-thinking to I-thinking, thus for we-intentions to an individualistic conceptual basis. This is because the collective B above is here left otherwise unanalyzed except for saying that it is constituted by the piano and the violin playing.[49]

4. GROUP AGENT'S INTENTION

So far I have discussed two of the three key notions to be dealt with in this section, viz., joint intention, we-intention, and a group's intention. Let us now consider an intention that can be attributed to a group agent. We consider a situation in which a group agent is taken to have the intention (or intended goal) to perform an action or to see to it that a certain state of affairs will come about (or continue to obtain or cease to obtain, etc.). The simple intuition here is the consensus intention: if an egalitarian group intends *as a group*, then its members *qua group members* must collectively intend to act as a group. In chapter 2, section 3, a deductive argument was presented concluding that when a group acts intentionally its members must (ideally) act in the we-mode. We can run essentially the same argument here by substituting "intends to act" for "acts" (with appropriate linguistic changes to make the text grammatical).

However, in the case of structured groups such as business corporations (e.g., Microsoft) or even political states (e.g., Germany), the matter can be viewed somewhat differently. The first and simplest case is *democratic groups* where there is a layered structure created by the group through its members authorizing some individuals (group members) qua position-holders to perform certain tasks and perhaps to be part of a group of individuals forming a hierarchical normative power structure. While here all the members participate in the formation of the power structure by their explicit or tacit acceptance, only some individuals wield the power in it. Let us assume for simplicity that there are only two hierarchical layers, the "upper" one consisting of position-holders authorized to make decisions (e.g., to accept attitudes such as goals, intentions, and norms) for the group. These may be called operative members (or leaders) of decision making. The other members, who take orders from the leaders, form the layer of nonleader (or rank-and-file) members who can still be operatives for action. In this kind of group the leaders, of course, lead, and the rank-and-file members are normatively assumed minimally to go along with the leaders' directives. Note that in democratic groups, viz., groups that can autonomously determine their affairs, all the members can be operative members, e.g., of decision making.

The next kind of group is the broad class of non-autonomous (and non-democratic) groups where a group, g, is externally controlled in some sense (recall the classifications made in chapter 2). An external authority (e.g., a single dictator or a group of persons having power over the group in question) may be able to determine the ethos of g and basic ways of proper acting as a group member. Here the group members might tolerate the use of power over their group (at least if not strongly coerced). The main point for the present discussion is that in this kind of case the external authority through its directives determines g's goals and intentions, possibly other attitudes, and what have you. The members of g are normatively required to go along with the orders and directives of the external authority. (Perhaps this administratively happens through the creation of levels of authoritative positions in g that are controlled by that external authority.)

The basic stylized setup here and in my account is this: there is an external authority that has the power to determine at least the ethos of a group, g, which may be a we-mode group. Within g we have a many-layered, at least two-layered, structure between operatives (leaders) who in g have the power of decision making (e.g., forming goals and intentions for the group) in the autonomous case. In the non-autonomous case they may have the power to decide about the execution of the goals and plans externally given to them and to order the nonoperatives to see to it that they are realized. In both cases the nonoperatives can be ordered to act by the internal leaders.

The following stylized account of group intentions can now be proposed of a structured group g, for example, a we-mode group:[50]

(GI) Group g *intends to see to it that X obtains* (or comes about, etc., where X is an action or state) as a group if and only if there are authorized operative members or individuals for decision making in relation to g such that

(1) either (a) these operative agents are internally authorized and, acting as group members in the we-mode, have formed the joint intention that g through its members will see to it that X, or (b) the operative members for decision making are externally authorized to see to it that X and have ordered some other group members (nonoperatives for decision making but operatives for plan-realizing action) to actually achieve or realize X having formed the shared intention to do it;
(2) in (1) there is a respective mutual belief among the operative members to the effect that (1)(a) or 1(b);
(3) both (a) in the internally and (b) in the externally authorized cases the non-operative members qua members of g group-normatively ought to accept as true that their group g intends to perform X (as specified in clause (1)), and go along with the group's directives);
(4) there is a mutual belief in g to the effect that (3), or at least this belief should be attainable by the members.

Clauses (1) and (3) express the most central ideas here. Clause (2) actually follows from (1) in the case of rational agents, for as has been established, mutual belief is central for carrying out joint intentions and, sometimes, for holding those intentions. Clause (4) expresses a rationality condition that might not always be fulfilled in the whole group but only in some subgroup, but when it is fulfilled it also tends to further motivate at least the conforming members to fulfill the going-along part of (3).[51] Note that in cases of external leaders or other authorities, viz., in the non-autonomous case, acceptance may be of the weak kind that I have called complying or going along with (see chapters 2 and 5). Here the external leaders determine g's intention, and the operative and other members of g go along with it.

It may also be noted that corporations (e.g., business companies) can in real life on contingent grounds (perhaps relating to cultural matters) operate on the basis of different kinds of "psychological modes", so to speak. Indeed, (GI) complies with this apart from some minor tinkering in that it does not specify the psychological mode, such as we-mode or I-mode thinking or some mixture of these, that the members should employ or exhibit. Thus, organized groups may be autonomous or non-autonomous we-mode groups (we-mode driven, so to speak), or they may be I-mode groups (I-mode driven).[52]

I will next illustrate the relations between the various collective-intention notions concentrated on in this chapter, i.e., the group agent's intention, the members' we-mode joint intention, and their we-intentions. This illustration will take place by exhibiting the main elements that may come up in the group members' reasoning, although the schema below need not represent an actual reasoning process. We consider an example of house painting and may assume that an external authority (e.g., the town council) has ordered that group g, the house-owning company, is to see to it that the house is painted and that this authority may have been able to impose the intention on g. In this case the group still has to accept going along with the intention and attempting to satisfy it. Similarly, in the case of an internally authorized leader, he basically determines the group's intention, and the members are assumed to go along and form the relevant joint intention. Alternatively, to consider the egalitarian democratic case, the members of g have noticed that house paint has peeled and that new paint is required, and they hence collectively form the intention for g to paint the house. Whatever the underlying source, g is assumed to have formed the intention to paint the house. The members of group g may make use in their reasoning of the following (potential) reasoning schema applicable to a member of g:

(a) Our group g intends to paint the house. (*Group intention*)

(b) We (i.e. the members or, alternatively, the leaders of g) accept collectively that we will paint the house jointly and hence accept as true for g the intention expression "We will see to it jointly that the house will be painted". (*Joint intention*)

(c) Each of us accepts the intention expression "We will paint the house jointly". (*We-intention*)

(d) I, qua member of g and a participant in our joint intention to paint the house jointly with the others, intend to perform my part (or contributory share) of our painting the house. (*Generic part-performance intention; the central intention-component of a we-intention*)

(e) My part being to paint the front of the house, I intend to do it and set myself to do it. (*Specific part-performance intention followed by intention-in-action that initiates action*)

Here (a) may be a social, coordinative reason for (b) when (a) is conceptually and justificatorily prior to (b)—such as is the case, e.g., in a leader's forming the group's intention on the basis of his assumed authoritative power deriving from either the members' authorization in the case of internal authorization or external authorization in other cases. However, in simple egalitarian cases (with no delegation of group tasks to specially authorized members), (a) and (b) can be regarded as truth-equivalent—the group's intention is formed by the members. Clause (b) may express a social (at least coordinative) reason for (c) in some cases (e.g., in the case of temporally preexisting external joint intention in the case of, e.g., newcomers), (c) entails (d) primarily on conceptual grounds, and (d) entails (e) on conceptual and situation-specific informational grounds. In the sense of this schema, group reason requires acting at least partly for the group. The group reason (a) here is explanatory and thus (a), especially in the case of non-autonomous groups, helps to explain (e) and thus the event of the house getting painted.[53] On the other hand, in egalitarian groups, (a) can usually be given a member-level bottom-up explanation in terms of (b).[54]

We can see from the present account that the nonoperative members can in a central way take part in the group's intention simply by functioning as group members who accept the operatives' joint intention—or at least they are assumed to recognize that they are normatively obligated to such acceptance. (In the non-autonomous we-mode case the external authority may determine the content of the joint intention.) The acceptance can sometimes simply amount to the nonoperatives' endorsing the operatives' (e.g., leaders') joint intention qua members of g, and they may simply be "in reserve" concerning the execution of the intention instead of actively participating in the performance of the required actions. For instance, the salespersons of a department store (an organization) can take part in the organization's intentions and actions just by doing their work and without knowing very much about what the company headquarters is doing. Accordingly, they need not actually, even in we-mode driven cases, have the relevant we-intentions; instead, they only take it to be the case that the operatives have accepted "We will do X" as "conatively" correct for the group. They still can be said to (weakly) participate in the group's intention. Furthermore, it is fully possible or even usual that the analysans of (GI) is satisfied even when some nonoperatives fail to accept "We will do X" for g and the participation intentions that this expression entails for them. Such persons may be dissidents, but other possibilities are available. Thus persons hired to help the group to achieve X might not accept this collective-intention expression.

As noted, collective intentions are spoken of in a variety of ways in the literature. Thus what have been distinguished as joint intentions, we-intentions, and a group's intention have all been regarded as collective intentions without really making the needed conceptual distinctions. As to a group agent's intention, in many cases (e.g., in the case of small informal groups) it may just be a group-level counterpart to the (current) members' relevant joint intention, but in some cases there is more to it; e.g., the group may make decisions purported to bind future members. Furthermore, in the case of large and hierarchically structured groups, group-level descriptions typically involve pragmatic simplicity and are instrumentally useful. The group agency account in this book is important primarily in the case of large organized groups, e.g., corporations and states, for it gives practical understanding and explanation of such groups' activities. This happens in a way that does not seem to be practically possible for theories taking as their starting point individuals and relationships between them and trying to give individualistic, often aggregative accounts of group attitudes and group action.

5. THE IRREDUCIBILITY OF WE-MODE ATTITUDES TO I-MODE ATTITUDES

The irreducibility of group-based states and activities to an individualistic basis depends on what one understands by reduction, since there can be reduction of different kinds. To mention some of the most important alternatives, one can speak of conceptual reduction, explanatory reduction, or ontological reduction. Methodological individualism is sometimes understood to require only the ontological reduction of collective agents to individual agents and their interrelations, but, since ontological issues about what really exists in the world ultimately cannot be decided without scientific theorizing backed by solid empirical support, the whole ontological reducibility issue is moot in the context of philosophical theorizing. Yet one can discuss the general setup for deciding about ontological issues and make educated hypotheses about what can exist in the world while the "scientific jury is still out". Sometimes conceptual reduction may proceed by explicit definition of group-level concepts by means of individualistically acceptable notions. Because of, e.g., the possibility that group-level properties are multiply realized, the general agreement is that explicit definability in general is not possible—it would at best result in an indefinitely long disjunction of individualistic realization possibilities. Let us instead consider the weaker, previously discussed alternative of conceptual *supervenience*.[55] Supervenience says, roughly, that it is necessarily the case that a group property cannot be changed without some change in the group members' individual properties or their interrelations. While supervenience is usually concerned with ontology, some supervenience claims may be true even on conceptual grounds. For instance, group cohesion seems to be a supervenient group property in this sense, if it is defined, as often in the literature, in terms of intermember attraction. Supervenience is compatible with the possibility of multiple realization. Explanatory reduction typically means theoretical reduction in the sense of a reduction of a theory concerning group phenomena to some set of claims formulated in the language of a theory that only contains individualistically acceptable predicates. It is often connected to ontological reduction, e.g., by the epistemic claim that best-explaining theories will find out what really exists.

Ontological reduction seeks to find out the fundamental existents of the world or at least what a true theory needs to postulate as existing. Groups (especially group agents) as social systems (interconnected structures formed out of individuals and their interrelations) seem generally to be ontologically emergent (i.e., involve qualitatively new features as compared with the individualistic basis) and irreducible relative to the individualistic, I-mode properties of our common-sense framework of agency and persons. This was argued earlier in section 2.1. Yet a kind of "holistic" and contingent relation of supervenience might obtain. There is also some empirical evidence for the ontological reality of we-mode states and processes, e.g., as stable explanatory behavioral dispositions manifested in certain experimental collective action dilemmas.[56] If indeed we-mode properties (mental states and dispositions, actions, etc.) are needed to complement I-mode properties for the best explanation of the social world and its ingredients, they can be regarded as prima facie ontologically irreducible.

To proceed to my present arguments for the *irreducibility* of we-mode concepts and states, consider this thesis:

> (IRRED) Propositions containing predicates (concepts) that express we-mode collective attitudes and actions or other related we-mode collective intentionality properties or activities (e.g., cooperation, collective commitment) in general are neither conceptually nor explanatorily or ontologically reducible to propositions containing predicates (concepts) expressing private (i.e., I-mode) intentions and actions and what can be conceptually constructed out of I-mode resources.

To defend a proper ontological irreducibility thesis, one would have to present an account of relevant ontological categories and show irreducibility relative to them. If the kinds of we-mode concepts under discussion are irreducible, then, as far as a priori argumentation goes, some of the generic social states and events to which they correctly apply can also be argued to be ontologically irreducible. Explanatory reducibility is often taken to entail and be required for ontological irreducibility, and my view concurs with this.

There is no direct route from language to what exists in the world—on pain of being committed to an unacceptable version of the Myth of the Given.[57] Accordingly, there might be ontologically idle we-mode concepts, and I need not claim ontological existence in a causal sense for *all* we-mode states and properties. This leaves additional room for group-relative collective acceptance of social facts as such and such. Standard examples of group-relative social facts are facts that involve institutional properties such as statuses like money, debt, private property, marriage, and profession (when used in institutionally appropriate contexts). Such institutional facts are real (epistemically objective) for the group in question, but they are still "mind-dependent" (viz., dependent on collective acceptance).[58] For example, a business corporation qua corporation can act and causally produce effects in the world. This is its a real property. But it can also legally responsible for what it does; and this is a partly fictitious property. (Recall chapter 2 for my discussion of group agents.)

Note, however, that features regarded as fictitious in the case of group agents and the we-mode are of course still created by real people functioning in the real world, so that nothing very mysterious is involved in this context. E.g. the notion of debt in the case of a financial corporation is ultimately constructed by collective human actions and need not be postulated to involve non-naturalistic features. Debt can be construed as a theoretical concept operative in a group-based sense but yet often with normative and other consequences that are naturalistic also for out-groupers (think of what people indebted to a bank have to do and normally are doing in relation to paying off the debt). Thus, for example, economic theories dealing with money, debt, and so on, as well theories in international politics (IR) dealing with states and various higher-order groups, are in the same boat with our naturalistic philosophical account.

Let me still present some other points against reducibility starting by reminding the reader of the argument presented in chapter 1 for the irreducibility of we-mode reasons for action to I-mode reasons for action in some collective action dilemma or coordination dilemma cases (also see chapter 7). It was argued that the set of *we-mode equilibrium-based reasons* for action in a Hi-Lo game differs from and is the set of (pro-group) I-mode equilibrium-based reasons and yields a group reason for action that the I-mode cannot yield. This result can be taken to support thesis (IRRED).

Also *collective commitment* gives a point against reducibility. We recall from Chapter 2 that in the purely private I-mode case a person is committed to herself to satisfying her intention, in the pro-group I-mode case she is committed to herself to participating in the satisfaction of the group's shared (I-mode) intention, and in the we-mode she is committed to the group to participating in the satisfaction of its intention as a group member. These differences in general entail dispositional differences concerning the behaviors to which the participants are committed, and again here the we-mode is seen to differ from the I-mode in a way suggesting that the we-mode is irreducible to the I-mode.

Note, too, that a group member may have an irreducible *group reason* to help other group members in a task, but he need not have a relevant, corresponding private reason—viz. one with the same content. We-mode group reasons accordingly need not supervene on I-mode reasons in this direct sense—in synchronic cases group reasons may change without a corresponding change in I-mode reasons—even in cases where the latter reasons are contingently group-based. (Recall the supervenience discussion in section 2 and also recall that supervenience does not entail explicit definability and the kind of strong reduction that it involves.) [59] As I have argued, people are generally able to engage in both we-mode and I-mode thinking and acting, but the we-mode is not reducible to the I-mode.[60] Furthermore, there is the simple general point that discussed in chapter 1 that the social world cannot be understood and accordingly cannot be fully explained solely in terms of I-mode notions without change of topic, so to speak. On the other hand, the social world can hardly be fully understood without I-mode notions, either. Human agents generally engage in both kinds of thinking or at least are disposed to do so, and our common-sense conceptual framework of agency does not seem to make either one of the perspectives conceptually primary—however, in some cultures but not in all the I-mode seems to be psychologically prior. As said, the group-based approach of this book is conceptually collectivistic, but ontologically it does not postulate full-blown, intrinsically intentional group agents with minds of their own—while recognizing the existence of social groups as basically irreducible systems. The present approach is ontologically individualistic in the sense that we-mode states and properties are attributed to individuals, severally or jointly, when they function as group members. Recall, furthermore, that my approach claims that people are the only ultimate agentive initiators of causal chains in the human social world.

The general conclusion of this section is that we-mode notions in many cases, if not generally, are not individualistically reducible without a conflict with liberal ontological naturalism and realism about the social realm.[61]

6. HISTORICAL REMARKS

6.1.

In this chapter I have discussed collective intentions and distinguished between joint intentions, we-intentions, and a group agent's intentions (intentions attributed to a group). I have also made several central distinctions concerning both the contents of collective intentions and the ways or modes of having intention contents and satisfying them. Various properties of social intentions were discussed. The we-mode/I-mode distinction was clarified in terms of the ways in which we-mode collective intentions differ from I-mode ones. A new account of we-intention improving on what I have in my earlier publications said about it was given in section 3. This account makes we-mode we-intention explicitly dependent on joint intention, a conceptually prior relational many-person intention holding between we-intending agents. Collective commitments were shown to arise primarily in the case of joint intention—and more generally in the case of joint psychological states and activities with the world-to-mind direction of fit. Accordingly, they may also be involved in the case of constitutive group beliefs that serve to ground the unity and identity of the group. At the end of the chapter a section was devoted to arguing that we-mode mental states and actions are irreducible to I-mode mental states and actions or (possibly interdependent) aggregates of them.

6.2.

Below I will make remarks on some early accounts of collective intentionality, namely collective intentions, group minds, and agents, relevant to the theory of this book. I have recently noticed that a rudimentary distinction between what I in this book call pro-group I-mode and we-mode thinking and acting has been discussed by some theoreticians since the times of Jean-Jacques Rousseau. This is interesting especially from the point of view of the present account, as modern literature on collective intentionality with the exception of my recent work does not discuss this distinction and its significance.[62]

I will start by some comments on Rousseau, who presented his account of collective will in the eighteenth century. He distinguished between *private will*, the *will of all*, and *general will*. General will (intention) represents the true interests that everyone has as a member of a civil society. Recall that a group's (group agent's) intention in the we-mode sense represents the members' joint intentions qua group members, although not perhaps as private persons. Rousseau's distinction between a private will and the general will clearly is a special version of the I-mode/we-mode distinction in the case of a state or nation: private will corresponds to I-mode goal or intention, and general will primarily corresponds to a group agent's (here: state's) intention, and hence to the members' we-mode intention qua group members (cf. the comments below on "corporate will").[63] Note that private will and general will are both notions that apply to single persons in Rousseau's account, as they do in the theory of this book.

In *The Social Contract*, Rousseau writes that every individual can personally have his particular or private will that contradicts or differs from "the general will which he has as a citizen".[64] (In this book we only consider what an individual's will as a member of *any* group is.) Rousseau continues: "There is often a great deal of difference between the will of all and the general will; the latter concerns only the common interest, while the former takes private interest into account, and is no more than a sum of particular wills".[65]

Accordingly, first, the general will is something the individual has as a citizen of a state, and, second, it concerns common interest. In the present we-mode approach we rely on the notions of we-mode collective intention, involving a group agent's intention, (the members') joint intention, and (a member's) we-intention. We assume that the we-mode collective intention qua group-centered reflects the common interest of the members through their collective acceptance. In addition to reflecting common interest, the we-mode joint intention and we-intention also represent the notion of group on the individual level. When a group member has an intention qua group member, he is supposed to satisfy it *as* a group member and *for* the group.

Besides private will, the will of all, and general will, Rousseau occasionally takes up the notion of *corporate will*. This is the notion that is closely connected to the notion of collective intention qua a group agent's intention in the case where the group agent is not a state (as it must be assumed to be in the general will case). It, so to speak, mediates between particular wills and the general will. It represents the agents' common objectives as members of a group ("corporation", "magistrate", etc.). According to Rousseau, the *general interest* of the group is the object of corporate will, and here the group is not a state. A person's private will can be in conflict with his corporate will, roughly his "we-intention" (e.g., when his desires are in conflict with his role). A conflict may also occur between the corporate will and the general will. In this latter case, according to Rousseau, the requirements of the general will should overweigh those of the corporate will.

I will finally comment very briefly on William McDougall's, Alfred Vierkandt's, and Ferdinand Tönnies's views. McDougall in his 1920 book considers the volitions that a group of pilgrims on their way to a city may have.[66] He discusses five cases with increasing strength of collective intentionality, five modes of conation, and five modes of collective action, as he says.[67] Among them are two (what I have called) pro-group I-mode cases (where the pilgrims function individualistically and act only partly for the group) and a we-mode case, a case where the participants truly identify themselves with the group and intend as a group. Alfred Vierkandt discusses McDougall's classification of collective will (recall the above discussion) and in that regard makes a distinction between a will that is joint ("*gemeinsam*") and one that is "societal" or "communal" ("*gemeinschaftlich*") mainly on McDougall's lines. Vierkandt's societal intention is a rudimentary version of a we-mode group intention in my sense, and his shared intention amounts to pro-group I-mode intention in my sense. [68] Alfred Tönnies in his later work also comes close to making the same distinction.[69] Both Tönnies and Vierkandt employ the notion of a group agent.[70]

APPENDIX: JOINT EQUILIBRIUM OF EXPECTATIONS

The factual dependency aspect associated with joint intention and joint action can in some cases be technically explicated in terms of the notion of a joint equilibrium of expectations, viz., goal-belief combinations that are in equilibrium on group-based grounds. Particularly, we have this: I will participate (or cooperate) given that (I believe that) you, my fellow group member, will probably also act jointly with me; and vice versa. This can express our group-based joint equilibrium. In general: Because of our collective commitment, the conditional probability that you will cooperate in the joint action given that I will cooperate is taken to be higher than your nonconditional probability of cooperating, and vice versa.

Let me define the notion of joint equilibrium for an interactive choice situation, for example, a case of a two-person two-choice Prisoner's Dilemma.[71] We say that the mutually known joint probability p (viz., the system p of shared beliefs) is in joint equilibrium if and only if there exist i and j (in the two-choice case $i,j = 1,2$), maximizing the players' expected utilities relative to the distribution p, i.e., such that

$EU_A(a_i)\ EU_A(a_k)$, for all k differing from i (here $k = 1,2$) and
$EU_B(b_j)\ EU_B(b_k)$, for all k differing from j (here $k = 1,2$).

Here $EU_A(a_i)$, the expected utility of action a_i for A, is defined as follows (assuming that the probabilities $p(a_i)$ and $p(b_j)$ are positive: $EU_A(a_i) = \Sigma_j p_A(b_j/a_i)u_{A,i}$ (and analogously for B).

We can accordingly define that in the cases of such a belief system in joint equilibrium, the strategy or action pair (a_i,b_j) is a joint strategy (or action) combination in joint equilibrium if and only if the corresponding system of beliefs p is in joint equilibrium in the just-defined sense.

4

Acting for Social Reasons

1. MOTIVATING SOCIAL REASONS FOR COLLECTIVE ACTION

1.1.

Human agents are reasoning organisms trying to cope with their physical and social environment by means of their reasoned actions and other behaviors. Cultural and probably also genetic adaptation to group life have been especially important in the evolution of humans. The broader motivational basis of collective activities is typically provided by the basic biological and cultural needs and desires that agents separately or jointly have. While group life is based on such needs and desires, and on the dispositions that they maintain, group life sometimes creates new need-based reasons, as well as "desire-independent" reasons for the members.[1] Thus, for instance, promises and moral and social norms can give desire-independent reasons for action, and so can the implicit or explicit agreement-making that is typically involved in the formation of collectively binding group attitudes. There are of course also desires and interests that are not tightly connected to coping with the demands of the external physical and social environment. Agents may be curious and try to acquire knowledge not only about their immediate environment but also to find out things that seem to have no practical significance. Such activities may be institutionally codified, and thus we may have society-wide enterprises committed to the pursuit of knowledge (as in science) or perhaps to artistic achievement. Here we have reason-based action (on both an individual and a social scale) that, however, is not strictly speaking a response to the demands of the environment.

The notion of reason is regarded by many theoreticians as a central notion for accounting for the attitudes and activities of agents, and many regard the notion as a conceptual primitive. So a central task for a theoretician is to elucidate the concept and its central functions, such as motivation and justification.[2] Motivation is typically connected to matters in the causal realm and the explanation of action, whereas justification is connected to the rationalization of action, which may be regarded as something dependent on implicit or explicit human acceptance in a broad sense.[3] The central difference between the two roles is that justification need not be as tightly connected to an agent's intentional behavior as motivating—which can be practically effective in bringing about and explaining intentional action. Thus one may say that intentional action normally is acting for a reason, and specifying the reason in question in general serves to explain the action.

Reasons can in general terms be said to "favor" the actions that they are related to. Here favoring can have both a justifying and motivating role. In addition to substantive reasons that are related to action, there are also logical requirements of rationality that have been called reasons or "normative requirements" by some philosophers.[4] The central focus of our discussion below is to explicate motivating social reasons and group-based reasons for individual and collective action. The topic of group-based reasons has not been properly investigated in the literature on reasons for action, where most emphasis has been laid on reasons for individual action. As to the general question of what a social reason is, reasons are fact-like and can, first, have social content (e.g., an agent's social reason for action can be that it furthers "our" group's goal). This gives a content-based aspect of a social reason. Second, a jointly held reason expresses another feature of sociality. Third, the social mode (e.g., I-mode or we-mode) in which reasons are held or "treated" in people's thinking and acting gives still another relevant aspect of social reasons. The above can be generalized by analogy to attitudes and other mental states as well as actions. Social reasons can have all or some of the above social attributes—that is, content, jointly or separately held, and held in the I-mode or in the we-mode or in another mode. I will below speak of private (or purely personal I-mode) social and nonsocial reasons, of social pro-group I-mode reasons, and of we-mode reasons, which are necessarily social.

A group agent's reasons are social, too, in the sense that they are directly or indirectly connected to group members' reasons qua group members. Accordingly, when dealing with social reasons that are group-based or group-related, we distinguish between a *group agent's reasons*, which are reasons that a group agent has for performing its actions, and the *group reasons* (conceptually group-based reasons) of its members for participating in the group's activities. There are motivating we-mode reasons that are conferred on the relevant individuals in virtue of the group's authority over its members, as well as the *private social* and other reasons of individuals, which are I-mode reasons that the members have independently of their membership in we-mode social groups. As I have said, there are also pro-group I-mode reasons that are I-mode reasons meant to promote a group's interests but processed in terms of individualistic (rather than collective or group) reasoning.

I.2.

Generally speaking, a reason is a fact-like entity, but it cannot be an agent's reason for action unless taken by the agent to be a reason for him to act. Such a recognized reason can, but need not as such, motivate. For it to motivate, the agent must be disposed to act because of it.

To proceed to a more detailed discussion, we first focus on motivating reasons of an ordinary human agent, which can be understood at first blush as states in her external or internal environment that have motivational potential. Such reasons—when they are facts in her external environment—must obviously be processed by her mental states to be truly motivating. These states (desires, beliefs, etc.) refer to and represent the external or "internal" (primarily mental) states expressible by that-clauses. They too must be similarly represented, human agents being reflective agents who may become aware of their mental states and the mental states of others. Although intentional states are always involved at least in this registering sense when the agent acts for a reason, typically mental states (qua states) do not have a more substantive reason-providing role—rather it is the contents of those states that rationalize behavior. Thus my desire to drink a can of paint may motivate me to go to the hardware store (here the representational content of the desire is at play), but, alternatively, it may motivate me to seek help from a psychiatrist—when I respond to my very mental state (or a higher-order representation of that state) rather than to its representational content.

However, sometimes reason attributions are merely about hypothetical rather than actual facts, since an agent may also have representational states whose contents are false. That I want to stay dry can be my reason for carrying an umbrella, if I believe that rain is forthcoming. Even if the content of my belief is false, it still motivates my action from a subjective point of view—in this case without objective backing.[5] Considering the rain example, we can say that the fact that it is raining is an objectively *justifying* reason for carrying one's umbrella. It also (when recognized by me) gives a *motivating* reason, in conjunction with my belief that carrying an umbrella will help me to stay dry (which I want). The salient motivational reason here consists of a justifying and motivating element in contrast to the false belief case. In that case we may speak of a purely *subjective motivating reason* (one without objective ground and objective justification).

Motivating reasons can be effective in bringing about action, and thus favor action—whether they are based on objective facts or not.[6] The favoring relation in question may be viewed from a descriptive (and "external") or from a normative point of view. The former is concerned, so to speak, only with how things *are* in the world, whereas the latter is also concerned with how things *should* be in the world. Below I will focus on the normative way of thinking about favoring, partly because it connects better to the fact that group reasons (for group members) are based on normative directing by the group. The other reason is the pragmatic one that we commonly speak in normative terms even about naturalistic cases (e.g., that one ought to carry an umbrella if it rains cashes out roughly as "If one doesn't do it, one will get wet"). To take up another example, that there is reason for me to keep the yogurt in the fridge relies on the fact that unless yogurt is kept in a cool place, it will spoil. One ought to keep the yogurt in a cool place, insofar as one does not want the yogurt to be spoiled. This merely "technical" instrumental connection is only weakly normative, and it is clearly distinct from the sense in which strongly normative reasons (e.g., moral or legal ones) direct action.

As to strongly normative reasons, they involve a properly normative ideal, typically something one *ought* to bring about or preserve, which does not strictly depend on whether the agent takes that ideal as her motivating reason. Strongly normative reasons include moral, legal, and prudential requirements, and they can be regarded either as categorical (viz., valid in all circumstances) or as pro tanto (viz., defeasible in the presence of stronger other, countervailing reasons). For example, under normal conditions, promising, qua putting oneself under an obligation, gives a strongly normative reason to keep the promise, but there may be circumstances where not keeping a promise is normatively justified (e.g., if keeping it would cause greater harm). In contrast, some moral requirements (such as the prohibition to cause unnecessary pain to another human being) may be regarded as categorical.[7]

Facts as such (including facts about people's mental states) are nonnormative entities, but we predicate reasons to them. The sentence "State of affairs s is a reason for action A" then concerns a reason for action in a predicative sense of the term "is (viz., "is a reason" is a predicate), not in its identity sense. That something is a substantive reason in this sense can be regarded partly as a human artifact, something depending on (explicit or implicit) human acceptance: *we* accept or *I* accept (perhaps only unreflectively through overt action of the right kind) that a certain fact qualifies as a (motivating) reason for that action.[8] This view applies to moral reasons (one ought to help people in need), to institutional reasons (a driver facing a red traffic signal must stop), and even to objective natural reasons (seeking shelter in stormy weather). Taking a fact as a reason in such cases involves the agent's functional acceptance of the reason as her reason (such that when had or accepted for action, it will de facto motivate the agent), but it does not require that the agent has more than a vague notion of reason, nor does it require that she reflect on the fact as her reason.

1.3.

Human agents are disposed to respond not only to physical and mental states of affairs but—as seen—also to *social* reasons that are conferred on them by other human agents. Such social reasons often stem from the conformative or nonconformative attitudes and dispositions that human agents have, and they are rooted more generally in the need and desire to respond to the intentional states and actions of others. Human agents are at bottom social agents disposed to cooperate and to share intentional states with their kin.[9] This sociality, which is probably partly genetically and partly environmentally based, is a many-faceted thing.[10] Thus, people on the whole need, and also enjoy, the company of other human beings, and this motivates them to take into account what others think and do, especially their hopes and expectations as well rights and duties qua individual agents and qua group members. Others' private or collective approval and disapproval of one's ways of thinking and acting are especially important motivational elements, which induce strong elements of conformity and cooperativeness into human life that serve to tame natural egocentric desires and aggression. (In addition, anticonformative social reasons based on such things as envy and hate are important reasons that may sometimes induce egoistic action.)

The central question to be accounted for in this context concerns the institutional and cooperative basis that human civilization is founded on. Even most forms of conflict may seem to presuppose this (think of such things as legitimate warfare, competitive sports, or competition for economic resources in general). The nature of our subject matter justifies concentration on the somewhat brighter aspects of human sociality, although even conformist and cooperative behavior may sometimes lead to undesirable consequences (recall chapter 1 for comments on the moral and political aspects of human sociality). Examples of such effects are given by gang violence, the bystander-effect, and strong economic fluctuations based on conformative buying and selling behavior.[11]

Reasons for action can be had in the I-mode or in the we-mode. Briefly, an I-mode reason is a person's private reason for action, and in this section these reasons will be taken to have social content so as to better bring out their contrast with we-mode reasons. The central case of social reasons for action is where the others' thinking and acting in a group is a person's reason for conforming. We may introduce the technical notion of shared "we-attitude" (see below) to cover such reasons. In the I-mode the "we" in question is assumed to be only a weak "we" applicable to an arbitrary set of persons, without the assumption that these persons are disposed to function together. This contrasts with the full-blown, "togetherness-we" that the we-mode involves (recall chapter 2). Accordingly, both I-mode and we-mode reasons may be other-regarding reasons, but the central difference between the two is that we-mode reasons are conceptually based on the group's acceptance. Roughly, a person acts for a we-mode reason if he takes as a central reason for that action what his salient group wants, intends, believes, etc.—in general something that requires his participation as a group member.[12] Here the reason is based on collective acceptance rather than being simply intersubjective in an other-regarding I-mode sense. We-mode reasons are conceptually based on the group's reasons, viz., substantive reasons that the group has for its actions and for directing the contributory actions of its members in an appropriate goal-directed manner. Example: Germany's ("official") reason for deciding to close the nuclear power plants was, let us suppose, the fact that they pose a bigger danger for the people and the environment than previously believed. Citizens are supposed to go along with this (and, e.g., prefer using green energy and refrain from complaining about their higher energy bills) because it is the state's decision and perhaps because they themselves sincerely prefer the new energy policy to what they had before.

We speak of we-attitudes in two different ground-level senses.[13] There are plain we-attitudes and there are reason-based ones. Considering an attitude ATT, an agent has a simple or *plain we-attitude* (e.g., we-want) toward a content s, expressing, e.g., action, precisely when he has the attitude ATT(s), believes that the others have the attitude ATT(s), and, furthermore, believes that it is mutually believed in the group that the other group members have the attitude ATT(s).[14] A reason-based we-attitude in contrast is characterized as follows in a somewhat idealized sense: An agent has a *reason-based we-attitude* toward s precisely when he has the attitude ATT(s) and has it in part because, i.e., for the reason that the others have the attitude ATT(s) and that it is mutually believed in the group that the group members have (or, in some cases, ought to have) the attitude ATT(s). The activity that we here have given a reason for performing is the agent's forming his we-attitude, which in turn grounds ensuing action(s) based on that attitude. My interpretation of "because" (and "on the basis of" or "on the ground of") as reason-involving in the case of a reason-based we-attitude seems warranted because the agent is assumed to be intentionally responding to the reason fact. Thus more than plain causation is involved.

Note that the reason for the attitude ATT(s) above is only stipulatively and contingently connected to the attitude. Thus, the reason is not conceptually connected to the attitude and to the ensuing action, and hence the reason can at least in the I-mode case serve as an explanans for what it is a reason for.

A *shared we-attitude* can be a social reason for which the participants perform their parts of a collective social action. I have argued elsewhere that a central class of intentional collective social actions and social practices, including institutional ones, is formed out of actions performed because of a shared we-attitude (such as a socially shared goal or belief).[15] We-attitudes may be either in the I-mode or in the we-mode.[16] They may be further classified in terms of their direction of fit. The content of our shared we-mode intention (the content of our joint intention) is "that we will see to it that X". It is not the same as the content of our shared we-belief in which, in contrast to the conative "will" in the intention case, "will" is predictively used. The latter attitude, like any belief, has the mind-to-world fit, while the former has the world-to-mind fit. Collective acceptance may yield both kinds of attitudes. In the case of our acting for an order or directive in the "going along with" sense, a somewhat different formulation can be used: The fact, as accepted by us, that we have been ordered to perform X is our central reason for performing X.[17]

We can classify different cases of social action based on we-attitudes in terms of four explanatory categories:[18] (1) In the first or *commonality* category, the shared explanatory social reason involves a shared undivided goal (namely, a goal that has not been divided into parts for the agents to achieve). More precisely, the shared social reason is the content of an undivided shared we-goal (in an aggregative I-mode sense). Case (1) typically includes instances like people going for lunch to the same fashionable place for a social reason, a shared we-attitude or its content. (2) In the *I-mode mutual behavioral dependence* category, the explanatory social reason is based either on a mutual dependence belief, namely, a we-belief about dependence, or on such a we-belief plus a shared divided we-goal in the I-mode. Case (2) includes instances involving strategic action. Here the belief about mutual dependency is central because rational action requires responding optimally to the others' actions. For example, people walking in a narrow corridor make an effort to avoid bumping into each other (a socially and morally "unpleasant" consequence). (3) In the *jointness* category, the social reason may be a (pro-group) I-mode attitude, for example, an intended collective goal to act together, with entailed action dependence. In general, this category includes those cases in which the participants *act jointly*. Case (3) thus includes I-mode instances of joint action based on the participants' shared personal intentions and beliefs (and in some cases group interests and goals). For instance, some people may jointly tidy up a road after a storm. (4) In we-mode-driven *group action* and we-mode joint action, forming our fourth, group action category, especially action performed by a group qua group, shared we-attitudes come into play. In this category we also have cases where a group (e.g., a business corporation or a state) performs an action via its members (or via a suitable subset of them, the "operatives" performing a relevant joint action in virtue of which an action can be attributed to the group).[19] The group agent has some reason for its action, and the members act for the reasons that the group provides them with (see the next two sections). When a group acts in the we-mode-driven sense, the members (or in some cases their representatives) act jointly as a group.

In (1)–(4) we are in effect dealing with *action explanation in terms of a social reason*, an I-mode one in (1), (2), and (3) and typically a we-mode reason in case (4). In a sense these classes are increasingly stronger as more conditions have to be satisfied in each higher case.

It must be acknowledged that agents often act for a multiplicity of reasons, and the contents of those reasons may be complex.[20] My account can be extended to cover such cases, but I will not here work out the details. I have above concentrated on conformative we-attitudes, but there are also nonconformative (as well as "neutral") we-attitudes.[21]

The upshot concerning the classification of all motivating, explanatory social reasons is this:

(1) Motivating *I-mode reasons*: private, purely personal, and not conceptually group-based motivating reasons with social content (e.g., conformative "we-attitude-based" but not group-based reasons)
(2) Motivating *we-mode reasons* (viz., conceptually group-based *and* "we-attitude-based" reasons requiring action as a proper group member)
(3) Motivating *group-based reasons* that are either we-mode or I-mode reasons or mixtures of these (in some cases reasons based on state laws, etc.)

Instances of case (3) fall into (1) or (2), depending on whether they are in the I-mode or in the we-mode.

Moral reasons that have social content generally belong to one of the above classes. Group agent's reasons are we-mode reasons, given that group agents are taken to consist of members acting in the we-mode according to the group's directives.

2. GROUP AGENT'S MOTIVATING REASON FOR ACTION

2.1.

The general conceptual and justificatory (but often not the contingent empirical) direction in the we-mode is top-down rather than bottom-up, as has been noted in the early chapters of this book—whereas the direction of ontological dependence is bottom-up, from the individual-agent level to the group level. As the focus of the present chapter is on group reasons, it is appropriate to proceed from the group level to the member level when we are talking of we-mode reasons for action.

Authority-based member-level group reasons for participation are in general we-mode reasons in the sense of being based on a conceptual construction and acceptance of the group as "our" group (hence a thick "togetherness-we").

The idea of a group agent's reason is based on the analogy view of collective agents that was presented in chapter 2, according to which a group agent's actions are purposive and based on reasons in the same way that an individual agent's actions are. Thus essentially the same account can be given of a group agent's reasons as of the reasons of individual agents for singular, nonjoint action. Note, however, that whereas an individual agent has to coordinate only her private bodily and mental behaviors in order to respond to her reasons, the members of a we-mode group need to collectively coordinate their we-mode mental states and collective behaviors in order for the group agent to respond to its reasons. This idea of normative directing by the group may be introduced here in terms of a simple example. Suppose you and I are members (thus position-holders), in a we-mode group, which is planning to throw a party.[22] Our group wants to get a heavy table upstairs for the party and believes that it can do so when some of the members carry it jointly. Suppose its leader issues a directive, or our joint agreement entails one, with the content that that you and I qua members are to carry the table together upstairs. Our (the rank-and-file members') proximate motivating *group reason* for participation here is (the fact that there is) the group's directive (in effect some members' directive to others in the egalitarian case), and the motivating *group agent's reason* is that the party will be held upstairs.

As to the formation of a group agent's attitude, the group members accept it for the group roughly by answering the question, "What should *our group* want, intend, believe, and so on, concerning a state or event X?" rather than "What should *I* want, intend, believe, do, and so on, concerning X?" Answering the former, "we-mode" question aims at forming the attitude in question, and we can speak here of a member's "we-mode proposal" for the group's (voluntary) attitude. Such a proposal will become a group's attitude in general if collectively accepted by the members.[23] If there is collective agreement, we arrive at a group agent's attitude, an attitude attributable to the group agent, which can function as the group members' reason for performing their parts or shares of X. This attitude is formed by the members but need not be reducible to the members' we-mode views. The collective attitude that the members arrive at (when successful) is a product of their interaction and might not be a simple aggregate of the members' proposals for the group (nor an aggregate of their I-mode attitudes).[24] Consequently, although a group agent can function only through the functioning of its members (qua position-holders), its reasons are not reducible (even) to we-mode attitudes and proposals by the members because of the aforementioned interaction effect. (Cf. the discussions in chapters 3 and 5.)

Suppose that the group leader has issued an order or that the members have collectively formed an attitude for the group. This gives the members a reason for performing their parts of the group agent's action. For a member to have such a we-mode participation reason, she need not know what the group agent's reasons for its action are. Yet, for the group action to be functionally effective, she often has to know what the group aims at, thus, e.g., what it has as its goal, what it intends, or what the group's leaders, qua responsive to the group's ethos and its particular ethos-related reasons, have ordered or directed the members to do. A reflective group member's total we-mode reason also can be expected to take into account the group agent's relevant reasons in addition to her particular group-grounded participation reasons.

The upshot of the above remarks is that the group agent's reasons yield and warrant *member-level group reasons* for participatory action (recall the earlier example of Germany's giving up nuclear power).[25] The latter are collectively accepted we-mode reasons conceptually based on the group agent's reasons for action, and they are their reasons qua group members to participate in the group action in question.

While on the member level we deal with the group members' we-mode attitudes (conceptually group-dependent attitudes), in the case of the formation of a group attitude (the proximate motivating group reason) we have the members' we-mode proposals, viz., proposals concerning what the group should do or what the group agent's attitude should be. A group agent's attitude or action is in general formed or generated by the members' attitudes and actions compatibly with the group's ethos and its previously accepted reasons and principles for attitude formation and action.

2.2.

I will next give a detailed account of a group agent's motivating reasons in a context where it is intentionally responding to the "demands" of its environment (physical or social, including institutional, environment). Hence the focus will be on instrumental rather than strongly normative reasons, but the present account may also be applied to elucidate the motivating force of strongly normative reasons in circumstances where the agent responds to relevant "oughts" by its actions (which amount to appropriate collective actions by its members).

Suppose that the group's (e.g., club's) house is in need of repainting, and this is believed by the group (thus in general mutually believed by its members). The fact that the house needs to be painted (call this fact R), as believed by the group, can then be its (main) motivating reason for seeing to it that the house gets painted, provided of course that it takes that fact as its motivating reason by forming an intention to act on it. (Note that in the case of a paradigmatic, self-guiding we-mode group, R is also the members' reason to form the group's intention and to participate.)

The group's intention then involves as its content the goal that the house will be repainted, and directs it to form relevant subplans and to guide its members' conduct in the appropriate manner. Thus, insofar as the group does not yet have paint and other requisite materials, it may form a subsidiary intention to acquire them and proceed to paint the house on the basis of its intention. The end result of these actions taken together (if successful) is that the house gets painted as required. This outcome is mainly explained by the group agent's taking R as its reason and forming the intention to act on it. Briefly, we may say that the group thus acted on its "motivational set", viz., its salient as-if mental attitudes and possibly other motivating as-if mental states, in the situation in question. The attitudes must be about R or at least relevantly connected to R (e.g., to some fact contextually entailing or implicating R).

In view of what was said in section 1 of the case of single individuals' motivating reason, we may now give our account of a group agent's reasons in view of the assumption that a functional group agent can also "reason-wise" be viewed in analogy with an individual agent. So let me propose this simple account for an internally or externally authorized, thus either autonomous or non-autonomous, group agent (g):[26]

(GAR) State R was the *motivating reason for which group agent g performed action X intentionally* in situation S only if in S

(1) g had some want(s), belief(s), and (prior) intention(s), jointly conducive to its performing action X, and these propositional attitudes were either directly or indirectly connected to R (*Existence of motivational set*);
(2) g performed X intentionally on the motivational set (*Acting on motivational set*).

In (GAR), the motivational set requirement (1) is a rather obvious and common requirement for a motivating reason, except that it speaks about a group agent's attitudes—ultimately to be cashed out in terms of its members' joint attitudes.[27] Clause (2) assumed that the group agent acts on its motivational set, and thus in general for R (although a sufficient condition is not given for this in (GAR)), and such intentional acting in general requires the group's intention to perform X (or at least a "closely related" intention that guarantees the right kind of intentional action). This involves the group agent's appropriately guiding and monitoring its action relative to R.

A group agent's action on its motivational set requires that its members act as one agent, thus act together, for R or, for example, in a hierarchical group, for a reason, say R*, derivable from R. The "derivation" might amount to a leader's issuing an action directive to the members to do something that reason R requires. Their part actions may be different, but they must still serve the agents' joint intention meant to have been formed for obeying R in terms of the members' actions.

The upshot of our above discussion is that the reasons for which a group agent acts were clarified in analogy with the motivating reasons of an individual agent. In the present context, reason R can be taken to explain at least in part why, viz., for what reason, group agent g performed X—although relevant nonintentional factors may also need to be taken into account in a full explanation. So we have here an explanation why the group agent acted that also in part explains the members' actions, as seen from the present account, especially its first clause. I have argued elsewhere that, on conceptual grounds, if a group intentionally performs an action, it must intend to perform it (or a closely related action). Hence at least its operative members (including the special, degenerate case with only one operative), must share the joint intention to perform that or a closely related action.

2.3.

To end this section, I will illustrate motivating reasons in a choice-theoretic situation in terms of a coordination case that exemplifies the typical case of group action in which the members have to coordinate their actions for the group to act successfully to satisfy its ethos. Consider thus the following simple Hi-Lo game:

	Hi	Lo
Hi	3,3	0,0
Lo	0,0	1,1

In Hi-Lo, HiHi and LoLo are strategy equilibria yielding the individual utilities 3,3 (summing up to 6, which here might represent the group's utility) and 1,1 (giving 2 for the group), respectively. The group has to choose between the four outcomes HiHi, HiLo, LoHi, LoLo (see chapter 7 for more on the game-theoretic situation in question). Generally, realizing HiHi will trivially be better for the group than realizing LoLo, and accordingly the joint outcome HiHi is better for the members on the average. Now, considering a we-mode group g, it is motivated to choose HiHi, for example, on the basis of its being the result of the group's acceptance of a relevant goal in this situation (e.g., one simply to maximize its gain) that requires HiHi to come about.

The fact of its goal acceptance can qualify as g's motivating reason to choose the joint outcome HiHi. This outcome is an outcome of actions that form a Nash equilibrium. In coordination situations the we-mode account of group attitudes (intentions, beliefs, reasons, and the like) typically makes satisfying or realizing the group's collectively accepted attitudes equilibria for the group members acting qua full group members. The basic way to arrive at this result is through the satisfaction of the collectivity condition. The goal of gain maximization satisfies this condition with respect to reasons for acting because of this goal, and we get this: Necessarily, because of the members' collective acceptance of goal G (e.g., to fully satisfy the group's ethos or to maximize its gain) for their group and making it their unique goal in the situation, a member in the present case—where the action is required for G—has a conclusive reason to contribute to the fulfillment of G qua group member if and only if the other members have the analogous conclusive reason for action required by G. This result entails that in the coordination case contributing to the collectively selected group's goal G (together with the actions required by it) is a Nash equilibrium and that a member qua member thus has a sufficient reason to contribute (and not to deviate) at least as long as the others contribute. Similarly, coordination-involving group actions often are group equilibria in analogy with the present simple example. [28]

As we will see in chapter 7, the we-mode in some cases leads to a smaller set of equilibria in a choice situation than what pro-group I-mode correspondingly entails.[29] Thus if the group's choice alternative or goal X is an equilibrium for an I-mode group, it need not yet be an equilibrium for a relevant we-mode group. Indeed, that we-mode group might even consist of the same members as the I-mode group. So here we have a kind of intensional group property: X is an equilibrium and thus a local "stability maximizer" for an I-mode group, but it is not an equilibrium for an intensionally different we-mode group. This is so although the only difference between these two groups is that the members are operating in different modes, in the we-mode versus in the (pro-group) I-mode.[30] (Similar observations can be made in the case of group beliefs [acceptance beliefs], but I will not here discuss the details.)[31]

As to the pro-group I-mode case, a member here must generally share a group-related goal with the others but will also be at least to an extent self-centered (at least have an underlying disposition for such self-centeredness that might be manifest only in some circumstances critical for the individual's well-being). He will function as a group member because he gains enough from that to be motivated (while still possibly being prone to free-ride on what the group produces). Another problem of motivation concerns the group members and their purely private (thus group-independent) preferences. In a two-person Prisoner's Dilemma the members' private preferences (and payoffs) in general are best served by their choice of D rather than C (as long as the others, qua individually rational, are expected to choose D, DD being an equilibrium). But, on the other hand, they can in their minds and actions change the game into a more cooperation-friendly one and choose C if they adopt cooperation concerning the CC outcome as their central, ethos-like goal. [32]

3. GROUP MEMBERS' MOTIVATING REASONS FOR PARTICIPATION

3.1.

While (GAR) in the previous section gives my main account of group agents' reasons, it is appropriate to complement it by saying how the members are to function in that case.[33] To proceed to that account, I will first clarify and emphasize some relevant matters. An internally controlled we-mode group (a functional group agent) can form a goal on the basis of agreements between its members, or the members may have delegated the task of goal formation to some authorized operative members. The fact that a group has formed a certain goal can accordingly be a group reason for the group members to perform their goal-promoting actions qua group members.

The goals that a group forms are goals of a group agent. There may be an external state of affairs, e.g., that the house is in need of new paint, which is relevant to the promotion of the group agent's ethos involving the standing goal that the group's clubhouse is to look beautiful. The group may now take as its current goal painting the house and directing some of its members to do it. Those members, qua well-behaving group members, do it. In this case the members' proximate group reason is the group's authoritative members' (position-holders') directive to them to paint the house, while their distant reason may be that the house looks shabby and is in need of new paint. To take another example, a state can impose economic sanctions on another country because the latter has violated international trade rules. This may directly affect at least some of the citizens of the latter, but they need only act according to what their government orders without knowing the details of the matter (consider, e.g., "Do not buy goods manufactured in that other country").

If the members had enough information about the group situation in question and if they were functioning as egalitarian group members, then their total or full reason could be R (of (GAR)) qua collectively accepted by them as their reason. The ground for this is that as a group agent consists of the group members and if the group functions for the long-run benefit of its members (as it generally should do) then at least in the long-run case the members' total reason in egalitarian cases on grounds of dysfunctionality (the group acts through its members) should not differ from the group agent's reason. Yet they may lack that information and in actual practice have to take a weaker, but compatible, reason, R*, as their proximate reason that they have a pro-attitude to act for (this seems to be a rather typical case in hierarchical and non-autonomous groups).

3.2.

There can be we-mode reasons, viz., reasons conceptually based on the group agents' attitudes or activities, both for individual and for joint action.[34] I will below discuss the joint action case and focus on the fullest sense of joint action—joint action *as a group*. The group may have formed an intention expressible by "We will perform action X together" or a group belief expressible by "We believe that p", and so on. Thus, when acting as a group member, an agent will have to perform his part of X partly for the reason that he, as a group member, accepts as his (proximate) group reason the fact that the group agent intends X; and analogously for the group belief (as acceptance belief") case.[35]

Note that whenever there is a joint intention, there is a social group, at least a group capable of action as a group. A single member can take part in the joint intention without a bootstrapping problem (viz. the "Münchausenian" problem of arbitrary intention formation) arising for him.[36] This may be because the joint intention was formed much earlier, or the formation of the joint intention may have been due to authorized leaders.

To consider joint action, we first notice that, necessarily on conceptual grounds, there seems to be a group reason involved in any we-mode intentional joint action, as it must be activity undertaken *for a group* (e.g., in simple cases a group generated in effect by the participants' prior joint intention or perhaps joint-intention-in-action). This reason may be (or contain) the fact of their jointly wanting something relevant, or it could even be their (or their group's) previously formed joint intention required for making the action intentional.

I take it for granted that, on conceptual grounds and in analogy with the individual case, if a group agent intentionally performs an action, it must intend to perform it. Hence its members, at least the operatives (including the special case with only one operative), must share the joint intention to perform that action (or a closely related one) jointly. The process that leads to a joint intention may accordingly involve compromise-making that is against some participants' underlying wants (at least their "first choices"). Here the fact of the jointness of the intention is indeed informative.

Based on the account (GAR), I now propose the following stylized summary account (in terms of necessary conditions) of a member's *motivating* group reason for we-mode joint action (satisfying the three criterial conditions for the we-mode, viz., the group reason, collectivity, and collective commitment conditions) in a case where the we-mode group can be either autonomous or non-autonomous (recall chapter 2 for the qualifications concerning the non-autonomous case). R refers to the group agent's reason (a fact or fact-like state) and R* to the members' group reason (below, R* may coincide with the group agent's reason R):

(GMR) State R* was the *members' motivating group reason* for which they performed X jointly in the we-mode (either autonomous or non-autonomous we-mode) in situation S only if in S

(1) Group g intended (or instructed, directed, required, etc. through its relevant operatives or leaders) that the members perform action X. (*Group's intention or directive*)
(2) Because of (1), the nonoperative members formed some joint want(s) and/or belief(s), as well as, especially, a joint intention to perform X together such that these propositional attitudes were joint attitudes directly or indirectly connected to R* (e.g., being semantically about R*). (*Joint motivational set*)
(3) The members (at least the nonoperatives) performed their parts of X on the joint motivational set (2). (*Acting on joint motivational set*)

In (2) in the case of an egalitarian group the group's intention simply upon analysis amounts to all members' joint intention toward X and hence cannot ground it. But in other cases, for example, in hierarchical groups, the authorized leaders have the power to form an intention that gives the ground for the nonoperative members' (i.e., rank-and-file members') assumed collective acceptance of the joint intention concerning the members' performance of X.

The group members are assumed in (3) to act on the joint motivational set and for a common reason, R*. Let me emphasize that their part actions may of course be different depending on the division of tasks in the group. What is more, R* need not be their total reason for participation and their individual total reasons for participation may contain different private, I-mode reasons. (Note that clauses (2) and (3) have their counterparts in (GAR) but are member-level conditions.)[37]

Joint action being based on a joint intention, in egalitarian, same-status cases the agents must have formed the joint intention to perform or bring about X as a group—corresponding to the group's order in clause (1). Clause (2) hence must contain that joint intention. Clause (1) only gives a group-level description of this case, viz., the presence of the group agent's intention. R* and the group agent's reason R are connected: R* is relevantly derivable from the group agent's reason R by means of some relevant epistemic assumptions, as will be seen below.

A motivating group reason also involves the *normative* aspect that the group agent's intention (1), based on its reason R, requires that the group members perform their parts of the collective action. The members group-normatively ought to do what they have agreed on as a group. This is in analogy with, and is an extension of, the idea that membership in the group constitutively requires that the members promote the ethos of the group. (The intention in (1) might be part of that ethos.) The reasons provided by group authorities (including the authority of the group over its members in the non-autonomous case) are (strongly) normative, but they may still be trumped by stronger group reasons or by moral requirements.

While authoritative group reasons concerning group members' participation are group-normative (thus strongly normative), a group agent's reason for its activities need not be more than weakly normative. The group agent's ethos is either instrumentally or properly normative.[38] In a well-functioning group the ethos, importantly, is also a motivating group reason for its members to act as group members. (Notice that group members can of course decide to do things together that they like as long as these activities are compatible, although perhaps not required by the ethos.)

As an illustration of the role of a group agent's reason and members' group reason, the reader is referred to the simple schema of reasoning concerning house painting in section 4 of chapter 3. There the group agent's reason for house painting is the fact that the house looks shabby and is need of repainting, while the members' proximate group reason is the fact that the group intends to paint the house. The schema illustrates how the group reason affects individual members' reasoning and activities in the situation. It was also argued in chapter 3 that the group agent's reason serves as a partial explanans of the members' activities related to house painting. On the other hand, each member performs his part of the joint action, X, partly for the reason that the agents have the joint intention to perform X jointly and believes that they will appropriately act toward the realization of this joint intention by their own part performances.

3.3.

Let us next consider in some detail how the agents act on a joint motivational set and thereby connect their reasons to the performances of their part actions in a joint action and do it normally without the interference of "wayward causal chains". We assume that a group agent's reason R here is simply that the window frames lack paint and the action X is painting the window frames jointly. R is also assumed here to be the members' reason for participating in X, and it serves to explain X if the group members have properly acknowledged R and want to have a house with nicely painted window frames. That is, R will have to create the right motivational mental state in the members.

Assume for simplicity that there are only two agents, A and B, who believe that the window frames need new paint (R) and form the joint intention to paint them. As above, R is assumed to be the dyad's reason and also the members' group reason (i.e., the frames need paint, as mutually believed by them). Their joint motivational set includes their recognition and acceptance of R and all the relevant beliefs and background knowledge. We assume that they have come to jointly intend to paint the house on the ground that they are assumed to act act on the joint motivational set. Each of them thus plans to participate in the joint painting, and they agree that A will paint the front windows and B the side windows. Their prior joint intention together with the relevant beliefs can be argued to generate in them the right "we-willing" (a kind of "intention-in-action") to put their bodies relevantly into motion when the right point of time, call it "now", comes about. This possibly subconscious we-willing rationally involves reason R for joint action, that is, it is a rationality requirement for the agents to keep on acting for R until the completion of the joint action. This requirement can also be viewed as a necessary condition for the avoidance of *wayward causal chains*—because the agents are, so to speak, jointly in charge of the joint action from beginning till end, typically in a partly routine way.[39]

To elaborate, the joint action and hence its part actions are performed because of group reason R. When X is performed because of R, rationality requires in normal cases that R be observed until the action has been completed. The prior intention to act is an intention to perform X and, furthermore, to do it in accordance with and partly because of reason R. When that intention develops (gets applied to the concrete "here and now" situation) and becomes an energizing we-willing, the same group reason R can be taken—for rational consistency—to guide action ("We are now intentionally performing X jointly, as a group, because of our prior joint intention to perform X in accordance with reason R"). Rational consistency thus entails that we-willings and the joint action they are part of are grounded in R, relative to the assumption that the prior intention is grounded in R. To use the group-level conceptualization, the dyad (that has A and B as its members) can be said to bring about X through its members acting jointly, in unison (in a way resembling a single-agent action where one does something that requires using one's left and right hands in a coordinated way) and even so that a participant's we-willing cannot be satisfied without the other's successful participation. Each agent can be said here to cause her body to move in the right way because of R. This involves that agents' possibly causally interacting bodily movements are caused by their we-willings derived from their prior joint intention. (This usually requires learning to act appropriately on one's intentions.)

Note that we-willings as components of action cannot cause action but only e.g., neurally conceptualized bodily movements (broadly understood). The present account gives a kind of solution or outline of solution to the notorious wayward causal chain problem for both single-agent and joint action. This problem is one of accounting for the "right" way of acting and not only accidentally producing the intended outcome.[40]

Note finally that there are many other possible motivators for group members than those commented on above. Thus, a full-blown member is assumed to be group centered and in this sense "patriotic": He values the group and wants it to prosper. A prospering group is normally beneficial to most if not all of its members. Compared with an I-mode group, there is a stronger group reason based on the group authority endogenously conferred to the group by the members. A rational group reason, e.g., one leading to the choice of CC (mutual cooperation outcome) in a PD, entails collectivity in a cognitive "content" sense (the collectivity condition is satisfied) and a collective emotion of unity ("group spirit" or "we-feeling") is typically contingently present.[41] This kind of composite group reason (be it the ethos or something derived from it) also tends to increase cohesion, order, stability, and solidarity in the group, especially in a diachronic case.[42] All the elements mentioned here serve to bind the members together and to motivate them to act as group members.

4. AUTHORITY AND AUTHORITATIVE REASONS

The group reasons of the members of we-mode groups are based on the authority of the group over its members. The members are, so to speak, assumed to have at least temporarily given up or delegated to the group a relevant part of their authority and autonomy to act, and this entails that they are normatively bound to comply with the group's directives. The most central group reasons are those relating to the group's ethos, which the group members have collectively accepted for the group and are publicly available to the group members. On the basis of their membership in a we-mode group the members in general ought to act as proper group members and to put aside their countervailing private desires and interests. In general, uniform action is taken to be needed for the satisfaction of the group ethos, and this in part justifies group authority. For example, in the case of a state, the goals and values, human rights, justice, and member welfare that its ethos may contain are taken to require authorized group action, and this fact serves to justify the state's authority.

As mentioned, the conceptual and justificatory direction in the we-mode is typically top down, from group level to member level (although desirably interactively so, recall, e.g., the individual members' proposals concerning what in their opinion the group's attitude or action should be, called "we-mode proposals"), and proposals are supposed to result in we-mode group attitudes when agreed upon in the group. In the I-mode the conceptual direction is typically bottom up, viz., from member level to group level. Thus, that the group believes or intends thus-and-so can serve as a group member's reason to act in appropriate ways amounting to his part of the group agent's action. Acting as a group member in a we-mode group concerning ethos-related tasks is based on what the group, through its internally or externally authorized leaders, authoritatively decides, orders, or requires. In this section I will further clarify and elucidate authority and normative directing in the context of group activity especially in terms of preemptive reasons.[43]

An authoritative group reason under ordinary circumstances is preemptive (exclusionary) concerning countervailing private reasons. This is because the members have given up to the group a group-related part of their natural authority to act. This entails that they ought to act as the group requires of them, i.e., in accordance with preemptive group reasons that in general normatively preempt other reasons for the group members. Functionally, the group ought to be capable of acting as a unit in order to achieve its goals, and this requires that the members be socially committed to each other to perform their parts of the tasks that the group gives to them. Indeed, all the central we-mode criteria (briefly, the requirements of group reason, collectivity, and collective commitment) must be satisfied in full-blown we-mode acting, but I regard the quasi-moral commitment criterion—entailing the requirement of not letting the others down—to be the most central noncontingent condition speaking for the preemption idea. An authoritative group reason is not only a normative preemptive reason but in a properly functioning group also a motivating reason (when recognized by the members). Note, too, that authoritative group reasons are good examples of desire-independent reasons, i.e., reasons that typically are not generated by a person's private pro-attitudes (although when a group reason is a motivating one, it will generate a pro-attitude toward acting on the basis of that reason).

What in general suffices for ordinary members (e.g., citizens of a state) to participate in group activities is the fact that the group has, e.g., through its internally or externally authorized leaders, formed a group intention, and the members mutually know this. They are assumed to be able to infer that they should participate because of the fact that the group agent has that intention and that this involves a kind of directive (to satisfy the intention as a group) for the members. In some cases a specifically authorized representative of the group, a leader, may have the power to issue the directive. Consider the following stylized schema, applicable primarily to a hierarchical group with a leader, to illustrate this situation:

(1) The group agent's reason for performing group action Y (e.g., painting a house) was R (e.g., that the house was in need of more colorful paint).

(2) The group (through its leader[s]) formed the intention to perform Y and took the performance of Y here to require their issuing a directive D to the members (for instance: Do X′ if acting in position P, X″ if acting in position P′, etc.), with the expectation that the members' acting in accordance with it will generate Y.

Therefore,

(3) The leader(s) accordingly issued D.
(4) The members explicitly or implicitly agreed to perform their positional shares because of the group reason (call it R*) that (3) expresses.

Therefore,

(5) The members performed their shares X′, X″, etc., because of R*, and these part actions generated the joint action Y (that the house was painted by them) whose intentionality was in part based on reason R.

Here (1)–(3) in effect form a practical syllogism for the group (e.g., for its leaders or members collectively, depending on the case), the conclusion (step (3)) of which represents a group reason for the group members. Step (4) involves the members' joint intention to act because of reason R*, that is, (3), which is realized by their part performances generating joint action Y. Conclusion (5) is justified and factually explained by (1)–(4).

Continuing to focus on we-mode groups, we see that authority and authorization are central in the cases of group reasons, group action, group belief, and actively accepted attitudes in general. The authorization of an operative member may take place, e.g., by means of the members' collective performative speech acts, such as, "We hereby collectively accept that NN will have the authoritative power to give us directives and orders in group contexts C". Of special interest is the case where the operatives are leaders internally authorized by delegation to give orders and directives concerning group-relevant (basically ethos-relevant) matters.[44] The other members need only tacitly accept what (e.g., what intentions or views) the operative members have jointly accepted for the group and directed them to do. This "ought" is an institutional (viz., group-normative) obligation related to the authorization of operatives and to the group's functioning as a unit when it has the attitude in question. Put simplistically, if I have authorized you to make decisions for our dyad, I am obligated at least in this sense to accept what you decide for us. In view of our developments in chapter 2 and above, it should be kept in mind that we-mode activities can take place under external authorization, although the authority's exercise of power may alter the situation (I have spoken of non-autonomous we-mode groups in such cases).

As to the notion of power that I employ in this book, it builds on the standard idea that an authority's having power over some people means basically that he can get his will through to the people and get them to act according to his will. Accordingly, an internally or externally authorized leader can, on the basis of his power source (such as authorization), by his activities (e.g., directives and orders) get those over which he has power to obey him irrespective of whether the target persons (initially) want to act as ordered. We can speak of *power as social control* in this standard case. A refinement of this generally accepted view for situations of social interaction can be couched in terms of game-theoretic payoff or utility matrices of the standard kind (see chapter 7). I have elsewhere shown that in terms of such matrices one can in all many-person situations, speaking on an abstract level, find three basic types of power in the sense of social control and that indeed one can deal with degrees of social control in all those cases.[45] We accordingly deal with a participating agent's *control over his own payoffs*, his *control over other agents' payoffs* (and conversely the other agents' control over *his* payoffs), and his interactive or *conditional control over his own and others' payoffs*.[46]

In its core sense the we-mode approach entails that in the context where a member is acting as a group member, the salient group reason (for action X) is regarded as (motivationally) preemptive in the sense of excluding other conflicting reasons.[47] An authoritative directive accordingly is preemptive in the sense that it normatively excludes and replaces the agent's own judgment about what is to be done in the case in question. This entails that at least ideally there cannot rationally be two conflicting preemptive reasons for an action in a group (although there may be conflicting preemptive reasons between different groups, this resulting in intergroup conflict), because other (e.g., private) reasons that are in conflict with the directive are excluded.[48] From a normative point of view, the group must be taken to be unitary in the sense that it satisfies this condition. From a descriptive point of view the situation is different, although the groups or at least the group authorities de facto tend to make their orders and directives preemptive by the use of suitable sanctions if needed.[49]

Let us consider a case where a group agent has a motivating reason to perform an action X. The members' will here have a membership-based group-normative obligation to participate in the performance of X as a pro tanto rather than an all-things-considered one (cf. the military case where a sergeant gives a detrimental or immoral order to the soldiers). The pro tanto construal gives better expression to the fact that the members of we-mode groups are socially connected persons with private desires, interests, and obligations that may conflict with group demands. A soldier's moral duty not to kill prisoners or civilians may thus override his group-based obligations as judged by him and perhaps by others as well.

The above suggests that group-external reasons should theoretically be taken to matter at least in some cases and give valid excuses not to participate in the group agent's action. While at least in an egalitarian group the members will have the pro tanto reason to participate, it is conceptually possible that they all on a certain occasion have valid excuses for not participating now (or perhaps ever, but in that case they really should leave the group). If the group had the obligation to do X, it will still continue to be obligated, as was claimed in chapter 2.

One of the central arguments for the we-mode approach is that the massive implicit and routine social "capital" and skills that it involves makes we-mode acting computationally more efficient than reflecting on one's private, I-mode reasons in quickly changing conditions. While there may be special urgent cases where private reasons can rationally and/or morally be taken to count, in general when an individual needs to make a quick decision in a group context, she may not have the time and other resources for detailed deliberation. Then she will have a rational reason to function in the we-mode that may lead her to act routinely or on "automatic pilot".

As I have said, it still seems reasonable and commonsensical to accept that people can occasionally weigh group reasons and urgent private reasons against each other when acting as group members.[50] In such a case the group reason is regarded as not preemptive concerning all private reasons or concerning we-mode reasons based on another group's directives, etc. For instance, in our military example an agent will have to decide one way or another in each eventuality (also if preemption concerning the I-mode does not hold in this particular case). If there is even partial comparability, weights might in principle be given to these reasons and some kind of weighted sum (or perhaps product) could be proposed as a motivational account here. If there is no comparability, the agent must frame the situation in one of these ways (viz., we-mode versus I-mode or morality) and act accordingly. Which way to go can in real life be viewed as a contingent psychological matter, or it can be regarded as a conflict between individual and collective rationality (or morality), or simply as a conflict between incompatible we-mode reasons. Given the above, I still require on group-functional grounds that a group reason be so strong that it tends to dominate or at least should dominate over the I-mode in standard circumstances but not necessarily over other salient we-mode reasons or over moral reasons.

The upshot is that the Razian normative regulations may be relaxed to yield more real-life freedom to group members. In all, we can say that ethos-respecting group reasons are in general de facto preemptive with respect to I-mode reasons and even with respect to other we-mode reasons as long as no stronger group reasons (group-internal or perhaps group-external ones) emerge. As to the latter eventuality, in the army case, for example, a sergeant's order in general is pro tanto preemptive, i.e., preemptive unless, say, an officer happens to interfere and give an order to the contrary.

An ethos-compatible directive is said to have *full normative authority* in the case of a we-mode group if the authorization is internal (viz., based on collective acceptance in the group), but if it is external it need be regarded as acceptable by the members only in a weaker sense such as complying or going along with the directive. A normatively authoritative directive has de facto authority in the group when most—or a substantial number of—the group members indeed regard the directives issued by the operatives as at least pro tanto preemptive reasons for action and are disposed to act for them.[51] The substantive ground of the directive in general is that it authoritatively represents something supposed to promote the group's ethos. In ideal cases justified authoritative reasons should be both substantive and have normative and de facto authority.

In general a justified reason need not be a good reason in all relevant aspects. By definition, the reason must be procedurally good in the sense that the operatives function correctly according to the accepted principles of decision making, etc.; but it need not be good in other respects, e.g., it may lead to morally bad actions. Indeed, the above account does not as such impose moral restrictions on group activity, although of course in civilized societies that is what we must have. In this book, I concentrate on the group's efficient functioning rather than on the central moral aspects that in general should not be violated in our civilization.

Note that there can be authority without specific (internal or external) authorization, for instance in egalitarian cases, where all the members are operative and where they form an intention for the group to do X. This involves the members' joint intention to do X (or at least something that generates X), and the existence of this joint intention serves as the group members' shared authoritative group reason for intending to perform their parts of X and for carrying out this intention. This is because the members' joint intention in this simple case amounts to the group's authorized intention to perform X.

In the I-mode case some people can agree to build a bridge together but still function as private persons in the sense that their private desires and beliefs are decisive—while they can accept, e.g., compromises etc. Individual rationality basically guides their activities, although also moral considerations and social customs, based on the I-mode framework, may well get involved. Their "collective commitment" is different from the we-mode case, as it is not necessarily based on functioning for the benefit of the group but rather and always at least in part for their private benefit. Group-based reasons, goals, utilities, beliefs, norms, etc. can be involved but only in the sense of being based on private acceptance (see chapter 2, section 5).

5. CONCLUSION

In this chapter reasons for intentional action have been discussed and informative truth conditions for statements attributing reasons have been stated for the individual and social, many-person as well as group agent cases. Social reasons in this sense have not previously been analyzed in the literature, at least not in detail. Normative and motivating reasons are distinguished at all the mentioned levels. Roughly speaking, R is agent A's motivating reason for action X if R is a reason that motivates A to perform X and thus serves to explain his performance of X. R is agent A's normative reason for action X if R is a reason that entails that A ought to perform X or at least that R is in some sense a right reason for him to act. A normative reason need not always be a motivating reason for an agent. (The many-person level and the group levels are accounted for analogously.)

All motivating reasons in the case of intentional action must be intentionally "processed" by the agent via his want-belief system and, indeed, accepted by him to be his reasons for action. The agent must form beliefs about facts that serve as his reasons, and he will have to have a pro-attitude toward potential facts that he purports to make actual. The engagement of the agent is already needed before acting: It is up to him what his effective reasons are, at least in the sense that he could have chosen to act otherwise than he did. (One cannot, however, always intentionally choose one's reasons.)

As to social reasons, the cases of both I-mode and we-mode actions were discussed, with a focus on the latter. We-mode joint action requires that the participants function as a group in a collectively committed and interdependent way on the basis of a shared group reason. Group reasons in two senses were distinguished: a group agent's (viz. the group's) reason and a member's group reason for participation. In a we-mode group that autonomously decides about its own affairs, group reasons are authoritative in the sense that they involve the group's authority over the individual. In cases of external authority the externally imposed group reasons might be accepted only grudgingly and not regarded as fully authoritative (e.g., morally fair) by the members.

Typically, members' group reasons cannot be aggregatively constructed out of their private reasons but are, rather, decided upon by leaders or by the collective acceptance of the group members. Group reasons, as authoritative, are group-normative in the sense of being the group's normative requirements for the members.

I have emphasized that in normal internally authorized cases the operative members have the legitimate authority and right to rule (concerning a specified set of topics) that entails a correlated obligation to obey for the members. There is thus appropriate justification for the nonoperative members to take the operative members' decisions (directives, orders, etc.) as desire-independent preemptive reasons for action, although they might not do so and fail to act as full group members. Indeed, to make the basic account more realistic, private reasons may play a role at the expense of group reasons, although strictly speaking this goes against acting as a group member—but human beings are not merely group members, and group reasons from other groups that a person is a member of may count, and so may private reasons.[52]

5

Collective Acceptance and the Formation of Group Attitudes

I. INTRODUCTION

The members of a structured group (such as a we-mode group) must be able to form collectively binding attitudes for the group because ensuring its temporal persistence and respecting its ethos and other established prior views and principles is at least a prima facie desideratum for a structured group. The group's continued existence may be dependent on its making up its mind on an important matter (e.g., we cannot build a bridge jointly unless we make up our minds about it).

Suppose now that a we-mode group has set as its task to form a goal or view (voluntary belief, "acceptance belief") for itself. The group may face a choice between several possible goals and views such that one of them has to be selected as the group's goal or view. These options themselves may be based on a prior group choice regarding the set of possible alternatives, or be based on the members' implicit background knowledge of the situation. The group's choice, or acceptance as I here say, is based on its members' collective acceptance. Such collective acceptance can be based on the group's representatives collective acceptance in a layered structure, where only the highest-level representatives are directly involved in making the collective choice. Below, however, I will below focus on the egalitarian case and assume that all the members are directly involved.

It can be argued that in order to secure reliable group functioning—including coordination of attitudes and actions among the members of the group—collective acceptance (concerning acting together) conceptually involves explicit or implicit agreement (understood in a broad sense) between them. An explicit agreement typically (but not necessarily) is a result of agreement making of some kind (e.g.. making a contract) such that the content of the agreement is explicit, in general stated in verbal (spoken or written) language, involving a joint obligation for the participants. There are several kinds of implicit agreement, and common to them is that the content of the agreement is not fully verbally (linguistically) stated and that the formation of a joint intention is a central element in the formation of the agreement. The participants can arrive at an implicit agreement in several different ways (e.g., by mimicry and gestures or even by mutual awareness of a shared history or experience). Both a sincere explicit agreement and an implicit one entail a joint intention for the participants to act together to satisfy the agreement in question. In the explicit case the content of the intention is explicitly stated and fortified, as it were, by a social or a moral obligation. In the implicit case the joint intention content is generally expressed only, for example, by bodily behavior or other implicit means, and there need not be an obligation involved.[1]

In all, it seems viable to take all collective acceptance conceptually to involve a process resulting in explicit or implicit agreement. (See the appendix for a more detailed summary account of these agreement notions.)

As to group attitudes, if the members of a we-mode group collectively agree about a group attitude toward a content for their group through their agreement making (the process through which the participants arrive at the agreement), they have collectively accepted that their group has that attitude. In my view collective acceptance involves acceptance of a content in a certain attitudinal mode (e.g., wanting, wishing, hoping, intending, believing, fearing) or, to use another terminology, with a certain direction of fit. Turning it around, the members can come by acceptance to want, wish, intend, etc., a certain content or that a certain proposition is true or satisfied. E.g., they can agree on a standing joint plan (containing at least a joint intention) to repair their house roof when needed. This is attitude formation by collective acceptance. The two sides of the coin are that they collectively agree to repair the roof if and only if they jointly intend to do it. Note that the formation of group attitudes requires that the members function as group members and, psychologically, that they have sufficient reliance on the other members' functioning in an equally group-oriented manner.

Even if an agreement between the participants to act together exists, there may still be some epistemic uncertainty among them about who is a trustworthy cooperator, even if it is a presupposition of the members that the other group members are cooperative. In real-life cases, however, some empirical checking by the participants concerning the other participants' continuous cooperativeness may be needed for successful joint action.

In the rest of this chapter, I will discuss a group agent's acceptance and group members' collective acceptance of a joint action or of an attitude. I will present the "Bulletin Board View" of group attitude formation to elucidate the manner in which group attitudes can be formed and group-based assurances arrived at. At the end of this chapter, I will present a weaker account of collective acceptance in terms of "going along" with a proposal and discuss some problems in relation to the rational aggregation of individual attitudes.

2. GROUP ACCEPTANCE AND COLLECTIVE ACCEPTANCE

There is an obvious need for agreement making in organized groups given that individuals need to coordinate their activities and to reach a consensus about what to do despite their possibly conflicting private preferences. The reason for this is that the group must be able to do what it wants or ought to do as a group, especially in order to promote and satisfy its ethos. As groups can act only on the basis of their members' action (we-mode action in we-mode groups), the members must collectively agree on what to do.

Rational collective acceptance must involve a "procedural" element, viz., some kind of agreement making or at least agreeing, where the members must fit together their "we-mode proposals" for creating the group's intention (or their collective intention). There is accordingly a process of *agreement making* or of *arriving at an agreement* as a result of which the content of the agreement (and thus of collective acceptance) will in a rational group be collectively accepted with the right kind of attitude (e.g., intending or believing).

In the we-mode case the participants are supposed to be group-oriented in a comprehensive sense and to take their basic question in the case of voluntary group attitude formation to be "Which attitude (e.g., want or belief, as the present case may require) should we accept for our group in this situation?" This indicates that "we-reasoning" will be the way to arrive at collective acceptance of an alternative for the group. The participants make their we-mode proposals and their joint task is to create the group's attitude by their we-reasoning and agreement making.

A we-mode proposal by a member entails a "precommitment" and an obligation to accept and promote the group agent's attitude that the group finally will arrive at through the members' decision making. Feasible kind of agreement making must by itself or together with plausible extra assumptions result in a we-mode collective acceptance of an attitude, e.g. an intention, for the group. We recall that this requires that the group reason, collectivity, and collective commitment criteria be satisfied.[2]

The main point of collective acceptance is to amalgamate member attitudes into a group attitude collectively binding the group members. I will below briefly consider some relationships between a group's attitude and the members' collective attitudes in the case of egalitarian and hierarchical groups. While hierarchical groups contain some operative members (leaders) authorized to make decisions for the rest of the group, in egalitarian groups all the members are operatives with an equal say about the views that the group will adopt. Sometimes the group's organizational design may be implicit or the group might not yet be organized, e.g., the members-to-be are getting together to form attitudes for the group for the first time and thereby to constitute the group by their collective acceptance.[3] Here I will not be concerned with what kinds of groups are ideal or preferable in social life, since there are various kinds of groups that seem to be suitable for different purposes and for different environments. Large groups typically require at least some distribution of power within the group to ensure fast and efficient decision making, but even small groups may involve power relationships and operative members (leaders). As to groups with hierarchical layers of personnel in various authority relationships, see the discussion in chapter 6.

A group's (a group agent's) acceptance and collective acceptance are distinct notions. To be sure, a group accepts a content through its members' acceptance, but the two notions are different. They are of course logically different because group agents are not mere sets of individual agents, but are also different for the reason that a group agent's acceptance can take place through the collective acceptance of an authorized subset of the group members in hierarchical groups (think, e.g., of France deciding to participate in the NATO air attacks against Libya).

The basic idea in my account of collective acceptance in the egalitarian case (where the participants are on equal footing) is this: the participants collectively accept a content (proposition) as true or correct for the group just in case they come, in a way involving their explicit or implicit agreement, to share a we-mode joint attitude as a group.[4] For instance, that a squirrel pelt is money can be true for a certain group but not for other groups in the sense of the proposition "A squirrel pelt is money" being correctly usable only in that group. Collective acceptance yields a joint attitude (e.g., joint intention) that also can be viewed as the group's attitude (e.g., the group agent's intention). As noted, the participants need not always constitute a preestablished group here, but they may sometimes only be on their way to forming one, while presently only being a collection of individuals making their proposals for a group's action. In a we-mode group the participants are assumed to function on the basis of the we-perspective and to be striving for an attitude applicable to the group agent as its attitude.

An attitude of the group agent has either the world-to-mind or the mind-to-world direction of fit, the members being collectively committed to what they have accepted. The world-to-mind case covers goals and intentions and the like, while the mind-to-world case basically covers beliefs and the like. In the group intention case, for instance, it is understood that at least the operative members in structured groups have the joint intention expressible by "We will bring about X together" (with a togetherness "we") when the group has the intention expressible by "Group g intends to bring about X". The institutional case is slightly more complex, especially in the case of constitutive group beliefs, and may be seen to involve both directions of fit. Taking up the example of money, an item such as a squirrel pelt may be *collectively made* money—by, e.g., a collective performative to that effect by the members assuming that they also extralinguistically behave accordingly (e.g., buy their food with squirrel pelts). Collective acceptance here has the world-to-mind direction of fit. *Given this*, a squirrel pelt *is* money for the group in question and is representable as money, where the representation has the mind-to-world direction of fit for the group. The members qua members are assumed to be disposed to satisfy the institutional proposition by their overt action, given the mutual understanding and knowledge about the proposition and its direction of fit.

I have earlier discussed group acceptance and collective acceptance. Here I will present a revised version of my account.[5] The central idea is to elucidate a group g's acceptance of a proposition p as true (or, if you prefer, taking p to be true or correctly assertable) in terms of its commitment to regarding p as true (in the mind-to-world fit case) or making it satisfied (in the world-to-mind fit case), which on the member level involves arriving at an agreement of a relevant kind.

The proposition p could be, for example, "We (conatively) will perform X jointly", "Grass is green", or "A squirrel pelt is money". Here g's acceptance of p is acceptance of p as "premisible" for the group (correctly usable as premise to act on in group contexts, e.g., when answering whether or not p is true or correctly assertable); thus it is the "group-perspectival" truth of p that is at stake ("g take p to be true or correct"). The group is here for simplicity's sake assumed to be an egalitarian group in the sense of the members having the same status, the group agent's acceptance amounting to its members' collective acceptance. The group is assumed to represent "us" in the sense of *group identification*: g amounts to "us" (which entails in the ideal case that the members are disposed to act fully as group members). It follows from this that the gap between third-person formulations and first-person plural formulations is bridged and also that they can in many linguistic contexts be used coextensively—e.g., "g intends to perform X" and "We will do X together" are equivalent even if the latter expression might be regarded as correctly assertable rather than as true.

The account can be summarized as follows for an attitude p and an egalitarian we-mode or an I-mode group g:[6]

(GA) Group g *accepts p as true (or correctly assertable) for itself* if and only if the members of g collectively accept p as true for g as a group.

To take up an example, when applied to our central topic of intentions (goals), (GA) deals, for example, with the case in which p = we will paint our house red. Here group g qua group accepts that p expresses its intention or goal and that it commits itself not to p but rather to seeing to it that the house will be painted red by the group members. Analogously, in the mind-to-world cases the group commits itself to using the attitude content in p (e.g., "The earth is flat") as a true premise and to acting accordingly.

Given the above discussion, I propose this simple account of collective acceptance for egalitarian (viz., same-status) cases:

> (CA) The members of a group g qua group members *accept p as true or correctly assertable for g* if and only if they (come to) jointly have an attitude expressed by p such that the attitude is for the "use" of the group (viz., for promoting its ethos or other accepted attitudes) and has either the world-to-mind direction of fit (one in the intention family of attitudes) or the mind-to-world direction of fit (one in the belief family).

In particular, we-mode collective acceptance here results in a jointly held attitude that satisfies the central we-mode criteria. However, the process that leads to this result may be individualistic, although the members are assumed to function from the we-perspective for the group. In the we-mode case the members' resulting joint attitude requires the satisfaction of the collectivity condition, the members being relevantly collectively committed to seeing to it that the attitude content is satisfied in the world-to-mind direction-of-fit case or in the mind-to-world direction-of-fit case to acting compatibly with the content of the belief-like attitude fitting the world, in conditions of common knowledge of what the direction of fit of p is.[7]

In view of (GA) and (CA) it holds for an egalitarian we-mode group g that it accepts that p if and only if its members (assuming all of them to be we-moders) collectively accept that p in the we-mode, with the central we-mode criteria being satisfied. This is entailed by the fact that a we-mode group's attitudes qua a group must be based on the we-mode attitudes of its members (and might in this attenuated or derivative sense be said to be in the we-mode). The members of g are assumed to be collectively committed to seeing to it in the right way (namely, in terms of action obeying the direction of fit associated with the content of p) that p is true or correctly assertable, given the mutual understanding and knowledge about p and its direction of fit. The overt action of satisfying p is both conceptually and practically important for indicating the sincerity of an attitude with the world-to-mind fit; and analogously for cases with other kinds of attitudes.

I have said that in (GA) the group need not be a we-mode group, although that is our main case here. When g is an I-mode group, the members' collective acceptance will be I-mode acceptance. There is also the intermediate case where g is not a full-blown we-mode group but only a collection of persons that is functioning on the basis of a we-perspective and can be expected to become a we-mode group. They can still collectively accept something p (p expressing, e.g., a group ethos-to-be). When they have succeeded in formulating an ethos attitude for their group-to-be and are collectively group-normatively committed to its satisfaction, they in effect have become a we-mode group that (normally) satisfies the conditions of the account (WMG) in chapter 2.

As we have seen, collective acceptance in the present context (e.g., in (CA)) can be regarded as a collective attitude state, typically with some acceptance action, e.g., suitable verbal action (like simply "We accept the proposal"). Furthermore, for the acceptance of a squirrel pelt as money to be socially in force, it generally requires some supporting action like the actual use of squirrel pelt as money to socially validate the collective acceptance and to give it popular support, so to speak, and this also applies to cases where collective acceptance is based on external power as long as the participants still act as intentional agents.[8]

Collective acceptance can be spoken of as a construction when it so to speak builds a group agent's view from the members' we-mode proposals, viz., proposals that when collectively held will express the group's relevant we-mode attitudes.[9]

It is not required that (CA) always deal with *collectively (*or *jointly) intentional* action, although the participants' acceptances in general must be intentional.[10] In we-mode cases, (CA) is based on explicit or implicit agreement (as clarified in the appendix) that is at least sufficient for collective acceptance, but is not here argued to be invariably necessary. Note that there need not be a joint intention (and still less an intentional agreement) to make the agreement.[11] The agents' individual we-mode or pre-we-mode intentions to try to arrive at a group agreement suffice.

Consider next the contrasting *nonegalitarian* case in which the group has different member roles given by the operative-nonoperative member distinction, and more generally, a division of labor for the members. If, for instance, there are operative members for goal formation in the group, they accept the goals for the group, and the other members, nonoperatives, are assumed to go along with the operatives' acceptance. More precisely, based on the fact that they have authorized and delegated the operatives to accept group goals, the nonoperatives are normatively expected to accept what the operatives are doing in their goal formation, but it is possible that they do not know which specific goals the operatives have accepted for the group. The analysans of (CA) should be reformulated analogously for the case with an operative-nonoperative division of members.

The collective agreement concerning a goal (etc.) can practically be reached in various ways, as will be seen. It is, however, required in (CA) that the *individual* parties do *not* enter the acceptance (agreement) fully *unintentionally*—thus, upon reflection, the acceptance should not come as a surprise to them. Overt individual performances by *each* party, however, are not required: It suffices that the parties in the agreement are aware of what is going on and do not refuse to adopt the possible obligations ensuing from it.

In the case of nonegalitarian groups we cannot realistically require that all the members participate in collective acceptance or even that the acceptance be based on a joint intention by the participants to accept the proposition in question—this matter depends on how the group is structured into positions and roles, which normatively and structurally connect individual acceptances (see sections 3 and 4). If, for example, the United States accepts that invading Afghanistan is necessary (say for peace in the region), this is compatible with many US citizens having no knowledge of this view or a great many refusing to take part in the acceptance. Still, they *ought to* accept it as the group's view and potential requirement for action partly because of democratic delegation of power in the state.

3. THE BULLETIN BOARD VIEW OF GROUP ATTITUDE FORMATION

3.1.

How can the members of an egalitarian we-mode group voluntarily acquire a (we-mode) joint attitude such as an intention (based on its members' joint intention) or a belief, especially an artifactual institutional belief? The answer given in this chapter is that such a procedural account must be based on (GA) and (CA), to begin with.[12] As earlier, the central question for the group is "What shall (or should) our group do in this situation?" or practically equivalently, "What shall (should) we do together in this situation?". In general, the participants will be group members or their representatives in the context of a democratic we-mode group that can autonomously form its attitudes. In democratic groups, at least, all full-fledged and adequately informed members must have a say (directly or indirectly) in group attitude formation. Recall from chapter 3 that the central conceptual elements that distinguish I-mode and we-mode accounts are that the we-mode in contrast to the I-mode requires that the three central criteria of the we-mode (viz. group reason, collectivity, and collective commitment) be satisfied in this case and the members are assumed to present their we-mode proposals as answers to the above question.

The bulletin board view, BBV for short, of the formation of joint intention gives a general schema for the manner in which some kind of agreement making is involved in the collective acceptance of attitudes for the group, although below I will focus on the intention case. This view also illustrates how collective acceptance in many typical cases takes place and leads to a joint attitude and a group attitude in an egalitarian group.[13] In an egalitarian group it holds true generally (with some exceptions) that an intention can correctly be ascribed to it just in case its members have that joint intention. BBV can be applied to both the (pro-group) I-mode case and the we-mode case of, e.g., joint intention, as will be indicated. I will below speak of joint intention in a mode-neutral way (unless something else is specified in the text).

As to the joint intention case, the basic idea in the model is that the participants give their answer to a proposal about what they should do together. The procedure gives as its result a joint intention involving the participants' sincere intentions to participate in a certain specific joint action.

To discuss an introductory example, suppose that one of the members of a community comes up with the idea of tidying up a park. This is the proposed joint action, which requires that the participants operate from a we-perspective, thinking of themselves as forming a group (or a group-to-be, a prospective group), and functioning for the goals of that group. That initiating person may publicly communicate the proposed joint action to the other group members. His action proposal can be thought to be written on a public bulletin board: "Members of group g are planning to tidy up the park next Saturday. Those who plan to participate, please sign up here". The ensuing (sincere) communicative signaling of acceptance by the participants (under the presupposition that sufficiently many others participate) may result in binding collective acceptance of this proposal, and in that case—given mutual knowledge about this—there will be an adequate we-mode joint intention to tidy up the park, provided that this was what the participants tried to achieve in this process. As a result the potential participation involved in a member's signing up turns into an actual, binding one.

For the procedure to correctly produce joint intentions and group attitudes various conceptual and factual (mode-relevant) presuppositions and background assumptions must be in place and hold true. These presuppositions must in a relevant sense and degree be understood by the participant. In the case of a we-mode joint intention at least the conditions specified in the account of joint intention and we-intention in chapter 3 should be included, plus other conditions to be mentioned below. BBV specifies on each occasion what the specific problem to be solved is, who the participants will be, etc., and how the participants are to function for a joint attitude to come about. In the (pro-group) I-mode case, the model builds in the conditions for I-mode joint intention respectively and proceeds analogously. The account assumes that there are some participants, a group that in the we-mode case is assumed to be either a we-mode group or a prospective we-mode group, a so far unorganized group. (If the we-mode group exists prior to BBV procedure, those members who actually do sign up will form a subgroup of it, but depending on the case, the tidying up of the park may still be attributed to the whole group.)

BBV relies on the participants' understanding that they aim at coming to agree on what to do together or what to accept as their view concerning a topic. Depending on the case, either an explicit or implicit agreement can be assumed to result. Joint promising, for instance, can take place if the task for the participants is to explicitly formulate and accept a joint intention (see the appendix to this chapter). Signing up for the activity may be the only concrete action needed in that case, and the analogous remark can be made in the case of implicit agreement making. The participants' having signed up, and thus agreed, gives each participant a group reason for participating in the agreed-upon action. Furthermore, it also gives a reason for each participant normatively to expect that the other participants indeed will participate. Thus, a participant has the right to expect that the others will perform their parts and is also obliged to respect their analogous rights. In this sense they are normatively socially committed. All this can take place in the I-mode or in the (prospective) we-mode, that is, on the basis of the we-perspective and with the aim and expectation that all the central we-mode criteria will apply to the product of the attitude formation (decision making). In particular, even in the we-mode case the decision making may take place in the pro-group I-mode, meaning that the participants function as private persons for the group or group-to-be and make their proposals for what the group's attitude should be.

The central thing about BBV is its general content, although I have used concrete, vernacular language to state the view—of course, no concrete bulletin board is needed for it to work. From a conceptual and theoretical point of view, this model of joint intention formation involves the following elements: *First*, what the proposed joint action is about must have been brought to the participants' attention in one way or another. I call this the topic issue. *Second*, the set of potential participants will typically be the members of group g (but group g need not exist prior to the occasion), and this must be knowable to the potential participants. *Third*, a related element is the "group-public" availability of the information about the intentions to participate; this aspect is also relevant to newcomers and persons who have to change plans. The potential participants pick up information about who is to participate, and this leads them to believe that those who have signed up will participate, given that sufficiently many have signed up and this is mutually known. What is more, they will also be able to acquire mutual knowledge about this, for they will come to know that the others know that those persons are willing to participate; and this can be iterated if needed. *Fourth*, when comparing we-mode BBV with (pro-group) I-mode BBV, there is the usual difference that exists between we-mode states and actions and I-mode ones; viz., they will occasionally yield different actions, and there is thus an analogous explanatory difference between the two accounts (see chapter 7). E.g., collective commitment in the we-mode sense will under certain conditions lead to predictions different from what shared I-mode commitments yield—concerning the persistence and resilience of joint action. The four basic features of BBV introduced above apply equally well to we-mode and pro-group I-mode collective acceptance and decision making.

It is a particular contingent feature of BBV that information gathering and delivery are centralized so that, for example, pairwise communication is not needed, and this makes the method practically applicable in large groups. However, this is a practical and epistemically relevant feature and not conceptually essential. But publicity in a group context is still philosophically central, as it creates a realm that is (epistemically) objective for the participants, and is likely to lead to actual objective knowledge.

In our somewhat metaphorical example, there may be information written on the board, and there may also be information in a special box beneath the board called "Presuppositions and Background Knowledge". In real-life cases often only situational information is written on the board, and the rest (for example, general background assumptions) is available in the presuppositions box, the contents of which need not be explicitly formulated.

We-mode thinking by the participants as such guarantees—on conceptual grounds and by our assumption that the members indeed are functioning in the prospective we-mode from a we-perspective—that their sought-after group intention and joint intention are in the we-mode. In standard cases the members form their (potential or proposed) participation intentions for the group reason that their group will achieve a relevant we-mode joint intention. These participation intentions-to-be can be pro-group I-mode intentions, i.e., when formed as private persons for a prospective we-mode group (see the comments in section 3).

Here is a recapitulation of the present account of BBV: (a) The we-perspective is assumed as the general background of BBV, which shows how a joint attitude comes about. BBV purports to answer questions of the kind: What shall we adopt as our group's intention? What shall we adopt as our group's view? What shall we do as a group? (b) The members should understand what it is for a group to intend, to have a goal or view and to act. In addition, the satisfaction conditions of such mental attitudes must be understood. (c) The contents that appear in the options for goals, views, actions, etc., must be understood by the group members, including the fact that they are to provide authoritative group reasons for the members, which serve to coordinate their activities in satisfying the group ethos. BBV will normally result in an explicit agreement about a group's attitude. (d) What it is to act collectively in pursuit of a collective goal and to be collectively committed to the relevant contents must be understood at least preanalytically, including an understanding of the group-social commitment to the other members relative to performing one's part. (e) Relevant skills and abilities are of course presupposed, including the ability to communicate with the others. Communication is often necessary so that the agents may arrive at the common knowledge that is required for them to rationally act in pursuit of the collective goal, or whatever is at stake. In addition, joint action skills must be presupposed, such as responsiveness to other's actions, coordination, and commitment to others.

The truth of some of these presuppositions might not be ascertainable before the BBV method has been applied and the metaphorical signatures gathered and the relevant information distributed to the participants.

3.2.

BBV has several advantages:

(1) It explicates collective and joint acceptance of attitudes (intentions, "acceptance" beliefs, and other voluntary attitudes) and does it by showing that the idea of a collective enterprise—for example, that some agents will have a joint plan or joint belief—is regarded as an underlying noncontingent presupposition for the formation of joint and group intentions to act (it applies to all possible courses of events, in contrast to a contingent condition—e.g., that the sun is shining). For example, that sufficiently many participate is a more concrete presupposition. If the presupposition fails, the members of course fail to form a (we-mode) joint intention and the participation intentions it involves (recall (WI) of chapter 3). But when it succeeds, it yields actual (not only potential) joint intentions and participation intentions that are *categorical*, unconditional.[14]

(2) When sufficiently many members for the planned collective action sign up and this is mutual knowledge in the group, BBV binds together all the participants in the pro-group I-mode case and especially in the we-mode case (because of the collectivity condition and the collective commitment requirement). A version of the collectivity condition is at play here, as the question is about the group's attitude.

(3) There is no need for a prior joint intention or agreement making (or, for that matter, team reasoning) for forming a joint intention. This is the case even if the joint intention's coming about is in general at least partly constituted by (sincere) agreement making, which is conceptually sufficient for the joint intention. (If the sincerity assumption fails, there will be no joint intention to fulfill the agreement

or rather "quasi agreement".) The aforementioned presuppositions direct the participants to form an intention for the group, and all they need to do is to sincerely signal their intention to participate (if the presuppositions obtain). Thus the participants' intentions to take part in satisfying a joint intention by their joint action are basically enough for entering one's signature on the board, given the truth of the required presuppositions of BBV that turns potential joint intentions and participation intentions into actual ones. The applies both to the I-mode and the we-mode application of it, and in both cases BBV assumes thinking and acting from a we-perspective, and in the we-mode case in addition the formed attitude must satisfy the three central we-mode criteria—often through adopting the full group-agency transformation (see chapter 7).

In the we-mode case the members have to have a mutual understanding to the effect that they indeed are prepared to function as we-moders, at least given that the others in the group are. In some cases children and other novices need first to be taught to function in the right way as group members.[15]

(4) BBV can treat the participants either symmetrically or asymmetrically with respect to their roles in attitude formation, depending on the demands of the situation.

(5) In principle BBV can be applied not only to small groups but also to large groups because of its flexible structure, as long as there are suitable devices and channels for propagating information within the group. The media may serve an important role in large national and supranational groups, as highlighted by the importance of independent national press and broadcasting companies.

As we have seen, in the case of BBV there is not much difference between participants functioning in the pro-group I-mode and those functioning in the we-mode. Still, in successful cases of group attitude formation the latter are collectively and not only privately committed to the formed attitude, and this will cause functional differences, e.g., concerning persistence in the task of group attitude formation, especially if several rounds of the use of BBV are needed (e.g., the task needs to be modified because the first round does not produce a result of sufficiently many forming the tentative intention). Furthermore, as will be seen in chapter 7, a pro-group I-moder will be more prone to private temptations in group projects.

Accordingly, it can be claimed that the formation of group attitudes in the we-mode sense is a desideratum for any group that wishes to ensure the continuation of its existence and activities and, on the other hand, to be sufficiently flexible as a group in the face of difficulties. For a we-moder who has truly internalized the we-mode we-perspective, there is hardly any excessive computational burden in comparison with the case of a pro-group I-moder.

3.3.

To end this section, I will consider a potential circularity problem facing the acceptance-based theory of this book. According to the theory, we-mode states and actions are conceptually based on all group members' we-mode collective acceptance (or, rather, a group's acceptance when these notions differ, e.g., in hierarchically structured groups). This collective acceptance is assumed to be in the we-mode in the prospective sense that the accepted attitude—viz., the intrinsic product of the acceptance that the group now has such and such an attitude—satisfies the basic criteria of the we-mode. We-mode collective acceptance in this sense does not require that the process leading to collective acceptance satisfy those criteria. It can thus be individualistic although undertaken from a we-perspective for the group. In the case of joint intention and action, the participants will not be collectively committed to the planned, jointly intended action in the we-mode sense until joint attitude formation has successfully been completed (and the presuppositions of BBV have become satisfied).

In general, mere I-mode or even pro-group I-mode collective acceptance does not suffice for the formation of a we-mode collective attitude. This conclusion can be based on the arguments against the reducibility of we-mode states to any kinds of I-mode ones in chapters 3 and 7.

The upshot is that what is missing is the members being precommitted and prepared to see and conceptualize the situation in terms of the *prospective we-mode* (ultimately in we-mode terms involving group agency as well as group thinking and reasoning as a group)—instead of their conceiving it in (pro-group) I-mode terms (with individual agents and individualistic reasoning for the group). When the participants function in the prospective we-mode, they are precommitted to accept a we-mode proposal, if the decision method (e.g., BBV) leads to it. Although functioning from the prospective we-mode is needed, as I have claimed, this need not result in vicious circularity.

4. COLLECTIVE ACCEPTANCE AND GOING ALONG WITH A PROPOSAL

As already seen—especially in the context of the bulletin board view, a group's acceptance of an attitude, e.g., a view or opinion, for itself can take place in many ways. In the case of small groups, especially informal and unstructured ones, group discussion (often involving negotiation and bargaining) is typical. The result of the process will be a joint attitude that in the we-mode case can be attributed to a group agent (because it has an attitude only if the members have the corresponding joint attitude). The process can at least in some cases result in explicit agreement, e.g., about what the group should do. In groups with hierarchical structure, those in power will generally have a weightier say than the rank-and-file members in decision making.

In large and organized groups, voting or voting-like attitude-formation mechanisms are often used. If the group is a democratic one, this poses some procedural constraints in addition to ordinary consistency and rationality conditions. In this section I will discuss a rather general approach to group attitude formation that is based on a logically weak kind of acceptance, viz., acceptance as going along with a proposal and group acceptance based on this idea.

Acceptance of a view or goal can be the kind of acceptance that at least "satisfices" the members' relevant goals without necessarily doing it maximally well. I prefer below to speak of *going along with a proposal*, in brief *ga-acceptance*, rather than satisficing. Ga-acceptance presupposes the members' understanding that they by their acceptance are in effect making an agreement to go along with the resulting joint decision. The ga-approach fits the bulletin board view of collective acceptance but has a wider scope and may apply better to realistic situations of group attitude formation (e.g., cases where a voting mechanism is in use). Ga-acceptance for rationally arriving at a group's attitude can sometimes be tacit agreement making, which is like explicit agreement but does not involve spoken or written statements, or it can concern implicit agreement, where agreement is achieved through nonverbal bodily behavior such as nodding. (See the appendix for explicit versus implicit agreements.)

A central justification for the ga-acceptance approach is not only that people often have different preferences but also that they are in different ways dependent on commitments and promises that they have earlier made; in addition, coercion may restrict the participants' choices and in this sense may force people to choose less than optimal alternatives. Ga-acceptance seems able to handle the above problems. It need not be based on the members' first choices, and this makes it weaker than acceptance as typically characterized in the choice-theoretic literature. Given the members' ga-acceptances of a proposal, the group's acceptance may be computed by the majority criterion or some other suitable aggregative means (unless there are ties). One can argue that the group's acceptance of an idea, view, goal etc., should be what best responds to the group members' acceptance in the ga-sense—this is a kind of adequacy requirement for connecting group acceptance with member-level acceptance. There might not be a uniquely best group response in the present sense or, on the other hand, a group response might not even come about because of differences in views.

I will now sketch what the top-down formation of group goals and views amounts to. We assumed that goals are states or events attributable to single or group agents, e.g., that agent A has goal g is equivalent to saying that A accepts goal g and it entails a pro-attitude toward g. Analogously A's having a view v amounts to A's belief-like attitude (but perhaps not a proper "experiential" belief) toward v or, equivalently, that A accepts view v.[16]

Consider the following simple framework concerned with agent goals and views. Let G be a set consisting of propositions expressing goals $g_1,\ldots,g_m$, or, in the general case, other kinds of attitude contents with the world-to-mind direction of fit; and let V be a set consisting of views $v_1,\ldots,v_k$, or, in the general case, of other kinds of attitudes with (at least) the mind-to-world direction of fit. P is assumed to be a set of profiles $<g_i,v_j>$. Acceptance of one of the elements of P for the group is the goal of the group's decision making here. Sometimes majority voting can be used, but there are viable methods that do not involve voting. If there are leaders in the group, they may present a proposal and the question, "Can you as a group member go along with this proposal for the group?" to the members. Notice that in principle a proposal may originate from members, leaders, previous history, Zeitgeist, generally accepted views and norms, etc.

I will below focus on proposals formed by members functioning on the basis of a we-perspective in the situation. These proposals express either the members' (pro-group) I-mode or their we-mode opinions. As earlier, I will speak of *we-mode proposals* or, more precisely, proposals made from within a we-mode perspective that—when collectively accepted as group attitudes—result in we-mode joint attitudes rather than, e.g., pro-group I-mode ones. We recall from the previous section that a member's acceptance of the proposal with a proper we-perspective involves her "precommitment", which upon collective acceptance turns into her full we-mode commitment and participation in the members' collective commitment to the proposal. E.g., collective acceptance may result in the joint intention to tidy up a park together. In the we-mode case the three central we-mode criteria will be satisfied for the resulting joint attitude but not in the pro-group I-mode case. As seen in the previous section, the genesis process of a we-mode joint attitude need not involve we-mode activity, but the end result must involve the kind of we-mode thinking and action that satisfies the three we-mode criteria—in general, a conceptualization of the situation in group terms. Notice that the present setup as such does not require we-mode proposals and that aggregation problems apply also to we-mode proposals, although the use of aggregative methods may not be as popular within we-mode groups as within I-mode ones.

Suppose now that several members or participants present proposals. In this case it may matter in which order the options are presented—e.g., if the first one is collectively ga-accepted by the members, it will be the group's view. But a group need not accept this rule but can allow that all proposals be taken into account.[17] Then the result may be that several options are collectively ga-accepted by the members for the group. In such a case, picking out randomly one option as the group's attitude might sometimes be considered, but in general a principled choice may be made on the members' preference ordering of the available alternatives. When the decision-making process continues, each member can be asked in the next round to select one of the collectively ga-accepted options as satisfactory (or perhaps the best) for the group. Then the relevant aggregation criterion can be used again to select the group attitude from among the options selected as satisfactory (or, alternatively, best) by the members. If a majority candidate is found, no further rounds are needed. If the second round does not give a group attitude, a further round is needed in which more (and, perhaps totally new) preference-based information from the members is used as an enriched information basis. And so on and so forth—the dynamic process may have to continue if no result is found. The earlier information (premises, input data) may in some cases have to be modified. One possibility then is to return to group discussion of the initial premises and to modify the members' first-order judgments or preferences over them.[18]

As we have in effect seen, the notion of going along with an alternative X (given that achieving a group attitude requires it) does not entail more in the sense of rational preferring than that accepting X is to be preferred to accepting not-X—but a total preference ordering of proposals is not required. One may be prepared to go along with X or with an alternative Y without being able to compare X and Y with each other.

Consider an example making concrete some central aspects of the ga-approach and focusing on a two-person group (consisting of you and me). The proposals are p_1, p_2, p_3, and p_4. My ga-set contains only p_1, while yours contains p_1 and p_2. So p_1 gets selected as the group's view. If, however, your ga-set did not contain p_1 but something else, there would be no common ground and no group attitude would come about in the first round. But, compatibly with what was earlier said about the dynamic nature of the ga-approach, we can enter a bargaining process and even change the set of original proposals so that we can suitably compromise on something. E.g., we might modify p_2 to p_2^* or simply add p_2^* as an additional profile such that I could include p_2^* in my ga-set. Then p_2^* would be the group's view or preference, provided that p_2^* is in your ga-set, too. Sometimes, though, the present method could be applied sequentially starting with one proposal that might have been chosen by a leader or that perhaps is randomly chosen. Then it may happen that that proposal is one that all members can go along with. Thus this proposal will yield a group attitude, and no further aggregation is needed. In other cases—when no proposal is in every member's ga-set—the situation remains open, but the proposed general dynamic method can then be applied. Or, alternatively, e.g., majority voting may be used.

Accepted proposals may not correspond well to each member's private attitudes concerned with what is preferable to a person in regard to her private well-being.

Furthermore, the we-mode proposal that gets accepted may be only some members' proposal for a group attitude. All that is required is that the accepted proposal belongs to a well-informed and sufficiently mature member's ga-set. The resulting group attitude may be suboptimal for the group because it is not based on all the information that could have been available in the situation. We recall from chapters 2 and 4 that in democratic groups, collective attitudes, at least voluntary ones, are generated by the members' or their internally authorized representatives' attitudes. Thus, basically the members' we-mode or pro-group I-mode attitudes determine the group's attitudes. Conversely, existing group attitudes on conceptual grounds conceptually determine individual members' we-mode attitudes.

I have not here proposed a foolproof method of choice that would always work. If the ga-set method does not lead to a solution, some of the standard formal aggregation methods used in the literature may be considered.[19] I will below briefly comment on recent research on majority voting, which is perhaps the most commonly used aggregation method.

5. GROUP AGENTS AND AGGREGATIVE ATTITUDES

The approach to group agency by List and Pettit in their recent book (2011) was already commented on chapter 2. Here I will consider some of their technical notions like supervenience and the aggregative construction of a group agent's attitudes.

The formal results of their book are mostly based on rational choice theory and emphasize the role of aggregation in the formation of binary-valued rational group attitudes. It is thus required by these authors, in accordance with methodological individualism, that the group's attitudes be fixed in some way by a suitable mathematical function in terms of the individual members' attitudes. The right kind of relation of determination (a general description of such a function) according to the book is the following kind of (holistic) supervenience:

Holistic supervenience: The set of group attitudes across propositions is determined by the individual sets of attitudes across these propositions.

List and Pettit argue that for their account of group agency to be vindicated, i.e., for group agency to be both real and nontrivial relative to their three proposed criteria concerning motivation, representation, and relevant action capacity (recall chapter 2), the supervenience relation must satisfy the following rationality criterion:[20]

> *Robust group rationality*: The supervenience relation determines consistent and complete group attitudes on the relevant propositions for any possible profile of consistent and complete member attitudes on these propositions.

Of the notions of supervenience considered by the authors only holistic supervenience is argued to be consistent with robust group rationality, whereas other supervenience relations (e.g., majoritarian or other kinds of proposition-wise supervenience) may lead to failures of rationality. As to my own account, recall the discussion of supervenience in chapter 3, where I argue that to be informative, supervenience should be of the "same-content" kind and be informative in this content-preserving sense. However, the same-content kind of supervenience does not hold between we-mode and I-mode properties, as shown in chapter 3. Here I agree with List and Pettit and can accept their notion of holistic supervenience to relate we-mode attitudes to I-mode ones with the drawback that holistic supervenience is a rather uninformative notion (although it serves as medicine against "free-floating group minds").

In this connection it is appropriate to mention an argument for a kind of group "autonomy" that List and Pettit present in the context of the discursive dilemma.[21] They show that concerning a combined proposition p&q, the group's attitude concerning it may be independent of the individuals' attitudes toward p&q. The group attitude concerning p&q is autonomous relative to the individual attitudes in that those attitudes are both insufficient and unnecessary for determining the group attitude. The group is here taken to decide autonomously whether to use the conclusion-based or the premise-based decision method. Still, the point against this autonomy argument can be made that it is nevertheless the members (or, anyhow, some individuals) who (collectively) decide about the group's decision procedure.

List and Pettit discuss some central conditions that recent choice-theoretic discussion has employed as constraints on rational collective decision making based on the aggregation of individual attitudes. These conditions originated from Arrow's famous investigations. There are the following four well-known general conditions for the aggregation of group attitudes that according to them cannot be simultaneously satisfied:[22]

> *Universal Domain*: The aggregation function admits as input any possible profile of individual attitudes towards the propositions on the agenda, assuming that individual attitudes are consistent and complete.
> *Collective Rationality*: The aggregation function produces as output consistent and complete group attitudes towards the propositions on the agenda.
> *Anonymity*: All individuals' attitudes are given equal weight in determining the group's attitudes. Formally, the aggregation function is invariant under permutations of any given profile of individual attitudes.
> *Systematicity*: The group's attitude on each proposition depends only on the individuals' attitudes towards it, not on their attitudes towards other propositions, and the same pattern of dependence holds for all propositions.

These conditions can be applied both to (binary-valued) attitudes with the mind-to-world direction of fit (e.g., views, beliefs, judgments) and to attitudes with the world-to-mind direction of fit (e.g., goals, preferences). List and Pettit prove the following result:

> *Theorem*: There exists no aggregation function satisfying universal domain, collective rationality, anonymity, and systematicity.[23]

So here we have the result that the aforementioned initially plausible four conditions cannot be satisfied simultaneously—while any three of them can. (It can be noted that a generalization of this theorem entails Arrow's impossibility theorem.). In such a case a group's attitude cannot rationally come about unless something in the situation is changed—e.g., new proposals expressing suitable compromises are brought into play.

To get out of the impossibility result, various strategies have been suggested. Indeed, any one of the four conditions of the impossibility theorem may be relaxed, and some such relaxations remove the impossibility.[24] List and Pettit primarily go for relaxing systematicity. There are also possibility results on majority voting (see below for some references) that involve such relaxations.

To comment on majority voting, I suggest that an "internal" view on the use of voting principles is in general needed: When using the majority principle the members must commit themselves to abide by what it results in. Generally, majority voting can be motivated by the consensus view according to which at least in egalitarian groups the best thing would be that all individuals agree on an option (attitude), which then will be the group's attitude. Majority and supermajority clearly to an extent approximate the consensus view and can get some justification from it. The other idea for justifying the majority view is the obvious one that it, like common aggregation methods, lets every member have his say and thus to enact his individual autonomy. This applies to the I-mode case in its fullest sense, for in that case the individuals function as private persons in a group context.[25] In the we-mode case the individuals are already constrained by the assumption that they function in the context of an organized group with an ethos to which at least most of them are collectively committed. The group attitude here is determined by the individuals, but the individuals must already function on the basis of the full we-perspective and be precommitted to the attitude that the group chooses on the basis of its members' proposals.

Majority voting is often used in large groups because the members cannot conduct face-to-face group discussion. As has often been pointed out in the literature, this procedure is beset by logical problems. For one thing, it does not satisfy the above four conditions for democratic group attitude formation, and it cannot as such solve the problem posed by cyclical preferences. In addition, the plain ga-approach faces analogous problems, although it fares better than approaches that require full individual preference rankings to be exhibited. Especially in hierarchical groups, where the leader(s) present the proposals to be voted on, it is practical if only one proposal at a time is voted on: the members either go along (e.g., in the sense of not explicitly objecting) or not, and going along immediately yields a group attitude in this case. List and Pettit also consider problems with majority voting and suggest some possible ways out:[26] A group "must either disallow certain profiles of individual attitudes, or permit less than fully rational group attitudes, or make one member dictator, or treat different propositions differently in determining the group's attitudes". List and Pettit regard the last two solutions as promising and take the last one to be the most attractive. As to the last category, the authors mention regular and distributed premise-based procedures and sequential priority procedures as examples of methods that satisfy both holistic supervenience and robust group rationality.

It may be pointed out here that there are interesting new possibility results for majority voting in fully general circumstances.[27] Let us also remember that there are methods like group discussion for achieving consensus and group decision. It seems that such methods typically need not be beset by inconsistencies and irrationality partly because of the feedback mechanisms often involved.

A general point on the research on aggregative group attitude formation is that it seems to be best suited for I-mode groups, as the strong we-mode criteria may well fail to be empirically satisfied, e.g., in folk referendums (but I do not claim that individualistic accounts of group attitude formation need to be aggregative in nature). Furthermore, aggregative group attitude formation need not be collective-intentionally *for* (the use of) the group (although some members may well vote for the group in the we-mode or in the pro-group I-mode), as individualistic conflicting interests may have a decisive influence how votes are cast. Finally, a separate argument is needed to show that the aggregated intentions or other attitudes in the List-Pettit approach indeed can be viewed as a group agent's attitudes. It seems to me that an aggregate of intentions, for instance, need not itself be an intention, and analogously for any attitude.

Last but not least, I wish to remind the reader that while the choice-theoretic literature has concentrated on the logical-mathematical problems involved in attitude aggregation, there are many kinds of contingent psychological and social psychological difficulties in forming group attitudes. In the case of the one man, one vote aggregation that typically is used in national elections and referendums, there are many problems related to the participants' personal or joint capacity to form good decisions for the group. A participant may not be mature enough to form a view of what is best for the group or even what is best for him as an individual. Furthermore, people often do not have the factual information needed to form an adequate opinion, and they may even be outright irrational in the sense of lacking the reasoning abilities that good decision-making requires, or they vote for the wrong alternative, one not even on the agenda (think of the much-discussed recent EU folk referendums in France, the Netherlands, and Ireland concerning the Lisboa treaty).[28] As to the deficiencies in participants' joint capacities, the so-called groupthink phenomena show how rational people can arrive at irrational group decisions. The above remarks basically apply to any group.

6. CONCLUSION

In this chapter I have investigated group acceptance and collective acceptance and have defended the view that group members' agreements, either explicit or implicit, typically underlie and are at least sufficient for the group's acceptance, at least in the case of egalitarian we-mode groups. Indeed, such an agreement trivially amounts to collective acceptance and the group's acceptance. This holds true also for the case of implicit agreements when these agreements are understood broadly in terms of joint intentions and relevant beliefs.

The chapter presented several ways of arriving at group acceptance. Thus the so-called bulletin board view, the ga-acceptance ("going along with" acceptance) model, and the aggregation view of group acceptance were presented and discussed. In that connection the recent account by List and Pettit was discussed and compared with the account of group agency and group attitudes of this book.

APPENDIX: EXPLICIT AND IMPLICIT AGREEMENTS

I will below present a stylized and condensed sketch of how to think of the notion of explicit agreement in an egalitarian we-mode group. Suppose the agreement concerns the members' seeing to it that a state X comes about (no arguments for the clauses of the account will be offered here). The following account gives only a sufficient condition:

> (EXPLAGR) The members of group g have made an *explicit agreement* to see to it jointly that a state X will come about (or be maintained, etc., as the case may be) if
>
> (1) The members have formed a joint intention to see to it that X—with the entailed result that g intends to see to it that X.
> (2) The members have publicly and sincerely jointly (and typically verbally) promised each other to participate in jointly seeing to it that X, where

joint promising entails that they have put themselves under the joint obligation to see to it that X, and (2) entails (1).

(3) Because of (1) and (2), each member has acquired the obligation and we-intention to perform his part of X as his part of their joint seeing to it that X.

(4) The members mutually know that (1)–(3).

In clause (2) of (EXPLAGR) the joint promise can be explicated in part by reference to the participants' interdependent promises to participate in the members joint seeing to it that X, where the promises are grounded in the participants' reason to try to arrive at a group intention concerning what to do, and they have here solved this task by making the agreement (in terms of joint promises) to do X and by accordingly (as (2) entails (1)) forming the joint intention to see to it that X. The joint promise, qua collectively sincere, thus is assumed to entail the joint intention of which the members' we-intentions are part and parcel (recall (WI) of chapter 3). As single-agent promises can be taken to involve the obligation to satisfy the promise, analogously a mutual promise will be seen to involve a joint obligation that entails their single-member obligations to perform their parts (but is not entailed by the conjunction of the latter). A joint obligation in this sense entails collective commitment. Explicit agreements are normative, while implicit ones need not be, as we will see.

Making an explicit agreement presupposes the participants' general understanding of an agreement as entailing their putting themselves under a certain joint obligation on the ground of their need or desire to answer the question "What should we do together and how should we do it"? (or, sometimes, "What should we accept as our group's attitude?"). The bulletin board view in section 3 and the ga-acceptance model in section 4 exemplify this procedure, although they also involve more complex elements—the latter model especially involves an inbuilt iteration procedure.

Next we consider implicit agreement, which complies with standard dictionary explications and which need not be normative:[29]

(IMPLAGR) The members of group g have *implicitly agreed* to see to it jointly that a state X will come about (or be maintained, etc., as the case may be) if

(1) The members have (largely) without spoken or written or other linguistic communication formed the joint intention to see to it jointly that X.

(2) Because of (1), each member has acquired the we-intention (in the sense of (WI) of chapter 3) to participate in the members' joint seeing to it that X by seeing to it that his part of X comes about (or is maintained, etc.).

(3) The members mutually know (or mutually correctly believe) that (1)–(2).

In this account the members need not voluntarily and reflectively control their very formation of the intention—they may in this sense arrive implicitly at it. The members may use gestures to affect an implicit agreement, e.g., by nodding. The content of the agreement maybe explicit, although written or spoken language is not used. Recall David Hume's famous example pointing out that two men who "pull the oars of a boat, do it by agreement or convention, tho' they have never given promises to each other".[30] Here agreement is implicit agreement in approximately the sense I presently mean. Another example: Some people may refrain from commenting on a sad event in their joint history. This kind of example may well satisfy the account (Implagr).[31]

6

Cooperation and Authority

I. INTRODUCTION

We can cooperate to carry a table, build a bridge, form an association, write a joint paper, sing a song, save energy, and we can cooperate with our fellow workers at a factory or other workplace. All these cases involve some persons who act together to achieve the same goal. This is indeed perhaps the most common sense of cooperation.[1]

My account in this chapter is based on the above kind of standard idea, although I will argue that the vernacular is ambivalent between two different senses of cooperation, a weaker and a stronger one. In my account they are explicated respectively as I-mode and we-mode cooperation. In this chapter I will mainly, but not entirely, focus on the strong, we-mode sense that may be regarded as the core sense of cooperation. The kind of group contexts that we-mode cooperation primarily concerns are situations of the following kind: People involved share some common goals, values, beliefs, norms, etc.. Most importantly, they view or "construct" themselves as a social group, capable of group action, in which they think and reason in terms of a nonaggregative "we". For example, "We intend X as a group, so each of us must contribute to X", "We believe that p as a group", "S is our institution".[2]

We-mode cooperation depends on full collective intentionality that involves joint goals and intentions, joint actions, group beliefs and knowledge, and, especially, collective acceptance and construction, as well as group reasons. In virtue of its connection to these, *we-mode activity (viz., acting fully as a group member) is intrinsically cooperative* basically because a we-mode group's action requires cooperation between the members for a satisfactory performance of its actions. In contrast, functioning in the I-mode is at best only contingently cooperative. This accounts in part for the functional superiority and the preferability in many contexts of we-mode activity over I-mode activity (see chapter 7). On conceptual grounds, we-mode cooperation, furthermore, seems to give a better account of hierarchical groups with positional structure than I-mode cooperation, and can account for full-blown actions attributable to a group, in contrast to I-mode cooperation.

Both we-mode and I-mode groups may have either group-internally authorized leaders or externally authorized ones. The central task of this chapter is to investigate cooperation analytically and do it within a framework involving authority, e.g., in the form of leaders directing group members to cooperate. This chapter extends and improves on my earlier account of we-mode cooperation and takes into account non-autonomous we-mode cooperation in the case of externally authorized leaders (e.g. a corporation).

The structure of this chapter is as follows. In section 2, I will give an account of I-mode cooperation, and section 3 accounts for we-mode cooperation that also applies to cases with autonomously or non-autonomously authorized leaders. Both approaches explain at least some kinds of cooperation, and giving a full account of human cooperative enterprises arguably requires appeal to both I-mode and we-mode approaches and also to group activities that can be realized in terms of mixtures of I-mode and we-mode "psychologies". The we-mode is required because much of both cooperative and strategic I-mode activity depends on a common cooperative core, which is basically a we-mode phenomenon. In sections 4 and 5 of this chapter, these two types of cooperation will be applied to account for hierarchical and positional groups, including social organizations. In section 6, I will argue (partly in view of some technical results to be presented in detail in chapter 7) that we-mode cooperation is functionally superior to, and indeed in many contexts preferable to, I-mode cooperation. In the end I will summarize my results.[3]

2. I-MODE COOPERATION

We intuitively think that some social actions are cooperatively performed while some others are not. For instance, carrying a table jointly and singing a duet together seem to be unproblematic paradigm cases of cooperation, whereas quarreling is basically noncooperative. What about playing a game of tennis? Is walking in a crowded street cooperative if the people intend to avoid bumping into each other? A philosopher of cooperation needs to know in more detail what is involved in examples such as these. We may try to imagine weak cases of cooperation to see what kinds of elements are or must be involved in cooperation and how weak cooperation can be. In this section, I will provide an account of a relatively weak form of cooperation called I-mode cooperation, which nevertheless satisfies a set of necessary conditions, which must be satisfied by any activity that is to count as minimally cooperative.[4]

On the most basic level, I-mode cooperation (in the two-person case) involves that they both adjust their means-actions and goals to the other participant's actions and (possibly also) goals, so as to further both the other's goal satisfaction and one's own goal satisfaction. Thus, for instance, we may cooperate in the I-mode so that my goal of going to Paris to take care of my business is connected to your goal of going to Rome to take care of your business by my adding to my antecedent goal the promotion of your business while in Paris, and analogously for you. Even if there is no behavioral dependence between our actions, they still are teleologically connected, and hence indirectly dependent on the same goals—your means-action will further the satisfaction of my goal, and vice versa. (Note that the above kind of cooperation could alternatively be performed in the we-mode.)

Cooperation is basically symmetric and other-regarding activity—you cannot cooperate with an unwilling partner, although you may help her in other ways.[5] But the benefits of cooperation frequently derive from the fact that the partners are in a nonsymmetric position with regard to some means-action alternatives relative to one another's goals—the partners may need help from each other to satisfy their goals. This allows each agent to draw benefits from cooperation that could not be gained by solitary activity. Hence there is at least a prima facie, situation-dependent prescription to cooperate and to be cooperative.

Indeed, I will argue in the next section that the we-mode case involves an intrinsic disposition to cooperate.[6] But the relatively weaker forms of cooperation that are at issue in this section do not involve such a disposition. In contrast to the we-mode case., cooperation in the I-mode is always contingent, and whether to cooperate or not is based on the situational states and dispositions of the agents who are involved. This makes I-mode cooperation more fragile and in some cases less functional than we-mode cooperation, as will be argued at the end of this chapter and in the next chapter.

Here is my proposal for simple egalitarian (viz., "same-status") I-mode cooperation, the analysans of which entails other-regarding (and in a group context, pro-group) I-mode action:

(CIM) A_1 and A_2 *(intentionally) cooperate in the I-mode* to achieve their goals G_1 and G_2 if and only if

1 A_1 and A_2 have respective goals G_1 and G_2 as their intended private goals;
2 they willingly perform interdependent means-actions x_1 and x_2 believed by them to be conducive (at least indirectly, via the other's action) to their

respective goals, G_1 and G_2, so that each adjusts her acting and goal to the other's action and goal with the purported result that the other's achievement of her goal is or may be furthered, and that, by the other's analogous acting, also the achievement of her own goal is or may be furthered;

3 A_1 and A_2 mutually believe that (1) and (2);

4 (2) in part because of (3).

Clause (1) specifies that the agents are indeed functioning in the I-mode. When they are functioning in an I-mode group, their goals, which might be the same, may be due to an either internally or externally authorized leader whose order they are assumed to be conforming to here. But in cases where the participants do not act for their group in the pro-group I-mode sense, each participant herself has the full authority to decide on her goals and actions (unless special agreements between the participants are made), and this is what she does in light of her awareness of the others' goals and expected behavior as well as relevant information pertaining to the environment. The agent here takes account of the others as agents functioning in the social world, whose actions have a possible effect on her environment and her goal satisfaction, but she need not think in terms of a strong "we", in the sense of a social unit irreducible to its parts and having collective goals in a strong sense.

Clause (2) specifies the nature of interdependencies that must be involved for a given sequence of actions to count as cooperative. Often these interdependencies require active participation from each agent on the other's behalf, but this is not always the case (when, e.g., non-interference as intentional omission of positive action might count as cooperation). The requirement of the adjustment of means-actions and goals is context dependent, as I have said, and in some cases even null adjustments seem acceptable—it is the intentional preparedness for adjustment that counts most.[7]

Cooperation in the present sense involves that the agents are disposed willingly to incur extra costs that the satisfaction of their own goals may not strictly require (this being rational as long as the costs of performing them are less than the gross gains accruing from the performance). Note also that cooperation requires that the actions x_1 and x_2 be performed intentionally, as nonintentionally and haphazardly doing something that will or might also further the satisfaction of the other's goal hardly counts as cooperation, even if it is mutual. But the above account of cooperation does not require that the actions be collectively intentional even in the I-mode sense.[8] Nor is it required that the cooperation be intended qua cooperation.[9] However, I will later present a characterization of strong, we-mode cooperation that occurs only in the context of group activity (even when there is a single individual who is actually performing in a behavioral sense, while the other group members are standing by in reserve). Accordingly, I-mode cooperation is only contingently connected to a shared goal, whereas we-mode cooperation depends on strong sharedness. We may apply the above account of I-mode cooperation to the (contingently) shared case by writing out the goals G_1 and G_2 as one identical goal, namely the shared goal G (= $G_1 = G_2$).[10] It is enough here that only types of goals are identical though tokens differ, in partial contrast to the we-mode case, where typically same joint token is required. Contributing to a charity foundation gives examples of both kinds of goal sharing. Note that cooperation in the present sense can be present even if the goals G_1 and G_2 are not achieved.

As to clauses (3) and (4), see section 3 below.

According to the above account, the agents perform the token actions x_1 and x_2 when they cooperate in the I-mode. We may now regard their set $\{x_1, x_2\}$, or in the n-person case $\{x_1,\ldots,x_n\}$, as an individually intentional cooperative many-person action or, using our technical terminology, as an intentional cooperative n-person action in the I-mode. Here we understand collective action in a weakly aggregative sense, which does not necessarily entail that the agents had a shared (distant) goal to which they intended to contribute. As to the variety of natural and institutional interdependencies that might be involved between the agents' actions in relation to (CIM), I will be brief here.[11] The goals G_1 and G_2 may be just the proximate goals conceptually inherent in intentional actions, namely, the "result" events of x_1 and x_2, respectively. Action dependence might also be due to antecedent goal dependence.

If the agents are truly cooperating in a case where G_1 and G_2 are the same, then the means-actions cannot rationally conflict, and A_1's action must contribute to A_2's goal, and vice versa. A case in point is two drivers coming from opposite directions and getting out of their cars to remove a fallen tree from the road; their shared goal is G (= $G_1 = G_2$), representing the state that the tree is removed from the road. Here we have a case of natural dependence such that the goals are connected to each other in a contingent, nonconstitutive way. We may also have conceptual or institutional dependence between the goals, as will be shown in the next section in the case of we-mode cooperation. For example, we cannot engage in a financial transaction without sharing the goal of making an exchange, although we may have a layer of strategic I-mode goals on top of this institutional goal (e.g., I may intend to mislead you about the value of the goods that we are exchanging). When performing one's part, the cooperative collective action must here be rational from the agent's private point of view, though possibly only in light of the results that are expected from the other's analogous performance of her part.

When people act together in the I-mode (in the sense of (CIM)), they do not act as a group in a strong sense, nor do they satisfy the constitutive we-mode criteria of group reasons, collective commitment, and the collectivity condition. In the

I-mode case, they act collectively only in an aggregative sense that possibly involves interdependent or shared means-actions and goals. Although the agents do not act as a group in the strong sense here, they may still function cooperatively as private agents in a group context. We arrive at such a case, which amounts to rudimentary *pro-group I-mode cooperation*, by assuming that G (= G_1 = G_2) in conditions of mutual belief and that this goal forms the ethos of a simple I-mode group that the participants here form. In more interesting cases, there is a preexisting group that the goals G_1 and G_2 serve (e.g., the ethos could be the goal of cleaning a yard, and A_i's goal would be to do what he reasonably can to help the goal being achieved). The end result of successful cooperation would be the achievement of the privately shared goal. As I have said, (CIM) takes into account leaders and hence the use of power. There does not seem to be much difference between I-mode and we-mode cooperation in this respect, and thus it seems to suffice to deal with authority and power more fully only in the we-mode case

3 WE-MODE COOPERATION

3.1.

Cooperation in its full sense must on conceptual grounds be intentional or at least involve intentional means-actions. Not all cooperation accordingly needs to be collectively intentional, as we have seen in the previous section on I-mode cooperation. On the other hand, any full-blown joint action—such as carrying a table or singing a song together—is intrinsically cooperative: the participants function intentionally together to achieve their jointly intended common goal. The joint action here is mainly generated by the joint intention (goal). The joint action need not involve behavioral interaction between the participants (think, e.g., of workers in a large business corporation working in different parts of the world).

As I have said, the we-mode can be regarded as intrinsically cooperative. Why? A central argument for this is that we-mode action is action as a group member and as an intrinsic part of the participant's salient) group's action. Any group action must in general be based on or involve at least a sufficient amount of intragroup cooperation between the members. Such intragroup or intermember cooperation is cooperation in the we-mode (viz., as a full-blown member of a group agent, i.e., a group properly organized for action). Thus cooperation in the we-mode is intrinsically cooperative. The "intrinsicness" here can be conceptual or normative. In this book I take the view that it is (constitutively) normative—based on the group's constitutive norms, especially the constitutive membership norm that required participation in the members' satisfaction of the group ethos. We can thus also say that group membership understood in this normative, ethos promotion sense is the central reason that makes all we-mode cooperation normatively intrinsic. This in-built cooperativeness largely accounts for the functional superiority of the we-mode over the I-mode, as will be argued in chapter 7. My view does not entail that one ceases to act in the we-mode if one occasionally fails to cooperate. Yet one is subject to criticism unless one has acceptable excuses for not being cooperative and participating in the group's joint activities.

As we have seen, we-mode thinking, reasoning, and acting are concerned with thinking and acting as a group member. In the we-mode case, an agent is supposed to identify with the group (or rather with being a group member) and to act as a full-fledged and well-informed member of the group, guided by its goals and norms. To think (believe, want, intend, or feel) and act in the we-mode is to see one's activities essentially as part of what the group is doing. Accordingly, an agent who fully functions in the we-mode is on this ground disposed to cooperate with the others—obeying the group-normative requirement concerning cooperativeness. This is the case even when she does not have full awareness of what the ethos (or other previously collectively accepted group goals) may require of her in the circumstances at hand. In contrast, I-mode cooperation is always more context-sensitive and situation-dependent because of being based on specific situational agreements concerning what each will have to do and because, furthermore, an I-moder must take his own efforts (costs) into account no matter how group-oriented he is.[12] In the (pro-group) I-mode case, the members acting as autonomous agents strive to achieve both their own goals and the group's goals (in some combination—recall chapter 3). Accordingly, I-mode cooperation tends to break down more easily and is in some cases less functional and less stable than we-mode cooperation (see we-mode argument (4) in section 6 for more on this). In contrast, in the we-mode case conflicting private interests ideally are laid aside, and in group contexts only the group's interests should matter for an individual. A we-mode group is organized and capable of action as a group as expressed in part by the members' disposition to cooperate. Basically, the strong disposition to cooperate within the group follows from the full-blown and wholehearted acceptance of group membership and the ensuing adoption of the group's point of view and thus acceptance of its ethos. The ethos includes collectively binding contents for the group members and serves to generate joint action between the members. Collective acceptance of the ethos as true or right for the members makes for the correctness of statements of the following kind: "We intend to achieve X", "We believe X", and so forth, which apply to the group members as a unit, viz., as the group that they conceptually and functionally reify and entify by the collective stand they take toward it.

As argued in chapters 2 and 4, group reason is the central underlying factor that accounts for we-mode cooperation on the member level. Group reasons are typically given by the collectively accepted ethos, by other collectively accepted group states (goals, intentions, etc.), or by leaders' directives and orders. Such reasons have authority over the members, and they ought to comply as members. As in chapter 5, collective acceptance is to be understood in the we-mode sense and generally as non-aggregative. It amounts to the members' becoming and being collectively committed as a group to the accepted content in the right way, that is, with the right direction of fit. The central element here actually is the group's acceptance, which on the member level in egalitarian groups basically amounts to the members' collective acceptance.

A rational group ought to try to satisfy its goals analogously with the case of an individual agent. Members of the group are thus bound by their membership to this kind of action as a group member and thus to actions for group reasons, and this makes a we-mode group intrinsically cooperative concerning member-level activities. *Group reasons* in the we-mode sense are supposed to generate members' cooperation partly because the collectivity condition applies to them. The members share group reasons in a sense satisfying the collectivity condition (or actually a normative version of it): Roughly, at a sufficiently general level of description that ignores, e.g., task division in the group, a member qua member can have an ethos-based or other authoritative group reason only if the others have it or at least ought to accept it as their motivating reason. The members are collectively committed to the content in question (which makes the group reason a motivating one), and this accounts for the rational functionality of we-mode cooperation (as will be argued below and in chapter 7). Collective commitment involves interpersonal group-social obligations between the members, and this makes it more stable than individual aggregative commitment, where such mutual bonds are missing (in the absence of further assumptions). Thus we here have the satisfaction of the three distinctive criteria or markers of the we-mode concerning the group members activities as group members (including mental states).

3.2.

To proceed to a more specific discussion of we-mode cooperation, my new account of (two-person) we-mode cooperation incorporates power considerations in the case of either internally or, which is new, externally authorized operatives or leaders:[13]

(CWM) A_1 and A_2 *intentionally cooperate with each other* (in the we-mode sense of cooperation) in order to bring about goal G if and only if

1 A_1 and A_2 intend jointly, as a group, to achieve G, a goal that can be jointly satisfied by A_1's and A_2's acting jointly as a group, and hence for the group, in congruity with the ethos of the group and for a group-authoritative reason;

2 A_1 and A_2 act purporting to achieve G jointly in accordance with and partly because of acting on this joint intention of theirs to achieve G together but in compliance with the appropriate authoritative reasons of clause (1);
3 A_1 and A_2 rationally mutually believe that (1), (2);
4 The truth of (1) and (2) is in part sustained by (3).

In clause (1) the phrase "as a group" signifies the we-mode, and hence the account (CWM) presupposes the we-mode and its intrinsic cooperativeness. The we-mode group of participants need not be formed and exist prior to the cooperative activity in question. (CWM) makes joint action and cooperative joint action equivalent in the we-mode case and, given a sufficiently precise account of joint action, shows this matter.[14]

The group reason in clause (1) can be (a) an informally formed authoritative group reason related to G, (b) a group reason based on the directive by an (internally or externally) authorized leader, or (c) a group reason based on a collectively accepted ethos, social norm, or rule directing the members to accept G as a group goal.[15] Clause (1) accepts cooperation both with and without a leader. In the paradigmatic, democratic we-mode case the leader is *internally* authorized, but as seen in chapter 2, *externally* authorized leaders can also be involved in cooperative contexts in the we-mode case. In the latter case we speak of cooperation in the non-autonomous we-mode, because in principle the leader can, in a stronger sense than in the case of internal authorization, use power to make the participants act against their earlier plans and ideas. However, as long as they can be taken to accept (at least to comply or go along with) the leader's orders, non-autonomous we-mode cooperation can take place. Of course, if an externally authorized leader constantly intervenes in the intermember cooperation, it will not achieve much if the members do not so comply. If the external authority's intervention is severe, the cooperativeness of the joint action will strongly diminish. (See our later discussion.)

Recall that any we-mode group (group agent) is assumed to have an ethos, which is basically just the constitutive "jointness" element shared by the members (e.g., a joint goal). In general, we are dealing with full-blown cases of joint action here, and it is uncontroversial that it must be based on a prior joint intention or a joint-intention-in-action.[16] I will not here specifically argue for the view that joint action requires joint intention. It is commonly accepted in the literature, and I have argued for it in my earlier work.[17] The notions of joint intention and joint action are here understood as we-mode notions in the sense informally explicated above.[18] In accordance with the irreducibility argument of chapter 3, (CWM) is irreducible to (CIM). As to the role of leaders, it will be explicated in more detail in the next section.

Given that the we-mode is intrinsically cooperative, the agents need not reflect on and adjust their private goals and performances, as they are already predisposed to perform as the group requires of them. Ideally, in we-mode cooperation incompatible private goals are completely set aside, and we-mode goals take their place. In this book I typically handle this matter by speaking of constitutive norms in the we-mode that serve to normatively exclude private goals. This contrasts with the I-mode case, where a conflict between private goals and the group's goals may occur—depending, though, on how the I-mode group's goals have been formed. But even in the we-mode case there may be conflict if what the group requires is unreasonable and strongly conflicts with the person's private interests, or contrasts with, e.g. what morality requires. In such cases we may be dealing with a "switch" from the we-mode to the I-mode, a switch to another group's ways of thinking and acting, or (often a weak-willed) lapse to the I-mode.

Clause (3) expresses a standard epistemic requirement: it is required of each rational member of the group that she believe that the other participants will indeed perform their parts of the cooperative joint action, and that she believe that the other participants have beliefs with the same kind of content (with the relevant kinds of loop beliefs included, or at least negative beliefs to the effect that she is not to have the belief that the others believe that she will not perform her part). The participants cannot realize their joint intention without the others' relevant contributions, and hence the intention contents in (1) are based on the (presuppositional) beliefs that the others will participate.[19] Mere hope is not in general sufficient (although admittedly in some cases one might rationally act on a hope, for example, when the matter is important and there is no other reasonable choice). Clause (4) says that the beliefs in (3) cannot be idle but function as a partial social reason for the agents' holding their joint intention.

As to the scope of (CWM), my claim is that it covers the fullest kind of cooperation. As is easily seen, it correctly includes standard tokens of full joint action such as cleaning the yard together or jointly carrying a table. But in addition to such uncontroversial cooperative cases, (CWM) is able to elucidate an important aspect of a range of activities where some conflict and competition is laid on top of a common cooperative core. We recall the cases of joint action and cooperation with only a joint action bottom, which is made up of some collectively accepted rules analogous to the constitutive rules of tennis or other similar games. The constitutive rules must be satisfied in all game situations.

(CWM) excludes weak cases of cooperation, which might nevertheless satisfy (CIM). Consider the following kind of case: people intentionally refrain from polluting the air by greenhouse gases with the hope that this may eventually prevent the climate from getting warmer. However, even if they believed that many other agents also similarly refrain from polluting and also believed that this collective activity may result in a reduction of global warming, all this need not yield cooperation in our sense (CWM). This is because the participants might not satisfy clause (1), as they might only have a shared I-mode goal here; and, of course, then clauses (3) and (4) need not be satisfied. All that we are sure to have here are contingent, less than fully intentionally connected individual actions contributing to the same goal. The agents need not here be collectively committed to the end, and they could interrupt their participatory activities without much criticism from the others.[20] The we-mode account covers cooperation independently of the size of the group—in principle the group members need not be counted and considered individually.[21] In the case of small groups, we are often dealing with unorganized, egalitarian collectives built around more or less spontaneous or task-relative cooperation, but even small groups may be organized and temporally persisting (think of a scientific committee consisting of specialists). With large groups, a higher degree of organization and temporal continuity is typically required, although we may also have spontaneous cooperation on a large basis. Such spontaneous large-scale cooperation may be either egalitarian or hierarchical, as witnessed by events such as the "masses" crowding the streets in demand for political reform, and local leaders and agitators arising here and there among the crowd. Both history and contemporary political climate lay witness to such fusion-based mass movements, where a strong we-feeling is involved. This kind of cooperation may evolve into more persisting cooperation, e.g., if a new political party is founded by the demonstrators, or by some subgroup within them. Yet there is no in-principle distinction between small and large groups in terms of the nature and type of cooperation.[22]

As to a group's capacity to act—recalling that such action generally involves intragroup cooperation—the nature and type of mental states and commitments involved may vary. Either we-mode and I-mode mental states or both may be at play. In the next section some arguments will be presented purporting to show that the we-mode gives a more natural and plausible account of cooperation in some large-scale groups, at least in situations involving authority relations and positional groups. Let me still note that (CWM) also covers cases where agents A_1 and A_2 are group agents given that intentional states can be attributed to a group (as they can in the case of we-mode group agents in my approach). Not even the wording of (CWM) needs to be changed for this application. An example is provided by some or all nation members of the EU cooperating with each other, for example, to help poor people somewhere, where, say, the second-order groups EU and NATO cooperate with each other, primarily through the authorized leaders of these second-order groups. However, I will not here discuss intergroup cooperation in detail.

3.3.

To end this section we consider situations that are cooperative in that they call for cooperation either on physical or normative grounds or because the people involved view them as suited for cooperation. In these cases cooperative situations are partly collectively constructed by us as the potential participants in cooperation. To use technical jargon, cooperative situations can be formed by "framing".

Let me say this to defend my idea: People can understand cooperation and other phenomena in the social world either in group terms (as the we-mode approach recommends) or individualistically, and this can take place by direct conceptualization of real phenomena in those alternative ways. When people use the group approach, they can (implicitly or explicitly) view themselves as forming a group agent. Such a group agent in general forms (adopts) attitudes toward the world through its members' or leaders' collective acceptance.

Collective acceptance can also help to create cooperative situations: the group members (say, the members of a linguistic community) can view (accept, construct) activities as cooperative. Let us assume that we are dealing with actions for which there are external criteria for whether or not they have been performed. Some of the group members may now collectively intend to see to it as a group that such a criterial event or state comes about, e.g., a table is carried upstairs by them or some others, a house is painted or is being painted, or a revolution has taken place through their efforts. In general terms, the group sees to it that a certain fact will obtain in the world. When the fact concerns collective activities, e.g., the painting of a house, the members form the joint intention to see to it (as a group) that the house is painted by them (or their delegates). This action as a group necessarily involves cooperation between the members, even if, e.g., a particular member will be the only person performing the actual painting.

My central point here is that in the paradigmatic we-mode cases the group members, by their collective thinking and acceptance in thought and action, can make a situation cooperative from a group's perspective. E.g., house painting will necessarily be cooperative if collectively accepted as the group's task and one that might be (directly or indirectly) performed by the members.[23] The group might hire people to perform the actual painting, and here the required cooperative element is merely the members' collectively seeing to it as a group that the house will be painted. Another case: Tandem bikes are obviously meant to be operated cooperatively, but there is no conceptual necessity involved here, although, so to speak, reality has been collectively (and artifactually) changed to fit the idea of cooperation and made the situation factually impossible for competitive cycling.[24]

As my approach contrasts with Michael Bratman's well-known theory of shared cooperative activity, let me here just make a couple of points.[25] In his account the basic cooperative intention has the form "I-intend that we perform joint action X", where X instantiates an individually shared goal G (recall (CIM)). His account does not make use of the constitutive feature of collective acceptance nor the other central elements of the we-mode framework. Accordingly, he deals with a weaker notion of cooperation than my notion of we-mode cooperation. His account seems to deal rather with "pro-group I-mode" cooperation and would seem to be a special case of my (CIM) account. To avoid the circularity involved in explicating cooperation by cooperatively loaded action types, Bratman makes a distinction between "cooperatively neutral" and "cooperatively loaded" action types. A cooperatively loaded act is one that entails cooperativeness, but a cooperatively neutral type does not, although some of its tokens may be cooperative. An example of the latter is given by Bratman: "There is, for example, a clear sense in which we can go to New York together or paint the house together without our activity being cooperative".[26] This may be right given a sufficiently weak notion of joint action. Bratman says the following in the context of trying to solve a potential circularity problem with his shared cooperative activity (SCA): "we will run into problems of circularity if we appeal to intentions that *we act together cooperatively*". Therefore he requires that the collective act types in his account be *cooperatively neutral* and not *cooperatively loaded*. His basic account of SCA goes as follows:[27]

> For cooperatively neutral J, our J-ing is SCA [shared cooperative activity] if and only if
>
> (A) we J.
> (B) we have the attitudes specified in clauses (1) and (2) [on p. 338 of Bratman's paper].[28]
> (C) (B) leads to (A) by way of mutual responsiveness (in the pursuit of our J-ing) of intention and action.

I find it odd that this account does not deal with such cooperative act types as consensual agreement making, cooperation, and discussion when they are understood in their full sense and thus as necessarily cooperatively loaded ("Let's cooperate to do X" entails that one cannot properly accept this and fail to cooperate). What kind of account we get or could get for cooperative act types from the Bratmanian account seems to be an open problem. Would he after all accept that J in the above account could be instantiated also by a cooperative act type—creating circularity?

Within the we-mode theory circularity is not an insuperable problem: In cooperation the participants basically are required to see to it jointly that some state comes about (or is maintained or prevented). This jointness is necessarily cooperative because of the intrinsic and irreducible cooperativeness of we-mode activities and states (recall my earlier account of such "intrinsicness"). The cooperativeness can be relatively small as, e.g., in an agreed-upon fight, but it still is there. The we-mode framework is learned by people early in life, and they get along with partly circular concepts as long as they connect to a rich framework and as long as there are clear-cut naturalistic events or states in what they denote. No conceptual reduction of cooperation thus seems needed as long as relevant action concepts are understood and used successfully in actual practice, which seems largely a true proviso. As emphasized, people can in principle decide in which circumstances they will cooperate (e.g., see to it jointly that a physical state comes about—say, that a blocking log is removed). This kind of collectively created cooperative situation may be largely independent of the nonintentional features of the situation in question and also independent of any "given" classification of act types into cooperative and cooperatively neutral.

4. GROUP ACTION AND AUTHORITY

4.1.

Under what conditions can a group act as a group? Can groups with externally authorized leaders act, or are only internally governed cases feasible? These are central questions to be answered in this section. An answer to them is needed for the following section discussing and illustrating social organizations and cooperation within them. The theory of this book needs an account of a group agent's action and its capability to act, in view of the centrality of group agents in the theory.

Roughly, an informal group acts as a unit if its members act with a joint intention and with the right understanding of what they are up to. In this section I will concentrate on groups in which decision making and acting are based on authorization of some members to carry out one or more of these tasks. Such groups may be regarded as institutionalized. The authorization can be internal or external. In the case of *internally* authorized operatives and leaders for a group, the authority they bear is given by the members, e.g., through their collective acceptance using one of the methods considered in chapter 5. The authorization concerns group-central matters and the authoritative powers are over the group members qua members. The case of *externally* authorized leaders is similar, but its source is group-external, e.g., based on another group's dominance. The externally authorized leaders might have the authority to use power—even in a coercive sense that harms the members. Leaders (in both internally and externally authorized cases) can give new directives and goals to the group members, and they typically also have the power to see to it that those goals are appropriately achieved by suitable means-activities. This may require that they impose sanctions and give various kinds of incentives to the members. They may also have to correct the members' part performances and perhaps ask somebody else to step in and help.

The members must obey their internally authorized leaders on pain of contradicting themselves relative to their earlier expressed will. Some coercion-resembling activity may be present here, and the participants may not be allowed to help each other extensively if that happens at the expense of the quality of the total performance (leader-directed cooperation). Even when the power use is overtly indistinguishable from domination and coercion in a proper sense, the leaders' activity is legitimate within the group as long as they act within the powers conferred upon them by the members. In the case of externally authorized leaders (e.g., in a hierarchical system of groups by authorities higher up in the hierarchy), coercion can be stronger. But even here it must be assumed that the participants in cooperation at least go along or comply with the leaders' directions and orders, and in this weak sense regard them as viable for the participants of cooperation to form the joint intention to act cooperatively.

It is typical that organized groups such as corporations involve hierarchical levels. Typically there is some functional basis for the division of authority within the group: the task that the group is performing may be too complex without hierarchical organization, or the members may simply appoint somebody to be in charge in virtue of her superior capacities. Consider the following simple example to illustrate an organization with a division of tasks: some people are searching for a lost child in a forest. They get organized, and someone who knows the forest well assumes the role of a leader and designs and coordinates the group's activities as well as he can. Similarly, a chamber music ensemble may choose one of the players to be the conductor of the ensemble, or it may accept an externally appointed conductor. The conductor's task here is gently to coordinate the players' activities in a "musical" way (for instance, the choice of tempi and phrasing is central here). Such a leader may solve coordination and bargaining problems between the members that could not be solved by their usual decision procedures.

Authority relations within a group in general give rise to the operative-nonoperative distinction, which may be task-relative and result in several kinds of authorized operative members. For instance, a member (or type of member, a position) may be an operative one for action (e.g., building a bridge) while also being subject to orders from another operative. Operatives for creating plans and goals and for directing members to act accordingly can be considered leaders. The authority system (all the operative-nonoperative distinctions for various tasks) can be hierarchical in a multilayered sense (organizations that involve groups as their elements), but it suffices here to present the main ideas for the two-layered case. The authority system can be codified and might thus consist just of a voting procedure or of the rule to act as in the past, and in such cases no specially authorized persons are needed. In this kind of case the authority may be external to the group but still tolerated and complied with. Note that authority may flow from the rank-and-file members to the leaders and down again, as when a (democratically elected) head of department appoints some subset of the staff to prepare the filling in of a vacancy in the department. In each case, we are dealing with a complex task-right system with authority relations that may be omnifarious.

As we have seen, internally authorized leaders derive their authority from the members, who must at least tacitly go along with what the leaders decide for them. The members give part of their "natural" authority to act to the leaders, who, e.g., have the right and corresponding obligation to adopt attitudes for the entire group. In virtue of this authorization, the group may be said to act when its leaders or leader-directed operatives act (cf. account (IGA) below). The ultimate foundation of group authority in the present sense is the members' collective acceptance and "construction" of the group's realm of authority, and in a derivative sense, of its directives and actions.

Allowing a gross simplification, the difference between groups functioning with internal authorization and those with externally authorized leaders amounts to the following: At one extreme there are democratically elected leaders, and they are to be contrasted with dictators whose power is based on external groups or on their having taken power by brute force inside the group. There are various other intermediate cases, e.g., externally nominated leaders of subgroups within a democratic group or in hierarchical organizations authorization from "above".

The discussion in chapter 2 is obviously relevant to the present topic of authority and authorization and also to internal autonomy (i.e., within the group autonomy) and group-external autonomy of a group's activities. We recall that a *paradigmatic* we-mode group (one capable of democratically controlling its activities) is ideally an internally and externally autonomous group that can determine its own ethos and can in principle satisfy it.

To give some justification for the group autonomy idea in the we-mode case with internal authorization, the conceptual starting point here is that the group functions as one agent and, e.g., accepts values and views for the group. Corresponding to the group autonomy desideratum on the member level we have free (thus noncoerced) and autonomous (not dependent on external authority) collective acceptance by the members. When collective acceptance has as its purpose and content the creation of an authorized leader (who could be a group member or an external, hired person), some restrictions to the members' autonomy obviously ensue concerning matters delegated to the leader. This often benefits the group's efficiency but perhaps not morality. Yet this matter, too, depends on what indeed the precise content of the delegation is (e.g., a person might be hired to take care of fair play and justice in group activities, possibly at the expense of efficiency).

4.2.

To be able to discuss (intragroup and in principle intergroup) cooperation and problems of authorities' power use more informatively, I will now proceed to give an account of actions performed by groups. The account largely bases group action on joint action performed by the operatives of the group, allowing for the basic case where all members are operatives in a natural sense because of their membership. As I have earlier discussed this matter, I will be brief.[29] However, let me emphasize that there is the new aspect in my present account that now authority and power, in the case of both internally and externally authorized leaders, play a central role. The interesting case here is that with layers of authorization. Presently only the operative-nonoperative distinction is assumed, and it creates two layers (think of, e.g., business corporations for the multilayered case). Considering normatively structured groups with positions (any we-mode group in fact is positional), we consider group action in groups characterized by positions (offices) and their interrelations. With filled positions we arrive at our central idea of a group action being based on its members' joint (and other) action, for groups can only act through their members' action (be it we-mode or I-mode or some mixture of modes). The members may have asymmetrical positions or roles (here: some of them are operatives for decision making—they are leaders—or for action realizing such decisions, and the others are nonoperatives). The operatives' joint action here basically suffices for an action (often the same type of action) to be attributed to the whole group. Here very little needs to be required on conceptual grounds on the part of the nonoperatives.

Consider now this account and its analogy with (GI) of chapter 3:[30]

(IGA) A group g *brought about an action or state X intentionally* (or, alternatively, saw to it that X was the case) as a group in the social and normative circumstances C if and only if in C there were specific (internally or externally) authorized operative agents $A_1, \ldots, A_m$ for action in g such that

(1) $A_1, \ldots, A_m$, when acting qua group members, intentionally together brought about X (i.e., there was an action Y such that these operative agents intentionally together brought about Y and this performance of Y generated X, and was correctly believed and purported by the operative members to generate X), or, respectively, these operative agents saw to it that X;[31]

(2) because of (1), the (full-fledged and adequately informed) nonoperative members of g, as members of g, tacitly accepted the operative agents' intentional bringing about (or seeing to it that) X—or at least ought to have accepted it;

(3) there was a mutual belief in g to the effect that there was at least a chance that (1) prior to action and to the effect that (2).

This account applies to all we-mode groups in the sense of chapter 2, and more generally to all groups capable of action. It also applies to non-autonomous we-mode groups, ones based on external authorization (with externally authorized leaders and officials). Among we-mode groups, the account obviously also applies to we-mode groups that have no specific prior normative structure (positional structure, task-right system) before the possible introduction of specially authorized operatives.

I wish to emphasize that the account does not require that the participants, let alone outsiders, have *specific* knowledge of who the operatives are and in general of the microstructure of the situation (clause (3) has to be understood in this way). This is obviously central in the case of large groups such as states performing actions.

The task of the (internally or externally) authorized operative members for decision making is to create normatively and publicly binding decisions (intentions, plans, etc.) and/or to act for the group in light of their collective acceptance (recall chapter 5 for various kinds of acceptance). The authorized operatives (leaders) may have the authorized power to issue directives and orders for the nonoperatives concerning the group action in question (e.g., the division of tasks). In the case of internal authorization, the latter are assumed to act as members of the group and thus to cooperate with each other in the standard sense, being group-normatively collectively committed to what they accept for the group. In this case, what they do is in the we-mode also when acceptance only amounts to ga-acceptance in the sense of chapter 5.

As has been said, in principle (IGA), qua positional, admits also the I-mode interpretation: the positional mode (viz., the right psychological mode or way of carrying out positional tasks) can be satisfied either by we-mode or by I-mode psychologies and sometimes mixtures of these if some agents are we-moders and others are I-moders (and perhaps some intra-agent mixing can occur in actual practice, although not in theory). It is a contingent empirical matter whether a group member is a we-moder or an I-moder even in the case of we-mode groups (because they can allow some I-mode functioning).

Generally, the acting group may have a power structure that can be iterated to create hierarchical layers of operatives (e.g., in the case of an organization such as a business company, which is a case typically involving external authorization). The members of the group can be taken to act jointly on the basis that the operatives for action act and the other members follow suit. In the we-mode case of internal authorization, the operatives for decision making (leaders), but only they, need to have an actual we-intention, hence a joint intention, in a strict sense. In general, they must have collectively accepted for their group the joint intention that is expressible by "We will do X". Note that clause (1) does not explicitly present this joint intention requirement but rather implicitly assumes that at least here the operatives' intentional action entails that they share the relevant joint intention in the we-mode case (and the plain intention to perform X together in less demanding cases such as the I-mode case). They act jointly as a group on the basis of the leaders' joint intention in question that in the simple cases represents the group's intention to bring about X (in cases where a leader has already determined that the group is to perform this action). In the case of external authorization, the operatives for group-internal decision making need to have a we-intention only relative to the group of externally appointed and authorized leaders. This contrasts with the case of internally authorized operatives who represent the whole group and whose "we" notion refers to the whole group and where it is at least a normative desideratum that all members have the we-intention in question. In the we-mode case, (IGA) represents the case of the group's action qua group agent.

In clause (2) we can also speak of the nonoperatives (or, equivalently, other members or rank-and-file members) being obligated to endorse what the operative members for decision making are doing for them. In the case of internal authorization, clause (2) can be required because, first, the nonoperatives have already authorized the operatives to decide and to act for them; thus, to be consistent, they should also accept the result of the action. While the nonoperatives need not have the full we-intention to see to it that X will be performed, they—if obedient—can still be understood to have a more generally and vaguely described we-intention; for example, "There is a joint end that we in this country are pursuing or ought to be pursuing, and that is why we should pay our taxes". So it might be suggested that they ought to have a participatory intention that amounts to a we-intention, at least in the above loose sense (with existential quantification over intention contents). If they then are aware of what exactly the operatives' joint intention (shared we-intention) is, a joint intention expression of the form "We will see to it that X" would apply to them. However, it need not, after all, be required that they have the we-intention or even the intention to perform their parts of the joint action—for instance, the nonoperatives might be in reserve for being operatives and thus only have the general pro-attitude towards X and the disposition to we-intend X.

In the context of (IGA), group g is assumed to act as a group (e.g., in the we-mode sense); in addition, this on functional grounds generally requires that the nonoperatives endorse what the operatives do. To illustrate what this involves, we consider a simplified societal case with a state involved. We actually need several hierarchical layers of operative members and groups consisting of them. In any case, we have an elected parliament making laws and the cabinet executing them via the various ministries. This is a case of internal authorization. The police and the army are enforcing agents controlling and monitoring the group members in accordance with the judicial system of the country. The state employees are mostly hired rather than elected members, but they might still be acting for the group and representing it. Ordinary citizens, who in a democratic society have authorized the mentioned operatives to act for them, are pursuing their private business. But while doing it, they also (perhaps unintentionally) participate in the public promotion of the ethos, E. They ought to respect the laws and standards that the operatives have made for them. Ideally there will be a grand societal collective action that amounts to the group's (society's, state's) seeing to it that E; the citizens' share is to intentionally stop at red lights, make their children go to school, pay taxes, and so on. They will thus have to have the intention to participate in the grand collective activity serving to promote E (whatever that assumes on the part of the citizens) but not necessarily under the description of "I intend to participate in our seeing to it that E" but perhaps rather "I intend to stop at red lights" and so on. The degree of reflection can vary (in some cases there may only be an unreflected intention-in-action in a routine action, and then the intention and the beliefs related to it form only a "presuppositional" reason), but many may be acting in the we-mode. While clause (2) can still be satisfied without the nonoperatives having the we-intention, the operatives (at least collectively) must have it. Thus, trivially, the legislators must we-intend and know that they are passing laws for promoting the ethos of the state.

The upshot of the above account is that in both small and large groups we can have intentional cooperative action that in the we-mode-driven cases has the following features (cf. (IG) of chapter 3): (1) In the case of a group involving operative members for both decision making and for acting and respective nonoperatives, it must be required that the leaders accept that the group is to perform X. In addition, the nonoperatives for action are required to perform X collectively. (2) These nonoperatives need not have the we-intention to do X or even the intention to perform their parts of, or to contribute to, the group's intentional performance of X. (3) Nevertheless, the nonoperatives pro tanto ought to tacitly accept the operative members' (for action) bringing about of X, where tacit acceptance involves a tacit pro-attitude toward what the operatives are doing (without necessarily knowing what it is).

5. AUTHORITY AND COOPERATION IN SOCIAL ORGANIZATIONS

In this section I will discuss social organizations as groups mainly in terms of common-sense examples. The purpose of the discussion is to illustrate the role of internal and external authorization in social organizations such as business corporations or in a public organization like the state, and thus also bring philosophical theorizing closer to people's daily working life.

In an organized group that is partly or fully governed and led by either internally or externally authorized leaders (operatives) with the power to issue orders and perhaps to determine the constitutive values, goals, and principles of the group—in brief its ethos—a problem of cooperation arises: Can the members cooperate with each other (which would be required for fully adequate group-level action), and can they cooperate with the leaders? Answering these two questions in a reasoned way is what the present section aims at after discussion of a few examples of the operation of social organizations. My discussion is based on a typical hierarchical view of social organizations.

To recall some features of authorization, let me first comment on the case of groups with internally authorized leaders. Such leaders have the legitimate authority and right to rule (concerning a specified set of topics) that entails a correlated obligation to obey. There is then appropriate justification for the nonoperative members to take the operative members' decisions (directives, orders, etc.) as "desire-independent" preemptive reasons for action, although they might not do it and fail to act as full group members. In addition, in the case of external authorization there is an obligation for group members to comply, but this obligation has external justification at best. In externally authorized groups justification may even be lacking (think, e.g., of the case of dictatorship based on brute force), but the members may still, perhaps grudgingly, obey the externally based directives and thus give factual legitimacy to them.[32]

Let us consider social organizations consisting of hierarchically embedded groups (or subgroups or teams, as you like) where only the largest collection of such groups, a "supergroup" such as society or state, in such a context might be internally authorized and the hierarchically ordered subgroups would derive their authoritative power from the supergroup concerning the group-relevant topics in question. Such cases may be based on external or on internal authorization. A democratic state is an example based on internal authorization at bottom, we can say, although it shares several features with externally authorized cases. In this kind of case the parliament and the government are under rather direct democratic control, but the state institutions (e.g., the educational system—schools, universities, etc.) are under the authority of the relevant ministries that derive their authority from the highest, supergroup level. In such a system, e.g., a university professor will have to take orders from the administrative bodies of the university, and their activities again are authorized and constrained by the orders of the ministry of education. Accordingly, while there is society-level internal authorization even for a professor's daily activities, functionally he could in some contexts act as if he had taken part in the authorization of those (lower-than-highest-level) leaders whose orders he is supposed to obey, although he has his say only in state-level elections and in the determination of the political values and views on the supergroup level. In real life there is typically a "democracy gap" between "local" authorization of the kind we may have in small groups and the more "global" case, the supergroup case.[33]

As to a business corporation as a social organization, it is typically based on external authorization, an externally created, hierarchical authority-power structure. An organization has a certain ethos (basic goals, values, standards, and so on).[34] Some organizations can be regarded as non-autonomous we-mode groups, viz., in cases where their members (or a substantial amount of them) collectively construct the group in we-mode terms and employ we-reasoning (ideally, for instance, "This is *our* organization and hence we are working together as a unit").

An organization typically consists of an ethos (central goal) and set of positions that are normatively interlocked with each other in terms of normative "task-right" systems.[35] Each position involves a task-right system for the position-holder concerning what he is supposed to do and what he may do when acting in his position. The interrelations between the positions contain power relations and informational relations. For instance, a position-holder can have the power to order the holder of another position to do something, and different position-holders may have differing amounts of knowledge concerning the organization's activities.

A corporation as a task-right system generally consists of owners (shareholders), the governing board, executive officers, and subordinate executive personnel. The executive personnel are hired by the corporation (and the same may apply to its governing board). The owners form an independent group, which can externally and internally freely decide about the ethos of the corporation. The owners' group might be—but need not be—a paradigmatic we-mode group. They have the power to select a governing board for the company, and the governing board has the power to select the position-holders (and also task-holders that are not position-holders). These functionaries range from the CEO to various kinds of managers, sales personnel, truck drivers, etc. These are the hired personnel taking care of the daily activities of the organization. It is in virtue of their action that specific actions are attributed to the organization. Thus the hired personnel can be seen as a subgroup of the full group.

The executive part of the corporation has only a limited freedom in deciding how to promote the ethos of the corporation, since the executives are authorized by the owners or the governing board and dependent on their decisions. Nevertheless, hired members of course have the freedom to give up membership in the organization.

In view of the positional power structure of the organization, those higher up in the hierarchy are responsible for those lower in the hierarchy (who in turn are responsible for doing properly what they have been ordered to do). The latter are lower-level operatives and, in a sense, nonoperatives relative to the higher level in the hierarchy. This kind of power and responsibility structure obtains because power flows downward in the hierarchy. In contrast, in the owners' (shareholders') group, everyone is an operative member and is self-authorized.

The hired persons might not be allowed to directly change the ethos of the organization, but they may influence or induce ethos change, although the owners' group is in the last instance responsible for such changes. The hired personnel can at best be a non-autonomous we-mode group (in the sense of chapter 2) rather than a full-blown we-mode group in our standard sense. This is because of the organization's external power structure (directives to the personnel coming "from above").

An organization's decisions are generally constituted by its authorized operatives' (leaders') joint decisions, and when it acts, it performs its actions in virtue of its authorized operatives' actions. The operative members may vary from one occasion and task to another, and they may also include nonmember operatives. Thus, when a business company does X—for example, sells a new brand of goods or constructs a new building for its own use—the operative members for decision making and action are different and may depend on context. Not all operatives need to be group members (cf. hired lawyers, cleaners, truck drives, etc.). The shareholders have the ultimate power in a business company. They collectively have the power to select a governing board for the company, and derivatively they have the power to select the functional position-holders—from the CEO down to a salesperson and truck driver. The shareholders' group may in some cases (e.g., family enterprises) operate as a we-mode group. Their group is a core-level subgroup within an organization, while the functioning operatives (the CEO, various kinds of managers, workers, and what have you) form its hired personnel and indeed another subgroup taking care of the daily affairs of the organization. It is by virtue of their action that specific actions are attributed to the organization, and in general they represent the organization in daily life.

In a typical business corporation, all the position-holders are hired ones and typically fill some codified positions (the shareholders are not position-holders in the organization itself). All of the mentioned subgroups, viz., the shareholder's group, the board of directors, and the upper-level managers (who relatively independently carry out their company tasks) may work together in a non-autonomous we-mode sense (although they do not on conceptual grounds have to). The rest of the hired personnel can in principle act together in a similar sense. Yet the business corporation under the present conception is a group of groups (or subgroups), of which only the subgroup of shareholders can function in an internally autonomous and authorized sense. The subgroup consisting of the board of directors and of (high-level) managers is externally authorized, as is the subgroup of plain selling personnel (and what have you on the lowest level). External authorization involves at least the possibility of exercise of power in a sense that contradicts a subgroup's autonomy (the capacity to function without interference by an external authority). Thus even when these subgroups adopt we-thinking and socially identify themselves with the organization, they cannot form a paradigmatic we-mode group but at best only a non-autonomous we-mode group (recall the discussion in chapter 2).

There is also codified social commitment between the position-holders: a position-holder may be responsible to another one (if they are interlocking positions or are somehow in a suitable power relation to each other). In any case, a position-holder is socially committed to the company to perform her tasks. All the position-holders who are hired by a company can be operative members or, when they are not members, operative "agents" for some tasks. However, hired agents who are not position-holders but only temporarily connected to the organization in order to perform some tasks are not operative *members* but rather are more like the company's "means" or "tools". As we have seen, the ultimate core of an organization is constituted on the one hand by its owners (if it has owners in the legal sense) and on the other hand by the positions that constitute it. The owners determine (often via suitable operative members) the ethos (and thus the general content) of the organization, and the position-holders act to achieve and/or maintain it. Some position-holders may in fact have as their task the reformulation of the ethos—within certain boundaries.[36]

In hierarchical organizations such as a typical business corporation or a university, authority flows downward. There may not be much difference on the level of practical activities in these cases, although the business corporation is typically externally authorized, while a university might be internally authorized. In both cases a group member may have to somewhat metaphorically give up some of his "natural" authority, involving often a simple trade-off, e.g., instrumentally offer one's services for money or for some comparable good. Often the same happens also because people may want to get a task performed that requires cooperation by several individuals, as emphasized earlier. This kind of (possibly only temporary) giving up part of one's de facto authority is typical and indeed necessary for much of social life. A requirement of autonomy in an ontological sense (that is, free from contextual empirical constraints) or in a moral sense can still be retained, but rather as a desideratum than a right that others are obligated to respect in all situations.[37]

The three criterial elements of the we-mode may be "approximately" satisfied in the *externally* authorized corporation case, although the full kind of autonomy that we-mode collective acceptance ideally can be taken to involve is missing. Thus, some externally authorized groups (such as business corporations) can in some cases be closely similar to (paradigmatic) we-mode groups if the group members have the right kind of attitudes based on the full we-perspective and have the possibility of exiting the group. They did not, however, choose the leaders or the ethos of the group, they just submitted themselves to the leaders for money (or something comparable).

Consider now the issue of intermember cooperation in social organizations. The case of an army unit is interesting, for in some cases the army is (part of) a democratic group in the sense of being a state institution and having been democratically formed. The ethos and the leaders are democratically determined in society at large. Still, an army clearly is not a democratic group. In an army unit, cooperation between operatives (such as officers and other leaders) and soldiers in principle cannot amount to more than compliance and perhaps non-autonomous we-mode cooperation (because of threat of coercion or of actual coercion that may destroy successful we-mode cooperation). However, there could still be we-mode cooperation at least between the rank-and-file members, as it might satisfy the main criteria of the we-mode (authoritative group reason, satisfaction of the collectivity principle, and collective commitment). Groups based on dictatorship can at best be non-autonomous we-mode groups, as such groups might in some cases be based only on brute physical force or threat of its use. In them free exit from the group is not possible, and the members have not chosen to serve the dictator for money or for efficiency or for any other comparable reason. Still, we-mode cooperation at least between some (or all) nonoperative members can take place in accordance with the group's ethos determined by the dictator.

In we-mode groups with internally authorized leaders there can also be genuine we-mode cooperation between leaders and rank-and-file members. In such cases some amount of sanctioning and coercion of the members by the leaders can be tolerated. As I have said, we should here perhaps speak only of *quasi coercion* because, as long as the leaders do not misuse their powers, they have the right to do what they have been authorized by the members to do, and they are in a sense delegates of the group members (of course morally impermissible kind of strong coercion—like coercive physical violence or threat of it—can be excluded on moral grounds). Thus, the members must tolerate what the leaders do within the bounds of delegation (authorization).

We have seen that in the case of external authorization, full we-mode cooperation between leaders and the other group members cannot, at least not always, occur because of the in-principle possibility of coercion, e.g., in cases where the leaders' orders go strongly against the participants' current shared will and disturb their cooperative activities. However, such full cooperation is possible in the internal authorization case where the leaders' act in a quasi-coercive manner (e.g., if the members' reliance on the legitimacy in the authorization is sufficiently strong).

Even in some cases of internal authorization, not to speak of external authorization, a leader can, by his use of power, block cooperation between the members, e.g., because he thinks that it would prevent the group from achieving its goal in an optimal way (recall our earlier orchestra case). In such cases the members' views of what are the best and most rational ways to achieve the goal may differ from the leader's view, and conflict in action (or at least action intentions and beliefs) may take place. Conversely, sometimes (e.g., in hierarchical military cases) leaders give poor orders and directives, and the members may both individually and collectively be morally or functionally better off by refusing to obey the leader's order. Note that while the members in a we-mode group ought to promote the ethos and obey the orders of the group's leaders, the "oughts" here are usually taken to be pro tanto; hence, depending on context, perhaps, it may be collectively rational and normatively acceptable to disobey, e.g., a leader's stupid or immoral orders.

6. ARGUMENTS FOR WE-MODE COOPERATION

We-mode cooperation basically applies to all kinds of cooperative situations partly because of the possibility of constructing the situation from the group's point of view, as we have seen. But I-mode conceptualizations also seem possible—at least in general. This section will collect the central arguments of this book for the we-mode approach and present some other central arguments for the we-mode approach in general, and for the case of cooperation in particular (cf. Tuomela 2007a, ch. 4; for other arguments, see especially chapter 2 of the same work). These arguments show that we-mode cooperation is not only conceptually and psychologically but also functionally (behaviorally) different from I-mode cooperation. Indeed, we-mode thinking and acting is individualistically irreducible and in some cases functions better than does the I-mode (including the pro-group I-mode). (Recall the argument from chapter 3, which I will not here repeat.)

Why do we need more than one argument? As we know, philosophical arguments depend on viewpoint and background and are never fully conclusive, in contrast to mathematical and logical arguments (and even they do not always rely on indubitable premises). This is my main reason for presenting several arguments. The arguments below are related to specific action-theoretic notions and topics in collective intentionality research (argument (1)); institutional practices (argument (2));

choice-theoretic matters showing that sometimes the we-mode improves over the pro-group I-mode (argument (3)); broader action-theoretic issues (argument (4)); and purely empirical and experimental results (argument (5)).

(1) According to the *group action argument* that was presented in section 2 of chapter 2, a group cannot act intentionally in an optimal sense unless its members (or their majority or the group's delegates etc., as the case may be) act cooperatively in the we-mode and satisfy the three central we-mode criteria: group reason, collectivity, and collective commitment. A further point to make is that when a group acts, it typically causes the action that it brings about. Even if the causation goes through the members *qua group members* causing or at least generating the intended result, we can use collectivistic language and say that the group caused that result, the group being in these circumstances indispensable for the result in question.[38]

(2) Consider next the case of *institutional cooperation*.[39] Suppose that a community has accepted the institution that silver coins are money. (The acceptance here might be either construction of a new institution or adoption of an established institution.) When the members use silver coins as money in their commercial exchanges, they usually cooperate at least in a weak sense through their monetary institution. Such exchange, e.g., selling and buying, can be of the individualistic kind of cooperation (cf. (CIM)) or sometimes of the we-mode kind (cf. (CWM)). There is, however, a broader sense of cooperation in the group that is involved. It is the sense in which institutional action in general is cooperative. Community members use money in many contexts and behaviorally independently of each other. Why can they be taken to cooperate? They operate and cooperate on the same collectively accepted goal or view, e.g., the institutional view ("acceptance belief") that silver coins are money.[40] Such a goal might in some cases be their reason for action, but usually it is rather a presupposition to be acted on.

Cooperation with respect to an institutional belief may satisfy (CWM). Consider this: Given the fact that silver pieces or coins are money in the group, a person functioning in the group context can normally expect that the others will take silver coins to be money (the converse statement also holds true; see (CAT) of chapter 8). Most centrally, this is not only an interpersonal matter of the members' beliefs about who takes those pieces to be money and who does not, but a group matter concerned with all actual and potential group members and others (e.g., visitors) functioning in that group. The group members should be relied on to act for (what a theoretician describes as) the desire-independent presupposition in the group (expressed by "These coins are money in our group") in order be trustworthy partners. They act on collectively accepted group intentions, norms, or a leader's orders and, e.g., use certain pieces of paper or kind of metal rather than other kinds to pay for their purchases, and are rewarded for their actions.

In general, (CWM) can in the money case be required to be satisfied by a substantial amount of group members.[41] This is because the stability that the we-mode has generated has come through the members' identification with the group (especially their collective acceptance of its ethos) and the resulting collective commitment involved. Financial loss or other harm may incur if the members do not act on the group view (e.g., use the right kind of money) or goal.

Another factor also motivating people to cooperate concerning the use of a certain kind of money comes from the collectively accepted group belief with the world-to-mind direction of fit when a change from one institutional arrangement to another has taken place, e.g., a switch from silver to gold coins or from the gold standard to "fiat" money. This typically requires organized decision making by the group, and in any case some we-mode thinking for the group concerning what it ("we") should do—and some we-mode action on this basis. Here we have another argument for we-mode cooperation in the case of institutional action such as the use of a certain kind of money.

(3) We-mode reasoning can explain *cooperation in collective action dilemmas (and coordination cases)*; for a fuller discussion see chapter 7. Collective action dilemmas such as the Prisoner's Dilemma are problematic for rational choice theory, since they generally entail that rational utility-maximizing leads to suboptimal solutions, and the only way to reach Pareto-optimal outcomes (e.g., mutual cooperation in the PD) requires individualistically irrational, out-of-equilibrium play, indeed coordinated play, by the parties. In a PD, cooperation by everyone is better than defection by everyone. In this sense Pareto-optimal outcomes can be seen as collectively rational to pursue.

In the group case the situation is different. The individuals here function as group members striving to realize the group's goals and interests (or to maximize group utility). Group members functioning qua group members are motivated to cooperate to reach them because they are group goals or at least are conducive to group goals to which the members are bound by their membership. The group here functions as the kind of coordinator required for arriving at the Pareto-optimal outcome. Thinking and acting as a group member in the we-mode is based on the reason that the group should reach its goals and will (ultimately) further also its members' private interests and goals. The we-mode approach is not reducible to the I-mode framework because it necessarily differs from it with respect to two facts: first, it is conceptually (but not causal-ontologically) based on a *group agent* as the basic agent (instead of the individual group member being the basic agent) and on viewing situations—including those that are collective action dilemmas when individualistically conceptualized—from the group's point of view. Second, it involves member-level *we-mode we-reasoning* instead of individualistic I-reasoning. These two features together, when game-theoretically elaborated, show dramatically that the we-mode and the I-mode approaches are rather different. For one thing, there is, e.g., no PD within the group-based we-mode approach relative to the utilities that group members qua group members have (although relative to their individualistic ["private"] utilities there may well be collective action dilemmas).

There are also other differences between the we-mode and the I-mode accounts related to cooperativeness assumptions and to the possibilities to free-ride and, importantly, to rational equilibrium behavior. The reader is referred to chapter 7 for these points.[42]

(4) In general, a we-mode group in many cases offers more *stability, persistence*, and *resilience* concerning the fulfillment of a joint project. Generally speaking, this is because of a we-mode group's nature as an "organic whole".[43] It is an inbuilt presupposition of the we-mode approach that the members will perform their parts of the joint project in a collectively committed way and that the project will be given up only on mutual agreement or consent or for some other good reason. In addition, *flexibility* in group action will be involved at least in the following sense: the group members will be disposed to help (or correct or pressure) each other when needed. And even the ethos of the group can be changed when the (external) circumstances so demand. In an I-mode group, helping and pursuing "emergency" tasks will often have to be negotiated and bargained, because a member's private costs are weighed against her private rewards, while a member's costs in a we-mode group are seen as "our" costs" for "our" rewards when the costs are fairly distributed. On the other hand, the individuals in I-mode groups have more action freedom in many cases (at the expense of functioning optimally for the group). Both I-mode and we-mode cooperation presuppose trust in the others' participation, and in the we-mode case, a strong kind of trust involving respect of the others' rights will be involved.[44] Still other advantages of we-mode thinking and acting are that it is often more economical—cooperation is the default when the group acts, and thus there is more routine thinking and action in the we-mode case than in the I-mode case. Finally, we-mode thinking and acting can involve organized creativity as much as I-mode thinking and acting, because the group can, perhaps even better, organize the infrastructure fruitful for *innovation* (cf. the US project in the 1960s to "get a man to the moon" that seems to have been largely a we-mode project).

(5) The we-mode approach and the pro-group I-mode approach are conceptually different, as seen in this book. It has also been claimed here that at least theoretically there are rational functional differences in behavior that are likely to become apparent in practical real-life contexts. There is much *anecdotal evidence* in favor of we-mode thinking and acting. People in many cultures have been brought up with what can be called the wisdom of the we-mode approach (be cooperative, think of your

group's best, be committed to participate in group activities for the common good). There are also *experimental results* concerning the role of "we" in social interaction. Thus, to mention a few, there are studies showing that identification with the group and group thinking plays or may play an important role in deprivation situations, in the case of situational adoption of speech style, in group polarization cases, and in in-group favoritism.[45] There are also studies pertaining directly to cooperation.

Let me mention a couple of relevant results. Empirical research supports the idea that identification with a group and commitment to it increases ethos-promoting intragroup cooperative action. Thus Marilynn Brewer argues on the basis of previous experimental research that when some individuals believe that they share a common group membership, they are more likely to act in the interest of collective welfare than individuals in the same situation who do not have a sense of group identity.[46] I take collective welfare to include acting for the group in promoting the ethos of the group. Hence identification with the group (and, most important, its ethos) tends to yield cooperative ethos-promoting action. Brewer also argues that identification with the group can elicit cooperative behavior even in the absence of interpersonal communication among group members. Functioning in an in-group context, individuals develop trust toward each other's participation and a cooperative orientation toward shared problems. Here we thus have empirical support for the claim that in group contexts, we-mode behavior (or at any rate pro-group I-mode behavior) tends to come about and to supersede selfish I-mode activities.

Recent experiments by Colman, Pulford, and Rose on collective action dilemmas show that over half of the participants use we-reasoning instead of I-reasoning in the dilemmas and thus end up choosing in collectively beneficial ways. In addition, Bardsley and coauthors find context-dependent support for we-reasoning in their experiments concerning subjects' views on focal points.[47]

Note, however, that because of the possibility of pro-group I-mode behavior, we may not get a clear and unambiguous evidential argument for we-mode we-thinking from the social psychological investigations conducted so far. But in any case, that we-thinking often is important or even indispensable for group projects, be it of the we-mode or the pro-group I-mode kind, does get support. (See also chapter 7.)

7. CONCLUSION

It has been seen in this chapter that we-mode cooperation is generally based on the requirement for the members qua members to contribute to the satisfaction and promotion of the ethos of their group and on other derived or otherwise related goals that also are collectively accepted by the members as their joint goals. In simpler cases some people need just collectively accept a goal, e.g., to clean a yard together and form the joint intention to do it. This collective acceptance suffices for their constituting a we-mode group and for cooperating in the we-mode to clean the yard.

Cooperation of this kind in general requires that for the group to be able to act adequately in a committed efficient sense, its members ought to act cooperatively from the full we-perspective that involves an irreducible "we", which can be regarded as referring to an intrinsically cooperative group and implies the members' disposition to act together cooperatively. A person acting from the we-mode we-perspective is disposed to use group-based we-reasoning, to be cooperative and reject free-riding in group activities for the group's action to be efficient and group-morally adequate. A we-moder should also be disposed to take part in forming we-mode groups. Indeed, for an ideal we-moder (one that fully identifies herself with the group) there in principle is no temptation to free-ride. For less than fully ideal we-moders, it anyway holds true that they should cooperate. If they fail to cooperate, they are subject to criticism by the others and may even be forced to leave the group.

A central new element in the account of full cooperation in this chapter has been to emphasize the role of authority (especially leaders) in contexts of intragroup cooperation. Leaders, be they internally or externally authorized, can have a central role in coordinating group members' actions by means of their power (e.g., orders and directives). Thus a new account of cooperation was given in section 3, after an exposition of the basic features of the we-mode approach to sociality and cooperation in sections 1 and 2. This analysis of cooperation is compatible with the exercise of authority in (we-mode) groups. Internal authorization entails the possibility and requirement of we-mode cooperation in the whole group (including especially cooperation between operatives and rank-and-file members). We noticed that some groups with externally authorized leaders may involve we-mode cooperation on the member level. Yet, in the whole group consisting both of leaders and rank and file members, full-blown successful we-mode cooperation is not always possible because power exercise by the leaders may lead to disturbances and a breakdown of cooperative activities.

The last section of the chapter presents five arguments for the desirability of we-mode cooperation at least in certain contexts. These arguments yield following conclusions:

(a) We-mode cooperation (including non-autonomous we-mode cooperation) is possible and has received experimental support. It is conceptually and functionally different from both plain and pro-group I-mode cooperation (see chapter 7). Indeed it is individualistically irreducible (recall chapter 3).

(b) We-mode cooperation (1) is often functionally more effective and collectively and individually more rewarding than pro-group I-mode cooperation (as will be shown in detail in chapter 7), (2) in several cases offers more collective stability and order (by eliminating individualistic equilibria) and also flexibility than (pro-group) I-mode cooperation (see chapter 7). This fact gives a *group reason* to encourage people to act in the we-mode rather than in the (pro-group) I-mode.

(c) Group action as a unit in a strict sense requires the members' we-mode cooperation.

(d) There is much anecdotal empirical evidence for we-mode cooperation, and, as noted, some experimental evidence for it exists so far.

There are many other aspects in which we-mode we-thinking and acting would seem to be superior to individualistic thinking and acting. See chapter 7 for a fuller discussion of these complex matters. What has been said above nevertheless gives support to my claim in chapter 1 that we-mode conceptualization and a we-mode account of cooperation are needed to complement individualistic (pro-group) I-mode account(s) in social science theorizing and experimentation.

7

We-Reasoning in Game-Theoretic Contexts

1. INTRODUCTION

As argued earlier in this book, people often think in terms of "we", referring to a group they belong to. When making decisions, they then frame the decision problem in a plural form: "What should we do?" instead of "What should I do?" This kind of "we-reasoning" has been studied in economics and in philosophical theories of collective intentionality. There can be we-reasoning both in the I-mode and the we-mode sense, and the same is true of I-reasoning. In this chapter the we-mode approach to group-reasoning (or, which here amounts functionally to the same, we-reasoning) will be connected to the recent work by the economist Michael Bacharach on "team reasoning". My philosophical theory provides a conceptual framework that augments Bacharach's theory. Indeed, his mathematical results can be taken to support my claim about the irreducibility of the we-mode to the I-mode.[1] In particular, it will be shown that group reasoning yields different results than pro-group I-mode theorizing, and in many cases it will be able to create more institutional order in the social world than I-mode theorizing.[2] When speaking of group reasoning, I below mean an autonomous we-mode group and the reasoning performed by the group agent. As, however, a group agent can only reason through its members, we arrive at the view that the members must we-reason, indeed we-reason in the we-mode. When speaking of group reasoning below, a we-mode group is focused on and the reasoning performed by the group (group agent). As, however, a group agent can only reason through its members, we arrive at the view that the members must we-reason, indeed we-reason in the we-mode.[3]

Furthermore, we-mode reasoning can help to give an explanation of human cooperative behavior in collective action dilemmas that is left unexplained by standard noncooperative game theory. That theory is not well equipped to deal with we-mode reasoning, but it can be extended by methods developed by Bacharach. I will argue that both standard game theory and Bacharach's theory require more attention to the information-sharing stages that precede actual decision-making. A stage-based model of we-reasoning will be described in which the first stage of we-reasoning concerns finding out and sharing information concerning the particulars of the decision-making situation, and the latter stages concern selecting actions based on that information.

To discuss joint decision making, noncooperative game theory is the most developed theory of rational decision making in situations involving several agents.[4] However, there are seemingly simple situations, describable as two-person normal-form games, that are problematic for the theory. Two well-known games of that sort, Prisoner's Dilemma (PD) and the High-Low game (Hi-Lo), have recently received much attention, because the predictions that game theory makes seem to clash with either empirical results or intuitive rationality judgments.[5] Two attempts to overcome these difficulties have been suggested, one based on what has been called *preference transformation* and another based on what has been called *agency transformation*.

The first approach starts from the observation that the experimental settings that attempt to represent a certain game, e.g., a PD, in fact do not necessarily have the PD structure as conceived by the participants' preferences. In experimental settings, the payoffs typically represent some objective features of the situation like monetary rewards. These *objective payoffs* are not necessarily equal to the *subjective utilities* that correspond to the agents' social and situational preferences, which are assumed to represent all the factors that the agents take to be relevant in the decision-making situation. In order to take such factors into account, various functions have been put forward for transforming objective payoffs to proper utility functions that represent the subjects' real preferences.[6] Such transformations may result in a game that is strategically different from the original game.[7] That may explain why people exhibit behavior that differs from the recommendations made for the original game. Furthermore, the resulting utilities can further be transformed in light of social interaction, group membership, and other related factors. Below this first approach for getting closer to what people really prefer in a situation will not be considered, partly because it does not seem to work too well.[8]

The second possibility is to rely on agency transformation.[9] This means that the individual agent conceives the situation not as a decision-making problem for individual agents but as a decision-making problem for the group conceived as an agent.

The idea is to conceptualize the situation, or "frame" it, from the group's point of view and ask, "What should the group (e.g., a team) choose if it were the agent making choices?" To answer this question, we need concepts that allow us to speak about what a group prefers; especially we need a notion of a *group's* preference. The we-mode conceptual framework of group agency employed in this book can be applied to this kind of choice context, and indeed this is the general approach of this chapter.

Both agency transformation and preference transformation (when the latter is applied to account for the influence of the group on an agent's preferences) can be seen as attempts to model we-thinking, thinking in terms of a "we" instead of an "I". Let us concentrate on practical we-reasoning (a subclass of we-thinking): Practical we-reasoning is we-thinking that aims at a decision about how to act. For instance, instead of asking, "What should I do in this situation?" the agents may ask, "What should we do in this situation?" The latter expression is ambiguous, however, since it can be understood in at least two different ways, as a combination of two questions: "What should you do and what should I do?" Alternatively, it can be understood as "What should our group, having you and me as its members, do?" An important task of the present chapter is to clarify these vague and broad characterizations of we-reasoning by distinguishing between two different types of we-reasoning: we-reasoning in the pro-group I-mode and we-reasoning in the we-mode. Pro-group I-mode reasoning answers the question "What should I do as a private person acting in part for the group?" while group reasoning (viewed as entailing we-mode reasoning) answers two types of questions: "What should our group do?" and "What should I do as a group member as my part of our group's action?"

There are several tacit assumptions in game theory, one of which is the presumption of the validity of a version of (explanatory) *methodological individualism*: Explanations of action and social phenomena more generally are to be couched in terms of intentional attitudes of individual agents and in general reducible groups (recall chapter 1). Furthermore, cooperation and collective intentionality phenomena can be adequately explained without reference to irreducible group attitudes. I will instead assume a mild version of collectivism based on irreducible groups (and group attitudes, etc.) and thus reject methodological individualism in the just-mentioned sense.

Another assumption, which concerns such static games of complete and perfect information as PD and Hi-Lo that can be represented as normal form matrices, is what we call the *givenness of preferences*: The preferences of the agents are antecedently given and are common knowledge among the agents involved in the situation. This assumption will be discussed later and relaxed for contexts where decision making occurs in consecutive stages.

The approach of this chapter is complementary to game theory since it largely focuses on cases in which the above two assumptions do not hold. The much richer conceptual framework of philosophical action theory, with the notions of reason, goal, and intention as well as collective intentionality concepts, is central and will be used to enrich game-theoretic reasoning. Furthermore, illustrative examples of processes by which preferences are communicated, modified, and brought into common awareness will be given.

Accordingly, the I-mode/we-mode distinction will be applied to collective reasoning and decision making and also be connected to Bacharach's theory of "unreliable team interaction".[10] Recall that thinking and acting in the we-mode is thinking and acting as a proper group member, group understood as "we" from "inside", from the members' point of view. It contrasts with the I-mode that concerns thinking and acting as a private person. Standard game theory is limited to I-mode type of decision making, but there is also a we-mode type of decision making. Moreover, this kind of decision making can lead to better results (in a sense to be explained) than the I-mode type.

A group's preferences are central to the present approach. They can be expressed by the group members as "Our group prefers that…" The question of where such group preferences come from has been commented on in our discussion of group attitudes in chapter 5. Below, a group's preferences are taken to be based on the collectively accepted attitudes of the group in question. These collective attitudes are themselves typically *results* of group discussion, deliberation, and decision making and thus cannot be assumed to exist prior to deliberation. Modeling this kind of deliberation is another reason for distinguishing between different stages of we-reasoning.

We can divide rational multiagent deliberation into reasoning immediately preceding a decision problem and reasoning within it. Furthermore, such reasoning can be either I-mode reasoning or we-mode reasoning. Standard game theory is basically concerned only with I-mode reasoning in a decision problem. The present approach, in contrast, deals also with I-mode and we-mode decision making *prior* to the existence of the decision problem—in addition to reasoning within it.

It will be shown below, first, that on the whole the we-mode account and Bacharach's team-reasoning account predict the same choices, e.g., in the Hi-Lo game. Second, when the game-theoretic approach is enriched with the conceptual apparatus of the we-mode approach, it can be applied to account for the stages that precede the one from which team reasoning starts. Third, it is an important asset of we-reasoning that it can provide the parameters that Bacharachian team reasoning presupposes, in particular, the group's preferences.

The outline of the chapter is as follows. In section 2, the I-mode/we-mode distinction will be related to Bacharach's theory of "unreliable team interaction," which attempts to extend game theory to situations in which groups can be viewed as agents and individual agents can reason as group members. His results are applied to show that I-mode decision making can produce different results than we-mode decision making: The equilibria in these cases may differ. In many cases suboptimal equilibria (e.g., mutual defection in a Prisoner's Dilemma) will be eliminated in favor of optimal but out-of-equilibrium outcomes, e.g., mutual cooperation in PD (the matter depends somewhat on the probabilities of being a we-moder). This is one way in which we-mode reasoning can produce better results than I-mode reasoning. Section 3 discusses the problem the empirical validity of the obtained results and in effect argues that Bacharach's framing approach ultimately does not go all the way to a full-blown group view (contrary to the we-mode approach).[11]

In section 4, the different stages of we-reasoning are discussed. Examples will be given of processes that lead agents to share information about their preferences and of processes that lead them to form group preferences. These preceding processes, in particular when they are of the we-mode type, can prevent agents from ending up in coordination problems with multiple equilibria and in collective action dilemmas with suboptimal equilibria. This is another way in which we-mode we-reasoning can produce better results than I-mode we-reasoning.

In section 5, the main results of the chapter will be recapitulated and their philosophical consequences will be commented on.

2. WE-REASONING

2.1.

Here we will study we-reasoning in a game-theoretic context and focus on we-mode we-reasoning rather than *pro-group I-mode we-reasoning*. First, we summarize some features of the I-mode/we-mode distinction and the we-mode approach and then proceed to a characterization of the differences between we-reasoning in these two modes. Then we present Bacharach's methods (in his 1999 paper) for extending game theory to account for decision making based on we-reasoning. Finally, we relate the I-mode/we-mode framework to Bacharach's game-theoretic account and argue that, given our "bridging" assumptions, Bacharach's results support the irreducibility of the we-mode to the I-mode. Our discussion up to section 3 is mainly conducted within noncooperative game-theory, viz., in the kind of game theory in which no binding agreements are present, even if communication between the participants can be allowed. Section 3 broadens the discussion and argues that at least some of the central results reported in the 2010 joint paper hold empirically, too.[12] In general, the main game-theoretical results below concerning the difference between the I-mode and the we-mode and the irreducibility of the latter to the former are "existential" in that they are shown to hold in *some* cases but not in all cases. But that suffices for showing the ("rational-functional") differences in question.

The we-mode framework is based on group concepts and especially a group's performative (and in this sense constructive) acceptance of attitudes (e.g., in linguistic terms, "We hereby accept G as our group's goal") and other group properties for the group, a paradigmatic we-mode group (recall chapters 2 and 5 for these notions). We assume that for everything that has been collectively accepted, it is common belief among the group members that it has been collectively accepted (a feature making possible collective action).[13] The group members take the facts that the group accepted certain attitudes or contents (e.g., that G is our group's goal) to be *group reasons* for their proper functioning as members. The members are assumed to recognize a group reason as an authoritative, hence generally preemptive and also presumptive (i.e., sufficient) reason for their action as group members. An authoritative group reason requires that the group members act appropriately, and it serves to direct their actions. We also recall that there are two other criterial conditions for we-mode activities, namely the satisfaction of the collectivity condition and the requirement of collective commitment. (Recall chapter 2 for the criterial conditions of the we-mode and specifically chapter 4 for group reasons.)

Traditional game theory, because of its commitment to methodological individualism, is confined to the I-mode: The individuals are the only agents, and they select actions aiming at satisfying their preferences in light of their expectations of the actions of the other agents who are also aiming at the satisfaction of their preferences. Game theory is neutral with respect to what the agents take into account in their preferences, and this makes it possible to accommodate some elements of we-reasoning in the theory. The preferences may be self-regarding or other-regarding, or they may aim at the benefit of the group's goals and interests. The last-mentioned case falls into the pro-group I-mode category.

A strategic aspect characteristic of the I-mode is that a rational agent tries to satisfy her preferences by selecting strategies that are *best replies* to others' expected strategies. In contrast, in the we-mode approach it is the group that is viewed as an agent that functions strategically in a decision situation. For illustration, compare individual-agent games from the point of view of an individual qua private person and from the point of view of the group consisting of all the agents involved: An individual agent can only select her *strategy*, but a group agent can in a sense select *joint outcomes,* because it can specify the strategies of all the agents in the group. In order to secure an outcome, it is necessary for an individual agent to act jointly with the others.

The selection of an outcome is based on what the group prefers, and this need not be a function of what the members privately prefer. The individuals who reason in the we-mode and act as group members then realize the outcome by selecting those strategies that lead to it, assuming that the other group members do their parts. We-mode we-reasoning does not inherently involve (individual) strategic thinking nor encourage it, as the I-mode does, although strategic aspects may sometimes be relevant—in particular when some individuals in the group are reasoning in the I-mode or when there is more than one group involved.

Whereas game-theorists talk about the selection of a strategy, philosophers interested in practical reasoning talk about the formation of an intention. Similarly, a group's selecting an outcome corresponds to its forming a collective intention, indeed an intention attributable to the group. The individual agents realize the intention by performing their part actions. The house painting example presented and discussed in chapters 3 and 4 illustrates this.

The I-mode/we-mode distinction will be applied below to decision making in situations that can be described by normal-form game matrices. Processes of we-reasoning concentrating on the difference between we-mode reasoning and pro-group I-mode reasoning will be focused on. The difference is not in the aims of the agents because in both cases the agents aim at the benefit of the group. Rather, the difference is in the reasoning process: It is individualistic in the I-mode case (both plain I-mode and pro-group I-mode). In game-theoretic terms, agents reasoning in the plain I-mode select actions that, given their expectations of the other agents' actions, best satisfy their preferences, which may be other-regarding in the sense of being affected by the others' preferences. Agents reasoning in the pro-group I-mode select actions that, given their expectations of the other agents' actions, best satisfy their preferences, which are group-regarding in the sense that they are partly constituted by the group's preferences. An agent reasoning in the we-mode selects an action that is her component in the outcome that best satisfies the group's preferences. We concentrate on the we-mode case in which the agent fully adopts the group's preferences as her own and commits herself to acting as a full-blown group member—thus "identifying herself with the group".

The above distinctions can also basically be extracted from Michael Bacharach's game-theoretic framework (see subsection 2.3 below).[14] We-mode reasoning corresponds to (or is a counterpart of) Bacharach's notion of team reasoning (although not all cases of we-mode reasoning are cases of team reasoning in this sense), pro-group I-mode reasoning corresponds to his notion of functioning as a "benefactor" to the group, and plain I-mode reasoning corresponds to what Bacharach calls individualistic reasoning with "egoistic" utilities. Making use of Bacharach's mathematical framework, I will soon argue that I-mode and we-mode decision making may produce different results, and that, in general, the we-mode helps to overcome collective action dilemmas.

2.2.

I will now comment on Bacharach's idea of the generation of group identification that goes in terms of the notion of *interdependence (I)*. He defines for some sets of states, S and S*, in a game-theoretic interaction situation or game (G):[15]

(I) For some S, S* the players have common interest in, and copower for, S* over S, and sol(G) contains outcomes in S.

Bacharach's Interdependence Hypothesis—which seems apt for rational agents—amounts to this:

(IH) Group identification is stimulated by the perception of feature I.[16]

The notion of sol(G) here means the set of the Nash equilibria of the game. To give an example, we consider the following Prisoner's Dilemma (PD):

	C	D
C	3, 3	1, 4
D	4,1	2, 2

(PD) with the preference ordering DC>CC>DD>CD

Here the players have *copower* over the Paretian (viz., Pareto optimal) outcome CC: (only) by suitably choosing their actions, they can between them, viz., by each of them choosing C, bring about the Paretian outcome. But all joint outcomes trivially satisfy this unless "can" is restricted to what one *individual rationally* can achieve (not explicitly required above). However, Bacharach also imposes the condition that the players' actions *not be assured*.[17] This involves that from the point of view of individual rationality there are better choices available to the agent (for instance, D in PD). C thus is not an assured action. With the assumption of nonassuredness added to the notion of copower, we may get at best a *sufficient* (but not a necessary) condition of group identification for rational agents. Bacharach emphasizes that if a game has feature I, individualistic reasoning cannot be relied upon to deliver s*, i.e., a Pareto-superior (joint) outcome.

Feature I is possessed by common collective action dilemma games such as PD and Chicken but also by, e.g., Stag Hunt, Hi-Lo, and Battle of the Sexes. As to the empirical applicability of I, it may seem rationally somewhat demanding. As the nonassuredness feature may not be very easy to detect in real-life games, imposing a weaker requirement might empirically work better—e.g., a requirement that the participants' preference rankings be highly correlated in addition to the common interest, viz., Paretian requirement.[18] This would be a competing hypothesis to the above I. In any case, there could empirically be several compatible sufficient conditions for group identification and—for that matter—for adopting the kind of group conceptualization that will be discussed later in this chapter (especially in section 3).

2.3.

To proceed to further comparison of the we-mode with the I-mode, the former, in contrast to the latter (including the pro-group I-mode), also guarantees the achievement of Pareto-optimal equilibria in coordination games with one Pareto-optimal outcome, for instance in the Hi-Lo game

	Hi	Lo
Hi	3,3	0,0
Lo	0,0	1 1

Intuitively, a we-mode reasoner chooses her part action on the basis of the outcome that benefits the group most. In general such reasoning presupposes the existence of a group utility function. We will later discuss the nature and formation of group preferences and group utility functions, but here we just assume that they exist. The following practical inference schemas illustrate the difference between the two cases. In the we-mode an agent would reason as follows:

1. We intend to maximize group utility.
2. Outcome HiHi uniquely maximizes group utility.

Therefore,

3. I will perform my component in HiHi, that is, Hi.

Reasoning in the pro-group I-mode, she would arrive at an impasse as follows, assuming that in this case she has fully adopted the group's utility function (and operates within the constraints of noncooperative game theory and operates within the constraints of noncooperative game theory such as a lack of effective communication; cf. connection thesis (2) below):[19]

1. You and I intend to maximize group utility.
2. If you choose Hi, my choosing Hi maximizes group utility.
3. If you choose Lo, my choosing Lo maximizes group utility.

Therefore,

4. I will perform what?

First, only we-mode reasoning strictly entails some kind of conclusion, and, second, given that you reason analogously, only the we-mode can strictly guarantee in the nonprobabilistic case that we succeed in maximizing group utility.

Bacharach gives several reasons for why the pro-group I-mode (the "benefactor mode") is inferior to the we-mode.[20] He speaks of refined instead of mere benefaction here. The first reason is that, according to him, the *payoff dominance principle* (choose your action from a Pareto-superior equilibrium outcome, one that gives a better or at least equal payoff for the participants) was originally introduced to deal with the Hi-Lo situation.[21] So it would seem to be question begging to add this principle, as we already intuitively think in its terms and appeal to this principle. The payoff dominance principle sometimes, as in risky Stag Hunt, clashes with the individualistic risk dominance principle toward which our intuitions in many cases lean, and thus payoff dominance does not apply at least to all contexts. Next, Bacharach argues that it is a merit of the team-reasoning model that it allows us to derive conformity to payoff dominance from assumptions about our more basic tendencies to team reason. Bacharach is right: there are independent and deeper reasons to accept we-mode thinking and reasoning (team reasoning, in his terminology), as argued earlier in this book. Bacharach's final reason is that one of his basic mathematical theorems (called the Central Theorem below) applies quite generally and does not rely on the assumption that the group utility function is Paretian. According to him the fundamental key to the relative success of team reasoning over group benefactor reasoning is independent of the specific objective of the group (its utility function), the key here being that team reasoning removes coordination problems within the group—independently of the group utility function and the individuality of the reasoners. Taken together, Bacharach's arguments are forceful against mere payoff dominance and in favor of the full we-mode framework.

To be sure, our we-mode approach has not been game-theoretically formalized, and partly because of its conceptual richness it goes much beyond the narrow framework of game theory. Even our central criteria of the we-mode—viz., group reason, the collectivity condition, and collective commitment—seem not to be properly formalizable within that framework. Yet the we-mode and the team-reasoning approaches at least partly share some features concerning, e.g., collective reasoning and the action recommendations they give. Thus, Bacharach's distinction between team reasoners and benefactors of a team (in his 1999 paper) can be related to the respective notions of the we-mode and the pro-group I-mode in the context of noncooperative games. Although we-mode reasoning has more conceptual content (especially as concerns the three central criteria of the we-mode) and covers, e.g., large groups with authorities, still in simple cases the relationships between the two accounts can be stated concisely in the following, somewhat stipulative *partial* connecting theses (which give a kind of "projection" of the we-mode approach into the team-reasoning framework by in effect leaving out the three central we-mode criteria):

(1) We-mode reasoning and Bacharach's team reasoning yield the same action recommendations in game-theoretic choice situations.

(2) Pro-group I-mode reasoning—here the kind of reasoning in which the agents adopt the group preferences—and Bacharach's reasoning as a team benefactor yield the same action recommendations in the present Bacharachian game-theoretic setting.

Claims (1) and (2) are assumptions that partially, but only partially, translate our framework into the game-theoretic one giving mathematically speaking a kind of partial nonnormative "reduct" of the we-mode approach to the team-reasoning framework. We do not claim strict entailment in any direction between we-mode reasoning and team reasoning or between pro-group I-mode reasoning and reasoning as a team benefactor.

The we-mode approach is typically discussed without the use of probabilities in a technical sense. Rather the kind of common-sense thinking that the we-mode involves uses vaguer notions such as tendency. Yet a clarification of tendency notions (e.g., a person's tendency to be a we-moder, to be considered together with her tendency to choose a certain alternative in an interactive choice situation) can in principle take place in terms of epistemic probabilities that are grounded in objective facts. With complete reduction of uncertainty all such probabilities can be assumed to reduce to ones or zeros if—as current knowledge seems to entail—the macro realm does not contain objective probabilistic processes (only the micro realm is objectively indeterministic).

Bacharach's theory, in contrast, assumes that individual agents have in-built objective probabilistic features ("probabilistic brains" as it were) and various parameters to go with them. These features make a precise comparison of the two approaches difficult. In the sequel, though, I will not eliminate epistemic probabilities but will use them in calculations when they can be assumed to be pragmatically both "sufficiently" nonarbitrary and objectively grounded by our current knowledge.

With respect to (1), both reasoning methods, viz., Bacharachian team reasoning and we-mode reasoning theory, have the same pattern: Given the group's preference ordering, the agents choose their part actions on the basis of the group-preferred outcome. With respect to (2), in both pro-group I-mode reasoning and Bacharach's team benefactor reasoning, the agents adopt the group's preferences and reason rationally in standard game-theoretic fashion: They predict the actions of the others and then select strategies that are best responses to the other agents' predicted actions. In addition to similar reasoning patterns in Bacharach's team-reasoning account and the we-mode theory, further parallels (related to the three criterial features of the we-mode) can be drawn between the two theories: Group utility in Bacharach's account plays the role of group reason, team-reasoning because of its shared reasoning and shared outcome correspond to the collectivity condition, and his notion of group identification has collective commitment as its partial counterpart in the we-mode theory.[22]

Given the connections stated in our theses (1) and (2), it will be shown later in this chapter that the pro-group I-mode and the we-mode in many cases do not entail the same equilibrium behaviors. This is shown by comparing Bayesian games in which the players share the group's utility function (which each is trying to maximize individually) with games in which the players acting as a group try to maximize (expected) group utility in the we-mode sense (that is, by each selecting the best outcome in terms of group utility and then inferring their own part-actions). This gives a strong argument for making and applying the distinction between the we-mode and the pro-group I-mode in one's theory. A simple nonprobabilistic example that illustrates the result is the Hi-Lo situation presented earlier: If the members are acting for the dyadic group, the we-mode approach only accepts the HiHi equilibrium, whereas the pro-group I-mode account also allows for the LoLo equilibrium to be realized.

2.4.

To proceed into more detailed discussion, we will repeat some of Bacharach's definitions, but partly in the terminology of this chapter.[23] Thus, when Bacharach talks about team reasoning, we will usually speak of (we-mode) we-reasoning and, parallel to our terminology elsewhere in this book, we will speak of groups (group agents) instead of teams. Similarly, where Bacharach speaks about agents that lapse from their team and play self-centeredly for the singleton team consisting of only the individual agent himself, we will say that agents reason in the I-mode. And when Bacharach talks about agents reasoning as team benefactors, we speak of reasoning in the pro-group I-mode.

In Bacharach's theory, an *unreliable team interaction* (UTI) is a structure $<M, A, U, S, T, \Omega>$, where

$M = \{M^1,\ldots, M^K\}$, where for each $k = 1,\ldots,K$, M^k is a subset of $\{1,\ldots,N\}$, is the set of group agents, viz., teams, which are collections of individual agents,

$A = A_1 \times \ldots \times A_N$, where for each $i = 1,\ldots,N$, A_i is a set of acts of i,

$U = \{U^1,\ldots, U^K\}$, where $U^k: A \to R$ is the utility function of M^k,

$S = S_1 \times \ldots \times S_N$, where S_i is the set of outside signals of i,

$T = T_1 \times \ldots \times T_N$, where for each i = 1,...,N, T_i is a subset of {1,...,K}, is the set of participation states of i (that is, the value k of a participation state or mode t_i of individual i indicates the group agent M^k that i reasons for: in the I-mode case $M^k = \{i\}$ and in the we-mode case it is a larger group, typically {1,...,N}), and Ω is a probability measure on $Z = S \times T$.

Note that although groups have preferences over the possible outcomes, acts are defined only for individuals. Thus groups act only through their individual members. Bacharach defines an *agent protocol* as a function from an agent's outside signals to actions and a *protocol for group agent*, viz., the *team*, M^k as an ordered tuple of agent protocols of the agents in M^k specifying the acts of each agent in the group. An agent, i, follows the protocol of the group she is active in, that is, the group as denoted by her participation state t_i. Thus, supposing that the protocol for M^k is $\alpha^k = (\alpha^k_i)$ for each agent i in M^k, then for each t_i in T_i and act a_i in A, if $t_i = k$, then $a_i = \alpha^k_i(s_i)$.

An *equilibrium* of a UTI is now a profile of protocols for each team such that each protocol is optimal for its team given the protocols of the other teams. Assuming that the signal space S is finite, expected utility is defined as follows:

$EU^k = \Sigma_{(s,t)\ \text{in}\ Z}\ \Omega(s,t)\ U^k(\alpha_1^{t1}(s_1),\ldots,\alpha_N^{tN}(s_N)) = V^k(\alpha)$.

Then α^* is an equilibrium of the UTI $<M, A, U, S, T, \Omega>$ if and only if α^* maximizes $EU^k(\alpha^k,\alpha^{*-k})$ where α^{*-k} denotes the acts of every other agent except k in protocol α^*.[24]

The kind of we-mode reasoning in which the agents select actions directly on the basis of the group's utility function may give results different from those obtainable from pro-group I-mode reasoning, in which the agents transform their preferences by adopting the group's utility function as their own. To see this, we consider Bacharach's results further. Bacharach proves a lemma saying that if α^* is an equilibrium of a UTI $I = <M, A, U, S, T, \Omega>$ then for each k and each i in M^k, α^{*k}_i maximizes EU^k subject to the conditions that $t_i = k$ and that each $j \neq i$ follows α^*.[25] This is needed to prove Bacharach's main result (called the *Central Theorem* below) showing that UTIs differ from Bayesian games with the same utility function. Proceeding to a discussion of it, Bacharach specifies what it is for a Bayesian game to be generated by a UTI as follows: The Harsanyi game generated by I is the Bayesian game $H_I = <M, A, U, S, T, \Omega>$, where all other components are as in I but the utility functions depend on the signal so that if $t_i = k$ then $U_i = U_{Mk}$, that is, the signal (here taken to represent the type of the agent) specifies the group whose utility function the agent will adopt. With probability ω an agent will be a *team benefactor* (pro-group I-moder) and adopt the group utility function as her own, whereas with probability $(1 - \omega)$ she will be what Bacharach calls an egoist (plain I-moder) and maintain her own individual utility function.

As an example, consider the Bayesian game generated by the UTI given above. The following matrices will represent the structure of the game with probabilities ω^2, $\omega(1-\omega)$, $(1-\omega)\omega$, and $(1-\omega)^2$, respectively:

(1)	C	D
C	3, 3	2, 2
D	2,2	2, 2

$p = \omega^2$

(2)	C	D
C	3, 3	2, 4
D	2, 0	2, 2

$p = \omega(1-\omega)$

(3)	C	D
C	3, 3	0, 2
D	4, 2	2, 2

$p = \omega(1-\omega)$

(4)	C	D
C	3, 3	0, 4
D	4, 0	2, 2

$p = (1-\omega)^2$

We can now calculate the expected utilities to find out the equilibria of this game, and with $\omega = 0.9$ it turns out that the equilibria are $(C_B D_E, C_B D_E)$ and $(D_B D_E, D_B D_E)$, where, for instance, a strategy $C_B D_E$ means that given the signal that one is a benefactor, one should choose C, and given the signal that one is an egoist, one should choose D. In this example, the result is that an egoist should choose D but a benefactor may rationally choose either C or D. Thus, this kind of pro-group I-mode reasoning is incapable of eliminating the Pareto-inefficient equilibrium. The situation resembles Hi-Lo-type games but is perhaps even more perplexing. Even in the following game (which is the same as the above matrix in which both agents share the group utility function), individualistic reasoning cannot uniquely recommend the strategy C to the players because in addition to CC, DD is also an equilibrium:

	C	D
C	3, 3	2, 2
D	2, 2	2, 2

Intuitively, C is the only rational strategy, because here, unlike in Hi-Lo, there is not even a conditional reason to select D instead of C because C always gives at least as high a utility as D.

Bacharach's central theorem that is illustrated by the example above can be rendered as follows:[26]

> *Central Theorem*: (1) for all UTIs I, for each equilibrium α of I there is a Bayesian equilibrium of H_I with which α agrees; (2) for some UTIs I there is a Bayesian equilibrium of H_I with which no equilibrium of I agrees.

To put the above in plain English, the Central Theorem entails that the pro-group I-mode and the we-mode, probabilistically construed concerning mode adoption, do not entail the same equilibrium behaviors. In the proof of the theorem this is demonstrated by comparing standard Bayesian games in which the players share the group's utility function (which each is trying to maximize individually) with games in which the players acting as a group try to maximize expected group utility in the we-mode sense (that is, by each selecting the best expected outcome in terms of group utility and then inferring their own part-actions). The resulting outcomes may differ since the former, individualistic case admits Pareto-suboptimal equilibria that will not be equilibria in the we-mode case. (Put somewhat differently, not all equilibria of Bayesian games generated by a UTI I are equilibria of I. In other words, optimal group decision rules [rules for maximizing expected group utility] provide Nash equilibria for pro-group I-moders, but not all Nash equilibria for pro-group I-moders are results of optimal group decision rules.) This result can be taken to show that rational we-mode action is not functionally equivalent to pro-group I-mode action where the agents adopt the group utility function but reason rationally in individualistic fashion.

Given our assumptions (1) and (2) above, the Central Theorem warrants the following thesis:

(3) I-mode and we-mode reasoning, even when aiming at maximizing the same utility function, may produce different equilibria. Furthermore, the we-mode tends to create more collective order than the I-mode: It can decrease the number of equilibria, but it cannot increase them.

Since similar examples can easily be multiplied, the theorem gives an important rationality-based argument for the we-mode superseding the (pro-group) I-mode, that is, for the following claim:

(4) Given that the group utility function is Paretian, then in some cases we-mode reasoning is more rewarding for everyone in the utility-maximizing sense than is I-mode reasoning.[27]

This claim is partly an empirical one. It means that in some cases of social action dilemmas the we-mode yields a better result in terms of maximization of expected individual utility for group members rationally acting as group members than does the (pro-group) I-mode.[28] Together with the assumption that rational agents aim at maximizing utility, it entails a prescriptive recommendation according to which *at least in some specifiable situations agents should reason and act in the we-mode rather than in the I-mode.*

In cases where group members begin by conceptualizing social situations in individualistic terms, they may ultimately switch to we-mode thinking and reframe an originally individualistically conceived situation in we-mode terms. Such a switch involves viewing the situation from the point of view of a group agent and its preferences and utilities. This together with the Paretian assumption can be seen to lead to group-rational mutual cooperation in such situations, which without reframing would be identical to games with mutual interdependence of interests such as PD and Chicken, to the highest joint outcome in the Hi-Lo situation, and so on. In other words, it leads to optimal choice for the group and tends to enhance its members' well-being, ceteris paribus. More precisely, this switch needs to occur at least in a certain proportion of the group members, not necessarily in all of them. Bacharach has investigated several situations in which the switch is expected to occur, given the relative frequency probability of switch that he, contrary to us, at least in his 1999 paper takes to occur due to external circumstances.[29] (See section 3 below for related discussion.)

Finally, (1), (2), and (3) warrant this thesis:

(5) We-mode reasoning is not reducible to pro-group I-mode reasoning, i.e., it is not definable by or functionally constructible from I-mode reasoning. This is because it employs a different reasoning mechanism that relies on groups as the (theoretically) basic agents of reasoning and that in some cases leads to different results than the latter.

To show the irreducibility of the we-mode to the pro-group I-mode, it suffices to show, and has indeed been shown above, that there are cases where the we-mode necessarily leads to different equilibria than the pro-group I-mode. Bacharach's mentioned theorem shows precisely this, given our bridge assumptions (1) and (2).

As will be argued in more detail in section 3, we can also subscribe to the empirical claim that in many cases (e.g., Hi-Lo cases and some instances of PD) our account of we-mode reasoning gives a more correct description of how people actually reason than the I-mode description given by traditional game theory. This claim can be supported by existing empirical studies the results of which are better explained by the hypothesis that people use we-mode reasoning instead of competing I-mode hypotheses that are based on, e.g., utility transformations.[30]

Bacharach's theory allows game-theoretic modeling of both I-mode and we-mode decision making, unlike traditional game theory that is only concerned with I-mode decision making. His extension of game theory is a generalization of standard game theory in the sense that in cases in which the only agents are individuals and groups play no role, the individuals can be modeled as singleton groups with a group utility function that is identical to the agent's utility function, and the original Nash equilibria are preserved. The result can be interpreted as saying that relative to the present game-theoretic setup, I-mode thinking is a special case of we-mode thinking in which the "we" is limited to the agent herself.

It should be noted, however, that Bacharach's theory has some quasi-technical problems (that do not pertain to the we-mode account). One, which Bacharach mentions himself, is that the probability of agents acting in the we-mode is an exogenous variable; it is fixed beforehand and does not vary with agents or depend on the interaction situation. As he notes, the probability of an agent's identification with the group that stimulates team reasoning is affected by the perceived features of the interaction situation.[31] Another problem (that he does not mention) is that defining equilibria in terms of expectations makes his theory sensitive to changes in parameter values in the sense that changing the utility values can sometimes change the equilibria even though the preference orderings are preserved.[32]

Most of the discussion in this chapter and indeed elsewhere in the book has been based on the assumption that the individuals being discussed are disposed to function either in the I-mode or in the we-mode in general or in a specific context. The disposition to select a certain mode (e.g., in the I-mode/we-mode case) seems to be strongly influenced by the underlying culture.[33] In at least some cases mode selection can be intentional action, or so at least common sense and anecdotal evidence suggest. I take the common-sense view that not only can the mode sometimes be intentionally selected by an individual but in some cases it can also be rationally intentionally selected. For instance, a person will adopt the group's view in almost all group contexts and act in the we-mode (e.g., when participating in an important meeting for the sake of the group), but sometimes urgent private matters may interfere, resulting in I-mode action.

Which people are I-moders and which are we-moders in general, or in a given situation, is a contingent matter that has not been much investigated empirically (but recall chapter 6, and see the next section).

3. DISCUSSION AND AUGMENTATION OF THE RESULTS OBTAINED

3.1.

Suppose that the members of group g are disposed to act as a we-mode group (a group agent) and to act as one agent on the basis of we-reasoning and intend to maximize g's group utility. The group members conceptualize from the group perspective. The physical-social situation is taken to be conceptualizable in different ways, viz., the conceptualization is not a priori metaphysically determined, but rather the situation is open to different interpretations.[34] It is thus conceptually and psychologically possible to view, e.g., a dilemma situation in we-mode terms irrespective of whether any utility transformation (of individual utilities into we-mode utilities) actually take place.

As an example, consider the case of two firms (or single agents, two wealthy persons) both owning a factory by a lake. The lake will be badly polluted if both factories let out their waste into the lake, but it is not very badly affected if only one factory does it while the other one cleans up its waste. When individualistically conceptualized, the situation can be seen as a PD. But it can alternatively from the start be seen from the point of view of the group consisting of the owners of the two factories. In this latter case the we-mode approach may lead to joint action concerning the four combinations formed out of (polluting, not-polluting), and the feasible group-friendly joint actions chosen might consist of the participants alternating polluting or both refraining from polluting. In examples like this agents' preferences can at least sometimes genuinely rationally change when they learn more about their surroundings (e.g., that the others are all we-moders). Maybe an agent's preferences were only conditionally of the we-mode kind and required the right kind of information from his surroundings to get deconditionalized (whether intentionally or nonintentionally).

In this section I will discuss the question whether, or to what extent, people de facto are capable and disposed to act as a unitary group agent in social dilemma cases rather than individualistically as agents who act in a partly self-centered way. Thus also free-riderism and other sources of motivation for activities going against group unity will come up as factors tending to lead the participants away from group reasoning and unitary group action.

In technical terms, I will below comment on the applicability of the Central Theorem to real life and especially on the extent of we-reasoning and we-action that we can expect in dilemma situations—test cases for we-mode action. I adopt the following stylized characterizations of the *ideal* (or, if you prefer, "extreme") we-mode and (pro-group) I-mode cases, with rational participants:[35]

(*) *We-mode*: The members fully identify with the group agent and thus function as ideal we-moders, the trio of we-mode criteria (the requirements of group reason, collectivity, and collective commitment) being satisfied and the members engaging in group reasoning in order to find out what they should do as a group to satisfy the group's interests (ethos) and hence their own interests qua group members. The members' relevant private interests should either coincide with their group's interests or else are left completely aside.[36]

(**) *I-mode*: The members act fully autonomously and attempt strategically to satisfy their individualistic (viz., "private") interests that in the pro-group I-mode case involve at least functioning in part for the group's interests while engaging in individualistic group reasoning, viz., group reasoning based on individual agents' reasoning for a distributive "we" (e.g., an I-mode group).

The "ideal type" concepts of the we-mode and the I-mode involved above are conceptually and normatively rather strict, and my theory in this book does not require quite so strong statements for all real-life group contexts. However, (*) and (**) make the discussion here simpler and have import in clarifying a theoretical approach in the way idealized limit cases (like frictionless surfaces) in science do. If the claims to be tested apply to some such cases, that will suffice for our purposes.

(*) and (**) are respective reducts of the we-mode and I-mode approaches to the Bacharachian game-theoretic setup. As earlier in the case of the bridge hypotheses, in (1) and (2) I assume here as my presuppositions that in the we-mode case the we-mode criteria must be satisfied (as (*) says and that, e.g., the pro-group I-mode notion similarly must concur with in previous analysis). Yet the projection assumption involves that, e.g., the normative features of the we-mode remain static and only underlying features here.

Note that the nonrestricted we-mode approach leaves more room than (*) for individual interests and thinking and restricts them only normatively and not conceptually when there is a strong social reason for that (e.g., the prevention of free-riding).[37] We will below operate with the interpretation of the we-mode involved in (*) that free-riding is forbidden for a member qua group member on constitutive normative grounds (thus both conceptually and normatively), once the (we-mode) *group agency* conceptualization or framing has been accepted (see below the T(a) cases in (T)). We recall that the group agency interpretation involves in this book a functional group with an ethos that it purports to satisfy or maintain, as the case may be. As to the members, there are norms that obligate the members to act accordingly. Note that if the members just act as a group and are not regarded as forming a group agent but rather as *acting jointly in the we-mode*, free-riding is conceptually possible in proper collective action dilemmas such as PD (although typically normatively prohibited). This is because then we are still operating with the individualistic utility matrices (e.g., the Bacharachian cases of section 2, below termed T(b) cases).

Recall that the Central Theorem entails that in many dilemma cases and situations we-mode reasoning and acting leads to different action equilibria than does reasoning in the I-mode sense. In neither the we-mode nor in the pro-group I-mode case are fully binding (i.e., all-things-considered) agreements possible within the classical game-theoretic setting, but agreement making in general is possible in a looser sense leading to an obligation to perform one's part.

Given (*) and (**), I now state my *Empirical Validity Thesis*:

(T) We-mode group conceptualization ("framing") and reasoning with ensuing intragroup cooperation can occur and at least in some cases (especially common interest, Paretian cases) indeed does occur in real-life situations that are individualistically conceptualizable as collective-action dilemmas. We-mode reasoners conceptualize them as situations requiring for optimal intragroup cooperation between the members at least with the purpose of satisfying the group's ethos that (a) the *group agent* choose between outcomes that are joint outcomes in the individualistic I-mode conceptualization *or* that (b) the *members function jointly* (at least in the sense, any intragroup action needs to be joint) and do it in the we-mode but yet are not thought of as forming a group agent.

The central difference between T(a) and T(b) is based on the fact that in T(a) a group agent, as viewed by the group members, is assumed to act, and this group agent often contains fictitious elements (e.g., thoughts and actions attributed to the group agent). T(a) is thus concerned with the group agency conceptualization of a situation that is individualistically conceptualizable as a collective action dilemma, e.g., a commons dilemma like cod fishing, the arms race, etc. (dilemmas with the PD structure), or a coordination case (e.g., Hi-Lo). These group agency cases are not Bacharachian cases, discussed in section 2, for in his approach the individuals as choosing agents and I-mode alternatives are always included in the utility matrices. In those cases the we-mode members choose as a group, and this alternative concerning the member level is covered by T(b) and concerns member-level conceptualization in the we-mode. The underlying idea in these different conceptualizations is that there is something (usually a real physical or institutional situation) common to the participants that can be conceptualized or construed differently, viz., either in terms of T(a) a group agent's action, or in terms of T(b) the group members acting as a group. It is generally up to the group members which of the two stances toward the group situation they will take—think, e.g., of the Apple corporation or of an army unit. Given (*), T(a) entails T(b), but the converse may fail to be true (e.g., even for the simple reason that the members might not accept that there truly are group agents even in a functional sense—although the (CAT) principle of chapter 8 might still be satisfied and the group agents in question might epistemically objectively).

Experimental tests concerning group reasoning (thus we-reasoning) in collective action dilemmas tend to support thesis (T), especially T(b), by showing that group (or team) reasoning and action based on it indeed is taking place. Especially interesting are the recent experiments by Andrew Colman and his team.[38] Those experiments concerned fundraising (a "give-some" PD game) and opposition to a genetic modification test site. Monetary payoffs were used in these games, which all had a unique Nash equilibrium and a collectively optimal, Paretian out-of-equilibrium joint outcome. The majority of the participants chose the collectively rational strategies (as we may say, the we-mode framing, and acting according to it). The authors regard the results as consistent with the theoretical assumptions made by Bacharach, and the results seem also compatible with the claims of the present chapter.[39] They also show that the positive results for group reasoning (or team reasoning), viz., the choice of the collectively rational strategies by the majority, seem not all to be explainable by individualistic reasoning (such as value-oriented payoff transformations).[40] The experimental tests of collective-dilemma situations are still scarce, but they do show substantial behavioral support for the group-reasoning thesis (T)(b) (apparently through conceptualizing the situations in the we-mode rather than in the I-mode).[41] As far as I know, there is no direct experimental work concerning the group agency cases T(a), where only groups qua groups make choices.

3.2.

To proceed to a more detailed discussion, I will below contrast we-mode groups (qua group agents) with I-mode groups, no matter what kinds of I-moders (e.g., plain or pro-group I-moders) there are, and consider the real-life validity of the results obtained. I will occasionally also consider the kind of motivation that might lead we-moders to deviate from (*) and lapse into intentionally satisfying their private interests (when different from the group's interests and thus their interests as group members). This is conceptually, or perhaps better (because of the feature of construction) quasi-conceptually, prohibited by (*) because it basically means ceasing to function as a group member (but only as a nonmember, making thesis (T) not applicable).

I will here consider paradigmatic we-mode groups that have preferences accepted for them by their members when functioning as group members, viz., in the we-mode. The members of such groups are assumed to reason in the we-mode on the basis of these preferences (compatibly with (*)). To be rational a group has to have synchronically consistent preferences in accordance with which it acts, given the appropriate information (beliefs, or subjectively estimated epistemic probabilities) it needs for action. A we-mode group has an ethos that can often be taken to express its most preferred state of affairs, or perhaps even its full central utility function(s). In simple cases, though, a goal, for example, may suffice, and in the game-theoretical setup at least the group utility, a goal-like entity, must be there. In addition, the group also needs specific instrumental beliefs for realizing, promoting, and maintaining its ethos (as the case may be).

In ideal group agency cases T(a), the principle (*) quasi-conceptually prevents free-riding, and thus free-riding here would amount to leaving the group. In T(b) cases, (*) does not pose such a conceptual barrier to free-riding (defection). Yet in this case free-riding is normatively prohibited in a (group-)constitutive sense because of group membership (and, e.g., not only by a contingent social norm).[42] A group is capable of rational action if it can take action to satisfy its preferences—ideally to satisfy the highest preference in its ranking. This requires that its members have adequate motivating reasons for a unitary group action—recall the comments on this in chapter 4.

Recall from chapter 6 that the full notion of cooperation is in part based on the group's general belief according to which for it to be able to act adequately in a committed and efficient sense, its members ought to act cooperatively on the basis of the we-mode we-perspective that involves a "togetherness-we" (which is inherently cooperative and hence implies the disposition to act together). The group agent's reason might be, e.g., that it needs to build a house for its activities. This might, according to the group agent's belief, require its members' effective cooperative action, compatibly with its ethos and other goals and principles. So the group decides to undertake the task and asks the members (e.g., through its leaders) to participate. As to a member's participatory action, in general a person acting in the we-mode on the ground of his membership in the group, ought to promote the group's goals and interests and hence ought to use group-based we-reasoning, *be cooperative and reject free-riding (defecting)* in group activities given that he expects that the others will cooperate *with sufficiently high probability* (or technically speaking, within the Bacharachian probabilistic approach the commonly known value of the probability ω is high enough for the participants).[43] A particular member's reason for acting so as a group member is that these activities will, according to his belief, contribute to the efficiency of the group's action compatibly with the group's ethos. So he will cooperate as a group member in what it takes, e.g., to get a house built and do it by the above kinds of cooperative actions appropriate to the task.

For an *ideal* we-moder (one who wholeheartedly identifies with the group) there is no temptation to free-ride in order to satisfy his private interests. For less than fully ideal we-moders it holds true that they either should cooperate or else they will be criticized or may even have to leave the group. This notion of cooperation entails that in a game with the objective payoffs of a PD the players still cannot be in a PD if they are we-moders and satisfy the above requirements.

Consider next the Hi-Lo game (recall chapter 4 and, above, section 2). The group has to choose between joint outcomes. Conceived so, realizing HiHi will trivially be better for the group than realizing LoLo, as the group gets more from it, and as the joint outcome HiHi is better for the members on the average. In the group agent case, a group g chooses one of the joint outcomes. Group agency framing will change not only the game utilities but also the structure of the (individualistically conceived) game in that there will now be a (group-level and higher-order) decision situation merely for the group agent g. Yet as a group agent can act only through its members, it is important to have a member-level account as well. For instance, in the above Hi-Lo situation we assumed that g prefers HiHi to LoLo (unless this happens to contradict its ethos) and accordingly the members as a group each choose Hi. This or something else (like the use of the payoff dominance principle) is needed because without agreement making (or something comparable) the Hi-Lo game has no purely individualistic solutions: the individual players are caught in the regressive dilemma "I will choose Hi if you choose Hi but you will choose Hi only if I choose Hi…" (and analogously for Lo). But when they choose as a group, there is no such irreducible conditionality, and the joint outcome HiHi comes about.

This is what the following kind of simple we-reasoning brings about: Group g decides, i.e., its members' jointly decide or arrive at the joint intention to perform Hi, and this means in terms of the members' reasoning that they accept the premises "We will choose the joint outcome HiHi as a group" (expressing the group's intention, and thus commitment) and, in the case of you and I being the members of g, "We cannot choose HiHi as a group unless I choose Hi and you choose Hi" (expressing a group belief collectively accepted by the members). So I conclude my practical reasoning with "I should choose Hi", which in normal situations leads me to form the intention to choose Hi (recall the discussion in chapters 3 and 5). Thus, from my subjective point of view, I will choose Hi unless something outlandish occurs and prevents me; and similarly for you.[44]

An I-mode group is formed out of suitably interconnected and interdependent members, but partly because of the possibility of free-riding made possible by individual autonomy, it cannot act fully as one agent (even in a case based on mutual promises), in contrast to an ideal we-mode group. While a we-mode group uses group framing to conceptualize a situation as a decision problem for itself (i.e., for a group agent), an I-mode group conceptualizes that same situation individualistically, at least initially. As to the game-theoretic case, the I-moders operate on the basis of the original, individualistic matrix in terms of their individualistic reasoning (even in the pro-group I-mode case). This induces the possibility of strategic action in relation to other group members and thus uncertainty in the situation concerning how they will act. This can happen even if the epistemic joint action probability ω equals 1. Even in that case we are left with the individualistic equilibria in PD and Hi-Lo.[45] However, the Central Theorem does not in all cases (not in Hi-Lo) entail a motivational reason for I-moders to choose a strategy leading to a certain equilibrium outcome rather than to another. Such reasons might be based on special situational and context-dependent information.

As we have seen, a group agent conceptualizes a situation (e.g., a PD or Hi-Lo, as individualistically framed) from its own point of view and requires its members to cooperate within the group. In the full-blown we-mode case dealing with group agents, there is no Hi-Lo game (and a fortiori no PD either): the primary choosing agent in the we-mode case is the agents jointly conceived, and they choose between the outcomes HiHi, HiLo, LoHi, and LoLo. If rational, the members will jointly choose HiHi, which consists of each member choosing Hi. The conclusion is that the we-mode approach group-rationally leads to the members' choice of Hi in both the T(a) and the T(b) cases.

Finally, we recall that the set of I-mode equilibria and the set of we-mode equilibria may differ because the we-mode set is a subset of the I-mode set. This can be commented on as follows: In the we-mode case, in contrast to the I-mode case, there is committed *intragroup we-reasoning (as a group) and group-based cooperation (grounded on group membership requirements)*. In the I-mode case, in contrast to the we-mode case, there is the possibility of using *strategic thinking to advance a single person's interests* in partial opposition to the other members' chances to satisfy their interests. Such strategic intragroup acting in the game-theoretic setup—and, more generally, also in a group-constituting normative sense—contradicts the we-thinking (team reasoning) that binds together the members in the we-mode case. These two elements, member-level cooperation in the we-mode case and the possibility of member-level antagonism based on strategic thinking in the I-mode case, of course pull in opposite directions, although on pain of losing one's membership a we-moder can in a factual situation decide not to participate in the we-reasoning at some point. Recall that our empirical thesis (T) requires the occurrence of at least some we-mode cooperative action based on we-mode reasoning.

3.3.

The Empirical Validity Thesis (T) is concerned with what the Central Theorem assumes and covers, and thus not with cases where the participants are allowed to communicate and, more importantly, to make binding agreements. Recall that in chapter 5 it was argued that collective acceptance requires agreement—but not necessarily the action of agreement making.

In contrast to the we-mode case, cooperation is not a constitutively normative presupposition in the case of pro-group I-moders, although it may be a normative assumption in an I-mode group. Nevertheless, I-moders can make individualistically acceptable agreements (one's failing to satisfy, e.g., the collective commitment and other requirements of the we-mode) to share a goal (e.g., to choose Hi in the Hi-Lo) by mutually promising each other to perform a certain action. We next assume that in both we-mode and I-mode groups the participants are allowed to communicate and explicitly agree in a sense that will be normatively binding either all-things-considered or pro tanto. Such an agreement need not always change the preference structure of, e.g., Hi-Lo, although it will have an effect on the preference intensities in making the utility of choice of Hi higher than in the case where payoff dominance is a mutually used principle of action. Let us also assume that the members of both we-mode groups and of pro-group I-mode groups have goals and share them. In the pro-group I-mode case the members' shared goal of choosing Hi functions as their group's goal, and if realized it gives a solution to the Hi-Lo situation in a group-preferred sense.

Employing the payoff dominance principle, we replace the earlier schema (recall section 2) for pro-group I-mode reasoning by the following schema that in effect incorporates payoff dominance and where you and I form a distributive "we" and where we can both perform the following kind of reasoning (I here write it out from the perspective of "I"):

1. I share with you the intention (goal) to maximize group utility.
2. I and you mutually believe that the shared goal HiHi increases both our individual utilities and group utility more than does LoLo and thus maximizes group utility.

Therefore,

3. I and you both take Hi as our respective individual goal in view of clause (2), and mutually believe this and, being rational, I and you will both perform Hi.

The present schema represents the kind of practical reasoning that ordinary people might engage in, and it normally works—if it did not, people probably would not as often act on their mutual beliefs and shared utilities as they do.

In general, I-moders can of course make (individualistically conceived) agreements to do something together. Such an agreement is meant to lead to the other individuals' or group members' participation (cf. (2) and (3) above). As we have seen, a central difference in the case of an I-mode group compared with the (ideal) we-mode case is that an I-moder may still think strategically vis-à-vis the other group members, and there will accordingly be a temptation to free-ride in collective action dilemmas (such as public good provision problems). In the we-mode group agency case T(a) there is no such incentive apart from leaving the group. In the we-mode cases corresponding to the earlier T(b), there is often the conceptual possibility of acting differently. At least in relaxed group agency or (mere) we-reasoning cases, defection may in real life be a tempting alternative and may not lead to the free-rider having to leave the group, in contrast to the group agency case.

The I-moders will in all cases choose as individual persons rather than as a group (in the sense of the we-mode approach). This may lead to defecting unless the participants in addition *trust* that the others will obey the agreement and are collectively committed to satisfying the agreement. As to trust, depending on context, a strong kind of trust termed "social normative trust" arguably is entailed by the we-mode—but not by the I-mode.[46] That means that the we-mode participants will trust (instead of merely believing or predicting) that the other group members will participate.

3.4.

To summarize, this section has shown that the Empirical Validity Thesis (T) has experimental (and also common-sense anecdotal) support at least in some T(b) cases (no experimental results seem to be available concerning the group agency cases T(a)). Confirmation for T(b) as such does not confirm T(a), as that case might contain fictitious elements that are not present in T(b) that may prevent the group agency case from being reducible to the joint-action case T(b) (see chapter 2 for fictitious elements that, understood in the broadest sense, include the group agent's imagined thoughts and actions). There is nonetheless reason to expect that we-mode groups in several kinds of collective action dilemmas reason and act in the we-mode in accordance with the Central Theorem and realize Paretian equilibria (especially in cases without binding communication and agreement making). As we have seen, we-mode reasoning can prevent collective action dilemmas such as PD from occurring, and it can also, through a switch from individualistic conceptualization to we-mode conceptualization, dissolve an existing dilemma. Rational players do not cooperate, at least in single-shot a PD, but they may dissolve a PD by reconceptualizing it in the we-mode (e.g., a commons dilemma such as fishing or hunting endangered species). Thus cooperation is relative to conceptualization in this sense. Furthermore, the we-mode case often fares better than the I-mode in collective dilemmas like PD and Stag Hunt and in coordination games like Hi-Lo. More research is required for more precise empirical assessments of we-mode reasoning and acting.

In cases with agreement making that go beyond the scope of the Empirical Validity Thesis, pro-group I-mode groups may do well, although the threat to the group of free-riderism is often present. Agreement making and the acceptance of goals in the framework relaxes, and of course changes, the strict game-theoretic assumptions, opening up a more realistic way of comparing the we-mode with the (pro-group) I-mode. There are still further reasons related to the central we-mode criteria, especially group-based collective commitment, for claiming that the we-mode even here has an edge over the pro-group I-mode. Accordingly, we-mode conceptual "tools" are needed in the social sciences in addition to I-mode tools.

4. THREE STAGES OF WE-REASONING

4.1.

In this section we will study the *processes* that may lead to situations describable as game-theoretic decision problems, that is, situations that can be modeled in terms of decision matrices the contents of which are common knowledge (or true belief) among the agents involved. These processes can be described as processes of we-reasoning, leading to new public information of a normal form game-theoretic matrix. Here we concentrate on the we-mode case and assume that there already is a group that has collectively accepted goals, in particular the goal of creating a collective preference matrix, a mapping of their individual preferences for the use of the group. In the I-mode case there need be no group goal but only individuals with a (shared) goal of creating a matrix. We consider a (we-mode) goal X that is based on collective acceptance and that satisfies the three criteria of authoritative group reason, satisfaction of the collectivity condition, and collective commitment Accordingly, first, goal X gives a member a "favoring" reason to perform her part to satisfy X. Second, she cannot satisfy X for herself only. Third, she participates in the members' collective commitment to X.

Here we apply the we-mode goal approach to the collective-reasoning process, that is, to we-reasoning from beginning till end. The participants' *first* goal is to acquire reliable information concerning the different action alternatives and their evaluation. The *second* goal is to form a joint intention on the basis of the information acquired in the first stage. The *third* goal is to satisfy the joint intention acquired in the second stage. Only the third goal directly involves interfering with the external course of events. The first two can be regarded as cases of collective problem solving.

This three-stage division can be made very clearly because each of the stages ends with the *satisfaction* of the corresponding goal. The first one ends when the parties have acquired the new information and when this is information is common knowledge. The second one ends once they have reached the joint intention to act, and the third one ends once this intention is carried out. In game-theoretic terms, the first goal is to create a decision matrix, the second goal is to choose an outcome from the matrix, and the third goal is to satisfy the chosen outcome. The we-mode goal account not only provides clear criteria for distinguishing different stages in "the stream of we-reasoning", but also serves as a unifying framework for accounting for the entire process.

Accordingly, the collective-reasoning process that leads to the satisfaction of the joint intention is divided into three different stages of we-reasoning, WR1, WR2, and WR3 for short. For logical reasons, each preceding reasoning stage must have been carried through before any subsequent process can begin. The accomplishment of WR1 is a presupposition for WR2, and the accomplishment of WR2 is a presupposition of WR3. Each of the three stages of we-reasoning aims at giving a solution to a different problem for the group.

Section 2 was concerned with the decision-making stages, that is, WR2 and WR3, which are the stages that game theory and Bacharach's theory of unreliable team interactions deal with. *Individual preference matrices* are taken as given in game theory, and their creation is discussed below.[47] Group members often end up in situations where joint action could be desirable, but they are not aware of how other members would rank the available outcomes. When the agents try to deliberate privately, by themselves, they may end up in incomplete matrices, or, even if they manage to create a complete normal form matrix by themselves, e.g., one that mirrors the objective payoffs, they do not know if it would serve as a trustworthy basis for further deliberation and action, or they do not know if the others are aware of it. In these cases they can join forces to find a solution in the we-mode by adopting a we-mode goal to create a matrix. For simplicity, we talk about the creation of a matrix, but it of course need not be produced in written form, let alone in matrix form. Game-theoretic matrices are tools for modeling; what the agents are sharing and producing is the information represented in the matrix.

Here they have two possibilities for a we-mode goal: the members might decide to create a standard game-theoretic matrix, viz., an *individual preference matrix*, or they might attempt to create a *group preference matrix*. The difference between the two is that in the latter case there will be a single common preference ranking that is collectively accepted for the group. In the former case, the members have their separate preference rankings that are acknowledged by the others. These separate rankings may, but need not, converge, and a collective choice can be attempted on the basis of them without trying to create a common group preference ranking. We will here discuss the formation of such individual preference matrices, and the formation of group preferences is discussed in subsection 4.2.

Consider a two-person two-choice case where the players are you and I. First we have to find out what each of us wants to be the case, thus what our individual all-things-considered preferences are concerning the outcomes CC, CD, DC, DD. Note that WR1 could have been preceded by another type of we-reasoning concerning what in fact is possible for the agents to do on a given occasion, i.e., what the external opportunities for action are. However, which of these possibilities are relevant is up to the agents. Accordingly, they can "we-reason" to produce a list of the relevant options that are available. This we-reasoning could be termed WR0. However, even though the relevant available options would be set and known at the outset, what need not be known is how the agents value these options, and WR1 deals with this.

The we-reasoning involved in WR1 can be represented by a syllogism that concerns means and ends. Here we consider the case where the parties are collectively committed to constructing a matrix mapping their individual all-things-considered preferences, of which there will be common knowledge. The following simple practical inference describes each participating person's we-reasoning in the first-person form:

> We intend to achieve a genuine common matrix of our preferences and to acquire mutual awareness of it.
> Unless (a) I rank the available outcomes into a preference order, and unless (b) I sincerely express my preference order to you, we will not achieve this goal (the genuine matrix of which there is common knowledge).
> Therefore,
> I intend to see to it that (a) and (b).

This pattern of reasoning can be considered as "conceptually binding" (if one accepts the premises, one cannot rationally consistently deny the conclusion). Suppose that the parties have succeeded in carrying out the conclusions of their corresponding practical reasoning. As a result, given that the flow of information is not blocked or distorted, they have obtained a matrix, M1, the contents of which are common knowledge. Matrix M1 may represent everyone's preferences, in which case WR1 is over and the members proceed to WR2 on the basis of M1. But it may also contain information that leads to a preference transformation, in which case M1 is transformed into another matrix, M2, and they continue on the basis of M2, or M2 is transformed to M3, and so on.[48]

We say below that the resulting matrix is a *genuine preference matrix* if and only if the order of the individual utility figures matches the order of the all-considered preferences of the individuals. If a group member lapses from the we-mode and strategically announces a false preference order, the resulting matrix will not be genuine, even if the other group member would falsely believe so. One can always try to arrive at a matrix by I-mode reasoning, but in that case the resulting matrix need not be genuine, as the parties can keep their true preference rankings to themselves.

A good game-theoretic model should describe the features of the interaction situation, not as they are realized in the world, but as they are perceived by the decision makers. To reach such a description in experimental situations, something like the we-reasoning process of stage WR1 could be simulated by allowing the subjects to exchange information about their preferences over the possible outcomes until these preferences stabilize. Accomplishing this in practice involves several difficult questions such as how to ensure that the subjects communicate their actual preferences, and, if this is solved, how to design experiments in which the subjects end up in final matrices representing situations that the experimenters are interested in, for instance, PD-type situations. However, these problems should be addressed if one wants to make any kind of comparison between game-theoretic predictions and people's actual behavior. In order to be able to draw accurate conclusions about people's behavior in various interaction situations, it is necessary to make sure that the experimenters know what the game is that the subjects are playing and upon reflection take themselves to be playing.

Theoretical accounts of collective-action dilemmas typically start with some matrices, e.g., PD, Chicken, or Hi-Lo. Given these matrices, they may discuss various reasoning patterns or matrix transformations that lead to different collective or individual choices. "Where the matrices come from" is not usually considered a problem that requires explanation. To account for the WR1 process is to account for the emergence of the matrices. Sometimes the situation is so obvious (the matrix is given and the parties are mutually aware of it) that the parties can directly begin with WR2. Sometimes it is enough to find only one mutually satisfactory or "satisficing" action alternative.[49] Sometimes there is no agreement over a description of the situation, or the agents realize that none of the alternatives will be mutually satisfactory and they return to stage WR0 to expand the space of alternatives. We have emphasized the WR1 stage because in standard accounts this stage is often overlooked or fused together with the subsequent stages, and this is apt to produce confusion.

In general, the following argument (which makes more precise our earlier discussion in chapter 6 and section II of this chapter) shows that we-mode reasoning can prevent the agents—in the nonprobabilistic case—from framing an interaction situation as a PD even though the objective payoffs form a PD structure:

1. In a genuine single-shot PD, individually rational agents defect.
2. It is not necessarily the case that rational agents frame the objective situation individualistically as a PD.
3. If one reasons in the we-mode and adopts a group perspective, the situation is not framed as a PD.

Therefore:

4. The we-mode prevents the emergence of a PD.

So far we have shown that *we-mode reasoning at stage WR1 can be more beneficial than the I-mode on three accounts*: (1) It can account for the emergence of the normal form matrix in cases where the I-mode fails. For example, privately they only succeed in creating an incomplete matrix. (2) It guarantees that the resulting matrix is genuine in the sense of expressing the participants' true preferences. (3) It can prevent the emergence of collective action dilemmas.

The prevention of collective action dilemmas can take place in various ways. For example, some agents "by nature" persist in framing interactive situations as cooperative: they are "disposed" to identify with their group and to team-reason accordingly.[50] For the present chapter, the most interesting possibility of preventing collective action dilemmas is the we-mode creation of *group* preferences. This will be discussed below.

4.2.

We now proceed to a discussion of the creation of a *group preference matrix*. As seen in chapter 5, a group's preferences (in our strong sense) can be taken to be based on the collectively accepted goals and other intentional attitudes of the group. My account is based on the simple idea that a group prefers an action or outcome X to an action or outcome Y when its members so collectively accept when acting as group members.[51] Of any two outcomes the one that better promotes these goals can rationally be taken to be preferred by the group, and assuming that the group's preferences satisfy the standard axioms of utility theory, a group's utility function can be derived. As a simple example, consider a business firm the only goal of which is to maximize profit. This entails that the outcome that maximizes profit is the preferred outcome for the group.

As argued earlier, the group's preferences are not necessarily functionally dependent on the group members' individual preferences, especially not if the we-mode view of a group agent accepting attitudes for itself is adopted. In the case of a business firm, its personnel may be required to act as group members in order to achieve the firm's objectives. If the firm's only goal is to maximize profit, the preferences of the personnel need not affect the group's preferences at all. However, the hired personnel can be seen as a subgroup of the whole group. The latter includes the owners, who have the power to decide about the goals of the firm. The preferences of the firm cannot in all cases be reduced to the preferences of the owners, since the owners may change without the change being immediately reflected in the firm's objectives. (See chapter 6 for organizations.)

Group preferences can be based on goals and other collectively accepted attitudes, but sometimes the group preference ordering itself can be collectively accepted. Above we discussed the WR1 process where the agents created an ordinary game-theoretic preference matrix. In a similar vein, the agents reasoning in WR1 may take reaching a group preference matrix as their goal. Here each group member gives her "we-mode proposal" for the group's preferences: "According to me, the group should put the joint outcomes in the following order: . . . " As intermediate results we may get different suggestions for a group preference ordering, and these suggestions may be transformed on the basis of other agents' analogous suggestions and group discussion. In terms of matrices, the ultimate aim is to reach a matrix with only one number for each outcome, representing the group's utility function.

The group preference ordering concerning certain outcomes is not necessarily reducible to individual preference orderings concerning those outcomes, for several reasons: First, the formation of group preference requires collective acceptance. Second, once collectively accepted, a preference ordering remains the group's preference ordering until it is collectively changed, even though individual preference orderings may change. Third, the collective acceptance of a preference ordering with respect to certain outcomes $O_1,...,O_n$ need not be based on individuals' preference orderings concerning these outcomes but on their opinions on what preference ordering the group should adopt, and these two things may differ.

Note that in addition to individual and group preferences, Bacharach's UTI matrices require the objective probability function Ω. We will here concentrate on the group members' shared (perhaps averaged) view or estimate, Ω*, of an objective epistemic probability Ω. So Ω* can be interpreted as expressing the group's view concerning the probability of group members selecting actions on the basis of the group preferences. The value of this parameter can be estimated in the WR1 process similarly to the formation of the preferences. After the group preferences have been agreed upon, the group members can give their estimates of Ω. If the estimates converge, all the information required for describing the situation as a UTI becomes available and common knowledge. Moreover, the estimate of the values of Ω now depends on the interaction situation described in the matrix, unlike in Bacharach's original theory, in which Ω is an exogenous variable.

In everyday life these kinds of estimations occur frequently. A group first evaluates the outcomes and then it estimates the number of group members who are willing to participate in reaching the preferred outcomes. These parameters, the group utility function and the probability function, then define the equilibria that specify whether it is rational for the group to pursue the most preferred outcome or some other outcome.

If the group members can agree on a group preference ordering, they can collectively accept it so that it satisfies the three conditions of the we-mode. If they then reason in the we-mode in accordance with these group preferences, their intragroup situation cannot be described as a PD or any other collective-action dilemma.

The jointly produced matrix M1, that is, the result or the output of WR1, of which there is common knowledge, serves as input to WR2. The second we-goal would be to choose an outcome from the matrix; viz., the second goal is to reach a we-intention to act jointly. This goal is satisfied when the agents succeed in forming a we-intention with the content of satisfying a particular outcome. Once the outcome is collectively fixed, the parties are committed to achieving it, and they can proceed to WR3, in which the agents select their part actions that together result in achieving the outcome. Note that the reasoning processes in stages WR2 and WR3 can be performed by the individual agents autonomously, as generally supposed in non-cooperative game theory. In particular, in cases in which there is a unique outcome that maximizes group utility or in cases in which there is a unique UTI equilibrium, agents reasoning in the we-mode will be guaranteed to reach the optimal outcome. If there are several equally good alternatives, the agents will still face a coordination problem, and communication will be required in order to guarantee an optimal result.

5. CONCLUDING REMARKS ON WE-REASONING

In this chapter we have compared two kinds of we-reasoning in a collective decision-making situation: pro-group I-mode reasoning and we-mode reasoning. We have discussed these reasoning methods both in Bacharach's game-theoretic framework and in my framework or theory of social action and sociality. This chapter has highlighted the connections and differences between these two frameworks. The I-mode/we-mode theory of this book adds conceptual machinery lacking in Bacharach's game-theoretic framework, whereas the results obtained by Bacharach support my idea of the functional difference between the we-mode and the pro-group I-mode and more generally of the irreducibility of the we-mode to the I-mode. In addition, it has been shown by our stage model of we-reasoning that the Bacharachian parameters (and other a priori given elements in his theory) can be empirically provided. In particular this concerns the group's preferences. (Cf. also chapter 5.)

The main results obtained in this chapter concerning the differences between pro-group I-mode reasoning and we-mode reasoning are as follows:

1. Pro-group I-mode reasoning and we-mode reasoning can yield different action recommendations. For instance in Hi-Lo, we-mode reasoning in the case of rational groups entails a specific action recommendation, but strict pro-group I-mode reasoning compatible with standard game theory does not.
2. We-mode reasoning can in many cases lead to more beneficial results than the I-mode because it eliminates suboptimal equilibria and thus creates more collective order. This result basically follows from Bacharach's theory of unreliable team interactions, given our connection theses earlier in the chapter. His important mathematical result, here termed the "Central Theorem", means that the we-mode approach is in some cases capable of creating more collective (i.e. group-level) order than the (pro-group) I-mode approach is capable of, and it gives a better explanation of cooperative behavior. This result can be taken to mean that the we-mode is irreducible to the I-mode, because as shown in section 4 it concerns also attitudes and not only actions.
3. The Empirical Validity Thesis has received empirical support in many cases of collective-action dilemmas, especially when communication and agreement making are absent.
4. We-mode reasoning can in many potential dilemma cases lead to more beneficial results than the I-mode, for instance because it can prevent the emergence of collective-action dilemmas by leading the agents to frame the situation as a group's decision problem.
5. Even if the agents do not succeed in framing the situation as a group decision problem by creating a group preference matrix but instead end up in a standard game-theoretic decision matrix, the matrix genuinely reflects their preferences if it is produced in the we-mode.

As least in principle, these results can be applied to the design of social institutions. Because we-mode thinking often yields more collective order, it may be taken as a rational desideratum that, other things being equal, the design of social institutions be based on we-mode thinking rather than on individualistic thinking. The results should also be taken into account in social-scientific theorizing. If we-mode reasoning and I-mode reasoning produce different rational behavior and if, as the discussed empirical evidence for we-reasoning suggests, human beings sometimes reason in the we-mode, methodological individualism is not sufficient as a foundation of the social sciences in either a prescriptive, rational, or descriptive sense.[52] Theories that rely on the assumption of methodological individualism need revision or complementation. Adequate conceptualization, description, and explanation of social activities (especially joint activities) of intentional and rational beings require the use of group concepts and the we-perspective, especially in its we-mode form.

We may ask why whether collectivism (e.g., in the form of the we-mode approach) or individualism or some combination of these approaches should be preferred to the other alternatives in certain specific kinds of situations or perhaps overall. This question can be partly answered by empirical scientific testing (cf. above). This is the empirical output-side of the problem. The empirical input-side concerns how people come to acquire the disposition to be dominantly I-moders or dominantly we-moders. The answer may in part lie in evolution (gene-culture evolution probably) and in part in the upbringing and education of children on the basis of pertinent cultural values, traditions, norms, etc. I cannot here discuss this important but very broad and complex problem.

ACKNOWLEDGMENT

Much of this chapter is directly based on the 2010 paper "Two Kinds of We-Reasoning" that I wrote together with Raul Hakli and Kaarlo Miller. I am grateful to my coauthors for their permission to use chunks of our joint text in this chapter. Section 3 consists only of new material (for which my aforementioned coauthors bear no responsibility).

8

Institutional Facts and Institutions

I. COLLECTIVE PATTERN-GOVERNED BEHAVIOR AND SOCIAL PRACTICES

Social institutions and the facts based on them conceptually pertain to social groups (e.g., communities, societies), and I will accordingly regard them as necessarily being group phenomena. Social artifacts such as social institutions are created (not always intentionally) and maintained by "us" (the group members) for us, i.e., for the use of our group. My approach to social facts and institutions accordingly is based on collective acceptance explicating conceptual construction. In a world without human or human-like beings and their conceptual activities, there would be no institutional facts. Indeed, I will argue that social institutions in general should be taken to be based on we-thinking (in the we-mode) rather than I-thinking (I-mode).[1]

Social institutions (such as the institutions of money, marriage, and private property, as well as many social organizations) basically consist of a *norm* system and a system of *social practices* conducive to the satisfaction of these norms. Hence social institutions can be taken to refer both to the behaviors characteristic of institutional behavior and to the underlying social facts and norms that explain such behavior. This description refers to a fully functional social institution, although there might be institutions, such as social organizations with unfulfilled positions, where the norms cannot be fully satisfied because of the absence of relevant social practices or practitioners. Social institutions typically have as their general goal or at least function to create order in society by solving coordination problems and collective action problems involving conflict between individual and collective rationality. Institutional solutions are typically collectively beneficial for the community in question, and they also help individuals to satisfy their basic needs. A basic desideratum for social institutions is that people be able to rely on them, since lack of trust can jeopardize the functionality of the institution (e.g., the medical personnel of a hospital must be suitably qualified and trustworthy according to the standards of the community). Social institutions with their constitutive norms involving rights and duties, such as the examination rights of a professor, enable new kinds of activities to come about. Social institutions economize reasoning by making activities routine and computationally easier. The converse is also often true: routine behaviors and customs will often be institutionalized if they are widely shared in a community. They might not be instrumentally rational, e.g., in an optimality sense, although acting on the basis of them typically is socially rational. Institutionalization involves making existing social practices norm-governed and giving them a special status. Thus customs may develop into institutional norms through a process of institutional evolution. These diverse aspects of social institutions will be approached in this chapter, beginning with an account of *routine collective behavior*, which is typically nonintentional and in many respects analogous to the habitual behavior of individuals (except for the import of social norms and customs).

Accordingly, I argue that social institutions and institutional facts, in one way or another, in general depend on routine and non-intentional activities. I claim that there is non intentional but yet conceptually and teleologically meaningful behavior that forms the core of routine behavior and, I claim, of (collective) institutional behavior. This is behavior that I have called *collective pattern-governed behavior*.[2] I have elsewhere discussed and analyzed the idea of collective pattern-governed behavior as collective behavior that need not be intentional—and typically is not—but still is purposive and meaningful.[3]

To clarify my notions, a strictly *intentional action* is behavior that is done on purpose and is based on the agent's intention or decision, its purpose being what the content of the intention expresses. Such intentional action accordingly is performed in accordance with and (partly) because of the intention to perform that very action or a "closely related" action. The closely related action can be a part of the action in question, or it can be a whole that the intentionally performed action is a part of or a means to.

Next we consider an example of a *nonintentional action*.[4] Suppose a person scratches his nose while talking without paying attention to his own behavior. The action still is meaningful in the sense of being an understandable agent-controlled action with a teleological point—as contrasted with reflex behavior and the like. Nonintentional nose scratching is not a mistaken action or a slip or anything of the kind. It belongs to a larger action as an element that (perhaps) was not necessary for the pattern (say, talking to one's boss) but which is meaningful and perhaps expressive of the agent's nervousness and accompanying loss of control. This larger action is *not nonintentional* (in the sense, for instance, falling or slipping is nonintentional) or even *unintentional* in the sense making a mistake (which is based on an attempt intentionally to perform something right) is unintentional.[5] In our present terminology, the discussed kind of meaningful nonintentional action (a token action instantiating a type that might have, and typically has, only nonintentional tokens) is *pattern-governed behavior* (PGB). This term is used by Wilfrid Sellars, but I use it in a somewhat wider sense and, especially, focus on *collective* pattern-governed activity, which Sellars does not discuss.

Single-agent collective pattern-governed behavior can serve to ground intentional action in the public realm. Social practices typically involve pattern-governed behaviors, viz., pattern-governed behaviors are often embedded in social practices. I have argued that social practices come about because of shared we-attitudes. Here "because of" expresses a reason-giving causal relation, i.e., these attitudes have a causal influence and also serve to rationalize the social practice.

As to the collective case, as I have characterized it in my previous work, *collective social action* is action performed for a social reason, e.g., a shared we-attitude.[6] A we-attitude in its ideal form is an attitude that an agent has such that he believes that the others in the group also have it and that all this is mutually believed or known in the group. When a we-attitude is shared, all members have it. A *social practice*, e.g., a custom or a pattern of institutional action, can be regarded as *repeated* collective social action performed for a (shared) social reason.[7]

Pattern-governed behaviors (components of such social action) are meaningful and teleological because they are part of an intentional activity; and in the collective case they analogously exhibit collective intentionality (meaningfulness in the collective aboutness sense) and goal-directedness.[8] Each particular token of a social practice gets its teleological meaningfulness from the social reason for which it was performed.[9] Shared we-attitudes are public in the group in normal cases, although one may conceive of implicit cases where that is not the case and where the fact of sharing is thus epistemically shaky. A social practice (repeated collective social action) in its core sense may accordingly be understood as expressing the content of a we-attitude, which might also be a we-attitude-in-action.

In addition, mental activities can be PGBs and, in the case of collective wants, intentions and beliefs, they can form collective PGBs, which may make the mental (motivational and other) elements involved in customs and social practices routine. People's patterns of thinking and reasoning, e.g., on how to think about solving certain practical issues in their daily activities, may be as routine as the overt activities themselves to which they give rise or accompany. We might coin the term pattern-governed mental activities (PGMA) for them. Collective PGMAs, conceived as mental activities guiding social customs when the latter are collective pattern-governed behaviors or include such behaviors as their elements, seem to be common in real social life (think of how racist stereotypes might function in people's minds, as an example).

To summarize the role of pattern-governed behaviors in institutional practices, a collective PGB, first, is a collectively meaningful element of an intentionally performed collective social action (action performed because of a shared we-attitude). Second, the collective PGB has individual PGBs as its elements. Third, the collective social action in question (typically) is performed in part *because of* a shared we-attitude, at least a shared we-belief to the effect that that is what the participants are doing. Here the single-agent PGBs are either individual part actions or elements of the individual part actions that make up the collective social action in question. Fourth, a collective PGB is causally governed by an ought-to-be norm or standard (think here of a child learning to cross the street on green light, her perception of the light being the proximate cause and the norm is that it ought to be the case in the community that people obey traffic rules such as the green-light crossing rule).

A collective PGB is actionally nonintentional both in the collective sense (which entails lack of guidance and control by a shared collective intention) and in the individual sense (which entails that the involved singular PGBs are nonintentional). Nevertheless, it is collectively intentional in the aboutness sense, as the ought-to-be norm governing a PGB can be taken to represent a group goal. However, this does not require that individual participants (e.g., children) have the right representations or goals as long as their behavior is correct. Thus there need not be intentional aboutness on the level of individual participants.[10] Yet group goals are involved.

Consider now the example of the collective social action of making a certain kind of pot that requires a special ingrained skill, say, a special nonintentional hand movement (PGB), a bodily activity with a certain overt result. The hand movement de facto cannot be performed without the learned skilled action in which it is embedded. (The hand movement type can be a bodily action type—something that can be performed directly on purpose.) We can assume that every potter participating in this tradition and exemplifying a certain pattern-governed mental activity (a kind of mental "script" or directive for the practice of such pot making) believes that the others are also manufacturing pots in the same special way and believes that this is mutually believed in the group. The pot making thus is a collective social action in the sense of being performed in part because of a shared we-attitude. While the embedded special hand movements are PGBs, collective sanctioning or disapproval of norm violation might consist of individual PGBs (expressions of negative feelings) and the appropriate explicit or implicit we-belief.[11]

The genesis of a collective PGB can take place in terms of institutional or group design based on *ought-to-be norms* that express group goals, although it may also be the expression of some natural or social process of selection that has such ought-to-be-norms among its consequences. A given collective PGB can be the central causal behavioral component of a social practice that fulfills an ought-to-be norm (e.g., it ought to be the case that people cross a street safely and according to traffic rules). Upbringing, education, and teaching will typically play a major role in the maintenance of a PGB. The upholders of these ought-to-be norms will be parents and other educators, but these norms may be spoken about in an abstract sense without specifying exactly which persons or institutional groups are responsible for fulfilling them. In any case, collective PGBs are dependent on cultural and social values, traditions, norms, and the like. Their central function is teaching novices (e.g., children), e.g., by parents or skilled specialists. They need not as such be optimal responses to demands of the environment in which (or for which) they came about, but, because of conformity and coordination demands for collective behavior, they typically are "coordinatively" socially rational (think, e.g., of various ways of building a boat).

As collective social actions and the social practices built out of them are central for my account of social institutions, collective PGBs will also derivatively anchor them in routine patterns of behavior. Collective PGBs are central building blocks of the social world, especially in the sense of forming the routine ingredients in social practices (viz., repeated collective social actions), customs, and institutional behavior. Such routines generally come about because of repetition and learning. Such routine activities are frequently economic or functional, since they tend to save energy and effort for other, more demanding activities. They also create social order, and even invisible-hand activity can in some cases be regarded as a collective PGB, as well as some implicit social norms.[12] In a way, then, collective PGBs belong to socialized persons' "natura altera".

2. GROUP-SOCIAL FACTS AND ENTITIES

The primary conceptual and theoretical basis of institutions, qua special social norm-practice systems, is public collective acceptance, while various presuppositions must also hold true. Thus, there must be actual people, often of certain specific kinds or with special capacities, who are members of social groups and are, as group members, engaged in social practices or transactions promoting the group's goals and interests. There must also be suitable physical objects or structures, if the institutions need them for their functionality—e.g., in the case of money there must be some physical objects with properties practically suitable for economic exchange. However, regarding the conceptual aspects of social institutions, we-mode collective acceptance (construction) is the crucial conceptual explanans. This is highlighted in instances where the group members—correctly or not—take it to be up to them to construct social items that in principle are fully up to a collective or group of people to decide about, e.g., the group's collective artifacts such as money. This is the central case that we will be concerned with. As just said, this may require that certain presuppositions are in place. Such collective acceptance in general requires overt action and might in some cases consist only of such acceptance-as-action when the right conceptual and factual conditions are satisfied.

Let us start by thinking of the simple medieval Finnish case of the collectively accepted institutional content of a squirrel pelt being money, an example that conceptually does not depend, at least as much as modern institutions do, on other institutional structures or facts other than language. Assuming that the relevant factual presuppositions are mutually believed and true and that people have a grasp of what money in general is (e.g., storage of value and vehicle for exchange), we are here dealing with full *content construction* entailing that the group has the full power by its collective construction to create an institution or other artifact by its "arbitrary" choice (see below and see section 4). In our present example the practice of using squirrel pelts as money accordingly is self-validating—the actual use of money ultimately validates the constitutive principle that a squirrel pelt is money where such use is not accidental but based on the participants' collective acceptance involving their having reached a joint understanding about what their use of this kind of money incorporates.

Group-social facts (or structures) are conceptually group-based and group-constructed, and they include normative institutional facts as a subclass.[13] The account to be given here states a schematic necessary and sufficient criterion for group sociality in the sense of a proposition expressing a group-social fact, given that suitable factual presuppositions are in place.[14] Note that the class of intrinsically group-based facts, i.e., group-social facts, includes *institutional facts* as a central subclass. The latter involve normative elements, especially ought-to-be, ought-to-do norms, and status-specifying norms saying that something X counts as something Y.[15] Not all group-social facts, e.g., social practices, are (strongly) normative (e.g., in the sense of obligation to participate). The groups that are considered here are groups that can act, organized groups in something like the old Roman sense of *corporatio* and are typically we-mode groups.

I will now present my thesis expressing the central features of group-social facts and also making precise the old idea that in the social realm what is taken to be socially real is socially real. Here is the collective "constructivist" account formulated for the somewhat idealized, full-blown case that fits best the case of egalitarian groups and voluntary acceptance but that also allows at least weak cases of non-autonomous acceptance:[16]

> *Collective acceptance thesis for group sociality* (CAT): A proposition, s, is *group-social* and correctly expresses a *group-social fact* in a primary sense in a group g if and only if (a) the members of g collectively accept s as true or correctly assertable for g, and (b) necessarily, they collectively accept s as true or correctly assertable for g if and only if s is true or correctly assertable for the members of g functioning as group members.[17]

Basically, a proposition s counts as group-social if and only if when it is substituted for the propositional variable s in (CAT), the analysans is true *for group g*. We recall that the truth of a proposition for a group entails that the proposition is normally meant to further the group's interests and it is supposed that the members are disposed to make use of it in their we-thinking and we-acting in relevant cases. This does not apply to out-groupers: s is true only in an objective, third-person sense in their case but of course cannot be similarly used in their we-thinking for their group (e.g., a squirrel pelt is not money for their group). Accordingly, s expresses a "groupjective" (group-relative) rather than objective fact. (That the fact is groupjective here entails it is "epistemically objective" for g.)[18]

According to clause (a), we are dealing with the group-public collective acceptance of a fact-expressing proposition s that involves its being for the use of the group and hence involves an underlying group presupposition and reason for a member's action such as her use of a squirrel pelt rather than, e.g., a rat pelt as money (while her primary reason for buying something with the money might be that she needs it). Although (CAT) does not strictly require it, collective acceptance of s is below assumed to be in the we-mode in the weak sense of chapter 5, section 3. Accordingly, a collectively accepted artifact for a group is of course a collective matter in the group—the collectivity condition entails in our example case that, necessarily, a squirrel pelt is money for all members. The group can in principle be a non-autonomous group, but in that case an external authority will determine what the group members collectively accept and which group-social fact comes about. In the extreme case of a sole dictator determining what the group's acceptable social facts are (e.g. that this rather than that counts as money or property) may be dealing with imposed group facts without voluntary popular acceptance basis. Another case where genuine popular support might be lacking is the case of old institutions that a group created and accepted (at least for actual use) a long time ago but still today go along with it in a customary way in terms of their intentional or nonintentional pattern-governed activities.

All collectively constructed social propositions (and only they) satisfy (CAT), cf. below. In the case of squirrel pelts, that they are money cannot be true in g and for g unless collectively accepted by g-members as true for them. This is the truly informative part of clause (b). It is obvious that if something is collectively accepted for g, it is true for the use of g-members and thus for their we-thinking if the members' function on the basis of having knowledge of the collective acceptance.

As seen, the kind of constitutive collective acceptance satisfying (CAT) according to clause (b) entails the truth of a descriptive proposition s for the group members qua group members and its "premisibility" or correct usability in group contexts, in contrast to the out-group case. The first and main necessary equivalence "if and only if" expresses both conceptual and metaphysical necessity. It is conceptual as we are speaking of collectively constructed and constituted parts of social reality, and it is real in a group-relative sense because the construction is basically self-validating if generally "obeyed" by appropriate action, in the squirrel pelt case by its use as money. What is constituted exists as a practice-involving epistemically objective fact for the group. Collective acceptance in our present sense can be taken ideally to entail mutual knowledge in the group that s is accepted and is true for the group. Clause (b) entails the central truth that a *group-social* proposition s is reflexive in the sense that a squirrel pelt is not money unless it is collectively accepted as money. The converse also holds almost obviously, although the right presuppositions must hold true. Thus it cannot be rationally accepted that, e.g., mathematical functions or icebergs are money in the group—the physical transferability criterion for money would fail. To have another example concerning the role of true external assumptions, consider group identity. The collective identity of a nation presupposes that the citizens not only exist but share certain objective characteristics concerning such things as language and traditions. Thus, not all group-social features can be socially constructed out of the blue—to put it briefly, the right kinds of background assumptions must be in place.

The present constructivist account elucidates the distinction between what—according to the members' view and relative to some commonly accepted underlying presuppositions—is and what is not up to them correctly to make true or correctly assertable in the group-relative sense, and thus is *premisible* for them (viz., usable in group contexts as a premise in g). Those and only those propositions that satisfy the analysans of (CAT) are in a constitutive sense group-social and thus pertain to collectively constructed features of group life. (CAT) applies both to propositions expressing generic kinds of institutions (e.g., money) and to propositions expressing token institutions such as what is money in a group (recall the squirrel pelt example). In our example, the proposition "Squirrel pelts are money" (= s) qualifies as a (possibly idealized) actual group-social proposition collectively accepted among medieval Finns.[19]

Instead, group stereotypes like the belief that the earth is flat fail to be fully content constitutive in the group social sense and do not satisfy (CAT); i.e., such stereotypes do not have the required connection to collective acceptance. In our example, the connection between an object's being a squirrel pelt and its being money can be regarded as ontologically significant, part of the ontology of the institution of money. This is partly because (CAT) here makes squirrel pelts money in an epistemically objective sense, if people act accordingly and use squirrel pelts as money. Something that was not money in g earlier now is money an epistemically objective fact for the group (out-groupers can also accept it as a true that such a fact for the group exists).[20] The group-social fact that squirrel pelt is money has ontological significance reaching out to people's (not only the group members') ways of thinking and acting.

Note that, for instance, a true natural statement such as "Grass is green" does not satisfy the analysans of (CAT) because the necessity feature is not present—contingent coincidence of the sides of the equivalence in (b) would not be enough. It seems rather clear (in analogy with the squirrel pelt case) that the (CAT) account holds true equally well of leadership, marriage, property, financial, educational, and religious institutions (e.g., banks, universities, and churches as institutional systems when viewed in terms of their characteristic constitutive propositions).

We can also speak of *derived* group sociality.[21] Roughly, a fact-expressing proposition is group-social (e.g., institutional) in a derived sense if it is not social in the above primary sense but *presupposes* for its truth (for the group) that there are some relevant true (for the group) propositions that are group-social in the primary sense. For instance, sentences containing such terms as "power", "unemployment", or "wealth" are candidates for group-social sentences in the derived sense. Many (nonconstructivist) social propositions fail to satisfy (CAT) and may even fail to be group-social in the derived sense. Thus sentences expressing latent or unilateral social influence are features of the social world that would *not* be cases of even derivatively group-social features in the constructivist sense. The same holds for "natural" emotions such as fear.

The (CAT) account is applicable to all basic constructed collective attitudes, thus to the belief family and the pro-attitude family of concepts, which are directly relevant to (constructed) group sociality and institutionality and viewed in terms of relevant propositions (e.g., "G is our, g-members', goal").[22] As seen in chapter 2, the members' collectively accepted group attitudes might be taken to be the basis of the attribution of a (partly) fictitious group mind to the group agent. "Fictitious" here means simply that the group mind (collection of attitudes and mental states) of a group agent may appear to be real but actually is not, and the same in part goes for the group agent itself (recall section 7 of chapter 2). However, if by a group agent's mind we mean only the collection of the members' attitudes and mental states, no metaphysical quibbles about that should rise.

To conclude, the important thing for our discussion is that the group qua group and its attitudes qua group attitudes (and its mind) are collectively constructed features of the social world based on an intentional stance toward the group by the members and possibly others.

3. SOCIAL INSTITUTIONS ELUCIDATED

3.1.

In this section I will elucidate central kinds of social institutions, those involving special collectively constructed institutional properties or statuses. Because I have elsewhere discussed and clarified social institutions, I will here concentrate on some new points.[23] These include a more explicit formulation of institutions that makes use of the group agency framework of this book and that also emphasizes the positional structure of social institutions, especially in the case of social organizations conceived as institutions.

The main function of a social institution is to establish collective order and give individual guidance in a community and to help people satisfy their basic needs, such as needs related to food and shelter, sexual relations and reproduction, sociality, and social power. The aspect of collective order involves division of labor and tasks, as well as suitable joint actions, while individual guidance involves the "routinization" of habitual tasks and the economization of time and resources. Institutions in different areas of social life tend to arise with the aim of collective and individual need satisfaction: *familial*, *educational*, *religious*, *political*, and *economic* institutions. These are institutions that social scientists generally deal with, but only their organized forms can be institutions in the sense of my account, as will be argued below.

In actual life basic needs are in many cases difficult to satisfy for all—there is often a scarcity problem related to their satisfaction at least in some societies. Furthermore, when satisfaction for all is economically feasible, their instituted satisfaction is typically a public good, as the good is meant to be for everyone in the group. This makes for the possibility of free-riding and defection concerning the institutionalized provision process. Here individual interests or preferences conflict with collective ones. In game-theoretic terms, we are dealing with coordination dilemmas (e.g., on which side of the road people should drive), full-blown collective action dilemmas, for example, the PD and Chicken, in which there is partial conflict between collective and individual interests and preferences, and situations of full conflict (zero-sum situations in game-theoretic terms). Successful institutional solutions to these dilemmas create sanctioned norms that guide people to behave in a specific way to increase social order and to avoid defection.[24] In many cases the norms are self-sanctioning in that when obeyed they lead to equilibria. The host group of an institution (the group for which it is an institution and which can be said to contain the institution) may also provide sanctioning mechanisms. It is important to recall that genuine we-moders will, on the ground of their intrinsic group-centered motivation, set aside their private interests and refrain from free-riding.

Institutions do not only constrain people's behavior. They can also give people acting in certain roles or positions the institutional power to act in ways that are not possible without institutions. A person who becomes a judge may get the power to send criminals to prison, a professor can decide whether a student is qualified for a university degree, and so on.[25]

Institutions tend to facilitate, economize, and "routinize" activities and thinking about those activities—recall our earlier discussion of the creation and role of (collective) pattern-governed behavior and mental processes. Institutions create order by providing group reasons (and derived individual reasons) for acting in institutional contexts. Given such reasons, people do not need to engage in decision making each particular time a norm-governed situation is at hand, and this tends to make the institutional actions routine.

The notion of social institution is somewhat ambiguous, as the literature on the topic indicates.[26] Here I concentrate on standard institutions such as money, property, and marriage that we have in modern communities and treat them as normative practices in the first place rather than as entities. The communities (groups) in question must be organized for action and for creating norms for their members. Accordingly, I will speak mostly of we-mode groups and take them to be required as infrastructure-providing host groups for social institutions. Notice that we-mode groups can contain I-moders (at least as nonoperative members), as long as there are some we-moders or at least group-centered persons in operative positions. The requirement of we-mode host groups can be given a normative grounding (in effect already built into the account of we-mode groups given in chapter 2): The group ought to satisfy—and in typical cases also maintain—its ethos. But the group can satisfy and promote its ethos only in virtue of its members' appropriate ethos-respecting and normatively ethos-guided activities. The ethos of the group in part determines what has been called the "culture" of the institution-hosting group.[27] So at least some amount of we-mode action for the group by the members is group-normatively needed in the present context.[28]

We-mode collective acceptance creates, and is required for, institutional entities and practices. Return to the squirrel pelt example for illustration. While collective acceptance can be taken to have created it and to have been required for it, this case does not rely on previously formed social institutions (except language). However, the group members must of course have some understanding of money in general, and what it implicates, and what its use empirically presupposes (e.g., that it is a practically feasible medium of exchange and storage of value). While money might have come about through a trial-and-error learning process, ultimately collective acceptance must be in place for squirrel pelts to be money for the group members, including future members (see below). As soon as the members cease to collectively accept squirrel pelts as money, the item loses its status and function as money. A squirrel pelt as money is a token institution depending on the generic institution money. In addition, money in the generic sense (money as an institutional predicate) is based on collective acceptance and thus construction.

Institutions are full-blown group phenomena. It is plausible to think that we-mode we-thinking and acting must be present, as the group qua group agent cannot otherwise function adequately.[29] A distinction is made between acceptance that is fully content-constitutive and acceptance that is weaker. *Content-constitutive* collective acceptance (construction) concerns purely institutional cases, like the squirrel pelt example. To put it bluntly, here a group takes the matter of squirrel pelts being money to be up to the group, the external world in principle having nothing (or next to nothing) to do with the truth for the group of the view that squirrel pelts are money (however, recall the various presuppositions discussed earlier). For squirrel pelts validly to be its money, the group agent must make squirrel pelts money by its acceptance (forming an accepting attitude toward the claim in question or at least intentionally acting in the right way, viz.. the members must accept this matter by actual intentional use of squirrel pelts as money, which use also serves to reproduce the institution in question). Here the "money part" of the group agent's world is created in epistemically objective terms (in Searle's sense) by acceptance of squirrel pelts as money.

The group can thus validate the claim and maintain that validation by their actual use of money in the right way (given its initial acceptance of the claim). The group (often via its leaders or leading group, e.g., government) can "falsify" the claim by its decision or acceptance that what has been money to it no longer will be money. We can speak of a constitutive we-mode collective acceptance of a content here. We can also in an attenuated sense say that a group agent's belief or view (e.g., that a squirrel pelt is money) has a quasi world-to-mind direction of semantic fit, which here means that the truth of the view requires acceptance action. The term "quasi" here means that the world-to-mind fit is relative to an artificial (but epistemically objective) state of affairs, i.e., one collectively constructed by the group by its acceptance based on the members' assumed capacity to imagine and pretend things in general (a capacity that children start acquiring in their second year of life). The belief in question also has the mind-to-world direction of fit, as the group here can be taken to represent its constructed world as involving the institutional fact that a squirrel pelt is money and that thus the belief that a squirrel pelt is money also represents the group fact that a squirrel pelt is money.[30] (See section 5 for my comments on Searle's related account.)

To summarize, the constructed belief is made true simply by the group members' treating squirrel pelts as money in their thoughts and activities. No input from the group-external world is relevant to the truth of the belief (given that the discussed conceptual and factual presuppositions are in place). It is the group members' own activities that socially validate the belief and make it true for the group. This is what is meant by saying that group beliefs based on constitutive construction in the purely institutional case (where the content that, say, squirrel pelts are money is being created) have the world-to-mind direction of fit. After the validation they also have the mind-to-world direction of fit (for instance, *the* belief that a squirrel pelt is money also *represents* the group fact that squirrel pelts are money). The upshot is that the general form of content-constitutive collective acceptance is this: a group collectively accepts and constructs in a truth-determining way a content (a proposition or item analyzable as propositional) for the group. From a linguistic point of view the collective acceptance might be a performative success "operator" in that it achieves its content in real social life given that the target people act in accordance with the acceptance.[31] Its performativity contributes to the satisfaction of (CAT) by entailing that collective acceptance implies truth for the group of what has been accepted.

3.2.

When a we-mode group has conferred (in general, but not necessarily, intentionally) a special status to a social practice by its we-mode collective acceptance (construction) of a constitutive norm, a social institution is created. The ought-to-be norm that a squirrel pelt is money in the group entails the appropriate ought-to-do norms for the group members. An institution is a group phenomenon involving two key elements, constitutive norms and a social practice, where the norms confer an institutional (symbolic, social, and normative) status to the activity or to some item involved in the practice. Examples are money, marriage, and private property, as well as positional statuses like president, lawyer, professor, and shoemaker. The constitutive and possibly other basic norms often also specify the particular social practices required to uphold the status of the collective item, which is a collective good available to all in the group. A collectivity condition with respect to their enjoyment holds: Necessarily, a member can enjoy the institutional good if and only if the others in the group can.

The core of the constitutive norms in a social institution lies in their presuppositional nature: they have been collectively taken to be *conceptual presuppositions* of action. In contrast, other norms normally govern behavior in a regulative sense.[32] To structure our discussion, let me state my summary account of "standard" institutions where the notion of a proposition, s, expressing (or describing) a social institution qua normative practice is used:[33]

(SI) Proposition s expresses a *social institution (in the standard sense)* for group g if and only if

(1) s expresses or entails the existence of a g-based, collectively accepted social practice (or a system of interconnected social practices) and a norm or a system of interconnected norms (including some constitutive norms conferring a special institutional status on some item) that are in force in g, such that the social practice is governed by the norm (or norm system);

(2) the members of g rationally collectively accept s for g with collective commitment; here it is assumed that collective acceptance for the group entails and is entailed by the truth of s for the group.

As to the notion of a proposition expressing a social institution, see the illustration in the case of a business corporation in section 5. When a proposition s satisfies clauses (1) and (2), it correctly expresses a functional social institution qua system of social practices and norms (or in shorthand, a normative social practice). Speaking of general institutions such as money, marriage, and private property, the members of g are assumed to obey the norms for the reason that they are supposed to obey the institutional norms that they have accepted for themselves. If the institution is externally authorized and created for g but so that the members still *go along* with, and perhaps only weakly collectively accept and "go through the relevant motions" concerning the institutional requirements, we still have a social institution in the above sense.

Clause (1) requires the existence of a social practice that satisfies (conforms to and "obeys") some norms (including constitutive ones). This requirement involves the idea of normatively instituted behavior—without the behavior (social practices), an institution is just a system of norms that does not play a functional role in the group. In order for the social institution to work well, the notion of collective acceptance should be taken in the we-mode sense of chapter 5, section 2. As in clause (2), collective acceptance is assumed to be rational; this involves that the institutional activities are meant to be rational at least in the sense that they promote or at least do not violate the host group g's ethos and the underlying goals or reasons for g's having the institution. This entails only that there must be at least *some* relevant we-mode action in g, especially between its leaders. Other members can still act in the I-mode without the social institution falling apart. Clause (2) simply makes the same reflexivity point that (CAT) involves and that expresses social construction and a degree of conventional arbitrariness (the institution could have been different). Note, however, that while I regard it as possible to give a weaker, pro-group I-mode interpretation to the key notions in (SI), best-functioning social institutions qua group phenomena seem to require a we-mode understanding of them.

As indicated, account (SI) covers generic institutions like language, money, property, and marriage, but also specific ones like a communal mail system and a certain business corporation. Only group items that are represented (thus accepted in my acceptance-as-true sense) as existing by the group are institutional.[34] Thus an organization-expressing proposition (see section 4 for an example) must be reflexively collectively accepted for the use of the group (as (CAT) specifies). This entails that ideally the group reason and collective commitment aspects, based on collective acceptance, must be involved and that thus each member of the organization ought to function as a proper we-mode group member. Public good organizations (such as public radio and TV or a public postal system or medical service) serve as good examples of social institutions.

One can study the maintenance (and change) of institutions through the maintenance (change) of the institutional practices that they involve and do this mathematically in a way that respects the feedback processes that partly govern the features of maintenance and change. One way to do this is to think that institutional practices in the host group, which ideally is a we-mode one, are in general intentionally performed on the basis of the participants' reasoning (in some cases joint reasoning) related to their relevant institutional wants and goals. The reasoning leads to a joint intention to perform the practice at least in the case of some operative participants. The intention is realized by the social practice that normally amounts to a series of recurrent activities. These activities may satisfy the goals—or satisfy them only to a certain degree—and this information gives the participants feedback relevant to the question of whether to maintain the institution as it is or to suitably change or even abandon it. They may have reasoned poorly, e.g., on the basis of false information, or they may not have succeeded in acting appropriately on the basis of their reasoning. The (degree of) the group's capacity to act in these contexts can in part be measured in terms of how successful it is in its social practices, e.g., in defending its resources and gaining new ones.[35] I will argue in the next chapter that the more solidary a group is, the better it will be able to act successfully. All this leads to a dynamic view of institutional (and other) social practices.[36]

To recapitulate, a social institution qua a normative action system as defined by (SI) has the following *basic functions* that it at least under favorable conditions tends to achieve—whether they actually do so is a contingent empirical matter:

(1) Social institutions tend to solve (or dissolve) coordination problems and collective action dilemmas—in general, conflicts between collective and individual rationality—and give cooperative, collectively beneficial solutions to these problems in the face of the chaos and conflict that unfettered individual action tends to lead to. Social institutions accordingly tend to create order in society.

(2) Because of their capacity to normatively solve such collective dilemmas, social institutions help to satisfy human needs and interests in an orderly and economic fashion on both the collective and the individual level (in the latter case by offering we-mode group reasons for member action).

(3) Social institutions also make new kinds of behaviors conceptually possible relative to the preinstitutional situation (think of functioning as a professor). They create new normative institutional properties and statuses for persons or other elements of the social practices that they consist of.[37]

(4) Social institutions tend to make institutional activities routine and accordingly to make such activities psychologically and computationally rather undemanding, and here the role of pattern-governed behavior mentioned in the introductory section is obviously pertinent.

(5) Social institutions tend to take care of the division of labor in society so that a member of society can free herself from multiple tasks and can concentrate on those that she is best at performing, leaving room for innovation.

We might take these functions to be requirements that social institutions should meet, especially if an institution is intentionally designed. Functionally similar accounts in terms of the pro-group I-mode approach may be feasible to some extent, but, if we recall the general features of the we-mode versus the I-mode, they involve less in-built "actional" persistence and commitment and on these grounds tend to fare worse in terms of the creation and maintenance of collective social order. One additional criticism of them is that *they allow many individualistic equilibria (which requires additional decision making)* and in this respect are inferior to the we-mode account. (See chapter 7 on we-reasoning and game theory.) Individualistic equilibria do not further the group's ethos and need not create collective order. Let me note that we get from the proof of thesis (3) in subsection 2.4 of chapter 7 a precise functional argument for the claim that on functional grounds *a social institution can and should be regarded as a normative action system designed to be operated at least in part in terms of we-mode activities*. This is the case at least when a full-blown institution satisfying (SI) (or some closely related account) is at stake. Given the tenability of this argument, a we-mode social institution is able to give more social order than an I-mode social institution.

Accordingly, the we-mode account is needed especially for institutional design and also for institutional change, as I have argued earlier.[38] To be sure, social practices and, based on them, rudimentary (normative) institutions can arise spontaneously or through cultural evolution without the collective or collectively authorized design, especially in primitive cases. Yet collectively intentional construction is required in some cases, e.g., in the case of designing complex organizations and often also when making changes in an institution to accommodate new needs or interests. We-mode activities clearly have a place here. A reductive and purely individualistic account of social institutions (viz., an account in terms of I-mode concepts) seems not to be possible, given that we-mode concepts in general are not so reducible.[39] However, notice that institutional actions, i.e., actions by which institutional norms and requirements are followed and obeyed, can generally be either we-mode action or I-mode action. The former gives full-blown norm obeying because it requires understanding the true nature of a social institution and acting for the right reasons. Although not all institutional action needs be reflective, at least some people acting in institutional contexts of course must understand what institutions are in terms of their teleological point and function. To be sure, many users of the institution nevertheless seem to perform institutional actions in the I-mode mainly to promote their own private goals.

To summarize, the ontological aspects of social institutions are collectively constructed and involve objectively real constraints and presuppositions. Without human intelligence (or something similar) there would be no institutional entities and facts in the full sense. This is because social institution notions are heavily conceptually laden and also go beyond material entities and features. In saying this, I take a scientific realist standpoint concerning social reality and regard, e.g., macro-material entities (objects, properties, events, processes) as capable of occurring in causal contexts, regarding this as a central mark of ontological reality. When one takes this view, one is saying that the kind of material entities that the physical and biological sciences deal with firmly belong to the causal order. In addition, psychological states and properties can be grounded in the material world and be regarded as elements in the causal order.[40]

4. SOCIAL ORGANIZATIONS AS INSTITUTIONS

The notion of a group member largely abstracts from the individual features of the members of the group (especially in large groups), and this, together with the functional group agency idea and account, indicates that the we-mode account is well suited to describing the ideal functioning of social organizations, such as business companies and government bureaucracies. The position-holders promote the ethos of the group, and the ethos indicates what kind of positional structure the group should have. If the host groups that are resourcing the functioning of social institutions are we-mode groups, the above account (SI) of social institutions may be adapted to account for *social organizations*—organized groups with a constitutive goals or purposes and normatively governed social practices.[41] An example would be a typical business corporation like Apple.[42]

As a social institution essentially consists of a norm system and a social practice system, an entity like a we-mode group cannot literally be a social institution, but it can host one (i.e., provide infrastructural resources for its operation): It is rather the norm-governed group activities that form an institution in the sense of (SI). One may claim that ideally the host group of a social institution (in the sense of (SI)) should be a we-mode one, because it involves the right elements for being a host group, i.e., the relevant constitutive norms and the members who at least ought to promote the ethos. The actions by which the members promote the ethos qualify as the institutional practices that (SI) speaks about. As a we-mode group is based on autonomous or non-autonomous we-mode collective acceptance, (CAT) will be satisfied in this case for the content "Group g is a we-mode group" and also for its collectively constructed properties (the normative social practices of g, etc.).

The group's ethos gives the organization's central goal and, as just said, the members can be taken to occupy refillable positions. There are at least some normative, at least group-normative, connections due to the members being collectively committed to the group ethos and its promotion. The members' social commitments to one another are interlocking and form a simple task-right system (e.g., a member is obligated to perform his part and may normatively expect that the others perform theirs). This makes the group a social organization at least in a rudimentary sense.

A social organization can be viewed as an institution also when its host group is not a we-mode group: As to clause (1) of (SI), the organization has a norm system based on formal norms and there is a target group with an ethos that includes the central goals of the organization. The members of the group are assumed to obey the norms or at least to act in accordance with them in terms of their recurrent actions, i.e., social practices based on their shared we-attitudes (we-goals, we-beliefs, etc.), which in general are either in the we-mode or in the I-mode.

To recall our discussion in chapter 6, a central feature of organizations is that there are power relations based on authority. There are differentiated sets of positions defined by social norms (authority-based rule-norms defining overt structure) and rules for filling the positions in social organizations. There are also formal ought-to-do norms and may-do norms determining tasks and rights respectively for each position. Thus each position is connected to a task-right system applying to it. There may also be norms concerning how and when to follow the task norms and right norms. The set of positions of an organization forms a net connected by authority-based power lines and communication channels for exercising authority. In some cases there are also norms for recognizing and maintaining the above norms.[43]

To give an example of an organization as a social institution (in the sense of (SI)), consider the postal system created for a community to serve the needs of people in it. Such an organization consists of rule-governed social practices, which are part of the task-right system of the organization. These norms must have been collectively accepted—because the postal system is meant for "our" group and constructed by "us" (perhaps indirectly, through our representatives). The creation of the organization may have taken place a long time ago, and the original position-holders may no longer be around, although the positions must at least largely still be there. In a properly functioning organization the operative members who are responsible for making decisions and acting must collectively accept the institution-expressing proposition s in the account (SI).

Clause (2) of (SI) thus is required to be satisfied in the case of those organizations that qualify as institutions. This seems plausible for organizations designed for communities. The entailed for-groupness assumption must then be satisfied. In contrast to the postal system case, business corporations might not qualify as institutions in my sense concerning the wider host community, group g, because they need not serve the goals of g or be in this sense *for* g.

As to business corporations or companies, we already considered their structure and function in chapter 6. They may satisfy (SI) and be institutions in the organization sense. They may viewed as we-mode institutions, *if* their members (or a substantial amount of them) collectively construct the business in we-mode terms (as the phrase "This is *our* organization and we are working together as a unit" indicates) and act accordingly. If there are no we-moders in the company, it will not be a we-mode group but operates through other kinds of psychological assumptions.

The *constitutive* core of a business corporation could be expressed roughly as follows by means of the following institution-expressing proposition, s:

> s = There is a group of shareholders (owners), a governing body consisting of certain agent positions, and a positionally structured group of hired persons

called personnel such that the shareholders collectively create a specific ethos (a constitution, etc.) for the corporation and select the governing body to promote and realize the ethos of the corporation; and the governing body appoints a CEO and high-level managers as well as lower level ones, who in turn hire personnel to carry out various tasks for the promotion of the ethos of the basic group.

The preceding institutional proposition may be interpreted in more detail for actual institutions as follows: We add a normative ought-to-be operator to s so that the conceptual part of the account of a corporation formally involves the sentence $O_{be}(s)$. The full theory of the corporation could then be $O_{be}(s)$ & p, where p gives the factual, nonconceptual part in my tentative schematic account. What the group of shareholders minimally would accept, then, is $O_{be}(s)$, while what the whole host community, g, would accept, when adequately informed, is $O_{be}(s)$ & p. In other words, $CA_g(O_{be}(s)$ & p) holds true. Community g accepts the above account s as true, and it also accepts that p is true. If s and p are true, we are dealing with a business corporation. The normative statement $O_{be}(s)$ cannot be satisfied without the constitutive norm applying to the agents. Group g thus ought to see to it that s is true and that the norm $O_{be}(s)$ is in force in g. We can also require that the constitutive norm $O_{be}(s)$ entail an institutional ought-to-do norm for the functionaries of the organization.

Let me end by summarizing what has been said about the we-mode/I-mode issue in the present case. The shareholders' (or owners') group ideally is an autonomous group that can function in the we-mode and satisfy the three central criteria of group reason, collectivity, and collective commitment. In that case its members may engage in joint reasoning for the organization and identify themselves with the ethos. Unless the shareholders function as a group in the we-mode sense, they might not be able to create an organization that satisfies (SI). The other (sub)groups referred to in the organization-expressing sentence are not free groups, because of the external authority directing them from above. Their members are hired or work for a fee and may think and act in the I-mode. These subgroups can still be non-autonomous we-mode groups even though their leaders and their basic principles of functioning are not selected by the members.

5. SEARLE ON INSTITUTIONS AND ORGANIZATIONS

My account of social institutions bears similarities to Searle's account, although mine covers more ground. The element of institutional status is a central component in both accounts. An important difference is that in my account it need not always involve social power.[44] In partial contrast to Searle's account, I claim this:

Institutions are constituted by practices and norms (including task-right norms to govern task division) and are collectively constructed, basically real normative action systems.
Institutions are conceptually group-based phenomena with we-mode groups (ideally) as their host groups.
Institutions are conceptually based on we-mode collective acceptance, although they may involve much I-mode institutional action.
The ontology of the social world cannot be satisfactorily characterized by a priori philosophical reflection alone but should be informed by, and rely on, empirical social science research, too.

Searle's central thesis in his 2010 book is the following tripartite claim: "(a) All of human institutional reality, and in that sense nearly all human civilization, is created in its initial existence and maintained in its continued existence by a single, logico-linguistic operation. (b) We can state exactly what that operation is. It is a Status Function Declaration. (c) The enormous diversity and complexity of human civilization is explained by the fact that that operation is not restricted in subject matter and can be applied over and over in a recursive fashion, is often applied to the outcomes of earlier applications and with various and interlocking subject matters, to create all of the complex structures of actual human societies."[45]

The speech act of declaration is a central linguistic element for Searle: "They [declarations] change the world by declaring that a state of affairs exists and thus bringing that state of affairs into existence."[46] As to the creation of status functions Searle elucidates this with the following claim:[47]

1 We make it the case by Declaration that the Y Status Function exists in context C. (*Status Function Declaration*)

Status function declarations are speech acts that are taken by Searle to have both the mind-to-world and the world-to-mind direction of fit. Their performative character is indicated by the feature that they bring about an extralinguistic state of affairs (in the case of nonlinguistic institutions).[48] In the claim (1) some people (referred to by "we") create a status function Y by declaration. As I understand it, this declaration involves not only that Y is described as existing in the group (language-to-world or mind-to-world direction of fit) but also that when making the declaration the members must collectively accept as true—in thought and in action—that Y exists for them (world-to-mind direction of fit).[49]

I would like to emphasize that unless a declaration is taken to entail or presuppose the participants' appropriate commitment and nonlinguistic actions (or action dispositions), it does not fulfill its extralinguistic function and cannot be used to create institutional social reality. At best it can create concepts or conceptual features of institutional things or facts. Searle assumes recognition (or acceptance) of the created status function, but he does not explicitly require appropriate nonlinguistic actions. Thus, my first critical point related to his declarative account is that he downplays the role of (nonlinguistic) acceptance-supporting action. Furthermore, he does not clearly define what institutional social reality is and what the possibility of its creation ultimately involves and presupposes on the part of "us".[50] Thus, "we" cannot make physical events or states come about by mere declaration, but we can bring about institutional facts through our collective creation of relevant institutional ideas (e.g., that pieces of gold rather than pieces of silver will count as money for us if we are prepared to use them as money).[51] Searle's takes individualistic collective intentionality to suffice for social institutions.[52] This is compatible with the individualistic nature of traditional speech act theory (on which Searle relies). However, I argue that claim (1) only works with the interpretation that "we" refers to a functional group agent, or at least intrinsically involves "our" doing something together, as a group. I have argued earlier in this chapter and elsewhere that an individualistic account does not suffice for collective acceptance in the present context.[53]

An example of an institutional status is given by money. E.g., a gold coin may have the status of being money in the group, and some standard constitutive functions of money can be attached to it (e.g., the use of money in economic exchange and as storage of value). While my approach clearly separates statuses from the functions conceptually or contingently connected to them, Searle speaks of status functions and gives the following general account of them: A status function is a "function that is performed by an object (objects), person (persons), or other sort of entity (entities) and which can only be performed in virtue of the fact that the community in which the function is performed assigns a certain status to the object, person, or entity in question, and the function is performed in virtue of the collective acceptance or recognition, of the object, person, or entity as having that status."[54] This definition, however, does not distinguish between the *constitutive* and *contingent* functions that statuses have or may have.

Searle claims that his new account takes care of three topics that pose problems for his 1995 account. In Searle's terms these topics are *the ad hoc problem*, *freestanding Y terms*, and *institutional facts that do not require collective recognition*. I will below discuss these matters in turn while also taking up some other related issues.

The ad hoc problem. Searle says that a primitive tribe may come to accept a certain person as the leader of their group, giving the leader the usual apparatus of deontic powers and status functions, although there is no existing institution and no set of constitutive norms (of the kind "X counts as Y in C").[55] Searle's problem arose because he assumed preexisting constitutive norms. His solution is to argue that, in the absence of a preexisting constitutive norm, an appropriate collectively accepted status function declaration is required and will do the job. It creates the deontic powers needed for leadership (which powers are lacking, e.g., in the case of alpha male wolves). This seems right.[56]

Freestanding Y terms. Searle claims that Y terms, i.e., the status-carrying terms, can be freestanding in the sense that they do not require an X term (or property or object). Searle's standard formulation for a constitutive norm "X counts as Y" thus does not apply to all contexts. According to him, corporations are a case in point. As his example he uses the California Code section that concerns the formation of a corporation and says that anybody can create a corporation when certain conditions are met. Here is what the code says according to Searle: "One or more natural persons, partnerships, associations or corporations, domestic or foreign, may *form a corporation* under this division by *executing and filing articles of incorporation*". "*The corporate existence begins by the filing of the articles and continues perpetually*, unless otherwise expressly provided by law or in the articles".[57]

However, note that the law says next to nothing about what a corporation is. The law in question is a collective creation of the legislators (who presumably represent the broad "we" of the people in the society). We are dealing with a double Declaration here:[58]

2 We make it the case by Declaration that for any x that satisfies a certain set of conditions p, x can create an entity with Y status function by Declaration in C.

The actual creation of a specific corporation according to Searle is based on this:

3 We make it the case by Declaration that an entity Y exists that has status function(s) F in C.

Searle says that a corporation is a *fictitious* entity, above represented by Y: "the noun, 'corporation', carries both the name of an entity and the existence of the status functions".[59] He also writes: "Limited liability corporations do not have any physical existence (this is why they are called 'fictitious persons')".[60] But I think that this is not feasible: for a corporation to be responsible and, e.g., pay its debts, it must have the kind of physical existence that group action requires. Fictitious agents above do not exist in the causal sense required for them to be relevantly responsible and, e.g., able to pay their debts—at least some relevant institutional positions must be fulfilled by real persons that a mere declaration of course cannot achieve.[61]

However, in a different place Searle seems to be speaking against the fictitious character of corporations:[62] "Note that the whole point of doing this [making the Declaration specified in the California Code] is to create a rather elaborate set of power relationships between actual people. When one creates a corporation one thereby creates an entity that can do business and that has such positions as the president of the corporation, the board of directors, and the shareholders. When a corporation is created, its status functions accrue to actually existing people." So here Searle seems to be implying that a corporation is a *non-fictitious* entity, contradicting—or at least creating tension—with the former cited passage.

A corporation law does not entail the existence of a corporation—even if the existence of this law is an institutional fact. Even when an application to establish a corporation has been filed and accepted, the corporation does not exist according to my functional-causal view. Only when relevant positions have been filled by actual people does the corporation exist in a sense allowing it to fulfill its functions and thus to operate in the causal networks of the social world. Then also the required institutional power relations hold between the position-holders. In such a case of functional existence we can thus have a domain, say D, of position-holders and in some cases other, additional people and appropriate power relations between them. We may ideally conceptualize this as a relational system $<D, R_1,\dots, R_n>$, where the R_i, $i = 1,\dots, n$, represent the institutional power and other required relations between them. There will also be a description or, better, theory that specifies the nature of these relations and also says between which position-holders they hold (etc.). Partly on conceptual grounds the corporation theory will be true of a relational system $Co(t) = <D^t, R_1^t,\dots, R_n^t>$ (possibly with changed members) at each point of time t at which the corporation functionally exists and contains the right number of actual position-holders, and so on, in its domain so that the relations correctly hold between them—and so that all the nonrelational requirements, say, competence requirements and functional requirements, also hold.

The above account gives this:

4 A system $Co = <D, R_1,\dots, R_m>$ counts as a corporation, given that D is a domain of (actual) people and R_i are relevant power relations holding between them such that Co satisfies the corporation theory.

This is a kind of constitutive rule for the corporation having the form of a Searlean constitutive rule "X counts as Y." Given (4), the m + 1-tuple Co is an actual singular (or token) corporation that can perform the basic functions that the corporation theory specifies—that is Co selling and buying stock and doing business are such functions.

Searle's account was supposed to show that there can be institutions with freestanding Y terms. But I claim that my reformulation is not only more precise, but (in a sense) does fit the old format with an X term. It might even be suggested that the present way of modeling the situation is appropriate for all social institutions. For instance, in the case of money we need a description that gives the meaningful content of the institution, viz., what the predicate "money" means and what kinds of functions it on conceptual grounds must have and what kinds of consequences are likely to be contingently associated with it, e.g., inflation or recession. Here we have some people and powers and thus a social relational system. Note that what is typically created in the money case is a kind of thing (say dollar bills, coins, etc., as kinds) that counts as money, where each concrete dollar note is a token of the money so created. Generally speaking, the institution of money (monetary institution) consists of the functionally relevant norm-governed practices of the target people.

Searle's present account of the creation and maintenance of institutional reality is based on three central notions: collective intentionality, the assignment of function, and a language rich enough for the creation of status function declarations. While Searle's earlier account required constitutive norms of the kind "X counts as Y in C", the new account goes in terms of declarations. As status functions are taken to entail deontic powers, we get the following (at least for the corporation case):[63]

5 We (or I) make it the case by Declaration that the Y status function exists in C, and in so doing we (or I) create a relation R between Y and a certain person or persons, S, such that in virtue of SRY, S has the power to perform acts (of type) A.

Statement (5) makes it clear how status functions involve (positive, negative, conditional, etc.) deontic powers at least in such standard cases of institutions as money and private property. E.g., Y could represent money and R the relation of possession.

My earlier way of reconceptualizing the situation in the corporation case obviously can be applied here again, and there would thus be an "X term" in Searle's sense. In the case of money, the content of (5) can be embedded in an economic theory that also contains lots of contingent claims about the social antecedents and consequences (such as inflation or depression) of monetary activities.

In Searle's account, declarations and status functions are connected to the community members' thinking and acting in terms of individualistically conceived collective acceptance (recognition).[64] Such acceptance represents the individualistic collective intentionality element needed for the existence of an institution, while concrete institutional facts making the institution function require cooperation and hence individualistically irreducible collective acceptance. In my account I do not require I-mode collective acceptance in either case, but claim that we-mode collective acceptance in both cases (viz., the case of existence and cooperation in relation to institutional facts) is at least ideally needed and is functionally the best (recall chapters 6 and 7 for arguments).

My own account of social institutions does not depend on Searlean constitutive norms having the form "X counts as Y", which is the form that originally caused the trouble of freestanding Y terms. In my account (SI) the institutional term Y would be collectively agreed to exist (if it expresses an institutional object or entity) or to apply to the host group g (if it expresses an institutional property). Y is conceptually or nonconceptually connected to and implies some functions (e.g., in the case of money the function of usability in exchange and storage of value). In a technical account these functions, at least the conceptually required ones, can be represented by the outcomes that they lead to because of collective action. These outcomes generally are equilibria in the sense of section 2 of chapter 7. Note that in my account the constitutive norms are conceptual presuppositions created by the group and need not have any specific form as long as something in the real world is required about the applicability of Y.[65]

To use our earlier simple example, suppose that the group accepts a particular institution-expressing proposition, e.g., "In our group, g, it ought to be that the members use squirrel pelts as money", or perhaps "In g, a squirrel pelt is money". Using, e.g., the Carnap sentence, the predicate "money" will become functionally defined. Here it is taken to be an existentially quantified predicate with the right functional connections and one in principle applicable to squirrel pelts. As noted, a couple of the functional connections of "money" are that money is something that can be used for exchanging goods and also as storage of value.

In all, it can be said that in the tentatively proposed approach the Carnap sentence is taken to be accepted by the group as a normatively valid sentence (proposition) and thus as what ought to be taken as true of the concepts (predicates) involved. The introduction of institutional predicates is not geared to one particular version or form of a constitutive norm, because there may be different ways to account for the kind of conceptual truths in question.

Institutional facts that do not require collective recognition. Searle mentions recession as an example of the "fallout" of collectively accepted and created institutional facts.[66] These kinds of unintended and often unexpected fallouts are what social scientists are busy investigating. What Searle does not discuss in his 2010 book is that there are also social facts that are not institutional facts even in the derived sense and thus would not seem to be fallouts from people's collectively intentional activities. Examples are given by such naturalistic facts such as latent social influence and social emotions (e.g., envy).[67]

Searle's new account related to fallouts of intentional activities comes close to my (earlier and present) approach concerning *derived* institutional or group-social facts (see above).[68]

One of Searle's claims in his 2010 book is the explicit statement that a status function entails power.[69] This can be disputed. A counterexample to Searle's claim is provided by be the institution of a calendar system in a society—a system for measuring time in part on a conventional basis. Searle accepts that this case, which for him is a purely linguistic institution, does not involve deontic powers for individuals, and therefore is not an institution, contrary to what I would say. In my view a calendar system is a partly linguistic and partly nonlinguistic institution with a special status concerning the measurement of time. The nonlinguistic features concern the calendar system's essential connection to such real facts as that the earth moves around the sun and also around its own axis and that the moon circles around the earth. Thus the length of the year, month, and day have a naturalistic objective foundation, which can described in various institutionalized ways (think, e.g., of the beginning date of the year).[70] The upshot is that a calendar system can be regarded as an institution with a specific status including essentially both linguistic and nonlinguistic elements.[71] Note, finally, that a calendar system is based on collective acceptance and satisfies my account (SI).

I thus think that Searle's account of institutions in terms of deontic powers is too strict, although it does capture a central idea typically present in social institutions. But it does not comply with, e.g., ordinary dictionary accounts and common-sense understanding of social institutions.[72]

The upshot is that the difficulties concerning the problems of ad hoc constitution, freestanding Y terms, and institutional facts that do not require collective recognition are internal to Searle's 1995 theory. The new theory fares much better, although I have made some critical points against it. As to Searle's central theses (cited in the beginning of this section), I regard them as basically acceptable but only with some qualifications. Thus, we need an account of nonlinguistic representations that have the same logical form as status function declarations.[73] There is also the important qualification to be discussed that language cannot be created by status function declarations on pain of circularity.[74] Furthermore, while Searle regards language as a social institution, he does not in his work give an informative account of it. Indeed it seems that that task is hard if not impossible to perform in a noncircular way within his approach, because his notion of social institution analytically involves language (a representational system).

6. CONCLUSION

In section 1 of this chapter certain kinds of usually nonintentional routine activities called (collective) pattern-governed behaviors were discussed, and it was argued that they typically underlie institutional actions and social practices. Section 2 argued that institutional facts and entities and institutions are collective constructions created by collective acceptance "by us for us." It was accordingly argued that the notion of social institution at bottom is a we-mode notion. This section also gave an analysis of institutional facts, their presuppositions, and the nature of institutional reality. In section 3 social institutions were discussed in detail. The possibility of treating business organizations as social institutions was the topic of section 4. Section 5 discussed John Searle's recent account of "making the social world" and connected it to the central claims and arguments of this chapter.

9

Group Solidarity

All for One and One for All

1. INTRODUCTION TO GROUP SOLIDARITY

One may speak of the solidarity between two (or more) persons, with one or both acting solidarily (cooperatively, helpfully, fairly, etc.; see below) toward the other. One may also speak of a social group being solidary, where solidarity involves solidarity *between the members* of a group (be the group a community, a team, or some other kind of group) and solidarity at the *group level* (in a structural and explanatory sense, e.g., toward other groups including its subgroups or other parties). The former kind of solidarity between members (qua group members) involves disposition toward prosocial (e.g., helping) behavior. There is also a third sense of solidarity that is often called humanitarian solidarity. It is grounded in universal morality or altruism.[1]

My focus in this chapter will be *group solidarity*, which will be elucidated mainly in terms of relevant prosocial, solidary relationships between the members qua members and the explanation of such solidary actions in terms of the group's main structural principles. Group solidarity involves member action directed at the promotion of the group's main goals and interests (even when burdensome), and this entails solidary action qua members toward the other members. There are strongly solidary social groups and social groups that are solidary only to a small degree, but all groups that are capable of action must involve some degree of solidarity. A traditional family and a sports team often count as *internally* solidary groups much in the sense of the idea "All for one and one for all", whereas, e.g., a business corporation is generally less so. A group that is solidary toward another group or other groups is solidary in an *external* sense.

In this chapter I will apply the we-mode approach of this book to elucidate group solidarity. This chapter presupposes that the main notions of this theory are understood by the reader. My account will consider factual, rationality- and efficiency-based aspects as well as normative aspects of solidarity. Contrary to some views, I take it that group solidarity as such need not in all cases involve morality; and when it does, it often involves only "group morality", not necessarily full-blown morality based on universalization.[2] A reason for this group-basedness is that group solidarity implicitly or explicitly refers to out-groupers—to "them" in distinction to "us"—and does not extend the requirements of solidary behavior to behavior toward out-groupers, unless the group's goals and interests happen to require doing so. My we-mode account of group solidarity will show the importance of "we-ness" in this context, and it will explain the members' solidary behavior toward each other and show what group-level solidarity amounts to.

By group solidarity several things have been meant in the literature, and my account will involve most of the central aspects emphasized in that literature. Émile Durkheim made a famous distinction between mechanical and organic solidarity.[3] Mechanical solidarity refers to the ties between people in traditional societies where much in daily life is normatively shared, whereas, in contrast, organic solidarity concerns modern forms of community involving division of labor and individualistic thinking. For instance, an agricultural community qualifies as an example of a mechanically solidary group, while a modern society that involves a far-reaching division of labor and tasks can be an organically solidary group.[4] Durkheim may be right in making and emphasizing the distinction, but much also depends on how the analytic concepts are understood. It seems that in actual life there are groups that include both aspects, e.g., in an organically solidary group there can be mechanically solidary subgroups, and conversely.[5]

The central aim of this chapter accordingly is to give an account of what group solidarity amounts to. The analysis should encompass and account for several intuitive features of solidarity (such as belongingness, togetherness, and cooperativeness as well as a sense of unity; cf. the slogan "All for one and one for all"). There is also the additional task of giving an account of the central scientific as well as practical functions of group solidarity that may be considered: In what sense is the notion of group solidarity needed or useful for philosophical or social theorizing? Why should group members be solidary toward each other? We may also ask for a clarification of what kinds of evolutionary and psychological factors can be taken to explain and determine solidarity. Furthermore, we may ask how solidarity creates social stability and order—and whether it can resist lapses into free-riding and defection.

My main claim is that groups that function on the basis of "we-thinking" (and not merely on individualistic "I-thinking" or "I-mode" thinking) are solidary groups. To make the idea of we-thinking clear and to see why it tends to generate solidary groups, I will make use of the we-mode approach that I have presented earlier in this book. It might even seem that a separate account of group solidarity is not needed, because the concepts of collective commitment, group reasons, and collectivity understood in the sense of this book already serve to account for the unity and solidity of the group. Yet more will be said below.

In section 2, I will present some central intuitive features that an account of solidarity needs to involve. Section 3 presents my we-mode account of group solidarity and shows that groups based on a strong kind of we-thinking and acting tend to be solidary and indeed are paradigm cases of solidary groups. Section 4 tests the we-mode account, and finally section 5 discusses the kind of group solidarity that modern society in general seem to require. Section 6 deals with group emotions in solidary groups, and section 7 presents some closing remarks.

2. SOLIDARY BEHAVIOR

As to the kinds of solidary behavior between individual persons, Siegwart Lindenberg has recently presented a kind of typology of solidary behavior.[6] I find his typology good because it seems to capture the central features of solidary behavior between persons. I will below modify and apply these elements to *member behavior* in a solidary group and through that to group solidarity.

Briefly, Lindenberg's taxonomy is as follows: (1) Cooperative behavior in a common good situation. (2) Fair behavior in a situation of sharing a common good. Fairness here is distribution fairness. (3) Altruism in a need situation. This refers mainly to helping action. (4) Trustworthy action in cases of temptation to breach. (5) Considerate action in a mishap situation (in cases where one has the intention to cooperate that yet fails). Considerateness involves making up for mishaps one has caused. It should be added that to be nonarbitrarily and nonaccidentally performed, the above behaviors had better be intentional actions in general. Indeed, they should be performed for the right kinds of underlying reasons and motives compatible with our intuitive ideas of solidarity such as those involved in the saying "All for one and one for all". (See section 4 for my related, but modified list of cases for the group context.)

Let me still add that the above list also, mutatis mutandis, applies to intergroup cases, thus what a group's solidarity toward another group involves. However, in this chapter such intergroup solidarity will not be discussed in detail.

Lindenberg goes on to define the strength of solidarity as the sum of the legitimately expected sacrifices (in terms of money, time, effort) over all the above five solidarity situations. This sum is taken to indicate solidarity costs. The phrase "legitimately expected", of course, is normative. I would like to see also the de facto costs taken into account. This would involve taking solidarity in a group to involve the average of solidarity costs taken over the above situations and the members in the group. A problem here is that the solidarity costs seemingly must be relativized to some kind of base level that may differ from individual to individual (the phrase "legitimately expected sacrifices" might not without adequate elaboration be able to take this adequately into account). For instance, concerning case (3), an altruist's base level or zero level is quite different from an egoist's base level. I will not below be concerned with measurement of solidarity at all but will take the above kinds of behavior to be central to solidarity. They can be seen as exhaustive of solidary actions at the individual level. I will here take this as an underlying working hypothesis and build on it below.

3. GROUP SOLIDARITY AND THE WE-MODE

What is group solidarity? As was said in the introduction to this chapter, solidarity has many faces. There are aspects related to prosociality and others related to morality or at least normativity. The concept of solidarity historically derives from the notion of *obligatio in solidum*, and this latter notion amounts to joint and several liability.[7] Here the factual aspects related to the group's strength ("solidity") and cohesion as a unit can be discerned and obviously also a normative aspect related to liability.

There have been some attempts to account for group solidarity in the literature. Émile Durkheim's account of "mechanical" and "organic" solidarity was already mentioned.[8] (Some comments related to it will be made in section 4.) Michael Hechter has developed an individualistic theory of group solidarity.[9] According to it, group solidarity is a multiplicative function of the extensiveness of the group's obligations (a), and the rate of member compliance (b) with these obligations, thus: Group solidarity = f(ab). This account relies heavily on the group members' fulfillment of the group's obligations. Note, however, that in the case of fully compliant members b = 1, and in this case the extensiveness of the group's obligations is the only decisive matter. But one may think that this is not a very central aspect of solidarity by itself, since in a group where there are only a few or no cooperators (b is close to 0), the group with many obligations is at best only potentially more solidary than a group with fewer obligations.

Sally Scholz has presented a theory of political solidarity that aims at characterizing solidarity as a kind of unity by taking solidarity primarily as a moral notion.[10] She requires morality not only of intragroup member action but also of group action toward other groups and people in a society. Solidarity in her account is ultimately based on private (and not collective) commitments.

My we-mode account does not require full morality in general but only group morality. It expresses part of the mentioned idea of solidarity as *obligatio in solidum*. In our present framework that focuses on we-mode groups, joint and several liability entails group-based collective commitment. The member-level interdependence associated with group solidarity is basically due to the collectively accepted ethos (or other content) of the group to which they are collectively committed. The ethos is regarded by the members as providing group reasons to participate in collective action. The cognitive part of the reason-dependence is expressed by the collectivity condition, and its normative-actional part is given by collective commitment.[11] Collective commitment gives the "glue" that normatively (not necessarily morally) binds the members together in accordance with the group reason in a stable way.

There are two central aspects of group solidarity. *First*, the group members qua group members must be disposed to act in a solidary way toward each other, where their solidary actions can be classified in terms of the five discussed kinds of solidary actions. *Second*, the group qua group agent must ground and explain the members' solidary activities toward each other. A mere collection of persons or in general an I-mode group can be solidary only if, and to the degree that, its members are solidary toward each other, but this collective is not yet solidary as a group. To put the matter bluntly, this is basically because it need not satisfy the central we-mode criteria requiring the presence of a group reason to motivate the members' activities, group-based collectivity, and group-based collective commitment, which have a strong unifying function, as we have seen.

Another difference between we-mode solidarity and I-mode group solidarity may be brought out by distinguishing between *internal* and *external* group solidarity. As I have said, internal solidarity concerns the members' solidary actions toward each other. External solidarity concerns the group's solidary activities (qua group) toward group-external parties, which may be other groups or individuals. The more solidary a group is in the internal sense, the higher is its capacity to act successfully as a group in intergroup contexts.[12] The we-mode approach can account for external solidarity, while I-mode groups may not be able to act adequately as groups and hence may at best qualify for internal solidarity. Whether a we-mode group acts in a solidary way toward other groups depends on its ethos and various other factors and is in this sense a *contingent* feature. However, internal solidarity in a we-mode group is one of its *constitutive*, conceptually necessary features. This contrasts with

I-mode groups, where both internal and external solidarity are contingent features of social interactions. We-mode groups may also sometimes exercise control over how solidary their members' actions are. At least ideally, the members of we-mode groups will function in a group-centered manner, and they will act in a solidary way because of their wholehearted commitment to the group. When I below speak of we-mode solidarity, it need not entail full-blown solidarity in the wholeheartedness sense, but may simply amount to instrumental action based on going along with the group's directives.

I will now present a summary of my theory of internal group solidarity in view of the above discussion and speak of degrees of solidarity. This is done in terms of two requirements:

> (GS1) A group (e.g. paradigmatic we-mode group) is *(internally) solidary qua group* to the degree that it tends to satisfy and promote its ethos and thereby through its ethos to guide, ground, and contribute to its members' solidary actions qua members toward other members.
> (GS2) A group's members are *solidary* to the degree that they tend to function (broadly) cooperatively toward each other qua members in matters concerning group affairs (in paradigmatic we-mode cases, promotion of the group's ethos).

(GS1) gives a *group-level* requirement for group solidarity, whereas (GS2) concerns *member-level* solidarity. Furthermore, it can be added to the above requirements that, rather obviously, external solidarity in general requires internal solidarity.

(GS1) is partly concerned with task-relative effective group action toward the group's ethos and other ethos-compatible action. Such group agent action guides and grounds the members' actions and integrates them concerning ethos-directed functioning. In the we-mode case it also serves to explain contributory member-level (solidary) action, e.g., by providing a uniform group reason for the members' acts and also by requiring collective commitment to the ethos and what it entails and implicates. (GS1) accordingly guarantees at least in principle that the members act in a unitary way when the group acts. The members' acting qua members is central here, because this in effect makes their action intrinsically group-based action. Private member action would hardly have anything to do with how solidary the group qua group is. Indeed, a (paradigmatic) we-mode group intrinsically requires the condition in (GS1) to be true (cf. chapter 2), but I do not above require the group in question to be a we-mode one.[13]

(GS2) is of course central and seems to be the only aspect of group solidarity that is usually considered.[14] In (GS2) the broadly cooperatively performed actions are assumed to include the five Lindenbergian cases of solidary actions (expressing cooperativeness, fairness, altruism, trustworthiness, and considerateness) but without invariably assuming wholehearted motivation for those activities.

Notice that (1) solidarity between people does not in all cases involve social dependence. I can act solidarily toward you and similarly you toward me without our being properly socially dependent on each other. However, (2) a group that is solidary must involve behaviorally interdependent members for it to be a group that acts as a group (group agent). In the paradigmatic we-mode case, group tasks involve the whole group as the ultimate Hobbesian author, even if only some group members concretely bring about the outcomes that the task demands (e.g., a group may be in charge of keeping a road free from snow and ice—here not all members need to participate in the concrete work). Because of this, the group's goal creates reason-based interdependence between the members, and so (2) is true. As seen in chapter 6, in general, goals of people tend to generate action-dependency both when the goals are in conflict and when they jibe—a special case being shared and collectively accepted goals. In this latter sense people can collectively make themselves dependent on each other.

I will later argue in more precise terms that at least a paradigmatic we-mode group necessarily is solidary and will tentatively even propose that only a we-mode group can be fully solidary in view of its structurally in-built features. Indeed, (internally) solidary groups that satisfy (GS1) and (GS2) are necessarily solidary we-mode groups and the *only* (internally) solidary groups that satisfy the requirements (GS1) and (GS2) to a full (or almost full) degree (viz., in the sense of the analysantia being both necessary and sufficient conditions). Therefore I will already here speak of the we-mode account of solidarity and freely use the earlier we-mode concepts in the present context.[15]

In we-mode groups the members in general identify with the group and thus function in the we-mode as group members, satisfying the group's central requirements basically because of their group membership. Note that collective commitment toward the group's ethos entails that the group members ought to participate in the group's promotion of its ethos. As to the group-social normativity of (GS2), if the participants are collectively committed, they are also at least weakly normatively committed toward each other to perform their own part action and, e.g., to help (or even suitably to pressure) the others when needed. In addition, a group-moral (or strictly speaking an "almost" group-moral) aspect of helping is also involved—together with other intermember activities that increase the group's chances of promoting and satisfying its ethos.[16]

The group members' collective commitment to the group helps to account for the group-level cohesion (or bond, the way the members bind themselves to the group) that solidarity requires. The directed intermember we-mode social commitments basically account for the nature of intermember solidarity, as illustrated by the contents of the commitments (recall reasoning schemas (W1) and especially (W2) of chapter 3). As will be argued below, the central we-mode principles requiring the presence of a group reason and collectivity in addition to collective commitment require solidary actions in about the sense of the Lindenbergian solidary actions. As just seen, collective commitment also creates the normative dependence (including reason-dependence based on a group reason) that solidarity is taken to involve or be associated with in we-mode groups.

We-mode action—and thereby solidarity—is also related to the members' respect of each other's rights and to their trust. Normally when some participants cooperate in the (paradigmatic) we-mode, where the members hence are sincerely collectively committed toward the others to performing their parts, and where they mutually believe that this is the case, their relationship is one involving their mutual *respect of each other's rights* and also *normative trust* concerning their part-performances.[17]

I will below defend the following aforementioned general thesis: *Necessarily, a paradigmatic we-mode group is a solidary group*. That is, necessarily, because of its conceptually and normatively determined structure, such a we-mode group is solidary. I speak of a *wholeheartedly solidary group* if the members' motive for furthering the ethos is their wholehearted and "group-spirited" acceptance of it (as true or correct for the group) with ensuing group-centered promotion of the ethos rather than merely promotion on other grounds. As I understand wholehearted acceptance, it is sincere, noninstrumental acceptance that may be based on an emotion (e.g., enthusiasm). Notice that one cannot decide to *wholeheartedly* accept the ethos—while one in general can accept an ethos voluntarily.

However, as a we-mode group essentially consists of positions that can be filled by different individuals at different times, the extra strength to solidarity that is due to the members' motivation (especially wholeheartedness) might be only temporary, because solidarity may be partly based on their personal idiosyncratic features (but always partly on the structural features of the we-mode). The central matter here is the fact that any group satisfying the we-mode requirements is solidary, although not perhaps wholeheartedly so. This kind of basic group solidarity is positional in nature, and different position-holders may motivationally differ in their solidarity—so in the case of group solidarity psychological differences may play a role. Accordingly, group solidarity may be temporarily strengthened or weakened on the basis of the change of the "esprit de corps" in the same group over time.[18] Indeed, more individual solidarity in both extension and intension, as reflected by the willingness to bear greater burdens, may cause more solidarity to come about in other members, and a process of mutual reinforcement of solidarity comes about. This happens especially when the members act on a group goal to which they have collectively committed themselves. Note that in the case of *procedural* we-mode groups (in the sense of chapter 2) the members act to achieve their private, possibly antagonistic goals under some collectively accepted constraints and restrictions. Here the above solidarity point only applies to obeying the constraining rules, especially when there is temptation to breach them.

Wholehearted solidarity in general is based not only on wholehearted acceptance that normally involves valuing the ethos of the group (its constitutive and central principles including informal values and customs, etc.) Such acceptance in turn may also be motivationally based on shared individual emotions induced by the group, but the emotions still might not be fully collective in the sense of having been collectively accepted by the members (an example of the latter: we collectively accept shame in an overt, action-based sense for our group's having done X, but all of us might not phenomenally feel shame and be truly ashamed).

Morality is another important factor that can add to the strength of group solidarity. To have that, we need not here require universalizing morality (whose presence might even weaken group solidarity). Rather, the morality is group morality in the present case, and it is centrally involved in the collective-commitment aspect of the we-mode. Strictly speaking, the present account does not entail full group morality unless certain further principles adding to collective commitment are fulfilled.[19]

What about solidarity in the case of weaker groups than (paradigmatic and in some cases other autonomous) we-mode ones? A mere collection of persons or a mere I-mode group can be solidary only in the sense of its members being solidary toward each other, but this collective is not solidary qua group (in the sense of (GS1)). A pro-group I-mode group might on contingent grounds satisfy (GS1) and (GS2) (or come close to that, depending on how the concepts exactly are understood in them), but they do not satisfy these principles in the fuller, noncontingent sense that a (paradigmatic) we-mode group satisfies them.

4. Testing and Explaining the We-Mode Account of Solidary Group Activities

To show that a paradigmatic we-mode group (in the sense of chapter 2) necessarily is group-solidary, we first recall that the we-mode is based on the following trio of key features: authoritative group reason, collectivity (as based on the satisfaction of the collectivity condition), and collective commitment. The (paradigmatic) we-mode can be regarded as the "solidary mode", basically because the central agent is a group agent, referred to by the members by a "togetherness-we", rather than its being just an aggregate collection of individual agents. The members are assumed to be engaged in we-reasoning (e.g., "We as a group will X, and as this requires us to do Y, together we will do it"). This means that if the group functions properly as a we-mode group, its members must satisfy what is to be required of a solidary group: they uniformly promote the group's ethos and cooperate with each other in a way involving helping (when needed) and other kinds of behavior that we regard as following from collective commitment. *Crucially, they perform their actions for all of "us" ("our" group)* as the musketeers' famous (group) solidarity principle "All for one and one for all" also entails This is paradigmatic group solidary action. In this case the members' intentional object of solidarity is the others' activities and welfare, but their private, I-mode features also are contingently concerned, and indeed their I-mode functioning must be appropriate for their personal we-mode functioning as these modes are not factually independent. I will below show in detail that at least a paradigmatic we-mode group indeed inherently covers (although perhaps not from a wholehearted motivation) the aforementioned central kinds of solidary behavior proposed by Lindenberg and briefly discussed in section 2.

According to our first condition (GS1), the fact that a group g is solidary requires that it function as a unit in accordance with its ethos, viz., its basic goals, beliefs, norms, standards, and practices. When a we-mode group (that is paradigmatic and hence democratic in the sense of chapter 2) so functions, its members must function appropriately as group members.[20] What does this involve? What kinds of behaviors are relevant to group solidarity, and what does such action itself amount to in those situations? I will below discuss the central member-level features of solidary groups that I base on the above list by Lindenberg. However, those features are modified to explicitly adopt the group's point of view and the three central criteria of the we-mode. An account of a solidary group must be able to explain or a least sketch an explanation for the five features below explicating agent solidarity. That kind of explanation will have to make use of various contingent pieces of information depending on the situation. (The general sketch of house painting given in chapter 4 helps to see how the explanation might go.)

I will next show that my account of an ideally functioning paradigmatic we-mode group indeed satisfies the modified Lindenbergian requirements, the central member motivation involved being group-centeredness in all cases:

(1) *Cooperation versus free-riding*: When a group acts as a unit, its members, because they are members, must contribute to the group's aim to promote and maintain its ethos and to perform other ethos-compatible tasks that the group has decided to perform (in the egalitarian case through its members' collective agreement) and that the members take as their group reason for their participatory action. This involves that the members ought to cooperate—and do cooperate—with each other appropriately and, in general, purport to act toward achieving the group's goals (i.e., its

attempt to promote its ethos, understanding the ethos to be goal-like and thus to have the world-to-mind direction of fit).[21] Free-riding thus is normatively forbidden (and ideally absent) in a (paradigmatic and any autonomous) we-mode group because it is incompatible with the group's ethos—the normativity here is constitutive of the group, but on the other hand it is also partly morality-based. (Recall subsection 3.2 of chapter 7.)

(2) *Fairness*: The group should fairly divide the tasks to be performed by the members and the fruits of its cooperation.[22] The structure of at least a functional paradigmatic we-mode group (in the sense of chapter 2) guarantees the existence of fairness criteria, because a priori all members are in an equal position qua members of a "we". In an ideal we-mode group these criteria are fulfilled. From the group's perspective there is no difference between you and me; it is "us" that counts. The group members should in this egalitarian sense behave fairly vis-à-vis each other, e.g., a member's free-riding would be unfair to the others. In a we-mode group the members are to carry the burden of actions and other "costs" fairly. Accordingly, in an egalitarian we-mode group with equal member inputs (but relative to resources) the a priori default principle of distributive fairness concerning outputs would in general be *equality*. However, instead of adopting this a priori principle it might instead a posteriori decide to use the *equity* principle of fairness and take actual effort and successful contribution quantitatively into account.[23] To put this differently, the participants of we-mode joint activities (thus of we-mode group action in general) can be taken to "jointly own", and a priori be in the same position as to owning, what they have produced by their action. Accordingly the we-mode group, qua internally governing its action, may itself decide about what will be its a posteriori fair division principle, and so it may divide goods on the basis of need or of effort in some specific way.[24]

(3) *Furthering the group's ethos and helping its members*: A solidary group is committed to functioning in accordance with its ethos (its constitutive goals, interests, and principles) and its welfare in this sense. In particular, the members of we-mode groups are constitutively assumed not only to be collectively committed to the ethos but also to be directedly committed to each other concerning what the group is doing. Thus, they will have to help each other, if needed. We may here recall schema (W2) of chapter 3, section 3, explicating in part directed social commitment between we-intenders.[25] This schema explicates in part what collective commitment contains, and it also shows that the we-mode requires that the members care for each other or at least for their "inputs" concerning group tasks. In some other cases encouragement of others or putting pressure on them—or doing something required for the group's promoting its ethos—may analogously be required for the group to prosper in its efforts. Too much helping may result in a crowding effect (cf. "too many cooks spoil the broth"), and this cannot in general be allowed or at least is not ideal.

Psychological altruism toward others or the group is not required, however, but adequate obeying action for the right group reason instead of mere conformity to the group reason (and in general, the ethos) must take place in a paradigmatic we-mode group. Thus, in the case of a we-mode group a member's acting on private opportunistic or instrumental grounds constitutively does not count as right in the we-mode framework. In a solidary group (in a we-mode group in general) a member's solidary action is action for a group reason observed with *group-centered* motivation. If the motivation is intrinsically (e.g., wholeheartedly) group-centered, it results in a more stable solidarity than if based on instrumental or private opportunistic grounds. Indeed, a member of a paradigmatic we-mode group is normatively required to act for a group reason and not for a private one.[26] Acting purely for a group reason, that is, furthering the group's ethos, is solidary action because it is performed for "all of us", that is, for the group, as constitutively and normatively required by group membership.

(4) *Trustworthiness and loyalty*: The members in a solidary group ought to be trustworthy in their behavior toward other members and also when they represent the group as its delegates. When acting as group members in a we-mode group, the participants constitutively must promote and maintain the ethos of the group by their contributory actions or shares (even in the face of temptation to breach on private grounds). Being necessarily "in the same boat" in a collectively committed way, they are responsible for these actions to the other members; and they are constitutively required also to help other members when needed, and, e.g., give advice (and also themselves take advice from others). Similarly, it is constitutively entailed by group membership that the members keep the promises that they have made to each other and to the group concerning group affairs. Performing one's share of a group action for the right group reason is the key to trustworthiness and reliability.

The kind of constitutive group-normative "ought" that acceptance of the group ethos and group membership (at least according to my account) creates and thus entails can be understood sufficiently widely so that all goals and views compatible with the ethos are covered: the members should thus respect not only the ethos but also other goals and views, and so on, that the group has accepted for itself.[27] The ethos of a group may contain general and somewhat vague matters, and accordingly the members must possess the right kind of informal understanding of what these involve in concrete situations to be able to act in a loyal way. For instance, a member delegated to do something for the group in front of some out-groupers should represent the group loyally in his relevant thoughts, speech acts, and other deeds, and he ought not to do anything that shows disrespect for his fellow group members or to the group ethos.[28]

That the present requirement is satisfied by a (paradigmatic) we-mode group is part and parcel of the members acting for the same collectively accepted group reason (typically group ethos), which they are collectively committed to acting for. Without trustworthiness such action will not be successful. (Cf. Scanlon's loss prevention principle that is compatible with collective commitment although not strictly entailed by it.)[29]

(5) *Considerateness*: As Lindenberg puts it, the members should be considerate toward fellow members. When lapses and mistakes occur, the members ought to make up for them when acting as group members. This follows from the social commitment aspect of collective commitment of paradigmatic we-mode groups. In view of point (4), the members should take responsibility toward fellow members for their own actions as group members and also take responsibility in relation to outgroupers, because when acting as a group member every member in a sense represents the group (even when he has not been specifically and explicitly delegated to represent it).

The above five features of solidarity also apply, with small modifications, to relationships between group agents (cf. the EU and its "constitution").

I conclude that the above discussion shows or makes it plausible to accept that a paradigmatic we-mode group—when functioning ideally—will satisfy the constitutive and normative requirements of solidary member behavior that we have been discussing.

5. THE BASIC THESES ON GROUP SOLIDARITY

On the basis of the above discussion the following elucidations solidarity theses (GS1) are plausible:

(GS1a) A group is internally solidary if (and only if) it is a we-mode group.

(GS1b) A group is internally solidary (if and) only if—and in part on the ground that—the group's basic features can be taken adequately to help to explain the members' behaviors of the kinds (1)–(5) in the above list of requirements for solidary behavior.

(GS1a) says that (1) if a group is a we-mode group, then it is solidary, and it tentatively adds the converse that (2) a solidary group must be a we-mode group. Both of these subtheses rely on the somewhat stipulative notion of solidarity. Of them, (1) is rather well grounded in view of our earlier discussion. My basic intuitive idea of *strong* (or high degree of) internal group solidarity is given by the aforementioned musketeers' principle, "All for one and one for all"—e.g., families and certain work and sports teams often exemplify this idea in real life. Here we seem to have a kind of independent handle on what strong group solidarity is. The kind of solidarity expressed by this slogan involves strong "we-ness" (explicable in terms of the we-mode and thus its central criteria).[30]

Let me thus somewhat tentatively propose that in addition to supporting the solidary behaviors (1)–(5) in appropriate circumstances, the central we-mode features of authoritative group reason, collectivity, and collective commitment must also be present in a strongly solidary group. I will, however, here leave open the issue of supporting these we-mode properties by solidarity and the same goes for the only-if part of (GS1a).[31]

The only-if part of (GS1b) clearly seems correct: a theory of solidarity and solidary action is adequate only if it properly accounts for solidary behavior (basically the cases (1)–(5)), although it may of course be debated what such an explanation must involve in precise factual terms in addition to the conceptually central elements of the we-mode approach in the case of we-mode explanation. In any case I assume here that the statement of the group's basic features (especially its ethos) helping a theorist and others to explain the solidary behaviors performed *qua members* in question can be cashed out sufficiently precisely, but I will here largely bypass this problem area. Given relevant antecedent conditions, entailment (perhaps with the help of some relevant auxiliary principles) of the relevant descriptions of solidary behavior by the explanatory account (the "theory of the group") would of course be a classical starting point for handling the explanatory question. Adequateness here means at least the fulfillment of the requirement that the explanatory premises be true or acceptable as true and refer to some kind of underlying (causal) mechanism or reason for the entailment to hold true.

As to the tentative if-part of (GS1b), it is not true if the theory of the group just entails the behaviors without properly explaining them. I have argued that an explanatory social psychological we-mode theory also involving, of course, the basic features of the philosophical we-mode account is required for such an adequate explanation. The intertwined features of group reason, collective commitment, and collectivity will thus figure in practically all adequate explanation—as seen in our above five "test" cases.[32]

The if-part of (GS1b) can be regarded as true if the adequate explanation of solidary behaviors requires a we-mode group and if (GS1a) is tenable. Here are some considerations supporting the if-part of (GS1b). Let me recapitulate the earlier arguments (in somewhat different phrasing) for the fact that the social psychological we-mode theory envisaged here would give an adequate and as far as I can see the best presently available general kind of explanatory account of the solidary behaviors (1)–(5). To comment on these five requirements once more, requirement (1) of cooperativeness follows from the collective commitment and obligation to respect and promote the group's ethos. This collective commitment and obligation I take to follow from the very fact of acceptance of group membership. The practical inference schema (W2) that elucidates the intermember aspect of collective commitment is central. The a priori symmetrical positions of the individuals in a we-mode group can be taken to ground group fairness (requirement (2)) and to be reflected in (W2). The members' collective commitment to the ethos of the group contributes to their actually performing their parts in ways satisfying the accepted fairness norms that are based on the idea that every member of a we-mode group is an equal party of the we-ness involved in the group. (The rights and obligations may of course vary in content depending on the division of tasks and roles.) If there is a group asset, the members qua members are a priori in an equal position to share it. As I have said, the group may decide to take the amount of input into account in distributing the good (the group product), and this in general leads to an a posteriori equity principle. The individuals operating on the basis of this and other similar patterns of thinking must be able to take the point of view of the others at least as far as the we-mode requires for their flexibly taking part in the project in question. Clearly, (W2) covers helping behavior (requirement (3)) as already explicit in the formulation of the principle. I take schema (W2) to cover also the trustworthiness (requirement (4)) and the considerateness (requirement (5)) when viewed in conjunction with the collective commitment and obligation to respect and promote the group' ethos based on group membership.

The collectivity condition in the we-mode serves as a cognitive explication of the slogan "All for one and one for all" (e.g., necessarily, a member is prepared to help the group and thus its members if and only if this holds true of every other member and thus the group likewise). Intermember strategic thinking normally should not be involved, but the members must be able to take another member's position and view matters from that perspective in order to be able to help and support her properly. Altruism or being nice to the others is not necessary. What is necessary for solidarity is what the group's ethos and its current projects intrinsically involve. Given that a collective commitment to the group ethos gives an authoritative group reason for the members of a we-mode group to act, the members' group-based goals, beliefs, etc., are neither necessarily directly definitionally based nor (perhaps) supervenient on their private goals, beliefs, etc. When acting in the we-mode, the participants are supposed to set aside their private interests etc. Thus, in the we-mode, group reasons govern members' solidary actions and give them a uniform ethos-grounded direction, whereas in the I–mode, solidary actions are less secure partly because they are dependent on the private psychological states of the members and their interest in the achievement of the group's goal.

It seems plausible, to avoid "schizophrenic" member action, to require that the members not act radically against their private will and that their private interests and preferences not radically differ from their group-based we-mode interests and preferences. (If one can choose, a person should choose not to enter a group where the group's interests badly conflict with her interests.) The fulfillment of both (GS1a) and the present requirement against psychological chaos can be taken to result in an ideal paradigmatic we-mode group and an ideal solidary group. The members are fully solidary toward each other in such a group. The members of a we-mode group have a presupposed right and responsibility to monitor and sanction ethos-opposing actions and to help others when needed—this is relevant to the patterns of "mutual support" characteristic of solidarity (recall schema (W2) of note 25 and the above typology), and it gives the needed flexibility to the group for dealing with mishaps. Functionally, the solidarity of we-mode groups is likely to be more secure and flexible than that of I-mode groups. The evaluative and normative relevance of we-mode solidarity will depend on the contents of the group ethos.

6. GROUP SOLIDARITY AND ECONOMIC ACTIVITY

In this section I will comment on how the we-mode approach relates to solidarity in large groups (such as modern societies) and especially to economic activity in them. As we-mode groups mostly are self-governing and in this sense democratic (see appendix 1 to chapter 2), we are here typically speaking of democratic groups, e.g., paradigmatic we-mode groups.[33] For a group to be a democratic we-mode group it must be able to act autonomously as a group on the basis of its own reasons that the members or their authorized operatives have created. In a we-mode group at least some of the group members, typically its leaders, generally must we-reason on the basis of a group reason and arrive by their we-reasoning at accepting specific views (beliefs) or goals and intentions. Such reasoning, both collective and individual member reasoning, is often based on institutionalized mechanisms, such as voting mechanisms. The main dependence-creation between the members qua members in large groups takes place on the ground of institutionalized (or other) group reasons.

Interestingly, there seems to be a conflict between a group's being a we-mode one and a group's prospering economically. This is because economic activity may require a kind of individual autonomy needed for individuals and groups to enter contracts that is not available in very strongly solidary groups such as Durkheimian mechanically solidary ones. However, we-mode groups can be economically liberal, and so this need not be a problem in our case. Economic activity in modern societies can be argued to develop only through social differentiation of roughly the "I manufacture, you sell, he buys and consumes" kind. But this can, and has been argued to, weaken the strong solidarity that characterizes Durkheim's mechanical solidarity (recall the previous section). As argued especially by Max Weber and later, e.g., by Lindenberg, individual gain-seeking in mechanically solidary groups will be both factually and ethically strongly restricted inside the group even when there are gains from trade to be had, and it is ethically unbridled vis-à-vis strangers.[34] (Again, this need not apply to we-mode groups.) According to both Durkheim and Weber, there is a trend from mechanical solidarity within groups and enmity between groups to weak solidarity within and possibly between groups. These and many other authors seem to think that group solidarity generally will result in hostile or at least competitive relations with other groups. But as recent social-psychological research shows, that need not be the case (even cooperation between groups is possible in many of situations; cf. the EU). The characteristic change (say, in Europe) pertains to the ethics of gain-seeking: at first gain-seeking was restricted within the group, while it was unbridled vis-à-vis strangers. Thus exploitation of out-groupers was regarded as permissible, but economic contracting with strangers was very limited. Later gain-seeking came to be allowed both within and between groups but only within certain bounds.

Lindenberg makes a distinction between *strong solidarity* (primarily in the sense of mechanical solidarity) and *weak solidarity*.[35] According to his account, strong solidarity is based on *equality* as the distributional norm and the primacy of the group over individuals—and this is the a priori default in egalitarian we-mode groups, too, if a different collective decision is not made a posteriori. Furthermore, high expected sacrificial behavior for group members is required in case of need. Lindenberg mentions a firefighting team as an example, I would add families and family enterprises as typical examples. In contrast, *weak solidarity* involves *equity* as the distributional norm, individuals have primacy over the group, little sacrifice is expected of group members in case of need (for example, we may consider the partners in a law firm).[36] While we-mode group solidarity bears similarity to mechanical solidarity, it is broader and can include cases or aspects of weak solidarity—for instance, the possibility of employing the equity principle of resource distribution indicates this. There can also be solidary I-mode groups, but they involve solidarity in a weaker sense than we-mode groups. For instance, the members are only privately committed to performing solidary actions within them, and solidary I-mode groups in general as such are less stable and offer less homogeneous behavior than is to be expected in intrinsically solidary we-mode groups.[37]

A central question in this context is how individual gain-maximization can be systematically restrained without inhibiting contracting.[38] There is anthropological evidence that supports the view that strong solidarity is bad for contracting in the economic sense. Redistribution by leaders in strongly solidary groups becomes the most central form of economic transaction, and this works like a high marginal tax rate and may easily lead to underproduction.[39] As to we-mode groups, they can more successfully (but perhaps not fully) combine individual gain-maximization and economic contracting, as, e.g., modern Nordic welfare states indicate. (They may be seen as we-mode groups.)

To comment on some special cases, *procedural* we-mode groups in the sense of chapter 2 are compatible with greedy individual gain-seeking, although gain seeking is, or may be, limited and controlled by the group (recall the "joint action bottom" principles). For instance, the group members may agree to use the equity principle (instead of equality) in the distribution of common goods and also to accept individual gains acquired in concordance with and constrained by the joint action bottom principles (such as state laws). The upshot is that in a modern capitalistic or partly capitalistic society, economic prosperity seems to require the flexibility involved in weak solidarity (which can be we-mode solidarity) for good economic results for the group (society) to be reached.

Another special case in addition to procedural groups that are basically covered by my approach is that of *oppressed* groups. They are *non-autonomous* we-mode groups—recall the externally powered authorities in the B-type of cases in the classification of chapter 2. Such groups can yet be *solidary* in the sense that the ordinary members are solidary toward each other but often not toward the externally empowered leaders and the group that empowers them. This kind of situation is typically one where a "common enemy unites" the members. If their subgroup has some capacity to further their ethos, which may be a subethos of the ethos of a bigger group of which they are a subgroup, they may qualify as solidary we-mode groups.[40] The oppression is typically political or religious in these cases.[41]

Let me also note that there can be weakly solidary groups in the individualist, I-mode sense. In their case there is no collective commitment but only aggregated individual commitments to the group's shared goods (goals, projects, etc.). The shared goods can be, or generate, group reasons when the members have agreed on them. Solidarity is weaker (at least more precarious) in these cases mainly because the group members are not required to act as strongly committed group members, and the amount of solidarity exhibited by them depends also on their private interests.

Because collective commitment (as opposed to aggregated private commitment) is not present in an I-mode group, and because the participants thus in general are free to leave the group or a joint project when it ceases to be individually rational for them, there will be more stability and persistence in we-mode group activities. The idea of necessarily "being in the same boat" that is structurally present as the fulfillment of the collectivity condition in we-mode groups may well be missing in I-mode groups. When it and the collective commitment requirement fail, less concrete helping behavior probably will be present. In addition, the group morality involved in we-mode groups is likely to be lacking in I-mode groups because collective commitment is missing in them. The individual members may or may not behave morally and fairly towards each other. In all, many of the solidary features present in we-mode groups may be present in I-mode groups—but mostly only on contingent grounds.

7. GROUP EMOTIONS IN SOLIDARY GROUPS

Wholehearted we-mode group solidarity in normal cases also requires we-mode group emotions. My basic view of emotions in we-mode groups is the following. *Group emotions* (in the we-mode sense) in my account are emotions ascribed to groups and require their members' collective acceptance—and as such in general involve only voluntary cognitions of the kind expressible (but of course not necessarily expressed) by "The group is proud of its victory" and actions in accordance with this. I say voluntary, because in general people can, broadly speaking, be taken to function voluntarily in a we-mode group. Thus collective acceptance is voluntary and typically intentional. The cognitive and actional elements of emotions can be collectively accepted, the qualitative feelings and physiological arousal that are part and parcel of full emotions cannot in general be voluntarily collectively accepted.

As a group agent does not have a body and (qualitative) consciousness (nor a mind, therefore), it cannot have full-blown emotions involving feelings and emotional arousal. On the member level, a group emotion of pride in group victory has as its counterpart the members' collectively accepted, shared *collective emotion* expressible by, e.g., "We, the group members, are proud as a group of our victory" as true of them with their collective commitment to this proposition. In simple cases (e.g., egalitarian small groups) the emotion is attributable to the group agent if and only if the members collectively accept and thereby acquire (the cognitive and conative elements of) the collective emotion. A group emotion applies to a group agent, while the corresponding collective emotion logically refers to a group-based relational property between the members (all members in the above simple case).

As such, a (paradigmatic) we-mode group is solidary from the functional point of view even without wholehearted acceptance of the ethos and without the presence of we-mode group emotions in a full psychological sense involving appropriate phenomenal feelings, but these factors add to group solidarity if they are also present. Thus, while the criterial we-mode requirements are conceptual requirements for the presence of both a group emotion and its member-level counterpart, a collective emotion, the presence of feelings may yet here be an adequate contingent empirical requirement related to group emotions that can even be partially taught to children through reinforcements that bring about the right kinds of collective pattern-governed behaviors and, as it can at least be hoped, the accompanying feelings. (If a child is taught to say "I'm sorry" after having breached a rule, she will normally also come to truly regret the breach at some point in this learning process.)

The requirement of the acquisition of appropriate emotional feelings accordingly seems typically fulfilled in the case of psychologically normal people: They tend to feel in appropriate ways (a case in point is we-mode group pride caused by a group victory).[42] If such an accompanying feeling is causally generated by basically the same group fact that caused the we-mode group pride, the feeling can be regarded as a "we-mode feeling"—one contingently connected to the we-mode emotion and the group fact that in the first place brought about that emotion. In all, while the normative structure of a we-mode group does not require the presence of member feelings, its functioning may contingently require it. A person functioning in the we-mode with the right accompanying feelings can be regarded as a more wholehearted and more trustworthy we-moder than a person without the accompanying feelings.[43]

In adopting and applying a we-perspective with a rich "togetherness-we" the members come explicitly or implicitly to agree that the emotion expression applies to them qua group members, in the we-mode sense (making its central criterial conditions fulfilled). Sometimes such acceptance can be seen only through the members' overt activities, such as their expressing their pride and joy together during festivities. Such situations typically generate group reasons for members' action. For instance, in the case where the group has acted victoriously and the members have mutually recognized and collectively accepted this fact, it is a group reason for the members to be proud of the group and to collectively say, "We are proud of our group" and, furthermore, to behave accordingly because this group emotion exists, whether or not they really phenomenally *feel* pride (which normal people, however, normally do). These kinds of shared we-feelings may have a central motivating role in the production of appropriate action. They can be regarded as empirically appropriate and also as required in a normative ought-to-be sense in the case of education and socialization (e.g., children ought to be raised so as to satisfy the norm "It ought to be the case in the group that the members feel sorrow for the death of their beloved leader").[44] When, e.g., small children are socialized (in some cases by a reward-punishment type of conditioning) by their parents and their social environment to behave and react in appropriate ways, including emotional ways, they will later, as adults, find themselves endorsing certain values, beliefs, and emotional ways of reacting to social and other happenings. Here we have cases of nonvoluntary and nonintentional acceptance that will generate collective acceptance when mutually recognized.

Note that while a solidary group may stay solidary in the discussed basic sense should its members change, such changes in position-holders do not necessarily "carry" member-level feeling-involving emotions with them. For emotion transferral, the invariance pertaining to the existence of the same cognitive elements of emotions, and hence action based on these elements, must be there.

8. Concluding Remarks on Group Solidarity

It is a common and probably largely true complaint that modern societies have become more individualistic than before, that people are isolated (and even alienated) and concentrate on promoting mainly their own (and their family's) welfare, and that, as a consequence, there is much less sharing of old values, goals, norms, and practices than there used to be, say one or two centuries ago or even some decades ago.[45] Because of the size of modern societies, reciprocal face-to-face personal contacts seem to have become fewer and are replaced by communication at a distance, by email or some other Internet communication devices (this can be we-mode activity). Yet there are smaller subgroups that show face-to-face we-mode solidarity. Globalization (which seems to be a partial cause of individualization) has in recent decades brought about the loosening of intragroup social-psychological ties between people and has tended to homogenize the world by introducing similar values, especially to the young generation, resulting in shared commercially based values, "consumerism" (think of fast food, jeans, computer games, movies, and the like).

The positive side in such globalization is the generation of more peaceful relations between nations in many parts of the world, especially in Europe, and also increased economic prosperity (disregarding environmental damage). This counteracts nationalism and tends to promote internal and especially external group solidarity.

Serious threats to a group's existence and welfare will often raise group consciousness, and group-positive emotions and consequently strengthen internal group solidarity. At least internal group solidarity may depend on group-external circumstances and on such group-internal features as its leadership or the general cohesion and social atmosphere in the group. Thus not all group solidarity is based on structural group characteristics (such as the group's collective reasoning patterns or various institutionalized practices and the like). A group that is highly solidary today may be solidary in a somewhat weaker sense tomorrow although it still remains a we-mode group.[46]

As in effect suggested earlier, we may distinguish between the kind of *rule-following* group solidarity that is based on following laws, rules, and sanctions (cf. Kantian morality) from *wholehearted* group solidarity that is based on group-centered we-mode thinking and we-mode group emotions. Those members who wholeheartedly accept and endorse their group's ethos and are disposed to act accordingly are solidary in a rich and genuine sense, because such solidary functioning is based on the right kind of motivation.

Wholeheartedly solidary groups—involving wholehearted acceptance and endorsement of the group ethos and typically appropriate group emotions—will psychologically differ from groups with members who merely follow laws and norms either (1) because of fear of sanctions (instrumental acting) or (2) because of thinking that they have to obey the ethos as "A law is a law", without intrinsically valuing it and the group as it now stands. The psychological features present in wholeheartedly solidary groups may also enhance the group members' actions as group members: they promote the ethos better and help their fellow members to do their tasks better than is the case in some other group whose members fail to have these psychological features (e.g., the same group with all the members changed).[47] Groups may of course contain both wholeheartedly solidary and (merely) rule-following members—in real life all kinds of mixtures can occur. None of these kinds of solidary groups welcome opportunistic members, members who alternatively overtly act as quasi we-moders or I-moders depending on situation-dependent expected benefit.

Finally, as we have seen, we-mode group solidarity is a fairly strong notion even when not of the wholehearted kind. It has important practical value to groups, as it makes them better capable of uniform action and as it is useful to the group members who are in special need of help and to people who belong to oppressed or devalued minorities. Because of its importance for ordinary social life, it should be taken into account by social science that purports to give a truthful and informative account of the social world.[48]

NOTES

CHAPTER 1

1. See Baumeister and Leary (1995).

2. In this book the term "group" is used in a broad, partly technical sense encompassing not only small informal groups but also, and especially, organized groups such as business organizations and even states. In the case of, e.g., a state one might also speak of an agential social structure, but for the simplicity of exposition I will normally use the term "group" or sometimes "organized group" in all these contexts.

3. Concrete evidence for the important role of we-thinking (be it in the I-mode or in the we-mode) on the national level is provided by Hyyppä (2010) concerning the Swedish-speaking minority in Finland. He argues that the more we-thinking and we-emoting as well as interpersonal trust a group's "ground culture" involves, the more both structural and cognitive social capital it is likely to involve. According to his group's empirical research, we-thinking and we-spirit among Swedish-speaking Finns' ground culture has the mentioned features, and the social capital in this group is accordingly on a high level. That social capital grounds active cultural-social life, which in turn contributes to health and longevity. As a consequence, the Swedish-speaking Finns live longer and healthier lives than other Finns.

4. See chapter 2, section 7 for detailed discussion.

5. See Cornford ([1912] 2004).

6. See Runciman (1997). Such organized groups can be we-mode groups in the sense to be discussed below and especially in chapter 2.

7. Our view of collective agents as social systems bears some resemblance to the ancient Roman view of group persons, while the collections that were grouped together under the term *societas* correspond to the weaker conception of group agents to the extent a *societas* is organized for action.

8. Gierke ([1934] 1957), pp. 62–67.

9. See Cornford ([1912] 2004) and especially Hayes (1942, 2009) for discussion and for detailed references. I have myself written a paper on group agency to which I refer for some historical discussions of collective volition (see Tuomela 2013). See also Schmid and Schweikard (2013).

10. See, e.g., Tuomela (1992) for a discussion.

11. The phrase "as a group" can of course be linguistically used also in some I-mode cases, but in this particular context I rather use it to signify the we-mode in order to have a handy phrase to use in joint action contexts.

12. Acting in a group context is very common in the sense I am using this concept. For instance, voting in an election is a group context and so can painting a house together be—at least when properly organized in terms of tasks and responsibilities.

13. In this book I use the word "private" basically to mean (purely) personal. The central point for the use of this term is that according to my account there will be both I-mode and we-mode mental individual states. As both states apply to persons, we would have to speak somewhat confusingly of personal we-mode and I-mode states. That is why I call I-mode states private or *purely* personal (i.e., not intrinsically based on a social group's properties).

14. In the terminology to be used later in this book (see chapter 2), a we-perspective will be understood to contain at least the ethos of the group providing a group reason for action, collective commitment, possibly affective elements (e.g., "we-feeling"), and action based on these components.

15. I will later clarify these mode-notions in more precise terms. This results in somewhat technical notions, but they are still intuitively satisfactory and applicable to real life.

16. There are also other kinds of cases in which the we-mode may be more rewarding even in a utility-maximizing sense. See Tuomela (2007a), chapter 7, for an example in which the synergy effects and the collective commitment in the we-mode lead to this conclusion.

17. An I-mode group can involve many of the above features, but the we-mode group still is a conceptually and functionally stronger group because of the central we-mode criteria (listed above) fulfilled by it but not as such by an ordinary I-mode group.

18. See Callero (2009) for an accessible account of individualism from the point of view of social science. He speaks of individualism as a myth (p. 29): "The artificial separation of the self from society, and the belief in the primacy and superiority of the autonomous actor is the *myth of individualism*."

19. This is my construal of the elements that individualism will have to be concerned with. Not all theorists who have been labeled methodological individualists have included all these elements in their accounts (see, e.g., Udehn 2001). Also cf. Tuomela (2009b).

20. Predicates with an established use are or express concepts (whether "are" or "express" is employed here depends on one's underlying ontological views).

21. See Tuomela (2012a) for a more extensive discussion. Also cf. Schmid (2009).

22. It also faces problems in dealing with subintentional explanations of evolutionarily "rigid" and nonvoluntary forms of behavior (though the latter kinds of problems will not be the subject matter of this book).

23. See Udehn (2001) for detailed discussion.

24. When I here say irreducible I mean groups that might not even supervene on their members' individualistic (i.e., I-mode) properties and interrelations.

25. See chapters 3 and 7 for irreducibility arguments concerning the we-mode and chapters 2 and especially 4 for group agents' reasons versus group members' group-based reasons. E.g., a group agent's reason for painting a house may be that the old paint has faded, while the members' group reason here will be the group's decision and directive to the members' to paint the house. The members' dominant private reasons might be something else, e.g., to get appreciation from others for the members' participation.

26. See, e.g., Sally (1995), Colman, Pulford, and Rose (2008), Hakli, Miller, and Tuomela (2010), and chapter 7 of this book. I am assuming that, e.g., a game that is subjectively a PD as to its preference structure rationally requires defection (choosing the so-called defection alternative rather than the cooperative alternative) in single-shot cases. Thus explanation of cooperation in a game with objective PD payoffs requires explaining irrational action or explaining action in a game with subjective non-PD preferences.

27. I am here speaking of theories that are specific enough to be testable, and not just mere conceptual frameworks or untestable pseudotheories.

28. Recently Quante and Schweikard (2009) have discussed individualism and collectivism in an interesting but totally different way from mine. Still it seems that these two approaches are compatible or at least reconcilable. The aforementioned authors also discuss some political doctrines, making reference to individualism and collectivism. Of the doctrines discussed, viz., libertarianism, moderate liberalism, liberal communitarianism, and antiliberal communitarianism, the doctrine that seems to fit best the ideas of the present book is liberal communitarianism defined as follows: Liberal communitarianism awards high priority to the basic rights of individuals, but in principle these rights can be weighed against the ethical claims of social entities, where the state (or any other comparable social entity) is regarded not only as an instrument but also as intrinsically valuable. The considerations presented in this chapter can be viewed as compatible with this account, even the intrinsic value requirement when naturalistically understood.

29. As to the conceptual framework of my theory, the new additions (e.g., the inclusion of power considerations in a deeper sense than before) seem to make possible applications to philosophy of science—viz., to scientific communities as groups with central epistemic tasks (see the paper by William Rehg [2013], where my theory is applied to clarify Kuhn's theory, e.g., paradigms as group ethoses and incommensurability problems).

30. A weaker version of this thesis would be one claiming that we-perspective concepts either in the we-mode or in the pro-group I-mode are scientifically required in addition to plain I-mode concepts. In this book I will defend the stronger claim (1). In Tuomela (2007a) the weaker version of (1) is defended in some cases (such as the problem of the evolutionary origin of the we-mode) when evidence is too scarce to distinguish between the pro-group I-mode and the we-mode.

31. The we-mode account conceptually requires the adoption of a strong group perspective (or we-perspective, described from the members' point of view), but in the I-mode case the adoption of a weaker kind of group perspective is contingently possible—and in such a case we have the pro-group I-mode account.

CHAPTER 2

1. By the phrase "giving up part of one's authority to the group" to act is meant becoming normatively bound to the group. One still in principle preserves the de facto autonomy to act as one thinks best in the situation, and this will here require breach of the normative bonds.

2. Cf. world-language, language-language, and language-world rules as discussed by Sellars (1968).

3. See chapter 3 for comments on the precise relationship between the group level and the member level and see section 7 for a more detailed discussion of group agents.

4. See Tuomela (1998) for discussion.

5. Shared mental states of individuals are member-level phenomena (collections of individual states at bottom) and hence are not group-level states in my account.

6. See chapters 3, 6, and especially 7 for the arguments mentioned in this paragraph. Also see section 3 below for an analogy argument for we-mode action as a group member.

7. The notion of group is here to be understood in a comprehensive sense ranging from two people carrying a table together to corporations and states.

8. I have elsewhere given a naturalistic process account of groups that also covers structured groups like we-mode group agents (see Tuomela 2007a, p. 146).

9. The tasks related to a position are based on ought-to-be and ought-to-do norms and rights corresponding to dovetailing may-be and may-do norms (see Tuomela 1995, chapter 1). Needless to say, the positions may be functionally equivalent—a common case.

10. Although a kind of we-thinking can take place in pro-group I-mode groups, typically I will below speak of we-thinking in the context of we-mode groups unless otherwise mentioned.

11. In my account, work acceptance is acceptance as true (in descriptive cases or as right in other cases) of a proposition in the first place rather than, e.g., approval.

12. See Tuomela (2007a), chapter 9, for a discussion of the evolution of we-thinking. Also see the pattern-governed behavior account of chapter 8 of this book.

13. As to the notions of realm of concern, intentional horizon, and ethos (as well as subethos and "umbrella" ethos), see the discussion in chapter 1 of Tuomela (2007a).

14. Cf. Tuomela (2007a), chapter 1, for my original account that the present account modifies slightly. The earlier account does not cover we-mode groups based on external authorization.

15. Clause (1) speaks of a group's acceptance action and also of acting as a group member, and if all or sufficiently many members act as group members, the group acts as a group. Thus all groups that satisfy (WMG) are capable of acting as groups.

16. We can say that we-mode groups are based in part on their members' (or prospective members') collective construction. In this book I use "construction" to mean a kind of constitutive collective acceptance where something is put together from some elements; it is based on the capacity to imagine and pretend things and to entertain counterfactual contents and to hold them true in one's mind. In general, construction is understood to be veridical collective acceptance: collective acceptance entails the existence of what has been accepted—we do not merely pretend that there is a group when we construct it.

17. Collective acceptance of the ethos can here be taken to be conceptually analogous to a performative (or "declarative") speech act that has the world-to-mind direction of fit of semantic satisfaction and thus makes the ethos goal-like. As a consequence of this acceptance it will also have the mind-to-world direction of fit analogously to an assertion. (See chapter 5 for more on collective acceptance and, e.g., Searle 2010 for a declarative account, and chapter 8 for an evaluation of it.)

18. See appendix 2 for a functional-explanatory argument for introducing group agents.

19. For other qualifications and additions, see Tuomela (2007a), chapter 1.

20. I owe this example to Kaarlo Miller.

21. See the more technical account of the we-mode in chapter 3.

22. Psychological properties and relations may of course be important in social groups and may further group life, but in large groups the members may never meet, and the positional account is especially apt for those cases.

23. Note that organized I-mode groups, of course, can have such a structure, although in them it is not an intrinsic feature in the same way as in we-mode groups.

24. See chapter 8 and cf. Tuomela (2007a), chapter 8.

25. Private sharing of an attitude by some individuals can be just a rather accidental contingent fact, or a fact due to a common external cause, or it can be due to their agreement of some kind. I will not here further investigate the various possibilities. I-mode sharing is obviously weaker than we-mode sharing, which is conceptually group-based.

26. See Tuomela (2007a), chapter 1, for more comments.

27. The central reason for the nonsatisfaction of these conditions in the I-mode case is that the notions of collectivity, collective commitment, and group reason are conceptually group-based, contrary to what I-mode theorizing gives us (even if some conceptual connections can occasionally be built in).

28. As in the case of we-mode groups, the possibility of partly externally identified I-mode groups is logico-linguistically covered below by the "if and" put in parentheses.

29. Note that the analogy under discussion concerns only the central conceptual and functional aspects of the respective individual and group agents, not their ontological aspects or features, as group agents do not literally have bodies or phenomenal consciousness.

30. I will in fact below assume for the sake of simplicity that every intentional action is performed for a reason and thus ignore other cases—the issue depends on what one thinks reasons are; see chapter 4.

31. See Tuomela (2007a), chapter 6, for a discussion and rebuttal of the kind of bootstrapping looming here.

32. See Tuomela (2010a), where I argue for the existence of this kind of collective causation and for the explanatory power of such explanation in virtue of the collective goals underlying the group's activity. The central general thesis defended in that paper is that there are cases of irreducible collective social causation and hence of explanation based on a causal collective social explanans.

33. See, e.g., Tuomela (2007a).

34. See the treatment of group solidarity in chapter 9 below.

35. In simple egalitarian groups what motivates the group amounts to the same as what motivates its members, and in such cases, as contrasted with hierarchical groups, there is no special reason to distinguish between a group's reason and a group reason that the members have. Note, too, that what is a motivating reason for one member might not in reality motivate other members. If there is a leader in the group, he might form the intention to act for the group on the basis of a fact that motivates him but not the rank-and-file members (who might not be aware of that special fact). See chapters 4 and 6 for further discussion.

36. Cf. Tuomela (2007a), p. 48.

37. In the case of structured groups, the collectivity condition applies directly to the operative members, viz., members authorized for performing some special tasks. However, normally at least tacit or implicit acceptance of the nonoperative members is also assumed.

38. Cf. Tuomela (2007a), p. 50.

39. Also see Tuomela (2000), chapter 6, for discussion.

40. See Tuomela (2007a), chapter 2.

41. That the group is so committed can come about in various ways, e.g., through its leaders' effecting it or the group members' previous or current (and sufficiently extensive) collective acceptance, or by means of, e.g., some previously agreed-upon institutional mechanism.

42. As will be clarified in chapter 3, collective intention as used in this book is a broad umbrella notion covering a group's intention, joint intention, and we-intention. In the present context, joint intention can be meant in the sense of chapter 3. However, if one speaks of large groups, the "face-to-face" intimacy that we may intuitively associate with the term "joint" is missing. Thus the term "collective" may be preferred at least in such contexts, and this applies both to joint intentions and to joint commitments. A similar comment applies to collective versus joint commitment.

43. Gilbert in her 1989 book and later works has advocated joint commitment in a related sense (which, however, is not closely connected to joint intention). For a comparison of my functional entity view (which is not, or not merely, a "plural subject" account) with theoretical views on collective intentionality including Gilbert's plural subject theory, see my recent paper Tuomela (2013).

44. See chapter 3.

45. Social psychologists in particular tend to speak of group identification in the present kind of context. Obviously, this does not mean literally identifying (or partially identifying) oneself with a group—a whole of which members are parts. In my account, identification with a group basically amounts to functioning (thinking and acting) in the we-mode—as a full-blown group member—relative to the group in question.

46. Collective acceptance of the ethos can here be taken conceptually to be analogous to a performative (or "declarative") speech act that has the world-to-mind direction of fit of semantic satisfaction and thus makes the ethos goal-like. At the same time it will also have the mind-to-world direction of fit as being—or being analogous to—an assertion. (See chapter 5 for more on collective acceptance and, e.g., Searle 2010 for a declarative account and chapter 8 for an evaluation of it.)

47. Cf. the somewhat different account and defense of the importance of joint commitment by Gilbert in her 1989 book and later works.

48. The account of this book is compatible only with the attribution of an "as if" group mind to group agents (or with the attribution of a group mind that upon rational and philosophical reflection turns out to be a quasi mind).

49. This is the kind of basis that supervenience discussions in this field typically use. See chapter 3 for discussion of supervenience.

50. See Searle (1995, 2010) for the notion of epistemic objectivity. For group-level mind-dependence see the principle (CAT) of chapter 8 of the present book.

51. In saying this I assume that individual agent's intentional features are not fictitious and do not problematize them.

52. The organizations that qualify as group agents in general have structures with positions or offices that have to be filled for the organization to become an empirically viable agent. (See chapters 6 and 8 for discussion.)

53. This is a rather strong individualistic element in the theory of this book. I will not defend this feature that is compatible with my account of group agency.

54. In this book I will not much analyze the causal and explanatory powers as group agents, but see Tuomela (2010a) and see note 53 of chapter 3 for a simple sketch of causation by a group agent.

55. Below I make use of some formulations in Tuomela (2011b).

56. It seems that a central argument for this kind of autonomy view is the one based on the discursive dilemma on p. 70 of List and Pettit (2011). I do not regard the argument as very strong because it is actually the individuals who control the decision making in the situation.

57. See chapter 4 for a sketch of my earlier account of social power, i.e. power over persons, qua social control of agents' preferences (utilities, payoffs, or the like).

CHAPTER 3

1. The conceptual psychological architecture that this book works with contains irreducible reasons (R) as well, and thus we have minimally what we could call the belief-desire-intention-reason (BDIR) architecture in the single-agent case, and its collectivized version would minimally use collective attitude and collective reason concepts.

2. A goal of the action might be such a closely related state intended to be satisfied. Note that one may speak of weakly intentional action if a person does not nonintentionally do what he does. (One may comment on collective action similarly.)

3. Logically speaking, a group's intention is a monadic property of a group agent, while a joint intention is a relation between individual group members, and a we-intention an intention ascribed to a single member.

4. See Tuomela (1995), chapter 2, for my general account. To illustrate, the following central cases of intentional activity fall under an agent A's *seeing to it that* the window is closed (and, mutatis mutandis for all cases with nonagentive states):

(1) A has the "action-prompting" intention of closing the window or keeping it closed, if somebody (or something) opens (or tries to open) it.
(2) A closes the window, if it is open.
(3) A orders (or asks, etc.) somebody else to close the window and does so with success, or uses some other relevant means to bring it about that the window becomes closed (including refraining from preventing somebody from closing the window), if it is open.

Let us emphasize that in all the above cases A can be said to be in intentional control over the situation, so to speak. Even if he asks somebody else, B, to close the window and B intentionally complies, A retains his overall control. In such a case both A and B can be said to see to it that the window is closed, the latter helping A to see to it that the window is closed. (If B changes his mind or if something goes wrong with his action of closing the window, A will step in and do whatever he can to close the window and to keep it closed.)

5. I have discussed these in Tuomela (1995), chapter 2. The principles are well known at least to those who have worked on the logical properties of (single-agent) intention.

6. There is another way of analyzing the content of an attitude such as an intention. It takes the content to be an infinitival phrase such as "to paint the house" in the case of an agent's intention to paint the house. I will not here discuss this view.

7. Below I regard intentions typically as propositional attitudes. However, intention as states or events with action contents (e.g.. "intentions-in-action") may seem to be an exception to the propositional attitude view.

8. See Tuomela (1995), chapters 2 and 3.

9. See Tuomela (1984) and (1995) for my account of we-willing and "purposive causation".

10. See Tomasello (2009) and the relevant experimental work by his colleagues at the Max Planck Institute in Leipzig, e.g., Gräfenhahn, Behne, Carpenter, and Tomasello (2009). Tomasello also emphasizes the capacities for trust and tolerance. Trust is of course central in this book, because it inherently underlies the we-mode.

11. The terminology in the literature varies, but it is the distinction that is important here, not the terminology.

12. See chapter 5 for a detailed discussion of collective acceptance and group acceptance.

13. The professor's correcting activity is in an obvious local sense nonjoint (he is doing it in his solitary ivory chamber, so to speak). However, in a more general context, especially in the context of the university as an organization, his work is part of the general joint activity that keeps the organization going, so to speak.

14. Note that the present conditions of (WMI) apply to both intentions and goals, and indeed with some minor linguistic changes to all representational mental attitudes.

15. The notion of acting as a group member is analyzed separately for the we-mode case and the I-mode case in Tuomela (2007a), chapter 1. I will not here repeat my detailed analyses.

16. The above account gives only a sufficient condition for holding an intention in the we-mode. This is because in other similar cases some members' intentions might have content that is somewhat different from precisely P. It seems that such intention contents might entail or be entailed by P. However, I will leave this matter open here.

17. The reader is reminded that the notion of mode (such as the we-mode or I-mode) as a way of having an attitude should of course be kept strictly separate from the general view that attitudes have modes (e.g., are wantings or believings) and contents.

18. To be consistent with my earlier usage, in this book I will not use "joint" merely for the we-mode in general nor "shared" only for the I-mode, but in this chapter "joint" will normally refer to the we-mode. Note that when I use "as a group" I generally mean the we-mode. So used, the phrase "as a group" covers less ground than "jointly", which also applies to I-mode cases.

19. We can satisfy our intention in various ways. For example, we can paint the house together, I or you paint it alone, we hire someone to do it, you provide the paint and I pay for the job, and so on; see chapter 5.

20. The agent thus in general acts in part for himself and in part for the group (the prefix "pro" in "pro-group" amounts to about the same as "for" in the present context). In chapter 7 in our game-theoretic discussion we will mostly technically consider the extreme version of the pro-group I-mode where the agent has fully adopted the group's utility function and thus acts for the group. Yet I suggest that an I-moder in general might be taken to be disposed to change his utility function into one allowing for free-riding and defection, when the possibility arises (contrary to a strict we-moder).

21. We may also add that "for A" here entails "for the use of A", which in turn can be understood as meaning functioning for the satisfaction of A's goals and interests.

22. See the argument in chapter 6 that we-mode group action intrinsically (in a constitutive-normative sense) requires cooperative member action and normatively giving part of one's authority to act in a causally influential way to the group. See chapter 7 for a related discussion of the differing possibilities and consequences of free-riding in I-mode and we-mode cases.

23. The above definitions supersede those given in Tuomela (2007a), chapter 2.

24. One may ask whether one could consistently formulate a weaker notion of the we-mode by dropping one or two of the conditions in our list of the three conditions. I do not have a well argued answer to this question, but my intuitive answer is no. The we-mode way of thinking is rather holistic with intertwined concepts, and, as concrete examples indicate, the criteria seem be (or fail to be) fulfilled together.

25. The functional difference between the we-mode and pro-group I-mode will be discussed in chapter 7. See also Bacharach (1999) and Hakli, Miller, and Tuomela (2010).

26. One can even go further and present the following concise classification as a conceptual possibility: (1) IM(I, PJ), (2) WM(I, PJ), (3) IM (W, J), (4) WM(W, J). Here IM and WM mean respectively I-mode and we-mode as logical operators covering the contents within the parentheses. I and W respectively mean an I-attitude and a we-attitude, in our present example I-intention and we-intention, where the mode of the we-attitude determines the "strength" of the "we" involved in it. In the intention case, J means joint action as the content of a we-intention, and PJ means an individual member's participatory action involved in the members' joint performance of J.

27. To be sure, the imagined, collectively constructed properties also have causal impact on the group members' and other people's thinking and through it on their actions, and so on.

28. See List and Pettit (2011), chapter 2, and chapter 5 of this book.

29. In chapter 2 of Tuomela (2000) the distinction between constitutive "c-action" and means or "m-action" closely corresponds to the present distinction between literal or concrete participation actions and the activity (often only potential) by which a participant takes responsibility for the group's effort and the concrete participation actions.

30. See Tuomela (1984), chapter 5, and, for a newer account with an emphasis on functioning as a group, chapters 5 and 6 of Tuomela (2007a).

31. Here I am referring to the idea that a we-mode group has an identity that does not in all cases depend on the identities of the participants—as in some small face-to-face groups (like groups based on mutual friendship). A large group, at least, can and must be able to survive change of members. Thus the central matter here is the positions or offices they occupy or their roles as group members.

32. Note that we-moders need to be group-centered and cooperative but not necessarily nice to each other.

33. I-mode and we-mode intentions can be considered from "the moral point of view", the view that morality applies to all of humankind. A case in point is a distinction made by Wilfrid Sellars. In his 1968 book he employs subindices "I" and "we" in his intention-forming Shall operator, thereby obtaining two different modes of intending, and he writes: "The function of the indices is performed in ordinary language by the contrast between 'from a personal point of view' and 'from the point of view of the group' or, of more interest, 'from a moral point of view'". As for the contrast between the personal and the group's point of view, my account of the we-mode and the I-mode distinction bears similarity to Sellars's distinction, although in comparison his account is less detailed and focuses on the moral aspect of we-intentions, applicable to the case in which the group in question is "mankind generally".

34. I basically regard "jointly" and "together" to be equivalent but typically use the former for the case of intention and the latter for action.

35. To keep things simple, I will here consider in detail only joint intentions in egalitarian groups where the members are in symmetric positions. Many small groups are such groups. I will in this

book also speak of joint intentions in structured groups and large groups, and in those kinds of joint action cases I prefer to use the term "collective intention" rather than "joint intention".

36. This new account involves changes from my earlier view (e.g., in chapter 4 of Tuomela 2007a). The account is now more explicitly geared to joint intentions, and the account can be seen basically to satisfy the much-discussed *own action condition*, *control condition*, and *settle condition*. It seems that within the theory of this book we can apply these conditions to (functional) group agents unproblematically in the case of we-mode joint intentions and we-intentions instead of applying them to single individuals. This is because we-mode intentions are group-dependent and group agents are the basic subjects of we-mode collective intentions. E.g., the own action condition applies well as the agent is a group agent and the intended action is a group action. See Tuomela (2005), especially p. 354, for my earlier account.

37. A main reason can be regarded as one that is sufficient for the intention in question if considered alone. A somewhat weaker possibility would be that it be regarded as an "inus" reason parallel to Mackie's (1974) notion of inus cause.

38. Some commentators have misunderstood this matter and regarded participation intention as an I-mode individualistic notion merely because of the linguistic formulation of it as "I intend to perform..."

39. Given that X_i expresses an individual's collectively accepted (or anyway intersubjectively collectively acceptable) part (an action type) of X, and I and JI stand for single and joint intending, we can define A_i's we-intention (WI) as follows:

$$WIA_i(X) = (EX_i)\ (X_i \text{ is an action type that is } A_i\text{'s part of } X \ \&\ IA_i(A_i \text{ performs } X_i \text{ in accordance with and in part because } JI_{we}(\text{we will perform } X \text{ jointly})))\text{.}$$

40. For relevant discussion and comments on these patterns of reasoning, see, e.g., Tuomela (1984), (1995), and (2007a). Note that schema (W2) represents the kind of mutual responsiveness idea of cooperative intentions that, e.g., Bratman (1992) has advocated. What is also involved is a required understanding of the others' relevantly similar understanding of joint intention and action and hence their part performances (thus imagining how to play their roles in the joint intention and action). Neither of the patterns below need be explicitly reflected upon when acting. They rather represent skills that can be exercised subconsciously and in a routine fashion. (In the terminology of chapter 8, we can here speak of collective pattern-governed behaviors.)

41. Here is my account of I-mode joint intentions in my 2007 book, pp. 70–73:

(*IMJI*) You and I *share in the I-mode the intention to jointly perform X* if and only if

(1) I intend that we X in the external reason-based we-attitude sense (namely, I intend that we X in part because I believe that you intend in the external reason-based sense that we X and that we mutually believe that each of us so intends), and
(2) you similarly intend that we X in the external reason-based we-attitude sense,
(3) it is mutually believed by you and me that (1) and (2).

External reasons above are contingent (as contrasted with conceptually required) reasons for one's intention as explained in the cited context. Bluntly speaking, the other persons and their intentions are taken to be a contingent part of the intender's environment conducive to his own purposes.

42. The "only if" part in ($CoCom_{Int}$) is missing, for it might not hold for all standard we-mode joint intentions. If that happens, there must yet be some kind of we-mode shared intention present, as our present notion of collective commitment has the world-to-mind fit.

43. Searle (2010), p. 48.

44. Searle (2010), p. 50.

45. A view similar to Searle's present suggestion can be found in Tomasello et al. (2005) and Tuomela (2007a), chapter 9.

46. See the later arguments, especially in chapter 7, that show that one cannot do everything with the pro-group I-mode notions that one can do with full-blown we-mode notions.

47. See Searle (2010), pp. 51ff.

48. See p. 54 of Searle (2010).

49. Searle confusingly speaks of "collective B" as collective action on the one hand and as collective intention-in-action on the other hand (2010, p. 52).

50. See especially my accounts in Tuomela (1995) and (2007a). Note that authorization obviously can be layered: E.g. the group members authorize a leader, who in turn authorizes a subset of the people to act as his deputies.

51. Other group attitudes, such as group beliefs, can be given a similar account; see Tuomela (2007a), chapter 6.

52. I am arguing in this book, though, that overall the we-mode way of operating tends to lead to collectively better results, at least in dilemma cases. This will be discussed and argued in later chapters, especially in chapters 6 and 7.

53. Here is a simplified and rather obvious account of how a group agent can cause, and hence explain why and how certain events in the world, such as a house getting painted, can be caused by a group agent through its members' activities and causal powers:

Group agent g *intentionally caused event E* (e.g. that a house gets painted) if and only if

(1) g brought about E through its members' activities when acting as group members;
(2) the "mechanism" through the operation of which it brought about E, is the members' joint capacity to form joint attitudes such as goals, intentions, and beliefs in virtue of which they acted together intentionally and brought about the individual part performances and results needed for E to come about;
(3) event E would not have come about without g's (possibly emergent) actions (depending on the joint actions by the members in the sense of (2)).

In addition, cases of nonintentional and less than fully jointly intentional causation are possibly because of g's activities. Thus, e.g., cases where the members have only limited information about the coparticipants' activities, such as may be the case with a spy organization's activities, e.g. the Red Orchestra's World War II activities, fit in here.

54. Recall chapter 2 for remarks on explanation in terms of group agents and see chapter 4, section 3, for additional comments.

55. For a recent, accessible account of social supervenience, see List and Pettit (2011). Also see my comments in chapter 5 of the present book. List and Pettit assume that only ontological reduction is required for methodological individualism. Recall the discussion of supervenience in section 2 of this chapter.

56. See the comments and references in Tuomela (2007a); also cf. chapter 7 of this book.

57. See Tuomela (1988) for my views of this myth.

58. See Searle (1995, 2010) for institutional facts and also see my somewhat different account in chapter 8 below.

59. There is a different kind of irreducibility matter, independent of the we-mode/I-mode distinction, concerned with the fact that a group may be able to do things that on logical-structural grounds its members cannot do. This fact gives an irreducibility argument for joint actions and group actions. Thus, for instance, multiple rebels can surround a castle, while individual members cannot. Other examples of such irreducible joint action types are singing a duet or dancing a tango.

60. Indeed, in the stylized game-theoretic framework of chapter 7, even the opposite holds true, viz., that the I-mode mathematically comes out as a special case of the we-mode. In that chapter several irreducibility arguments are presented. (Also see the final section of chapter 6.)

61. See Tuomela (1985a) for my realism—a kind of internal realism.

62. In my 2007 book I made the pro-group I-mode/we-mode distinction and discussed its functional effects. See chapter 7 for a technical game-theoretical discussion related to this matter.

63. "Will" is used in a somewhat vague sense in the historical literature. In some contexts, "want" might be a better translation.

64. Rousseau ([1762] 1979), Book I, chapter 7. Ripstein (1999) argues that Rousseau's general will in part consists of shared ends of citizens and regards citizens' intentions to cooperate to satisfy them as we-intentions akin to Sellars's notion of we-intention (which is less collectivistic than mine). See Miller and Tuomela 2013, for a more extensive account of Rousseau's views.

65. Rousseau ([1762] 1979), Book II, chapter 3.

66. McDougall (1920).

67. McDougall (1920), p. 56.

68. Vierkandt ([1928] 1975). He also has a kind of notion of we-intention as, e.g., the following passage clearly shows: "Gruppenwille bedeutet dabei ein Wille der in alle (oder den massgebenden) Gliedern lebendig ist und von ihnen wiederum als 'unser' Wille erlebt wird" (Vierkandt 1949, p. 56). Also cf. (1928), pp. 352–53. The quote says, in effect, that a group will is active or salient in the members and is experienced as "our" will. Reading "in the members" distributively, we are here dealing with a central feature of a we-intention.

69. Tönnies ([1887] 1996).

70. See Tuomela (2013), where I give a detailed account of the aforementioned authors' views with textual evidence.

71. See Tuomela 2000, chapter 11.

CHAPTER 4

1. See, e.g., Searle (2001) for these.

2. See Scanlon (1998).

3. See Dancy (2000).

4. Broome (2004).

5. See Dancy (2000), p. 125, for a related conception and for examples similar to that of the paint can.

6. See Dancy (2000) for the notion of favoring. Dancy also discusses the weaker kind of "enticing" reasons in his 2004 book.

7. This chapter concentrates on reasons that can be weighed against each other as contrasted with normative requirements in Broome's (2004) sense. My notion of reason is viewed as primitive and hence a conceptually irreducible notion. Accordingly my accounts below do not attempt to give old-fashioned analyses in terms of noncircular necessary and sufficient conditions.

8. See Tuomela (2002b) and chapter 8 below for a collective acceptance account of social institutions and a discussion of other things that are in the meant sense up to us to collectively create and maintain.

9. Cf. Tomasello (2009).

10. See Richerson and Boyd (2005) and Tomasello et al. (2005) for recent discussions defending the importance of cooperation and (in the latter text) also shared intentionality as evolutionary adaptations characteristic of humans as species.

11. With some qualifications, people tend to be cooperative in in-group contexts but competitive and even hostile in out-group contexts, as social psychological experiments demonstrate.

12. See Tuomela (2007a), p. 17, for my earlier account of I-mode and we-mode reasons. Let me emphasize that a group member's general reason for acting as a group member on the whole is the simple one that he is a group member and backing that reason there may be the motivating reason that he joined the group and is motivated to continue as a group member because he likes the group's goals and social atmosphere.

13. See Tuomela (2007a), chapter 3, for a detailed account.

14. Mutual beliefs must under an *iterative* construal involve loop beliefs of the kind "I believe that you believe that I believe that s", and thus it cannot be strictly said the agent x here is responding to his environment. The agent's own belief state is built into the notion of an iterative mutual belief. However, if this is considered to be a problem, mutual beliefs must be understood differently—e.g., in terms of a *fixed point* analysis (which is only at the infinite limit equivalent to the iteration analysis; cf. Balzer and Tuomela (1997) or in terms of my weaker account in chapter 1 of Tuomela (1995). Alternatively, the mutual belief could be taken to be a still weaker one, e.g., "general belief" in the group, without assuming the iterative account of this notion.

15. See Tuomela and Bonnevier-Tuomela (1997) and Tuomela (2002b). Also see chapter 3 of Tuomela (2007a).

16. We recall from chapter 2 that we-mode and I-mode attitudes and actions need not differ with respect to their contents but rather with respect to their mode of having or sharing them.

17. This paragraph owes to comments by Kaarlo Miller.

18. I have discussed these categories in detail (except for the group action category) in my 2002 book (Tuomela 2002b).

19. See Tuomela (2007a), chapter 6 and recall chapter 3 of this book.

20. See Tuomela (2007a) for various other cases where the social reason is based on others' attitudes different from ATT.

21. Social norms and obligations can also function as social reasons in the present account. What we have been discussing above are pro tanto reasons, i.e., reasons that do not in general strictly entail that the agent categorically ought to do the action that he has the reason for. In contrast, in the case of social norms and sincere promises we are dealing with an "ought". E.g., when one fulfills the promise to do A, then, *for the reason of having promised*, one does A. That one has promised here is a desire-independent reason (i.e., normative requirement) for performing A. Analogously, institutional actions are in part normatively required and in that sense given reason for by institutional norms.

22. Any we-mode group's members are position-holders in a general sense and in this capacity represent the group. The group members' group-reasons are at bottom reasons for position-holders' actions as group members.

23. This general statement is too blunt and needs qualification, e.g., concerning the decision method and the specific nature of the we-mode group, e.g., concerning the authorization of its leaders. See the relevant discussion in chapters 2 and 5.

24. See Tuomela (2007a), chapter 4, and (2011a).

25. The warrant concerns relevant social coordination, not necessarily substantive features of the members' group reasons.

26. This account is closely related to that in Tuomela (2012b). Below I make use also of some other formulations of that paper but in a revised form. Below I only give a partial account of a group agent's reasons and only for cases where action is successful. Of course an agent can have a motivating reason that never gets acted on.

27. See Tuomela (2007b) for acting on a motivational set.

28. The present notion of equilibrium is a special case of the joint equilibrium of the notion defined in the appendix to chapter 3. The present notion does not consider probabilities at all.

29. This is a consequence of the "Central Theorem" (my term) based on Bacharach's (1999) work.

30. Because all group-based or we-mode equilibria also are I-mode equilibria, but not conversely, we must here take into account all the equilibria in the game. Hence we can argue that collective causation or bringing about an action that is based (justified and explained by) on a group goal produces more and better collective order into the social world than does I-mode causation and bringing about.

31. The grounds of the group's functionality, that is, we-mode preferences, goals, intentions (and the like), and their I-mode counterparts should not strongly conflict with each other in a we-mode group, because that would diminish the group's attractiveness and motivating power. The actors in general know this and prefer to choose their we-mode groups accordingly, if possible.

32. See chapter 7 for a detailed discussion of the PD case and its group-based transformation into a cooperation-friendly game. (See, e.g., Tuomela 2000, and McMahon 2001 for the assurance game and other related cooperation-friendly games.)

33. There is a direct, rather mechanical way to do it by applying the general account of a group agent's attitude in Tuomela (2007a), chapter 6, to a group agent's reason. However, I will below proceed somewhat differently.

34. A full-blown group reason (we-mode reason) must satisfy a collectivity condition expressing the participants' "common fate" due to their collective acceptance of the reason as their group agent's reason.

35. See e.g. Tuomela (1993) and (2007a), chapter 6, for a group's belief as a voluntary *acceptance belief*, in contrast to group's belief as its members' shared nonvoluntary we-belief.

36. See Bratman (1987), chapter 2. See my comments in chapter 6 of Tuomela (2007a) on when bootstrapping in the joint case is avoidable.

37. As to individual group members' *action motivation* qua group members, the personal psychological characteristics of agents may of course contingently play a role concerning how prone they are to defect. An important feature about the I-mode and the we-mode is that individualistic, I-mode reasoning (including pro-group I-mode reasoning) is concerned with individual rationality and interests rather than group rationality and the group's interests, whereas we-mode reasoning concerns the kind of group rationality that follows from a group's functioning rationally on

the basis of its members' group-centered we-reasoning. Such group rationality has the effect of gluing people together, and this contrasts with the (pro-group) I-mode case.

38. This actually depends on what aspect of the situation you look at—the member perspective (group-social obligation) or the group agent's perspective (only an instrumental perspective). This note owes to Matti Heinonen.

39. We-willings, as I have characterized them in Tuomela (1984), are act-relational, i.e., make existential reference to means-actions. The notion of a reason-preserving account of causation (termed "purposive causation") that I developed in Tuomela (1977), with an extension to the social case in the (1984) book, is compatible with the present account. However, the present account lays more emphasis on agent causation than the earlier one.

40. This is approximately how I account for this kind of situation in Tuomela (1977, 1995, 2012a). Searle (1983, 2011) has used a somewhat similar formulation, although he employs the stronger, semantic requirement that the reason be in the *content* of a relevant intention-in-action (a counterpart to my notion of willing). I do not see a strong ground to prefer the semantic requirement to the present *rationality* requirement. Wayward causal chains do not seem to be primarily a matter of what the agents are doing but rather how rationally they are doing what they are doing (although this is not all that they involve). In addition, of course, external forces affect the causal chains initiated by humans, but that matter is not in our present focus.

41. I say normally, because emotions cannot be voluntarily acquired in a direct sense, but in certain situations they tend to come into existence in normally functioning persons.

42. How to define all these notions? *Cohesion* is based on collective commitment and collective we-feeling (contingently present, in contrast to the required feature of collective commitment). *Order* comes simply from acting as a group member, which requires orderly intragroup cooperation. *Stability* concerns a diachronic setting: the group continues to function resiliently in an orderly fashion despite some perhaps unexpected obstacles. Stability in this sense is a robustness feature. Stability in part follows from an equilibrium and resulting equilibrium behavior. *Solidarity* entails intragroup helping behaviors—in part involved in collective commitment and such reasoning patterns as (W2) for we-intenders.

43. Raz (1986).

44. The characterization of commission authorization in Kavka (1986), pp. 389–90, can with some small modifications be proposed as a viable elucidation of authorization: A *authorizes* B to do X if and only if

(1) A has a (permission, noninterference, or aid) right to do X; and
(2) A (perhaps revocably) transmits use of his right to do X to B; i.e.,
  (2a) A obligates himself to not interfere with B doing X, and
  (2b) A transfers to B others' obligations to A to not interfere with or to aid in, the doing of X; and
(3) A (perhaps revocably) assumes responsibility for B's doing of X, as if he had done it himself; i.e.,
  (3a) A takes on himself any obligations entailed by the doing of X, if B does X; and
  (3b) A obligates himself not to blame or punish B for doing X.

In my application A will typically be the set of rank-and-file members (or in some cases, all the group members) and B the set of operatives (or to-become-operatives through the present authorization) of a group, although the verbal formulations may seem somewhat clumsy for this kind of collective case. Note that if A respects the ethos of the group in its thoughts and actions (which at least ought to be the case), then B also ought to function congruently. If B intends to do X on the basis of the authorization given to it, and if X requires that A acts in a certain way, B is entitled to give directives to A to that effect. Those directives are authoritative group reasons for member action. (For discussions of internal authorization, see Tuomela 1995, chapter 4, and 2007a, chapter 6.)

45. See Tuomela (1985) for a technical development generalizing the two-person theory by Kelley and Thibaut (1978) to the many-person case; see also Tuomela (2000), chapters 8 and 9, for a perhaps more accessible treatment and the formulation of relevant dependence indices for cases with the presence of social control.

46. I have accordingly defended the following general thesis (Tuomela 2000, p. 231):

> (C) In the case of every interactive social interaction situation and all acting agents, assuming that the agents are mutually aware of each other's choice alternatives and the resulting outcomes (utilities) and act on that information, there are in (potential or actual) causal operation—in varying degrees—three components of social control, *viz.*, control over an agent's own wants (utilities), control over other agents' wants, and conditional (or interactive) control between the agents' wants.

(See the mentioned source for the details on which (C) is based.) Note that the first component of control expresses the old idea of power as a capacity to intervene with the external (social world), the second, viz. control over others' utilities, explicates the standard idea of social power (see text). The third component has been less discussed. According to it, power in general is dependent on the situation so that, e.g., the target people may have control over the authority with power and ability to resist his use of power (although their power source may be based only on situational constraints).

47. Cf. Raz (1986) and his later work.

48. Consider the following explication of Raz's notion of preemptive reason, making the point that it is really the recommended actions that should be regarded as conflicting:

> If R is a preemptive reason for doing X, it "overweighs" the reasons for doing not-X.

However, this claim seems too strong for group reasons, as will be argued. Some private actions may not be overweighed (see the text). This note owes to Kaarlo Miller.

49. I have briefly discussed this matter in Tuomela (2007a), chapter 6.

50. I will not here try to define what urgent cases are, but we might tentatively consider taking them always to belong to the realm of general escape conditions for obligations (see, e.g., Beran 1987). E.g., moral reasons belong here. This move to "pro tanto we-mode" can be made also in the case of characterization of the we-mode for game-theoretic contexts in section 3 of chapter 7.

51. I speak of pro tanto reasons because, e.g., morality might require otherwise and be motivationally stronger.

52. See chapter 7 for a game-theoretical result that shows that in some cases the rational action recommendations coming from we-mode group reasons are different from those that I-mode reasons especially pro-group I-mode ones give.

CHAPTER 5

1. By "agreement" many things can be meant according to dictionaries. For instance, the following possible use of this term comes close to my idea of implicit agreement, the core of which is joint intention: "oneness of opinion, feeling, or purpose" (*Webster's Third New International Dictionary*, 1966). Analogously, the recent *Merriam Webster's Collegiate Dictionary* (11th ed.) uses the phrase "harmony of opinion, action, or character" for agreement that is weaker than contract or compact. See the appendix to this chapter. (For example, two views or beliefs can be in agreement without there being any agreement making, either explicit or implicit.)

2. If the group does not yet exist as a we-mode group, this is not literally true. However, assuming that the members-to-be are operating with the we-perspective, that perspective will still contain their goal of forming a group, the specific nature of which yet is to be collectively constructed. This goal functions as a kind of collective reason. Their group can be regarded a *prospective* we-mode group.

3. Cf. List and Pettit (2011) for the notion of organizational design.

4. In Tuomela (2007a), chapter 7, I speak of the "premisibility" of a collectively accepted proposition within the context of group activities.

5. See especially Tuomela (2007a), chapters 6 and 8.

6. Note that I below use the qualifier "as a group" although the account does not exclusively deal with we-mode groups. Earlier in the book this phrase marked the we-mode. Note too that our group identification assumption may be true of the pro-group I-mode cases as well.

7. The present account is closely related to the formulation given in Tuomela (2007a), p. 127, but corrects a slip in it.

8. See Tuomela (2007a), chapter 8, for more on collective acceptance as attitude.

9. Such construction will be illustrated below in the case of the "bulletin board view" and "ga-acceptance," as well as in section 2 of chapter 8.

10. In my preferred terminology, we speak of "jointly intentional" action when the action is in the we-mode, and this entails that the action is performed because of a joint intention. As in the present context, I-mode collective acceptance is also conceivable, and the broader term "collectively intentional" is appropriate.

11. Intuitively, handshaking between participants in general means making an agreement. Some kind of counterpart of handshaking arguably is present at least in standard cases of collective acceptance. My view does not strictly require agreement making but rather the conceptual truth that all collective acceptance entails agreement (that is, the participants agree on the content of collective acceptance). See the appendix.

12. See, e.g., Tuomela (2007a), p. 127. However, my view on the role of agreement making for collective acceptance has changed somewhat since writing the 2007 book. Note that groups can only have voluntarily acceptable attitudes in my view; see Tuomela (2007a) for arguments. For instance, it cannot have proper "experiential" beliefs but only "acceptance" beliefs (accepted views, etc.), although the group members can *share we-beliefs* in the standard sense of belief.

13. I have developed and discussed the bulletin board view in Tuomela (2000 and 2002b) and also in (2005) and (2007a). The presentation below is a condensed and somewhat modified version of the earlier version.

14. Such participation intentions avoid the kind of "I will do X if you will do X but you will do X..." regression that in principle threatens typical coordination cases. See the discussion in Tuomela (2007a), chapter 3.

15. Such functioning can in its first stages take place as "pattern-governed behavior" (see chapter 8) and without the subjects having the right concepts and without their deeply understanding the underlying reasons why they are taught so to function.

16. This account in a sense reduces meta-level talk about the fact of A's acceptance of something p to object-level talk, viz., to the fact of A's psychologically relating to p in a certain way (e.g., in the pro-attitude way or in the belief-like way, so to speak). Let me note, too, that familiarly, goals and beliefs, e.g., can in certain ways of speaking be regarded as contents of attitudes that some agents have. Thus a belief such as that the earth is round is a content that somebody is assumed actually or possibly to have and believe.

17. If the first collectively ga-accepted option will be taken as the group attitude and if a particular member or a set of members is allowed to determine the order, strategic factors may come in.

18. Accordingly, I agree with the "straw-vote" procedure that List and Pettit (2011), chapter 3, propose. It goes as follows:

> Consider the propositions on the agenda one by one in a sequence, which may reflect either a temporal order or some order of priority.
> Take a majority vote on each proposition considered.
> If the attitude formed is consistent with attitudes already formed, let it stand as the group attitude.
> If the attitude formed is not consistent with these attitudes, consider all the different possible ways in which previously formed attitudes or the new attitude could be revised so as to restore consistency.
> Take a vote under a suitable procedure, or deliberate on which of the possible revisions to make.
> Assign suitable members or deputies to enact the resulting group attitudes.

19. The method of Approval Voting that is in use in some organizations resembles my ga-set method, but also it has its drawbacks.

20. Robust group rationality and holistic supervenience are discussed in chapter 3 of List and Pettit (2011).

21. List and Pettit (2011), pp. 69–70.

22. For a non-formal survey, see List and Pettit (2011), and for a more technical one, see, e.g., Gaertner (2006) and List and Puppe (2009).

23. See List and Pettit (2002). A generalization of this theorem entails Arrow's impossibility theorem (see Dietrich and List 2007).

24. See List and Pettit (2011) for discussion.

25. When the agents act in a group context they might act as group members of a collective they form in the decision situation. In that case it must be assumed that they act in part for the reason of promoting the ethos of their group that they privately accept and are privately committed to and thus privately socially ought to promote. For instance, in the case of national elections the distinction between voting to satisfy one's selfish preferences versus voting for the welfare of one's country may make a big difference.

26. List and Pettit (2011), p. 59.

27. See Dietrich and List (2010) for some of these results.

28. See, e.g., Caplan (2008) and Shenkman (2009) for discussion and arguments.

29. Recall note 1.

30. Hume ([1740] 1965), p. 490.

31. First and foremost I wish to thank Kaarlo Miller for incisive comments on this chapter. In addition Raul Hakli, Matti Heinonen, Mikko Salmela, and Maj Tuomela made good critical remarks.

CHAPTER 6

1. The *Oxford Dictionary of English* takes cooperation centrally as "the action or process of working together to the same end".

2. It can be argued that cooperation, especially we-mode cooperation, is based on cultural-biological coevolution. Man needs his fellow men to keep alive and to prosper. Partly because of this, human beings have lived in groups and seem to have cooperated about as long as they have existed. This has helped people not only to satisfy their basic needs but also, starting about fifty thousand years ago, to develop into cultural beings. See, e.g., Tomasello at al. (2005) and Tomasello (2009), as well as Tuomela (2007a), chapter 9, for discussion.

I have in a congress paper (Tuomela 2007b) defended the following argument for the gene-culture coevolutionary basis of cooperation:

(1) Culture-gene coevolutionary group selection favors groups that function well and thus have the capacity to act persistently and resiliently as functional group agents toward their goals.

(2) To function in a well-functioning group requires that the members function on the basis of the shared group perspective (either I-mode or we-mode we-perspective) and thus collective intentionality.

(3) The members' functioning as group members requires that they cooperate with each other, that is, it requires intragroup cooperation.

(4) An optimally well-functioning group requires we-mode intragroup cooperation (and relevant collective intentional mental states).

Therefore,

(5) Coevolutionary group selection optimally results in we-mode groups and makes them winners over other kinds of groups.

3. Some passages in this chapter are based on ideas and material (in revised form) from Tuomela and Tuomela (2005), M. Tuomela (2006), Tuomela (2007a), especially chapter 7, and Tuomela (2010a).

4. A more detailed account of I-mode cooperation has been presented in Tuomela (2007a), chapter 7, from which account I draw on below.

5. One is sometimes said to "cooperate" with a norm or order in some institutional cases, but even here there is the implicit assumption that there are others in the community who at least are supposed to act similarly.

6. Along with several other theoreticians I have argued in Tuomela (2007a), chapter 9, for the culturally and probably also genetically evolved cooperativeness of humans.

7. The present account is slightly weaker in this sense than that given in Tuomela and Tuomela (2005) and Tuomela (2007a), chapter 8.

8. See my account of shared I-mode intentions in chapter 3.

9. This last point contradicts my aforementioned earlier account. The reason is that because cooperation at its edges is a somewhat vague notion, one had better avoid legislating very much on the use of language about cooperation.

10. In the shared-goal case, making clause (2) a bit more explicit will make my account nearly equivalent with Michael Bratman's (1992) account of cooperation. The mutual adjustment of the actions can be formulated as a kind of "meshing subplans" requirement that we have in Bratman's account. As intentions (at least in my view) entail commitments, it can be argued that they account for "cooperative stability" in his account. I have written a somewhat critical appraisal of Bratman's theory of cooperation in Tuomela (2000), chapter 3, to which I refer the reader (although I do not now fully subscribe to my point there about meshing subplans).

11. See Tuomela (2007a), chapter 7, for some sharper and stronger formulations of action dependence.

12. Recall chapter 2 on collective commitment.

13. For my earlier account of I-mode cooperation, see chapter 7 of Tuomela (2007a).

14. I will not here discuss joint action in detail—see Tuomela (2007a), chapter 5, for my account.

15. I typically use "as a group" in the we-mode case for "jointly" and use "jointly" as a we-mode notion even when not accompanied by "as a group". Instead, I typically use "shared" to signify I-mode sense.

16. See Tuomela (2005), for a lengthy discussion of the requirement of the presence of joint intentions (goals) in cooperation.

17. See, e.g., Tuomela (1995).

18. Recall chapter 3 for joint intention, and for a detailed account of joint action see Tuomela (2007a), chapter 5.

19. There is thus a connection on the levels of both intended goals and relevant means-end beliefs, because the agents must of course also be disposed to realize their joint intention (goal) in the we-mode case. Indeed, there is a kind of joint equilibrium situation concerning the proximal intentional mental background, i.e. the underlying motivating reasons, of joint action here. It is neither rational nor "group-socially" beneficial for one of them to defect, at least as long as the other one does not defect. A participant cannot defect without being legitimately criticizable by the other. Note that in the we-mode case of an authoritative group reason to cooperate that the participants accept, each tends to believe that the other will cooperate if he himself does. This need not involve a causal connection between the participants, but it will typically be an effect of the *common cause* that their group reason provides. (See chapter 4 for the closely related notion of group equilibrium. Also see the technically formulated appendix to chapter 3 for a related notion of joint equilibrium of probabilistic expectations.)

20. While I interpret the central psychological terms used in (CWM) as referring to we-mode states and activities, it seems possible in principle in a different context to take those terms to refer to I-mode states and activities, in order to give an account of pro-group I-mode cooperation.

21. Cf. Bratman's (1992) account of cooperation that is based on interindividual relationships.

22. Bratman (2009b) might be taken to suggest such separation in his account of what he calls "modest sociality", when saying that his account is geared to small groups.

23. If the group members are legally prohibited from painting a house, they cannot legally view

painting it as a cooperative situation for them. Thus, not all situations that were not originally viewed by the group as not cooperative situations can in practice be made cooperative.

24. To take yet another simple example, people eating breakfast in the morning can be viewed as a collective activity. Normally it is only I-mode activity, but if the people collectively decide, e.g., to do it at the same time as a group, it will generally be we-mode activity.

25. See Bratman (1992).

26. See Bratman (1992), p. 330.

27. Bratman (1992), p. 339.

28. This clause refers to Bratman's conditions that we need not discuss here.

29. This account was developed a long time ago and has improved during the years. See Tuomela (1984), and especially (1995) and (2007a).

30. I presented basically this account in Tuomela (2007a), chapter 6, but without the element of external authority. (IGA) is analogous to the account (GI) of a group's (group agent's) intention in chapter 3, although my formulation here uses somewhat different phrasing.

31. In general Y is assumed either to causally generate X or to conceptually constitute it. Often Y and X are the same action, and for simplicity I will make the sameness assumption below.

32. Consider this example of an external leader: An army unit or a school class may be ordered by a leader (respectively an officer or teacher) to act as a group, and they may do so, perhaps based on a group reason different from the whole group's ethos. They might be told that only the whole group's, rather than single individuals', achievements will be rewarded (or, in some cases, negatively sanctioned). These kinds of situations may motivate a group to act as a group (team) even under external authority. Those who are skilled and good at the task involved will help the weakest, and such help is collectively rational. This is how we-mode groups in general act and exhibit strong solidarity (cf. chapter 9).

33. Of course, the professor can resign from his job if he cannot agree to take orders from his immediate supervisors—he has retained this kind of freedom to exit from the group.

34. See the mathematical account in Tuomela (2002b), chapter 7.

35. Task-right systems have been analyzed in Tuomela (1995) and in precise terms in Tuomela (2002b), chapter 7.

36. What kinds of commitments are there in an organization when it can be regarded as a we-mode group? At least ideally, there is codified collective (hence social) commitment that involves the position-holders binding themselves qua position-holders to the organization to perform certain tasks and indeed to obey the task-right system pertaining to their positions. This codified collective and social commitment is based on the obligations and rights involved in the organizational norms. In addition, there may be uncodified we-mode collective and social commitment involved in the freely chosen joint and jointly accountable activities that the position-holders choose to perform (but which still further the organization's ethos).

37. I distinguish between the kind of metaphysical freedom and autonomy (independence) that, e.g., intentional action in principle presupposes, and de facto freedom (and, on the other hand, dependence) that social life as a matter of fact normally involves.

38. See Tuomela (2010a), where I argue for the existence of this kind of collective causation and for the explanatory power of such explanation in virtue of the collective goals underlying the group's activity. The central general thesis defended in that paper is this:

> (GC) There are cases of irreducible collective social causation and hence of explanation based on a cause-expressing collective social explanans.

39. See the discussion in chapter 8 below and in Tuomela (2007a), chapter 8.

40. See Tuomela (2007a), chapter 8, for such institutional beliefs.

41. I discuss this case in chapter 8 of Tuomela (2007a).

42. However, see section 3 of chapter 7 for two relevantly different interpretations of the we-mode.

43. Stability is the broadest notion, and it might be taken to include the features of persistence and resilience. Here I mention all three and will not enter into a deeper discussion of these notions, which can be given systems-theoretical explications.

The readers are referred to Balzer and Tuomela (2001, 2003) and Tuomela (2002b), chapter 7, for a mathematical investigation of self-guiding groups in a simple case where the group, interpretable as a group agent, takes feedback from its performances of its practices, and is capable of maintaining or changing them and accordingly of controlling its activities and creating behavioral stability.

44. The reader is referred to Tuomela and Tuomela (2005), where the relationship between cooperation and trust is examined in detail from the perspective of the account of trust developed by Maj Tuomela (2006).

45. See Brewer (2003).

46. See Brewer (2003).

47. See Colman, Pulford, and Rose (2008a, 2008b) and Bardsley et al. (2010) for the research referred to above.

CHAPTER 7

1. When discussing Bacharach's work I will concentrate on his 1999 paper, although the 2006 book is also relevant. I will speak of group reasoning instead of team reasoning, because my account will also cover large we-mode groups that can hardly be regarded as teams (paradigms of which are sports teams and business teams).

2. In Tuomela (2007) I discussed the functional differences between the we-mode approach and the pro-group I-mode approach in the context of cooperation. When writing that work I was not yet aware of Bacharach's (1999) paper. Only after I was asked to review the posthumous book by Bacharach (2006) did I come to study his important 1999 paper. In Hakli, Miller, and Tuomela (2010) my colleagues and I make precise the connections between my theory and Bacharach's theory. This chapter describes the results of our joint paper.

3. Occasionally I speak of we-mode thinking performed by the members. We-reasoning is a special kind of we-thinking. In this chapter we work with a rather traditional idea of reasoning as argumentation proceeding from premises to a conclusion about what should be done.

4. As I understand noncooperative game theory, it does allow for communication and negotiation as long as no binding agreements between the participants come about. Strictly mathematically or logically binding agreements can at best be standards of criticism of failure, but no more. But there one can deal with weaker notions. A standard way of taking them into account is to change the game in question by adding to it the choice alternative that an agreement (joint commitment) is made. It can either be obeyed or violated.

5. See, e.g., Sally (1995); Colman, Pulford, and Rose (2008a, 2008b).

6. Griesinger and Livingston (1973); Tuomela (2000), pp. 279–89; Guala (2006).

7. However, transformations do not strategically help in the case of coordination games—see, e.g., Tuomela (2007a), p. 158.

8. See Colman, Pulford, and Rose (2008b) for arguments.

9. "Agency transformation" is the term used by Bacharach (2006), p. 90.

10. See his 1999 paper.

11. The material in section 3 is not dealt with in Hakli, Miller, and Tuomela (2010).

12. Hakli, Miller, and Tuomela (2010).

13. We are speaking of an ideal group publicity requirement here. All group matters should in principle be knowable to all the members. In the case of collective acceptance, this requirement translates into the requirement that the fact that something p has been collectively accepted in the group must be mutually known (or correctly believed).

14. Bacharach (1999, 2006).

15. Bacharach (2006), p. 85.

16. Bacharach (2006), p. 86.

17. Bacharach (2006), p. 86.

18. See Tuomela (1985b, 2000) for a technical account leading to such a measure of preference correlation.

19. This reasoning parallels the indecisive situation that we get if individualistically thinking person argues that I will choose Hi given that you choose Hi, and I will choose Lo given that you choose Lo. But as I do not know whether you will choose Hi or Lo I cannot rationally on the basis of factual information make any choice (e.g., tossing a coin would not in this sense properly solve the problem).

Recall the definition of the pro-group I-mode from chapter 3, according to which, in partial contrast, it suffices that a person acts only in part for the group. This wider notion will be considered also in section 3 below.

20. Bacharach (1999), p. 136. Here I use my terms "we-mode" and "pro-group I-mode."

21. For discussion, see Harsanyi and Selten (1988), pp. 355–57; see also Bacharach, (1999), pp. 135–37, and Colman, Pulford, and Rose (2008a, 2008b).

22. See the discussion of we-mode reasoning in collective action dilemmas in chapter 7 of Tuomela (2007a), as well as Bacharach (1999) on team reasoning in such cases.

23. Cf. Bacharach (1999). The material below in the text is rather technical, and therefore some readers may want to move directly to the Central Theorem toward the end of the section.

24. See Hakli, Miller, and Tuomela (2010), pp. 303–5 for a lengthy example that illustrates the role of the we-mode and I-mode in the above setup.

25. Bacharach (1999), Lemma 1.

26. This is Bacharach's (1999, p. 129) own formulation of what he labels Theorem 2.

27. For a precise definition of a Paretian utility function, see Bacharach (2006), p. 88.

28. See also Tuomela (2007a), chapter 7.

29. To study the effects of different types of reasoning as in the previous example, Hakli, Miller, and I have formulated a spreadsheet file by means of which the changes in expected utilities and their maximization in arbitrary two-person games can be calculated as a function of the probability of being a we-moder versus being I-moder given the same shared group utility in both cases. The file is available at http://www.cs.helsinki.fi/~hakli/uti-equilibria.xls. It is easy to check that, e.g., with p = 1 and closely related probability values, it gives the kind of results concerning equilibria mentioned in the text.

30. For recent results and discussion, see Brewer (2003) (who is somewhat ambiguous concerning the distinction between the we-mode and the pro-group I-mode, which distinction she does

not make) and the discussion of Brewer in chapter 2 of Tuomela (2007a); Colman, Pulford, and Rose (2008a, 2008b); Krueger (2008); Sugden (2008); Van Lange (2008); Bardsley et al. (2010), as well as Guala et al. (2009) and Colman and Pulford (2012). Also see the next section.

31. See Bacharach (1999) and (2006), chapter 2.

32. See Hakli, Miller, and Tuomela (2010), pp. 308–9, for discussion and examples.

33. In chapter 9 of Tuomela (2007a) I argue that the disposition to think and act in the we-mode is a product of gene-culture coevolution.

34. See Tuomela (1988). The reinterpretation of an interaction situation bears analogy to the ambiguous duck-rabbit picture in which one can often at will change what one sees.

35. Below I focus on paradigmatic we-mode groups and functioning in the we-mode in the sense of chapter 2.

36. Here we have an ideal type characterization of the pure we-mode. It lacks realism because in real life most people are probably disposed to act also on their private interests, and so there is in many cases a tendency for a conflict between we-mode and I-mode interests. On the other hand it is obviously instructive to try to see what pure we-mode and pure I-mode involve and lead to.

37. The group's normative directives implicit in the above ideal type characterization (*) need not always be regarded as all-things-considered requirements but can contextually be viewed by the addressees as pro tanto requirements. This applies also to explicit group norms of the kind "One ought to do X in C". Furthermore, with a liberal interpretation of "pro tanto", there will be lots of cases in real life where a group agent's directives, as commonly viewed, need not be obeyed—e.g., if there are weighty private or moral reasons against them—recall the discussions in chapters 2 and 4. (For standard escape clauses allowing for deviance, see, e.g., Beran 1987.)

38. See Colman, Pulford, and Rose (2008a, 2008b). Also see Bardsley et al. (2010) for similar results.

39. Colman, Pulford, and Rose (2008a), p. 395. Indeed, game-theoretically the illustrative examples used by Bacharach resemble the payoff matrices used in these experiments (see, e.g., Bacharach 1999, pp. 129–30, 136–40). While the theory of this book seems more collectivistic than Bacharach's, the two theories are comparable (recall section 2). Thus if Bacharach's collective theorizing gets experimental support, that seems transferable to the we-mode approach (as long as the experiments do not drive an experimental wedge between them).

40. See the arguments in Colman, Pulford, and Rose (2008b).

41. See also the references mentioned in note 30 above.

42. In real life this is still compatible with we-mode members occasionally breaching the norm and lapsing into the I-mode in order to satisfy their own private interests.

43. Bacharach (2006), p. 132, considers a PD with the following payoff matrix:

	C	D
C	a,a	s,t
D	t,s	b,b

He shows that the value of the critical value of the probability ω to be exceeded for rational cooperation is $\omega = 2b - (s+t)) / ((a+b) - (s+t))$.

44. No I-mode utilities are at play in the group agency case (*): The group operates as a group on the basis of its own utilities, and the members' we-mode utilities are based on the group's utilities.

There may be a case in which the group orders some members to perform C, and the rest to perform D. In such cases, the group might change the game payoffs so that there is a stronger incentive to act for those who are ordered to choose C. However, my general idea is not to base the group members' motivation (thus utilities) on their private motivation but on their motivation as group members and thus as derived from group utility, from the value that the group members realize for g by their action as group members, as one agent.

Note that the group members' joint decision in general is not allowed within noncooperative game theory if it leads to binding action obligations, while arriving at a joint intention, e.g., spontaneously or because of a common history is allowed. As truly logically binding obligations are not possible in real life, it is not that clear where to draw the boundary between noncooperative and cooperative game theory.

45. This is illustrated by the spreadsheet program referred to in note 29. In the we-mode case only the HI (or HiHi) cases become equilibria when the probability of acting for the group is maximal, viz., $\omega = 1$. In contrast, in the corresponding Harsanyi game also the LoLo cases are equilibria.

46. See Tuomela and Tuomela (2005), p. 80, for an argument. The group's acting as one agent involves the participants' collective intention to act in the right way, and this is fortified quasi-normatively by the presence of collective commitment. Thus the participants will have the ground to expect that the others will participate. Full-blown *normative trust* in turn requires also a close personal relationship that need not be involved, e.g., in large groups.

47. Bacharach's UTIs presuppose, in addition, group preferences and the parameter Ω; see Hakli, Miller, and Tuomela (2010) for a discussion.

48. See Hakli, Miller, and Tuomela (2010), section 3, for a detailed example clarifying these patterns of reasoning.

49. Recall my "bulletin board view" discussed in chapter 5 and also cf. the "offer-acceptance" model by (Bach 1995).

50. Cf. Bacharach (2006), chapter 2.

51. See the account of the group's preferences on p. 160 of Tuomela (2007a).

52. See note 30 for references.

CHAPTER 8

1. In Tuomela (2007a), chapter 8, I argue for the basic we-mode nature of social institutions in terms of we-thinking, identification with the group, change of institution, and instrumental rationality in action dilemmas. Below I will not repeat these arguments but rather refer to Bacharach's Central Theorem in chapter 7, which gives a new argument for the we-mode character of we-thinking.

2. See Tuomela (2002b), chapter 3.

3. The notion of pattern-governed behavior was to my knowledge introduced by Wilfrid Sellars (1973). My discussion owes to his treatment. However, he did not specifically consider *collective* pattern-governed behavior (in a nonreductive sense). Furthermore, he defined pattern-governed behavior as essentially nonintentional, which I do not require. My own discussion of collective pattern-governed behavior is to be found in chapter 3 of Tuomela (2002b), and here I rely on that treatment.

4. Below I will draw on my treatment in Tuomela (2002b), chapter 3.

5. Driving a car often involves pattern-governed behavior. Driving on "automatic pilot" seems to involve pattern-governed behaviors as its elements.

6. See, e.g., Tuomela (2002b), chapter 4. Here is a simple and stylized example of an I-mode we-attitude: I have the we-attitude to achieve goal G if and only I have goal G, and have it in part because I believe that the others in the group have G, and it is a mutual belief in the group that all have this goal. A we-attitude in the present sense is shared simply when the others in the group have it as well. For shared we-attitudes in the we-mode sense, see Tuomela (2007a), chapters 3 and 6.

7. See Tuomela (2002b), chapter 4, for a detailed account of these notions.

8. Collective social actions in general are not reducible to aggregates of individual actions or pattern-governed behaviors (cf. Tuomela 1995 and 2002b, ch. 4).

9. See Tuomela (2002b) for discussion of these issues.

10. See Tuomela (2002b), chapter 3.

11. In Tuomela (2002b), chapter 3, further examples are provided and analyzed.

12. In Tuomela (2002b), chapters 3 and 4, I discuss Wittgenstein's, Heidegger's, and Bourdieu's views on conceptually and psychologically undemanding behaviors that have to some extent functions similar to pattern-governed behaviors.

13. See, e.g., Tuomela (2002b), chapters 6–7, and (2007a), chapter 8.

14. The basic idea in my account of collective acceptance leading to (or in many cases, mounting to) group acceptance lies in the members being committed to going along with certain proposals for group decision contents. Very roughly, a proposal p for acceptance is suggested, for instance, by a leader, and the members are asked to consider whether they qua group members can go along with the proposal (here compromises are possible). If sufficiently many (for instance, the majority) do, a group decision concerning p (for instance, a goal) comes about, possibly involving discussion and feedback-based iteration—but perhaps no voting. Consistency with the ethos is required, at least initially. (See chapter 5.)

15. See Searle (1995, 2010) for counts-as norms.

16. The presentation below uses some formulations drawn from Tuomela (2007a), chapter 8.

17. In logical terms, the CAT formula can be rendered as follows.

(CAT*) s is group-social (in a primary constructivist sense) in g if and only if
FG(CA(g, s)) & FG(N(CA(g, s) <->s)).

Here N stands for artifactual (viz., group-made) conceptual and metaphysical necessity; FG(CA(g, s)) means that group g collectively accepts s for the group. Thus, if s is social, it will satisfy what comes after "if and only if" in (CAT*), and conversely. Condition FG(s) entails that s is true (i.e., true in a perspectival sense in the group) in g with a certain direction of fit based on its meaning or interpretation. CA must be a "performative" achievement-expressing notion that entails the truth of what has been accepted, and "acceptance" is general enough to cover both the creation and upholding of s and has achievement conceptually built into it. Thus the equivalence in (CAT*) expresses a kind of conceptually necessary, constitutive connection. I assume that FG distributes over necessary equivalence, equivalence that holds in all situations within the group's realm of concern. (CAT) also applies to the fact that a group believes thus and so (this can be expressed by s here).

18. See Searle (1995) for the latter notion.

19. Note that some people can accept through their overt activities that their group is a we-mode group. Thus they operate in accordance with (CAT), but they need not do it reflectively (although the in-principle capacity of such reflection must be assumed). The unreflective case is of course typical in two senses: people do not often or at least not always reflect on their activities, and they are not normally theoreticians familiar with (CAT) or analogous theoretical accounts.

20. All readers might not like my group-relative notion of truth and the accompanying merely epistemic group-relative objectivity. If objective truth is preferred in all relevant formulations, this can be achieved by using the expression "A squirrel pelt is money in g" for my above "A squirrel pelt is money" is true for g, where true for g concerns perspectival truth. In the resulting substituting account it must be added that in group g the group members take it to be up to "our" group ("us") to make it correct to use the proposition as a premise and to use squirrel pelts in actual exchanges taking place in g. (I wish to thank Kaarlo Miller for critical comments on (CAT). They resulted in some additional clarifying remarks in the text.)

21. See, e.g., Tuomela and Balzer (1999) and Tuomela (2007a), chapter 8.

22. See Tuomela (2007a), chapters 6 and 8.

23. I will not here comment on the variety of other approaches in the literature; see Tuomela (2002b), chapter 6, and (2007a), chapter 8, for such discussion.

24. Recall chapter 7 on this.

25. Recently Searle (2010) has strongly emphasized the enabling function of social institutions.

26. See, e.g., my survey in chapter 6 of Tuomela (2002b).

27. See, e.g., Miller (2011) for a discussion. What other elements belong to the culture of the institution-hosting group I cannot here discuss—as quite a few of both general features (such as the cultural climate) and social psychological factors (such as the background and interests of the group members) must be taken into account.

28. This macro-matter can be formulated for the group member level. Let me here without further discussion produce a quasi-deductive argument for the we-mode requirement based on what the group's ethos, E, implies (cf. note 62 to chapter 8 of my 2007 book):

(1) It ought to be the case in g (and for g) that E is fulfilled (that is, satisfied by the group members' actions qua group members' conducive to E).
(2) The group (and group members collectively), perhaps via their authorized operative members, ought to see to it that the ought-to-be norm expressed by (1) is satisfied.
(3) The group members ought to commit themselves to (possibly recurrently, as the case may be) intentionally performing actions conducive to E.
(4) The group members indeed have collectively committed themselves to E in view of (1)–(3), and they act purporting to fulfill and promote E.
(5) Intentionally performed actions purporting to fulfill E are actions qua a group member involving for-groupness and hence group reason (which together with the assumption of collective commitment in (4) will satisfy the collectivity condition).
(6) In view of (4) and (5), the group members' (intentional) actions conducive to E in this case are we-mode actions.
(7) The institutions of g must not contradict E and must in general be conducive to E.
(8) An institution of g must involve at least some we-mode acting, which by definition must be based on we-mode beliefs or we-mode we-intentions and possibly on other we-attitudes, purporting to uphold E.

29. See Tuomela (2007a), chapter 3, and chapter 6 of this book for various arguments for the we-mode claim, and see especially chapter 7 of this book for a game-theoretical argument for the claim that we-mode rather than pro-group I-mode thinking and acting should lie at the theoretical and conceptual bottom of social institutions, including the actions maintaining and revising them.

30. In the case of group stereotypes, such as that the stars determine our fate, the truth of the stereotypic belief is dependent on the way the external world is and not on what the group accepts or decides. Yet the group agent here can be said to create the state of belief or state of believing and maintains it by its norms and sanctions. The content is immunized from external evidence by the group members, viz., evidence that is crucially relevant to the truth of the content.

31. This might at least sometimes be achieved in terms of a performative linguistic speech act such as "We hereby accept that squirrel pelts are our money" (not to be confused with the simpler notion of collective acceptance, which is performative in the simple sense of entailing the truth of its content).

32. See Searle (1995), where he also emphasizes the idea of a special status function involved in an institution. In his account, status functions entail power, whereas this does not hold for my account. See section 4 below for some of the new features of Searle's theory, as expressed in his 2010 book, and for a brief comparison of his and my theory.

33. See Tuomela (2007a), chapter 8. Also see that chapter for an account using role- and task-division in the group, repeated below.

(SI*) A proposition s expresses a *social institution* (in the standard sense) for a normatively structured group g if and only if

(1a) the operative members of g, say, $A_1,\ldots,A_m$, when performing their (we-mode) tasks in their respective positions and due to their exercising the relevant authority system ("decision making" system) of g, collectively accept s, and because of this exercise of the authority system they ought to continue to accept it, at least until (new) reasons not to accept it emerge;

(1b) collective acceptance for the group entails and is entailed by (the truth of) s;

(2) there is a mutual belief among the operative members $A_1,\ldots,A_m$ to the effect that (1a);

(3) s expresses or entails the existence of a g-based social practice (or a system of interconnected social practices) and a system of interconnected norms (including one or more constitutive norms) in force for g, such that the social practice generally is performed at least in part because of these norms;

(4) because of (1), the (full-fledged and adequately informed) nonoperative members of g tend to tacitly accept—or at least ought to accept—obeying the normative content of s, as members of g;

(5) there is generally a mutual belief in g to the effect that (4).

Also see Tuomela (2002b), chapter 6, for a wider discussion and p. 229 of that book for a precise mathematical systems-theoretic account.

34. See Searle (1995 and 2010).

35. See Tuomela (2002b) for this way of measuring the success of the group's activities. Turchin (2007) in this interesting historical study investigates the waxing and waning of a large group's (like a nation's) ability to act and uses the Arabic notion of *asabiya* for the notion of the capacity

of a social group for concerted collective action.

36. I have mathematically investigated the dynamics of social practices in Tuomela (1995) and later, especially in the joint work with Wolfgang Balzer in Balzer and Tuomela (2001, 2003) and in my book (2002b).

37. Searle (1995, 2010) has emphasized this central feature.

38. See Tuomela (2002b), chapter 6, and (2007a), chapter 8.

39. See Tuomela (2007a), chapter 4.

40. For my own detailed account of mental causation, see Tuomela (1998).

41. See Tuomela (2002b), chapter 7, for a technical account.

42. Business corporations generally are *corporate agents* and involve law-based elements that makes them legal persons. Every corporate agent can be taken to be a group agent, but—depending on what one means by incorporation—not every group agent needs to be a corporate agent.

43. For a precise logical account of organizations as social institutions, see Tuomela (2002b), especially the final summarizing account on p. 229.

44. My account in this section draws on my paper in *Analysis* (2011a). I have added my comment on Searle's replies to my basic claims in this section.

45. See Searle (2010), p. 201. I will below depart from Searle's usage to capitalize his technical terms except, of course, when directly quoting his text.

46. Searle (2010), p. 12.

47. Searle (2010), p. 99.

48. Searle (1985, 2010) takes all performative speech acts to be declarations. See Grewendorf (2002), Harnish (2002), and Martinich (2002) for comments on the connections between declarations and performatives and for criticisms of Searle's account. In contrast, I do not in my account rely on the technical notions of speech act theory and thus do not have to take a stand on the controversies just referred to. The second reason is that while I occasionally make reference to performative speech acts (cf. the performatively used expression "We collectively accept that a squirrel pelt is money"), they are irreducibly collective in relevant cases, but so far we do not have an adequate linguistic theory of them by linguists. See Tuomela (1985a) and (2002b) for my views on language and especially chapter 3 of the latter book for my account of nonverbal representations, which are often relevant in institutional contexts.

49. See chapter 5, section 3, where I argue that it is possible to have both the world-to-mind direction of fit and the mind-to-world direction of fit if a suitable asymmetry is created concerning the two kinds of fit. Searle's account seems to be subject to the inconsistency (or regress) that one cannot simultaneously bring about fit in the sense of these two opposite kinds of fit (see Laitinen 2013).

50. I have discussed this matter in Tuomela (2002b), pp. 144–148, in terms of the objective powers that people have for creating institutional facts, facts that are up to them to create.

51. Cf. my earlier distinction in Tuomela (2002b), chapter 5, between states of affairs that are fully "up to us" to bring about and those that are not.

52. Searle (2010), p. 57. Recall from chapter 5, section 3, that my account of collective acceptance even in the we-mode case can be based on a rather individualistic process that need only be in the prospective we-mode.

53. Recall the discussion in this chapter and see the arguments on pp. 208–210 in Tuomela (2007a), and for a recent argument based on group-reasoning in a game-theoretic frame see Hakli, Miller, and Tuomela (2010) and chapter 7 of this book.

Searle (2011) criticizes my (2011a) *Analysis* paper by saying that "Tuomela thinks that he can get equally powerful results by treating institutional facts as solutions to coordination problems in the game-theoretical sense." However, while I have used game-theoretical tools to discuss collective action problems and coordination problems (recently in Hakli, Miller, and Tuomela 2010), my account of institutional facts and institutions is given in sections 2 and 3 of this chapter. That account, also summarized in aforementioned review paper, does not make use of game-theoretic tools, contrary to what Searle claims.

54. Searle (2010), p. 94.

55. Searle (2010), p. 19.

56. See my 2002 and 2007 books, where I do not assume preexisting constitutive norms.

57. Searle (2010), p. 97.

58. Searle (2010), p. 100.

59. Searle (2010), p. 100.

60. Searle (2010), p. 115. In his reply to my *Analysis* (2011a) paper he objects to my use of the phrase "fictitious entity" by saying that corporations as entities are real (recall section 7 of chapter 2 for my view). However, e.g., on p. 100 of his 2010 book he says that corporations are fictitious entities.

61. On the other hand a limited liability corporation is a candidate for being an irreducible social group, partly because its members are normally in a nonaggregative and nondistributive sense responsible for the corporation's undertakings.

62. Searle (2010), p. 98.

63. Searle (2010), p. 102.

64. Searle (2010), pp. 56–58 and 102.

65. See Tuomela (2007a), p. 201.

66. Other similar cases of institutional phenomena that I have earlier discussed since the 1990s in various publications are inflation, unemployment, wealth, social discrimination, etc. (see Tuomela and Balzer 1999; Tuomela 2002b and 2007a). These are *derived* cases of institutionality as opposed to the *direct* or *primary* cases dealt with by my collective acceptance thesis.

67. This sentence corrects a slip in my list of cases that are not even fallouts of collective intentional activities (in Tuomela 2010b, p. 713).

68. Terminologically, for Searle such consequences of institutional facts (in my sense, primary institutional facts) are not themselves institutional facts. This is presumably because they do not involve deontology that people have collectively created for them on purpose. As my own account does not invariably impose the deontology requirement on institutional facts, I can go on speaking of institutional facts also in this case.

69. See, e.g., Searle (2010), pp. 23 and 103.

70. I have elsewhere (in chapter 6 of Tuomela 2002b) presented an example in terms of the "Sunday Match" soccer game where no power is involved and where we yet are dealing with an institution in the sense we ordinarily speak of them and dictionaries define them.

71. See Searle (2011) for recent comments where he claims that it is only a linguistic institution.

72. E.g., the *Oxford Dictionary of English* regards established laws and practices and even "well-established persons and customs" as institutions.

73. See Searle (2010), p. 13. However, Searle does not say what having the same logical form involves. Under a reasonable construction of the sameness of logical form as invariance concerning change of extralogical constants, a declaration must still be a declaration, thus at least a broadly linguistic speech act in which spoken or written language is not always needed.

74. Searle (2010), p. 111.

CHAPTER 9

1. The word "solidarity" is used in many other ways as well. Here I have mentioned only three categories of solidarity that have been perhaps most frequently considered in the theoretical literature on the topic.

2. Cases of group morality without full-blown moral implications come up when group solidarity is viewed from the point of view and focus of rationality and efficiency of group activities (instead of mere member-level interrelations), which involve the possibility of harming others when participants intentionally fail to do their parts. If the latter is emphasized, we are dealing with group-based morality, but not always morality in the universalizing sense (think of a Mafia groups where a member does not perform a killing that he had originally agreed to do). A group-moral norm need not be moral in the sense of traditional Kantian universal morality.

3. Durkheim ([1893] 1964).

4. Recall that in this book the word "group" is used very broadly to cover groups like families, work teams, small informal social groups like lunch groups, organizations such as universities and business corporations, and finally large groups such as societies and states.

5. There is also group solidarity called "workers' solidarity" that is primarily concerned with solidarity of oppressed groups as prompted by their struggle to free themselves from oppression by another group. My account seems compatible with this kind of solidarity concerned with this kind of subject matter, but I will not specifically discuss workers' solidarity below.

6. See Lindenberg (2006).

7. Liedman (2002), p. 3.

8. See Durkheim ([1893] 1964) and also Lindenberg (1988, 1998).

9. See Hechter (1987).

10. See Scholz (2008).

11. Suppose that you and I have formed the goal of painting a house; this goal gives us a group reason (and it is the ethos of our dyad, we may typically say). My part is to paint the front of the house, while you do the rest. Our part actions are connected and dependent because of our group goal that we are collectively committed to satisfying. Our goal that provides us with a group reason satisfies the collectivity condition and makes us cognitively normally also motivationally dependent on the end result of goal satisfaction, and our collective commitment makes us normatively and motivationally dependent.

12. This point, of course, relates to our earlier points about a group's power to act, e.g., in chapter 8.

13. In this chapter my theses usually (except in the later case of a suppressed we-mode group) concern *paradigmatic* we-mode groups, unless otherwise said. To what extent other autonomous we-mode groups (viz., the A-cases in the classification of the appendix 1 to chapter 2) are or can be solidary will not be discussed, nor will non-autonomous we-mode groups, except for a comment on oppressed groups. The obvious problem against full group solidarity in non-autonomous cases is the possibility of the external authority changing the group's behavior from solidary to nonsolidary by external measures (orders, etc.).

14. A group's solidarity concerning its members can involve more features than the requirements in (GS1) and (GS2) involve, especially because in structured groups the leaders may adopt additional principles concerning intermember solidarity.

15. Recall note 14.

16. Strictly speaking, for there to be group morality, mere harming is not sufficient for a morally bad event to have occurred. See note 19 below on Scanlon's (2003) moral principles and the extra features required for morality and group morality. When speaking of group morality in this chapter I usually assume that these features are present. The strict conclusion concerning the present we-mode account of group solidarity is that it does not as such quite entail group morality.

17. See Tuomela and Tuomela (2005) and note 40 of chapter 6.

18. Strength and weakness here refers to the (counterfactual) disposition of the group to cope with obstacles—it gets its tasks done even when extra burdens come up. Various factors may affect this (organizational matters etc.), but "group spirit" in any case is one of them. The notion of group spirit is vague, and except for recognizing its being an emotion at least in part, I will not use it as an analytic notion. As such it requires I-mode or we-mode *we-thinking* at least concerning its cognitive component.

19. Collective commitment as such is only quasi-moral not only because it concerns only a certain group and is not universal, but also because some other conditions are needed for proper morality. Scanlon (2003) gives some such additional conditions. For instance, the following principle of "loss prevention" is central but is not yet entailed by collective commitment:

> (Principle of Loss Prevention) If one has intentionally or negligently led someone to expect that one is going to follow a certain course of action X, and one has reason to believe that that person will suffer significant loss as a result of this expectation if one does not follow X, then one must take reasonable steps to prevent that loss.

This principle gives a sufficient condition for a moral "must" (whether this gives a truly overriding obligation is a moot point) and is compatible with differing personal motivations toward the actions in question.

20. I will below focus on democratic we-mode groups that determine their own ethos autonomously and internally control their life and serve their members' interests, so to speak. The theory of solidarity formulated in this chapter applies at least to all democratic we-mode groups in the sense of chapter 2—and "almost" to nonautonomous we-mode groups.

21. Note that the group goals can be of various kinds. For instance, to use familiar terminology, they can be of the "give-some" or the "take-some" type (e.g., contributing to the group's building a house versus contributing to the conservation of the group's common resources).

22. Note, in relation to the previous point, that the analogue of free-riding in the case of distribution is unfair grabbing of goods.

23. According to Lindenberg (1998), mechanical solidarity in Durkheim's sense is based only on equality. We-mode solidarity, as discussed in this chapter, can also make use of other principles.

24. Theoretically, a group may accept an "objectively" unfair principle as its fairness principle. I will not here discuss this issue but assume for our present purposes that it only accepts an "objectively" defensible fairness principle for its use.

25. I reproduce the schema here:

(W2)

(1) We will do X jointly.

(2) X cannot be performed by us jointly unless we perform action Z, for instance, teach, help, or pressure a group member to perform his part action.

Therefore,

(3) We will do Z.
(4) Unless I perform Y we cannot perform Z.

Therefore (because of (3) and (4)),

(5) I will do Y (as my contribution to Z).

26. One might say that if an action here is of the right kind but performed for a "wrong" reason, it had better be called quasi solidary rather than solidary—but I will not here be strict about language use, only about the underlying conceptual issues.

27. A constitutive norm typically is an ought-to-be norm, and it entails for normal cases that the members ought to act toward its satisfaction. Ought-to-be norms in the present context mainly relate to the group's functioning in relation to its ethos, whereas ought-to-do norms in some cases also concern other kinds of normative requirements concerning group members.

28. Note that one can act loyally and do something that is not legitimately expectable while trustworthiness concerns only legitimately expected action. (Cf. Keller 2007 on loyalty.)

29. Scanlon (2003).

30. This kind of strong solidarity is not to be confused with Lindenberg's notion of strong solidarity to be discussed in the next section.

31. For evidence of we-mode reasoning recall chapters 6 and 7 and the references given in them.

32. It is a central, nonobvious point of this chapter to study how the given constitutive criteria for a group to count as a we-mode group (group reason, collectivity, commitment) relate to the given constitutive criteria of solidary behavior (1–5). Further possible relations can be considered here: (1) conceptual connection (a we-mode group entails behavior B, and B counts as solidary); (2) normative implication (a we-mode group gives reasons for B or states that B ought to take place, and B counts as solidary); (3) explanatory connection (there is something in we-mode groups that explains why B is likely to take place, and B counts as solidary), and indeed this connects nicely to the previous point: B takes place because there are good reasons for it; (4) functional point (given some psychological constraints, etc., a we-mode group cannot function without B, and B counts as solidary). Why B occurs requires further explanation here; (5) empirical generality (we mode group typically leads to B, and B counts as solidary). (This note owes to Arto Laitinen.)

33. Recall, however, the point made earlier in a note that nonautonomous we-mode groups also can be solidary.

34. See Durkheim ([1893] 1964); Weber ([1923] 1961); and Lindenberg (1988, 1998) for the points in this paragraph.

35. See Lindenberg (1988, 1998, 2006) for discussion. His notion of strong solidarity is different and not to be confused with my notion of strong solidarity in section 3.

36. What according to Lindenberg remains outside the realm of both weak and strong solidarity are opportunistic relationships (in which everyone seeks to maximize his own outcome without concern for the other, such as spot market and authority relationships, for example, employer-employee relations).

37. See Hakli, Miller, and Tuomela (2010) and especially chapter 7 above for arguments distinguishing we-mode groups from pro-group I-mode groups by means of game-theoretic tools. The arguments in that chapter show that we-mode acting tends to lead to more orderly action in

collective action dilemmas and in institutional contexts in general. Briefly, the we-mode restricts possible collective action equilibria more than the pro-group I-mode.

38. This paragraph in part owes to Lindenberg (1998).

39. See the discussion in Lindenberg (1998).

40. See Tuomela (2007a), chapter 1, for such relevant notions as a subethos and nuclear ethos that can be used to analyze the case of suppressed groups.

41. Oppressed groups are often solidary—a common threat in general unifies a group and may accordingly make it more we-mode like and more solidary than it otherwise would be. Examples of oppression would be provided by the Soviet Union, where the communist ruler class oppressed ordinary citizens, especially citizens of Islamic states belonging to the Soviet Union; the Nazi regime, which oppressed Jews; and in Afghanistan the Taliban, whose rulers oppressed women. (Cf., however, my comments on the minority group of Swedish-speaking Finns in a note to chapter 1.)

Ann Cudd (2006) presents a philosophical account of what one group's being oppressed by another group involves. In her account oppression is taken to be a circumstance in which the following four conditions are satisfied (p. 25):

(1) The harm condition: There is a harm that comes out of an institutional practice.
(2) The social group condition: The harm is perpetrated through a social institution or practice on a social group whose identity exists apart from the oppressive harm in (1).
(3) The privilege condition: There is another social group that benefits from the institutional practice in (1).
(4) The coercion condition: There is unjustified force that brings about the harm.

42. Basically the same point applies to other group attitudes. While, for instance, group beliefs are really acceptances, normal people will typically internalize them and acquire what I have called "experiential" psychological beliefs.

43. The above arguments indicate that there can be both involuntary we-mode and I-mode feelings, distinguished by their cause rather than by their phenomenal qualities. Above I have discussed only we-mode feelings that may accompany (we-mode) group emotions.

44. Recall the discussion of collective pattern-governed behaviors in chapter 8.

45. Of course, individuals qua individuals have made important inventions and discoveries—but perhaps those individuals that function as group members have contributed even more.

46. What kinds of factors affect the degrees of solidarity? Here are a couple of relevant factors. First, groups may consist of we-moders, pro-group I-moders, and egoistic I-moders, as well as perhaps other kinds of members—such as opportunists who do not belong to any of the mentioned three categories (whether in general or not). In large groups we may want to speak of the probabilities of a member belonging dominantly to one of these categories—which information may be central for estimating how a person will act "here and now". Second, the firmness of collective commitment may get weaker in situations where free-riding is more attractive or when countervailing factors come into play that are more attractive to the group members (such as moving to another group). These kinds of factors lower the degree of member-level cohesion and hence the degree of solidarity of the group.

47. One may of course debate the matter. In moral philosophical discussion, Kant's deontological morality is based on following rules of the right kind. This is quite close to rule obedience in the case of group solidarity.

48. I wish to thank Arto Laitinen for excellent comments on an early version. Maj Tuomela also is to be thanked for her many insightful points. Kaarlo Miller and Matti Heinonen presented good criticisms of my group solidarity account, and Mikko Salmela deserves thanks for his critical comments on my account of group emotions.

REFERENCES

Bach, K. 1995. Terms of Agreement. *Ethics* 105 (3): 604–12.

Bacharach, M. 1999. Interactive Team Reasoning: A Contribution to the Theory of Cooperation. *Research in Economics* 53 (2): 117–47.

Bacharach, M. 2006. *Beyond Individual Choice: Teams and Frames in Game Theory*. Ed. N. Gold and R. Sugden. Princeton, NJ: Princeton University Press.

Balzer, W., and R. Tuomela. 1997. A Fixed Point Approach to Collective Attitudes. In *Contemporary Action Theory II*, ed. G. Holmström-Hintikka and R. Tuomela, 115–42. Dordrecht: Kluwer Academic Publishers.

Balzer, W., and R. Tuomela. 2001. Social Institutions, Norms, and Practices. In *Social Order in Multiagent Systems*, ed. R. Conte and Chrysanthos Dellarocas, 161–80. Dordrecht: Kluwer Academic Publishers.

Balzer, W., and R. Tuomela. 2003. "Collective Intentions and the Maintenance of Social Practices." *Autonomous Agents and Multi-agent Systems* 6: 7–33.

Bardsley, N., J. Mehta, C. Starmer, and R. Sugden. 2010. Explaining Focal Points: Cognitive Hierarchy Theory versus Team Reasoning. *Economic Journal* 120 (543): 40–79.

Baumeister, R., and M. Leary. 1995. The Need to Belong: Desire for Interpersonal Attachments as a Fundamental Human Motivation. *Psychological Bulletin* 117 (3): 497–529.

Beran, H. 1987. *The Consent Theory of Political Obligation*. London: Croom Helm.

Bratman, M. 1987. *Intention, Plans, and Practical Reason*. Cambridge, MA: Harvard University Press.

Bratman, M. 1992. Shared Cooperative Activity. *Philosophical Review* 101 (2): 327–41.

Bratman, M. 2009. Modest Sociality and the Distinctiveness of Intention. *Philosophical Studies* 144 (1):149–65.

Brewer, M. 2003. *Intergroup Relations*. 2nd ed. Philadelphia: Open University Press.

Broome, J. 2004. Reasons. In *Reason and Value: Themes from the Moral Philosophy of Joseph Raz*, ed. J. Wallace, M. Smith, S. Scheffler, and P. Pettit, 28–55. Oxford: Oxford University Press.

Callero, P. L. 2009. *The Myth of Individualism: How Social Forces Shape Our Lives*. Lanham: Rowman and Littlefield.

Caplan, D. 2008. *The Myth of the Irrational Voter: Why Democracies Choose Bad Policies*. Princeton, NJ: Princeton University Press.

Colman, A., and B. Pulford. 2012. Problems and Pseudoproblems in Understanding Cooperation in Social Dilemmas. *Psychological Inquiry* 23: 39–47.

Colman, A., B. Pulford, and J. Rose. 2008a. Collective Rationality in Interactive Decisions: Evidence for Team Reasoning. *Acta Psychologica* 128 (2): 387–97.

Colman, A., B. Pulford, and J. Rose. 2008b. Team Reasoning and Collective Rationality: Piercing the Veil of Obviousness. *Acta Psychologica* 128 (2): 409–12.

Cornford, F. M. (1912) 2004. *From Religion to Philosophy: A Study in the Origins of Western Speculation*. Mineola: Dover Books.

Cudd, A. 2006. *Analyzing Oppression*. New York: Oxford University Press.

Dancy, J. 2000. *Practical Reality*. Oxford: Oxford University Press.

Dancy, J. 2004. *Ethics without Principles*. Oxford: Oxford University Press.

Dietrich, F., and C. List. 2007. Arrow's Theorem in Judgment Aggregation. *Social Choice and Welfare* 29 (1): 19–33

Dietrich, F., and C. List. 2010. The Aggregation of Propositional Attitudes: Towards a General Theory. In *Oxford Studies in Epistemology*, volume 3, ed. T. S. Gendler and J. Hawthorne, 215–34. Oxford: Oxford University Press.

Durkheim, E. (1893) 1964. *The Division of Labor in Society*. Trans. W. D. Halls. New York: Free Press.

Gaertner, W. 2006. *A Primer in Social Choice Theory*. New York: Oxford University Press.

Gierke, O. (1934) 1957. *Natural Law and the Theory of Society 1500–1800*. Trans. E. Barker. Boston: Beacon Press.

Gilbert, M. 1989. *On Social Facts*. London: Routledge.

Gilbert, M. 2006. *A Theory of Political Obligation*. New York: Oxford University Press.

Grewendorf, G. 2002. How Performatives Don't Work. In *Speech Acts, Mind and Social Reality: Discussions with John R. Searle*, ed. G. Grewendorf and G. Meggle, 25–40. Dordrecht: Kluwer Academic Publishers.

Griesinger, D. W., and J. W. Livingston. 1973. Toward a Model of Interpersonal Motivation in Experimental Games. *Behavioral Science* 18 (3): 173–88.

Guala, F. 2006. Has Game Theory Been Refuted? *Journal of Philosophy* 103 (5): 239–63.

Hakli, R., K. Miller, and R. Tuomela. 2010. Two Kinds of We-Reasoning. *Economics and Philosophy* 26 (3): 291–320.

Harnish, R. M. 2002. Are Performative Utterances Declarations? In *Speech Acts, Mind and Social Reality: Discussions with John R. Searle*, ed. G. Grewendorf and G. Meggle, 41–64. Dordrecht: Kluwer Academic Publishers.

Harsanyi, J. C., and R. Selten. 1988. *A General Theory of Equilibrium Selection in Games*. Cambridge, MA: MIT Press.

Hayes, M. (1942) 2009. *Various Group Mind Theories: Viewed in the Light of Thomistic Principles*. Washington, DC: Catholic University of America Press.

Hechter, M. 1987. *Principles of Group Solidarity*. Berkeley: University of California Press.

Hume, D. (1740) 1965. *A Treatise of Human Nature*. Ed. L. A. Selby-Bigge. Oxford: Oxford University Press.

Hyyppä, M. 2010. *Healthy Ties: Social Capital, Population Health and Survival* Dordrecht: Springer.

Kavka, G. 1986. *Hobbesian Moral and Political Theory*. Princeton, NJ: Princeton University Press.

Keller, S. 2007. *The Limits of Loyalty*. Cambridge: Cambridge University Press.

Kelley, H., and J. Thibaut. 1978. *Interpersonal Relations: A Theory of Interdependence*. New York: Wiley.

Krueger, J. I. 2008. Methodological Individualism in Experimental Games: Not So Easily Dismissed. *Acta Psychologica* 128 (2): 398–401.

Laitinen, A. 2013. Against Representations with Two Directions of Fit. Forthcoming.

Liedman, S. E. 2002. Solidarity www.eurozine.com.

Lindenberg, S. 1988. Contractual Relations and Weak Solidarity: The Behavioral Basis of Restraints on Gain-Maximization. *Journal of Institutional and Theoretical Economics* 144 (1): 39–58.

Lindenberg, S. 1998. Solidarity: Its Microfoundations and Macro-Dependence. A Framing Approach. In *The Problem of Solidarity: Theories and Models*, ed. P. Doreian and T. Fararo, 61–112. Amsterdam: Gordon and Breach.

Lindenberg, S. 2006. Prosocial Behavior, Solidarity, and Framing Processes. In *Solidarity and Prosocial Behavior: An Integration of Sociological and Psychological Perspectives*, ed. S. Lindenberg, D. Fetchenbauer, A. Flache, and A. Buunkd, 23–44. New York: Springer.

List, C., and P. Pettit. 2002. Aggregating Sets of Judgments: An Impossibility Result. *Economics and Philosophy* 18 (1): 89–110.

List, C., and P. Pettit. 2011. *Group Agency: The Possibility, Design and Status of Corporate Agents*. New York: Oxford University Press.

Martinich, A. M. 2002. On the Proper Treatment of Performatives. In *Speech Acts, Mind and Social Reality: Discussions with John R. Searle*, ed. G. Grewendorf and G. Meggle, 93–104. Dordrecht: Klüwer Academic Publishers.

McDougall, W. 1920. *The Group Mind*. Cambridge: Cambridge University Press.

McMahon, C. 2001. *Collective Rationality and Collective Reasoning*. Cambridge: Cambridge University Press.

Miller, K., and R. Tuomela. 2013. Collective Goals Analyzed. In *From Individual to Collective Intentionality,* ed S. Chant, F. Hindriks, and G. Preyer Oxford: Oxford University Press Forthcoming.

Miller, S. 2011. Social Institutions. *Stanford Encyclopedia of Philosophy*. http://plato.stanford.edu/entries/social-institutions.

Quante, M., and D. Schweikard. 2009. Leading a Universal Life: The Systematic Relevance of Hegel's Social Philosophy. *History of the Human Sciences* 22 (1): 58–78.

Raz, J. 1986. *The Morality of Freedom*. Oxford: Clarendon Press.

Rehg, W. 2013. The Social Authority of Paradigms as Group Commitments: Rehabilitating Kuhn with Recent Work in Social Philosophy. *Topoi* 32: 21–31.

Richerson, P., and R. Boyd. 2005. *Not by Genes Alone: How Culture Transformed Human Evolution*. Chicago: University of Chicago Press.

Ripstein, A. 1999. The General Will. In *The Social Contract Theorists: Critical Essays on Hobbes, Locke, and Rousseau*, ed. C. W. Morris, 219–37. Lanham, MD Rowman and Littlefield.

Rousseau, J.-J. (1762) 1979. *The Social Contract*. Trans. M. Cranston. Harmondsworth: Penguin.

Runciman, D. 1997. *Pluralism and the Personality of the State*. Cambridge: Cambridge University Press.

Sally, D. 1995. Conversation and Cooperation in Social Dilemmas: A Meta-analysis of Experiments from 1958 to 1992. *Rationality and Society* 7 (1): 58–92.

Scanlon, T. M. 2003. *The Difficulty of Tolerance*. Cambridge: Cambridge University Press.

Scanlon, T. M. 1998. *What We Owe to Each Other*. Cambridge, MA: Harvard University Press.

Schmid, H. B. 2009. *Plural Action*. Dordrecht: Springer.

Schmid, H. B., and D. Schweikard. 2013. Collective Intentionality. In *Stanford Encyclopedia of Philosophy*, ed. E. Zalta. www.plato.stanford.edu.

Scholz, S. 2008. *Political Solidarity*. University Park: Pennsylvania State University Press.

Searle, J. R. 1983. *Intentionality: An Essay in the Philosophy of Mind*. Cambridge: Cambridge University Press.

Searle, J. R. 1995. *The Construction of Social Reality*. London: Penguin.

Searle, J. R. 2001. *Rationality in Action*. Cambridge, MA: MIT Press.

Searle, J. R. 2010. *Making the Social World: The Structure of Human Civilization*. Oxford: Oxford University Press.

Searle, J. R. 2011. Replies. *Analysis* 71 (4): 733–41.

Sellars, W. 1968. *Science and Metaphysics: Variations on Kantian Themes*. London: Routledge & Kegan Paul.

Shenkman, R. 2009. *Just How Stupid Are We? Facing the Truth about the American Voter*. New York: Basic Books.

Sugden, R. 2008. Nash Equilibrium, Team Reasoning and Cognitive Hierarchy Theory. *Acta Psychologica* 128 (2): 402–4.

Tomasello, M., M. Carpenter, J. Call, T. Behne, and H. Moll. 2005. Understanding and Sharing Intentions: The Origins of Cultural Cognition. *Behavioral and Brain Sciences* 28: 675–735.

Tomasello, M. 2009. *Why We Cooperate*. Cambridge, MA: MIT Press.

Tomasello, M., M. Carpenter, J. Call, T. Behne, and H. Moll. 2005. Understanding and Sharing Intentions: The Origins of Cultural Cognition. *Behavioral and Brain Sciences* 28 (5): 675–735.

Tönnies, F. (1887) 1996. *Community and Society (Gemeinschaft und Gesellschaft)*. Trans. C. P. Loomis. New Brunswick, NJ: Transaction Publishers.

Tuomela, M. 2006. Rational Social Normative Trust as Rational Genuine Trust. In *Philosophy and Ethics: New Research*, ed. L. Siegal, 1–56. Hauppauge, NY: Nova Science Publishers.

Tuomela, R. 1977. *Human Action and Its Explanation*. Dordrecht: Reidel.

Tuomela, R. 1984. *A Theory of Social Action*. Dordrecht: Reidel.

Tuomela, R. 1985a. *Science, Action and Reality*. Dordrecht: Reidel.

Tuomela, R. 1985b. The Components of Social Control. *Quality & Quantity* 19 (1): 1–51.

Tuomela, R. 1988. The Myth of the Given and Realism. *Erkenntnis* 29: 181–200.

Tuomela, R. 1992. Group Beliefs. *Synthese* 91: 285–318.

Tuomela, R. 1995. *The Importance of Us: A Philosophical Study of Basic Social Notions*. Stanford: Stanford University Press.

Tuomela, R. 1998. A Defense of Mental Causation. *Philosophical Studies* 90 (1): 1–34.

Tuomela, R. 2000. *Cooperation: A Philosophical Study*. Dordrecht: Kluwer.

Tuomela, R. 2002a. Collective Intentions and Game Theory. *Journal of Philosophy* 106: 292–300.

Tuomela, R. 2002b. *The Philosophy of Social Practices: A Collective Acceptance View*. Cambridge: Cambridge University Press.

Tuomela, R. 2005. We-Intentions Revisited. *Philosophical Studies* 125 (3): 327–69.

Tuomela, R. 2007a. *The Philosophy of Sociality: The Shared Point of View*. New York: Oxford University Press. Paperback ed. 2010.

Tuomela, R. 2007b. Motivating Reasons for Action. In *Rationality and the Good: Critical Essays on the Ethics and Epistemology of Robert Audi*, ed. M. Timmons, J. Greco, and A. Mele, 176–97. Oxford: Oxford University Press.

Tuomela, R. 2009a. Collective Intentions and Game Theory. *Journal of Philosophy 106*: 292–300.

Tuomela, R. 2009b. Collective Acceptance, Social Institutions, and Social Reality. In *Neuer Mensch und Kollektive Identität in der Kommunikationsgesellschaft*, ed. G. Preyer, 272–306. Wiesbaden: VS Verlag für Sozialwissenschaften.

Tuomela, R. 2010a. Holistic Social Causation and Explanation. In *Explanation, Prediction, and Confirmation*, ed. D. Dieks, W. J. Gonzalez, S. Hartmann, T. Uebel, and M. Weber, 304–18. Dordrecht: Springer.

Tuomela, R. 2010b. An Account of Group Knowledge. In *Collective Epistemology*, ed. H. B. Schmid, D. Sirtes, and M. Weber, 75–117. Frankfurt am Main: Ontos Verlag.

Tuomela, R. 2011a. Searle's New Construction of Social Reality. *Analysis* 71 (4): 706–19.

Tuomela, R. 2011b. Review of *Group Agency: The Possibility, Design and Status of Corporate Agents*. *Notre Dame Journal of Philosophical Reviews* 38 (November).

Tuomela, R. 2012a. Individualism and Collectivism in Social Science. In *Selbstbeobachtung der modernen Gesellschaft und die neuen Grenzen des Sozialen*, ed. G. Peter and R.-M. Krauss, 128–43. Wiesbaden: Springer VS.

Tuomela, R. 2012b. Group Reasons. *Philosophical Issues* 22 (Action Theory): 402–18.

Tuomela, R. 2013. Who Is Afraid of Group Agents and Group Minds? In *The Background of Social Reality*, ed. M. Schmitz, H. B. Schmid, and B. Kobow, 13–35. Dordrecht. Springer.

Tuomela, R., and W. Balzer. 1999. Collective Acceptance and Collective Social Notions. *Synthese* 117 (2): 175–205.

Tuomela, R., and M. Bonnevier-Tuomela. 1997. From Social Imitation to Teamwork. In *Contemporary Action Theory II*, ed. G. Holmström-Hintikka and R. Tuomela, 1–47. Dordrecht: Kluwer Academic Publishers.

Tuomela, R., and K. Miller. 1988. We-Intentions. *Philosophical Studies* 53 (3): 367–89.

Tuomela, R., and M. Tuomela. 2005. Cooperation and Trust in Group Context. *Mind & Society* 4 (1): 49–84.

Turchin, P. 2007. *War and Peace and War*. New York: Plume.

Udehn, L. 2001. *Methodological Individualism: Background, History and Meaning*. London: Routledge.

Van Lange, P. A. M. 2008. Collective Rationality: The Integrative Model Explains It (as) Well. *Acta Psychologica* 128 (2): 405–8.

Vierkandt, A. 1949. *Kleine Gesellschaftslehre*. 2nd ed. Stuttgart: Ferdinand Enke Verlag.

Vierkandt, A. (1928) 1975. *Gesellschaftslehre*. 2nd ed. New York: Arno Press.

Weber, M. (1923) 1961. *General Economic History*. New York: Collier Books.

INDEX

List of named technical accounts and explications referred to in the book: